The Revels Plays
COMPANION
LIBRARY

E. A. J. HONIGMANN former editor

J. R. MULRYNE, R. L. SMALLWOOD and PETER CORBIN general editors

For over forty years *The Revels Plays* have offered the most authoritative editions of Elizabethan and Jacobean plays by authors other than Shakespeare. The *Companion Library* provides a fuller background to the main series by publishing worthwhile dramatic and non-dramatic material that will be essential for the serious student of the period.

Three Jacobean witchcraft plays eds. Corbin, Sedge
John Ford's political theatre Hopkins
The works of Richard Edwards King
Thomas Heywood: Three marriage plays ed. Merchant
Three Renaissance travel plays ed. Parr
John Lyly Pincombe
A textual companion to Doctor Faustus Rasmussen
Banquets set forth: Banqueting in English Renaissance drama Meads

======

Beyond *The Spanish Tragedy*

MANCHESTER
UNIVERSITY PRESS

THE REVELS PLAYS COMPANION LIBRARY

Beyond
The Spanish Tragedy
A STUDY OF THE WORKS
OF THOMAS KYD

LUKAS ERNE

Manchester University Press
Manchester and New York

distributed exclusively in the USA by Palgrave

Published by
Manchester University Press
Oxford Road, Manchester M13 9NR, UK
and Room 400, 175 Fifth Avenue, New York, NY 10010, USA
http://www.manchesteruniversitypress.co.uk

Distributed exclusively in the USA by
Palgrave, 175 Fifth Avenue, New York,
NY 10010, USA

Distributed exclusively in Canada by
UBC Press, University of British Columbia, 2029 West Mall,
Vancouver, BC, Canada V6T 1Z2

British Library Cataloguing-in-Publication Data
A catalogue record for this book is available from the British Library

Library of Congress Cataloging-in-Publication Data applied for

ISBN 0 7190 6093 1 *hardback*

First published 2001

10 09 08 07 06 05 04 03 02 01   10 9 8 7 6 5 4 3 2 1

Typeset in Sabon
by Action Publishing Technology Ltd, Gloucester
Printed in Great Britain
by Bookcraft (Bath) Ltd, Midsomer Norton

To my mother

VERA ERNE-SUTTER 1932–81

and to my father

FRANZ ERNE 1927–99

CONTENTS

ILLUSTRATIONS

GENERAL EDITORS' PREFACE

Since the late 1950s the series known as The Revels Plays has provided for students of the English Renaissance drama carefully edited texts of the major Elizabethan and Jacobean plays. The series includes some of the best-known drama of the period and has continued to expand, both within its original field and, to a lesser extent, beyond it, to include some important plays from the earlier Tudor and from the Restoration periods. The Revels Plays Companion Library is intended to further this expansion and to allow for new developments.

The aim of the Companion Library is to provide students of the Elizabethan and Jacobean drama with a fuller sense of its background and context. The series includes volumes of a variety of kinds. Small collections of plays, by a single author or concerned with a single theme and edited in accordance with the principles of textual modernisation of the Revels Plays, offer a wider range of drama than the main series can include. Together with editions of masques, pageants and the non-dramatic work of Elizabethan and Jacobean playwrights, these volumes make it possible, within the overall Revels enterprise, to examine the achievements of the major dramatists from a broader perspective. Other volumes provide a fuller context for the plays of the period by offering new collections of documentary evidence on Elizabethan theatrical conditions and on the performance of plays during that period and later. A third aim of the series is to offer modern critical interpretation, in the form of collections of essays or of monographs, of the dramatic achievement of the English Renaissance.

So wide a range of material necessarily precludes the standard format and uniform general editorial control, which is possible in the original series of Revels Plays. To a considerable extent, therefore, treatment and approach is determined by the needs and intentions of individual volume editors. Within this rather ampler area, however, we hope that the Companion Library maintains the standards of scholarship that have for so long characterised The Revels Plays, and that it offers a useful enlargement of the work of the series in preserving, illuminating and celebrating the drama of Elizabethan and Jacobean England.

J. R. MULRYNE
R. L. SMALLWOOD
PETER CORBIN

PREFACE

Thomas Kyd (1558–94) was among the pioneering figures of English Renaissance drama. Along with Christopher Marlowe, he paved the way for Shakespeare's tragedies. His masterpiece, *The Spanish Tragedy*, was probably the most successful play of the entire period up to 1642. It was revived over decades, provided with additions, taken to the Continent, translated, and several times adapted. It was printed no fewer than eleven times between 1592 and 1633, a number only exceeded by the anonymous *Mucedorus* which passed through fourteen editions by 1639. *The Spanish Tragedy*, the lost *Hamlet*, and *Soliman and Perseda* fully established on the English public stage the powerful traditions of the revenge tragedy, the tragedy of blood, and the tragedy of intrigue. Kyd's early successors did not ignore his importance. More than forty years after his death, the playwright Thomas Heywood referred to him as 'famous *Kid*', and Ben Jonson, in his poem on Shakespeare printed among the prefatory material to Shakespeare's First Folio in 1623, gave Kyd a place of honour among Shakespeare's early contemporaries:

> For, if I thought my iudgement were of yeeres,
> I should commit thee surely with thy peeres,
> And tell, how farre thou didst our *Lyly* out-shine,
> Or sporting *Kid*, or *Marlowes* mighty line.[1]

It is surprising then that interest in Thomas Kyd, whom T. S. Eliot called an 'extraordinary dramatic (if not poetic) genius', remains low.[2] Granted, critical essays on *The Spanish Tragedy* are published with regularity and have led to a significantly better understanding of Kyd's masterpiece. Yet, not one substantial study devoted to his works, rather than to a single play, has appeared in the last thirty years. Heywood's epithet 'famous' no longer applies today. The long-standing identification of Kyd as the father of the English revenge tragedy as well as the chief founder of English tragedy along with Marlowe has masked the fact that we essentially lack a sense of Kyd as a dramatic artist.

One of the problems that has bedevilled Kyd scholarship is that critics seem to disagree substantially to whom and to which works we are referring under the heading 'Thomas Kyd'. For example, Andrew S. Cairncross edited *The First Part of Hieronimo* and *The Spanish Tragedy* on the assumption that both plays are by Kyd and form a diptych. In the same year of publication (1967), Arthur Freeman, in his study *Thomas Kyd: Facts and Problems*, held that there is 'no longer any serious doubt' (pp. 175–6) that the extant *First Part of Hieronimo* is not by Kyd. Frederick Samuel Boas's edition of Kyd's *Works* (1901) is of little help as some of its assumptions are hopelessly outdated. Since 1967, nothing has been written that could help settle this dispute.

The question of what Kyd wrote should really be the starting point for any further investigation. I therefore reject the easy solution advanced by Peter B. Murray who, in a full-length study of *The Spanish Tragedy* with the misleading title *Thomas Kyd*, writes that 'a book about Thomas Kyd turns out to be a book about *The Spanish Tragedy*. And this is as it should be'.[3] I argue, on the contrary, that Kyd must not be reduced to his most famous play. He can be identified with some confidence as the author of at least five plays: *The Spanish Tragedy*, *Soliman and Perseda*, *Cornelia*, *Don Horatio* ('doneoracio' according to the theatre manager Philip Henslowe) of which a part survives in *The First Part of Hieronimo*, and the lost *Hamlet*.

Only when all his plays are considered can the sense of a dramatic *oeuvre* emerge. Towering at the centre of his extant dramatic works is Kyd's masterpiece to which all others are intimately related: one dramatises the events leading up to *The Spanish Tragedy* (*Don Horatio*), one expands the play-within-the-play of Act V (*Soliman and Perseda*), one inverts its basic pattern of a father seeking revenge for the murder of his son (*Hamlet*), and one fully explores its elegiac element, the protagonist's grief for the loss of the dearest kin (*Cornelia*). Kyd's dramatic interest is thus very focused. He explores a limited range of material which he keeps approaching from different angles. Not only *The Spanish Tragedy*, but all of Kyd's plays turn around a thematic pattern constituted of loss, grief, and revenge. Hieronimo as well as Andrea, Hamlet, Perseda, and Cornelia are protagonists in the strand of early tragedies that G. K. Hunter has labelled 'victim tragedy'.[4] Like Marlowe's plays of overreaching heroes, Kyd's plays place at their centre a certain type of character: the victim of adverse fortune trying to cope with his or her loss.

Kyd's plays show not only the thematic but also the dramaturgical fingerprints of their author. Apart from *Cornelia* which, as a translation and a closet tragedy, is in some ways in a category of its own, the plays dramatise intricately plotted novelistic material – the *favola intrecciata* of novella collections that found its way from Italy via France to England in the course of the sixteenth century – with an unprecedented attention to human causality and physical action.

Generically, the plays form a new and daring mixture. Far from merely providing 'comic relief', Pedringano in *The Spanish Tragedy* and Basilisco in *Soliman and Perseda*, are comic participants in the tragic main plot. Also, the generically mixed *Don Horatio* formed a diptych with *The Spanish Tragedy*, a pattern John Marston appears to have remembered when writing *Antonio and Mellida* and *Antonio's Revenge*.

The chief contention, then, of this study is that Thomas Kyd is much more than the writer of one masterpiece, *The Spanish Tragedy*, even though he is that. He is the author of a dramatic *oeuvre* that, subjected to critical scrutiny in its entirety, gives a fuller picture of the artistic achievement and historical importance of Shakespeare's most important tragic predecessor, besides Marlowe, than has hitherto been drawn.

Notes

1 Herford and Simpson, VIII, p. 391, ll. 27–30. Heywood is quoted from *The Hierarchie of the Blessed Angells* (London, 1635), S1^v.
2 *Selected Essays, 1917–1932* (London, 1932), p. 142.
3 (New York, 1969), p. 5. In his recent *English Drama before Shakespeare* (London and New York, 1999), Peter Happé has a subchapter entitled 'Thomas Kyd (1558–94)' (pp. 202–10) which similarly confines itself to *The Spanish Tragedy*.
4 *English Drama, 1586–1642: The Age of Shakespeare* (Oxford, 1997), p. 69.

ACKNOWLEDGEMENTS

I have received precious help from various quarters, and it is a pleasure to thank those from whom I have benefited. This study would not have been written without the unfailingly generous and encouraging support of Emrys Jones who supervised my work for three years. The Marquis de Amodio provided another *sine qua non* by granting me a Berrow Scholarship to Lincoln College, Oxford, for the same period. I owe both these men a tremendous debt of gratitude. I am grateful to the Rector and Fellows of Lincoln College for such a congenial environment in which to learn, and to my many colleagues for their stimulating companionship. I am particularly grateful to the College for the award of an Andrew W. Mellon fellowship which enabled a month's fruitful research at the Huntington Library, San Marino, California.

Richard Waswo's persistent generosity and assistance have proved invaluable in the final stages of the writing of this book. He, Balz Engler, Brian Gibbons, and Greg Polletta read my manuscript when it was submitted as a thesis, and I have benefited from their astute critiques. Neil Forsyth provided initial encouragement, and he as well as Martin Dodsworth, Katherine Duncan-Jones, Richard McCabe, Anthony Mortimer, Margaret Tudeau-Clayton, and Francis Warner read and helpfully commented on parts of my work. Malcolm Parkes kindly answered a query on a point of paleography while José Ramón Diaz-Fernández drew my attention to material which I had not considered. I would like to thank my friends and colleagues in Oxford, Geneva and Washington with whom I have discussed aspects of my work, in particular Pascale Aebischer, Saba Bahar, Guillemette Bolens, Steven May, Kirk Melnikoff, Bernard Schlurick, and Regina Schneider. I am grateful to Arthur Kinney for permission to print as chapter 1 a revised version of an article entitled '"Enter the Ghost of Andrea": Recovering Thomas Kyd's Two-Part Play' that first appeared in *English Literary Renaissance* (Autumn 2000, pp. 339–72), and the two anonymous readers for their useful comments. The general editors of the Revels Plays Companion Library have been persistently encouraging and helpful, and Peter Corbin and J. R. Mulryne have made a great number of incisive comments, suggestions, and corrections.

In addition, I wish to acknowledge my indebtedness to those scholars who have gone before me: I am particularly grateful to Frederick Samuel Boas, Philip Edwards, Arthur Freeman, George K.

Hunter and J. R. Mulryne for their important contributions to Kyd studies. The human and textual resources of many libraries have been consulted in producing this study. Accordingly, I wish to thank the staff of the Bodleian Library, the English Faculty Library, Lincoln College Library and Magdalen College Library, all in Oxford; the British Library; the Shakespeare Centre, Stratford-upon-Avon; the Shakespeare Bibliothek München, the Universitätsbibliothek Freiburg i. Br.; the Bibliothèque Publique et Universitaire and the English Department Library, Geneva; the Folger Shakespeare Library, Washington, DC; and the Huntington Library, San Marino, California. As this project was nearing completion, the Swiss National Science Foundation granted me a generous scholarship, allowing a prolonged stay at the Folger Shakespeare Library in Washington DC.

I owe special thanks to John Freeh, Tore Rem, and Michael Suarez SJ for giving so generously of their time, knowledge and warmth of friendship in personal and academic life. Finally, I owe a very special debt of gratitude to my wife Katrin for her endurance and encouragement.

THOMAS KYD'S LIFE AND WORKS: A CHRONOLOGY

1558	Thomas Kyd is born in London and baptised on 6 November.
1565–c. 1573/75?	Kyd Attends Merchant Taylors' School. In the following years, he may have served in the trade of 'Nouerint' (according to Nashe), i.e. in his father's trade as a scrivener.
1583–c. 1585	Kyd writes plays for the Queen's Men.
c. 1586/87	Kyd writes *Don Horatio*.
c. 1587	Kyd writes *The Spanish Tragedy*.
1587–93	Kyd is in the service of a noble lord (probably the Earl of Pembroke).
1588	*The Householder's Philosophy*, a translation of Tasso's *Il Padre di Famiglia*, appears in print.
c. 1588/89	Kyd writes *Hamlet* and *Soliman and Perseda*.
1589	In the preface to Greene's *Menaphon*, Nashe denigrates Kyd's *Householder's Philosophy* and his Senecan plays, alluding to *Hamlet* and, probably, *The Spanish Tragedy*.
1591	Kyd shares a single writing room with Marlowe.
1592	*Don Horatio* (seven performances) and *The Spanish Tragedy* (fifteen performances) are acted at the Rose by Strange's Men. *The Spanish Tragedy* and *Soliman and Perseda* are entered in the Stationers' Register and appear in print.
1593	On 12 May, Kyd has his room searched by officers of the Privy Council and is arrested for 'vile hereticall Conceiptes' found among his papers which Kyd claims he had from Marlowe. He is imprisoned and probably tortured. He loses the favours of his patron and, in an attempt to be restored to his employment, writes two letters to Sir John Puckering after being freed.
1593/94	During the winter, Kyd writes *Cornelia*, a translation of Garnier's *Cornélie*.

1594   *Cornelia* is entered and published with a dedica-
                tion to the Countess of Sussex.
                The Spanish Tragedy is reprinted.
                Hamlet is performed on 9 June at the Newington
                Butts theatre by the combined Admiral's and
                Chamberlain's Men.
                Kyd dies and is buried on 15 August.

1595   *Cornelia* seems to be selling badly and is reissued
                with a new title-page.

c. 1595–6   *Hamlet* is performed at the Theatre by
                Chamberlain's Men.

1597   Admiral's Men revive *The Spanish Tragedy*, possi-
                bly in revised form, for a run of thirteen
                performances.
                Soliman and Perseda seems to have been acted by
                Pembroke's Men at the Swan.

1599   *The Spanish Tragedy* and *Soliman and Perseda* are
                reprinted.

1601/02   Henslowe pays Jonson for additions to *The
                Spanish Tragedy*.

1602   *The Spanish Tragedy* is printed for the first time
                with additions (probably not those by Jonson).
                Further editions follow in 1603, 1610, 1615,
                1618, 1623, and 1633 suggesting that the play
                continued to be performed.

c. 1603/04   The Children of the Chapel appear to have appro-
                priated *Don Horatio* from the
                Chamberlain's/King's Men and, through extensive
                revision, turned it into the burlesque *First Part of
                Hieronimo*.

1605   *The First Part of Hieronimo* is published.

1668   *The Spanish Tragedy* is performed at the Nursery
                Theatre in Hatton Garden (reported by Pepys).

1744   Dodsley's *Select Collection of Old Plays* contains
                the first 'modern' editions of *The Spanish Tragedy*
                and *Cornelia*.

1901   The first and still only edition of Kyd's *Works* is
                published (edited by F. S. Boas)

1973   *The Spanish Tragedy* returns to the professional
                stage at the Mercury Theatre, London.

1978   *The Spanish Tragedy* is performed at the Citizens
                Theatre, Glasgow.

1982   Michael Bogdanov directs *The Spanish Tragedy* at the National Theatre.

1983   *The Spanish Tragedy* makes its professional début in the US at the Globe Playhouse in Los Angeles.

1986   The Riverside Shakespeare Company plays *The Spanish Tragedy* at the Shakespeare Center in New York.

1997   *The Spanish Tragedy* is performed by the Royal Shakespeare Company in Stratford-upon-Avon and London.

ABBREVIATIONS

The following abbreviations have been used for periodicals, works of reference, and publications of learned societies:

CE   *Cahiers Elisabéthains*
DNB   *Dictionary of National Biography*
ELR   *English Literary Renaissance*
ES   *Englische Studien*
JEGP   *Journal of English and Germanic Philology*
MLN   *Modern Language Notes*
MLR   *Modern Language Review*
MP   *Modern Philology*
MSR   *Malone Society Reprints*
NQ   *Notes & Queries*
OED   *Oxford English Dictionary*
PMLA   *Publications of the Modern Language Association of America*
PQ   *Philological Quarterly*
RD   *Renaissance Drama*
RES   *Review of English Studies*
RORD   *Research Opportunities in Renaissance Drama*
RQ   *Renaissance Quarterly*
SEL   *Studies in English Literature 1500–1900*
ShJ   *Shakespeare-Jahrbuch*
SP   *Studies in Philology*
SQ   *Shakespeare Quarterly*
SS   *Shakespeare Survey*
STC   *Short-Title Catalogue of English Books 1475–1640, 2nd ed.*
TLS   *The Times Literary Supplement*

The following works are ordinarily quoted by short-title only:

Arber   Edward Arber, *A Transcript of the Registers of the Company of Stationers of London, 1554–1640*, 5 vols. (London, 1875–94)
Boas   *The Works of Thomas Kyd*, ed. by Frederick Samuel Boas (Oxford, 1901, repr. with a supplement 1955)
Bond   *The Complete Works of John Lyly*, ed. by R. W. Bond, 3 vols. (Oxford, 1902)
Bowers, *Dekker*   *The Dramatic Works of Thomas Dekker*, ed. by Fredson Bowers, 4 vols. (Cambridge, 1953–61)
Bowers, *Marlowe*   *The Complete Works of Christopher Marlowe*, ed. by Fredson Bowers, 2 vols., 2nd edn (Cambridge, 1981)
Bullough   Geoffrey Bullough, *Narrative and Dramatic Sources of Shakespeare*, 8 vols. (London, 1957–75)
Cairncross   *['The Spanish Comedy', or] 'The First Part of Hieronimo' and 'The Spanish Tragedy' [or, 'Hieronimo is Mad Again']*, ed. by Andrew S. Cairncross, Regents Renaissance Drama Series, (Lincoln, London, 1967)

Carrère   Félix Carrère, *Le Théâtre de Thomas Kyd* (Toulouse, 1951)

Chambers   E. K. Chambers, *The Elizabethan Stage*, 4 vols. (Oxford, 1923)

Collins   Robert Greene, *The Plays and Poems of Robert Greene*, 2 vols., ed. by J. Churton Collins (Oxford, 1905)

Edwards, *Kyd*   Philip Edwards, *Thomas Kyd & Early Elizabethan Tragedy* (London, 1966)

Edwards, *ST*   *The Spanish Tragedy*, ed. by Philip Edwards, The Revels Plays (London, 1959)

Freeman   Arthur Freeman, *Thomas Kyd: Facts and Problems* (Oxford, 1967)

Greg   W. W. Greg, *A Bibliography of the English Printed Drama to the Restoration*, 4 vols. (London, 1939–59)

Harbage   Alfred Harbage, *Annals of English Drama, 975–1700*, rev. S. Schoenbaum (London, 1964)

Herford and Simpson   *The Works of Ben Jonson*, ed. by C. H. Herford and Percy and Evelyn Simpson, 11 vols. (Oxford, 1925–52)

McKerrow   *The Works of Thomas Nashe*, ed. by R. B. McKerrow, corrected reissue ed. by F. P. Wilson, 5 vols. (Oxford, 1958)

Mulryne   *The Spanish Tragedy*, ed. by J. R. Mulryne, New Mermaids, 2nd edn (London, 1989)

Sarrazin   Gregor Sarrazin, *Thomas Kyd und sein Kreis* (Berlin, 1892)

Wells and Taylor   *William Shakespeare: The Complete Works*, ed. by Stanley Wells, Gary Taylor et al. (Oxford, 1986)

Wood   *The Plays of John Marston*, ed. by H. Harvey Wood, 3 vols. (Edinburgh, 1934–39)

When not otherwise stated, *The Spanish Tragedy* is quoted from Edwards's edition, Kyd's other works from Boas, and the works of Dekker, Greene, Jonson, Lyly, Marlowe, Marston, Nashe, and Shakespeare from the above editions.

INTRODUCTION

Thomas Kyd was born in London in 1558, six years before Shakespeare and Marlowe. Like Shakespeare, but unlike most of his other contemporary playwrights – Marlowe, Thomas Nashe, John Lyly, Thomas Lodge, Robert Greene, and George Peele – he did not go to university. On entering Merchant Taylors' School in 1565 – four years after Edmund Spenser – the seven-year-old Thomas would have been expected 'to saie his Chathechisme and to read *p*fectly bothe Englisshe and Latyn and to wright competently'.[1] His subsequent life is a blank until the mid-1580s. We owe the next glimpse we get of Kyd to Thomas Dekker's *A Knight's Conjuring* (1607): The narrator describes an Elysian 'Grove of Bay Trees' in which 'Poets and Musitions' are assembled.[2] In the first bower dwell Chaucer and Spenser:

> In another companie sat learned *Watson*, industrious *Kyd*, ingenious *Atchlow*, and (tho hee had bene a Player, molded out of their pennes) yet because he had bene their *Lover*, and a *Register* to the Muses, Inimitable *Bentley*: these were likewise carowsing to one another at the holy well, some of them singing *Pæans* to *Apollo*, som of them *Hymnes* to the rest of the Goddes, whil'st *Marlow*, *Greene*, and *Peele* had got under the shades of a large *vyne*, laughing to see *Nash* (that was but newly come to their Colledge,) still haunted with the sharpe and *Satyricall spirit* that followd him heere upon *earth*.   (p. 156)

The passage establishes a chronology within which Kyd is conveniently placed. Chaucer and Spenser, whose *Shepheardes Calendar* had been published as early as 1579, constitute the 'first generation' of English poets. Thomas Watson and Thomas Achelley, who belong to the next group, are known to have been active from the beginning of the 1580s, while the chief creative period of Marlowe, Greene, Peele, and Nashe does not start before 1587. By grouping Kyd with Watson and Achelley and not with Marlowe, Greene, Peele, and Nashe, Dekker appears to regard Kyd as belonging to an earlier generation.[3]

We further learn from the passage that Thomas Watson, Thomas Achelley, and Kyd wrote plays in which John Bentley – 'a Player, molded out of their pennes' – performed. Bentley, one of the leading actors of the Queen's Men along with the popular comedian Tarleton, was buried on 19 August 1585.[4] The Queen's Men had been formed in March 1583.[5] Kyd then appears to have been among the playwrights for the leading adult company and indeed the only one whose skills have left a mark.[6] It may well be that the plays which Kyd wrote for the Queen's Men between their foundation in 1583 and Bentley's death in 1585 are irretrievably lost.[7] Nevertheless, the passage from Dekker leaves no doubt that Kyd had been among London's leading playwrights for several years when Marlowe left Cambridge for London in 1587 and Dekker's epithet 'industrious' may suggest that Kyd's output had been considerable.[8] Marlowe's arrival on the London stage was clamorous:

> From jygging vaines of riming mother wits,
> And such conceits as clownage keepes in pay,
> Weele leade you to the stately tent of War:

> > (*1 Tamburlaine*, Prologue, 1–3)

Kyd's first attempts were less resounding and have since perished. It has been argued that Elizabethan tragedy came 'out of nowhere' and was created 'in a year of two' by Marlowe and Kyd at the end of the 1580s.[9] Even though the scarcity of extant dramatic texts from the 1580s gives this impression, we may be confident that the reality was more complex. Kyd's lost early plays would no doubt constitute an important chapter in the missing genesis of English tragedy. T. S. Eliot pointed out long ago that Kyd has as good a title to the honour of being the father of English tragedy as Marlowe, a point that is supported by a close look at the chronology of their dramatic careers.[10]

There is little doubt that Kyd did not have his first experiences with the stage as playwright for the Queen's Men on their foundation in 1583 but considerably earlier as an actor at Merchant Taylors' School. Richard Mulcaster, the progressive headmaster, included the acting of plays in both Latin and English in the curriculum. The judge Sir James Whitelocke, who had been educated at Merchant Taylors', later reported that every year Mulcaster 'presented sum playes to the court, in whiche his scholers wear only actors, and I on among them, and by that meanes taughte them good behaviour and audacitye [i.e. self-confidence]'.[11] Kyd may have remained at Merchant Taylors' until 1573–75.[12] Mulcaster's students performed four times at court from 1573 to 1575 and Kyd may have been among the actors. If so, he would also have played in Merchant Taylors' Hall early in 1574 in front of a paying audience, the earliest known instance of a commercial boys' company.[13] Despite the absence of hard evidence, the likelihood is that Kyd, like Shakespeare, Jonson, and Anthony Munday, was once a player as well.

While the 1570s saw the beginning of strong opposition to the theatrical profession and the publication of several anti-theatrical tracts stressing the immorality of impersonation and disguise, the humanist education at Merchant Taylors' exposed Kyd to the belief that acting can teach 'good behaviour and audacitye'. Even for the University Wits, writing plays for the public stage instead of taking to a 'normal' profession to which their degrees entitled them was, no doubt, a questionable choice. Marlowe, after six years in Cambridge, became a playwright instead of taking holy orders. In *Greene's Groatsworth of Wit* (1592), Marlowe, Peele, and Nashe are exhorted to cease writing plays for the stage and to amend their lives. After his education at Merchant Taylors' under Mulcaster, Kyd's attitude towards writing for the stage was possibly quite different. Writing a closet tragedy (*Cornelia*), projecting a poem on the conversion on St Paul, and furnishing players with *The Spanish Tragedy* may have seemed more appropriate to Kyd than to most of his contemporaries.[14]

Thomas Kyd was a witness of and a participant in the first generation of the professional stage in London. He was fourteen when the 'Act for the punishment of vagabonds' forced players to secure patronage, may have acted before the Queen as one of Merchant Taylors' boys when fifteen, was eighteen when James Burbage had the Theatre constructed in Shoreditch, and was among London's leading playwrights at twenty-five. He was in the right position to contribute to the changes from amateurish beginnings to artistic and commercial success.

And contribute he did. In 1582, around the time when Kyd may have begun his career as a professional dramatist, the preacher and pamphleteer Stephen Gosson painted a bleak picture of contemporary stage craft:

> Sometime you shall see nothing but the aduentures of an amorous knight, passing from countrie to countrie for the loue of his lady, encountring many a terible monster made of broune paper, & at his retorne, is so wonderfully changed, that he can not be knowne but by some posie in his tablet, or by a broken ring, or a handkircher, or a piece of cockle shell, what learne you by that?[15]

Gosson mocks the random progression of the action in which one episode is followed by the next with a complete absence of stringent causality. Early romantic plays such as *Common Conditions* and *Clyomon and Clamydes*, written in deadly monotonous fourteeners (lines of fourteen syllables), have precisely this loose structure.

Kyd's extant plays, in contrast, introduced the complex intrigue plot characteristic of many later Elizabethan and Jacobean plays. Even the dramaturgy of Marlowe's main plays, with the possible exception of *Edward II*, shows a less radical break with the medieval heritage than Kyd's. The structure of *Tamburlaine*, *Doctor Faustus*, and *The Jew of Malta* is basically linear and shows the protagonist move from one episode to the other: from Mycetes and Cosroe, to Bajazeth, to the Soldan of Egypt, to the virgins of Damascus in *1 Tamburlaine*, from Valdes and Cornelius, to the Pope, to Rafe and Robin, to the Emperour, to the Horse-courser, to the Duke and the Duchess of Vanholt, to the old man in *Doctor Faustus* (1604), and from the three Jews, to Mathias and Lodowick, to the two friars, and to Bellamira and Pilia-Borza in *The Jew of Malta*. Structure and character constellation in Kyd's plays are altogether different. In *The Spanish Tragedy*, in *Soliman and Perseda*, and in *Hamlet* (assuming Kyd's lost play of that name resembled Shakespeare's *Hamlet* as seems indeed plausible – see chapter 6), the chief characters are introduced early on and the rest of the play develops a plot of intrigue and revenge in which the action does not advance in episodic linearity, but through tightly dramatised causality. As Aristotle put it in his *Poetics*, 'there is a great difference between happening next and happening as a result'.[16]

Kyd then is 'the first English dramatist who writes dramatically' in the sense that he is the first who skilfully represents human causality on stage.[17] A. P. Rossiter rightly pointed out that '[i]f we seek a sharp break between medieval and Renaissance ways with drama, it is to be found much rather with Kyd than with Marlowe.'[18] Lyly is in many ways a greater stylist than Kyd, but his is a drama of thought rather than of plot. Marlowe, even though the greater poet than Kyd, was not necessarily the greater dramatist, and the development from *Tamburlaine* to *The Jew of Malta* shows more traces of Kyd's influence than Kyd ever shows of Marlowe's.[19] Peele's plays, unlike Kyd's, show little interest in dramatic situation and characterisation and lack a tight dramatic structure. Likewise, Greene's plots, in the words of his editor, 'are too loosely constructed, his characters as a rule too sketchy, and his range too limited to entitle him to a high place among dramatists'.[20] More than anyone else, Kyd appears to have paved the way for Shakespeare's dramaturgy.

The numerous near-contemporary references to and quotations from Kyd's plays, in particular *The Spanish Tragedy*, are well documented and hint at Kyd's lasting importance. To instance only a few, Sly quotes Hieronimo's 'go by' (*The Taming of the Shrew*, Induction i.7), Don Pedro cites Lorenzo's 'In time the savage bull doth bear the yoke' (*Much ado About Nothing*, I.i.243–4), the Bastard refers to

'Basilisco' (*King John*, I.i.244), and Dol Common, as late as 1610, quotes the King's 'Now say Lord General, how fares our camp?' (*The Alchemist*, III.iii.33). In themselves, however, these passages say as little about the nature of Kyd's influence as the scraps of Seneca in countless Elizabethan plays indicate about the formative role of the Latin playwright. Too specific at one extreme, the relationship of later plays to Kyd's is in just as many cases too general to be one of real significance. For the revenge tragedy, the Machiavellian villain, the successful impingement of the comic upon the tragic, the mixture of Senecan theme and elaborate plotting, the crucial importance of the play-within-the-play, and possibly even the two-part play, Kyd set a precedent for later dramatists. *Titus Andronicus*, *Hamlet*, *Antonio's Revenge*, *The Malcontent*, *The Tragedy of Hoffman: or a Revenge for a Father*, *The Revenger's Tragedy*, *The Atheist's Tragedy: or The Honest Man's Revenge*, and *The Revenge of Bussy D'Ambois* all share definite generic features with *The Spanish Tragedy* and the lost *Hamlet*.[21] Lorenzo stands at the head of a list of Machiavellian villains that includes Barabas, Aaron, Edmund, Iago and many others. To argue, however, that Kyd is the 'source' for all the later plays that contain features first introduced by him is of course wrong-headed. As 'the first English dramatist who writes dramatically', he was followed by playwrights who had soon absorbed and in some ways developed several features of his dramatic method and made of it the stock of the well-plotted love-and-crime tragedy.

Shakespeare, perhaps more than anyone else, seems to have specifically profited from Kyd's works, especially in his tragedies of the 1590s. His first tragedy, *Titus Andronicus*, follows closely the structure of *The Spanish Tragedy*.[22] His second tragedy, *Romeo and Juliet*, did what only Kyd's *Soliman and Perseda* among extant plays had done before on the public stage, namely to place a conflict of love at the centre of a tragedy.[23] His third tragedy, *Julius Caesar*, covers the same period of Roman history as Kyd's *Cornelia*, and Shakespeare's Brutus may well owe something to Kyd's. Finally, the chief source of Shakespeare's fourth tragedy, *Hamlet*, is undoubtedly Kyd's work of the same name. The precise relationship between the two plays will never be known. Yet, even in the absence of Kyd's *Hamlet*, *The Spanish Tragedy*, its companion-piece, can be shown to contain far-reaching analogues. Like *Hamlet*,

[i]t has a background of wars and politics, with ambassadors going back and forth. Hieronimo distrusts the letter which reveals the murderer just as Hamlet distrusts the Ghost. He reproaches himself for delay, even

accuses himself of preferring words to blood. He has thoughts of suicide. His situation is reflected in that of other fathers as Hamlet's is in that of other sons. He takes one father for a spirit come to rebuke his tardiness. He arranges the performance of a play which is less innocent than it seems. Instead of mirroring the crime, as in *Hamlet*, this play presents the vengeance; yet the image of the crime is still there in the exhibition of Horatio's corpse, and the play, by effecting vengeance in the guise of an entertainment before an unsuspecting court, extends the analogy with Hamlet to include the fencing-match as well. In an ironic prelude to it the avenger and his destined victim, like Hamlet and Laertes, have a public reconciliation. For the rest, *The Spanish Tragedy* has a heroine whose love is opposed by her father and brother, and another woman, Hieronimo's wife, who goes mad and kills herself.[24]

Kyd's contribution to the dramatic architecture of Shakespeare's *Hamlet* was substantial.[25]

Despite his considerable influence on Elizabethan drama, Kyd was virtually forgotten after the Restoration and only occasionally referred to in cursory remarks as the author of *Cornelia*. Kyd's disappearance from literary history is best reflected by *The Lives of the Poets* in five volumes of 1753 – attributed to Theophilus Cibber though now believed to be by Robert Shiels – which contains portraits of Francis Beaumont, George Chapman, Samuel Daniel, John Day, Thomas Dekker, John Fletcher, John Ford, Greene, Heywood, Jonson, Lodge, Lyly, Marlowe, Marston, Nashe, Shakespeare, and of many others, but not of Kyd. *The Spanish Tragedy* remained anonymous until 1773 when Thomas Hawkins, in *The Origin of the English Drama*, quoted Thomas Heywood's *Apology for Actors* (1612): "'M. *Kyd* in *The Spanish Tragedy* [...]'" (II, p. 3). Kyd's plays were printed in Robert Dodsley's *Select Collection of Old Plays* (1744) and its various reissues (1780, 1825, 1874), but no scholarly edition of Kyd's works appeared before the twentieth century. The recently discovered volume entitled *Dramatic Works of Thomas Kyd* of 1848, now extant in the Folger Library, is in fact a re-binding of eighteenth-century editions to which only a title page was added.[26]

In the nineteenth century, it was John Payne Collier who did more than anyone else since the Restoration for a reappraisal of Kyd.[27] His evaluation was original in that it went far beyond the repetition of the clichés with which the few pages of earlier Kyd criticism had abounded. He was the first to recognise that

Kyd was a poet of very considerable mind, and deserves, in some respects, to be ranked above more notorious contemporaries: his thoughts are often both new and natural [...]. In taste he is inferior to Peele, but in force and character he is his superior; and if Kyd's blank-verse be not quite so smooth, it has decidedly more spirit, vigour, and variety. As a writer of blank-verse, I am inclined, among the predecessors of Shakespeare, to give Kyd the place next to Marlow.[28]

Collier found *The Spanish Tragedy* 'very powerful' and 'parts of it [...] in the highest degree pathetic and interesting', adding that '[Hieronimo's] grief is not as sublime, but it is as intense as that of Lear'.[29] While many twentieth-century critics agreed with this view, it had been pioneered in the first half of the nineteenth century.

Collier's judgement led to a gradual rise in Kyd's reputation which reached its passionate peak in A. F. Hopkinson's somewhat uncritical rhapsody on Kyd:

> In his time he was second only to Marlowe in his influence on the drama and the stage; in many things he was his equal, and in some his superior. His genius was of a sombre turn; and even his comedy has a sardonic cast – he frequently conveys a flash of lightning in a sunbeam. Nevertheless, his genius was of a high order, and he but wanted the one essential – possessed by Shakespeare – to have made his *Spanish Tragedy* as puzzling and as immortal as *Hamlet*. Death, unfortunately, carried him off at a very early age, before his unquestionably great powers had approached to anything like maturity. It is useless speculating, in the face of accomplished facts, as to what Kyd would have achieved had he lived another decade; but I am firmly convinced he would have conquered new realms of poetry and tragic passion, without trespassing on the regal dominions of Marlowe or Shakespeare.[30]

Serious scholarship on Kyd started late in the nineteenth century. Gregor Sarrazin's *Thomas Kyd und sein Kreis* (1893) is the first full-length study of his works. Most of it is now outdated, but it remains valuable for its chapter on *Soliman and Perseda*. A little later followed Gassner's edition of *Cornelia* (1894) and the first scholarly editions of *The Spanish Tragedy*, J. M. Manly's in old spelling (*Specimens of Pre-Shakespearean Drama*, 1897), Josef Schick's in the Temple Dramatists series (1898), the same Schick's much fuller edition in the German series of the *Litteraturhistorische Forschungen* (1901), and F. S. Boas's in *The Works of Thomas Kyd* (1901) – see the Bibliography.

Boas's Clarendon edition is the only edition of Kyd's works to this day. While it can claim the obvious merit of having laid the foundations for further Kyd studies, its inadequacies were commented upon soon after its appearance and, owing to the insights gained in the course of the century, have now become glaring.[31] Boas's extensive discussion of Kyd's *Hamlet* (pp. xlv–liv) is marred by the assumption that the first quarto of *Hamlet* of 1603 allows detailed inferences about Kyd's *Hamlet*. His text of *The*

Spanish Tragedy shows no awareness of Manly's old-spelling edition. *Soliman and Perseda*, on the other hand, adopts readings of a nineteenth-century type-facsimile and, even discounting this blunder, has been shown to be riddled with errors.[32] Boas erroneously includes the prose pamphlet *The Murder of Iohn Brewen* among Kyd's works and, in the appendix, prints Ayrer's poor adaptation of *The Spanish Tragedy* while hardly mentioning the much better anonymous Dutch adaptation. These are only some of the more serious flaws of Boas's edition. Kyd's works, perhaps more than those of any other Elizabethan and Jacobean playwright, need a competent new edition.[33]

A number of significant single-play editions of *The Spanish Tragedy* have been published in the course of the century: W. W. Greg's Malone Society Reprints of the first extant edition (1925) and of the first edition with additions (1948), Philip Edwards's for the Revels Plays (1959, still the standard edition), and J. R. Mulryne's for the New Mermaids (1970, 2nd edn 1989). Cairncross's edition of *The First Part of Hieronimo* and *The Spanish Tragedy* (1967) as a two-part play argues an interesting point but does so superficially. J. J. Murray's edition of *Soliman and Perseda*, finally, has rightly been described as 'extremely undependable, both textually and critically'.[34]

Of the remaining full-length studies on Kyd, four limited themselves to *The Spanish Tragedy*: P. W. Biesterfeldt's *Die dramatische Technik Thomas Kyds* (1936), Peter B. Murray's *Thomas Kyd* (1969), Frank R. Ardolino's *Thomas Kyd's Mystery Play: Myth and Ritual in 'The Spanish Tragedy'* (1985) and the same author's *Apocalypse and Armada in Kyd's 'Spanish Tragedy'* (1995).[35] Félix Carrère's *Le Théâtre de Thomas Kyd* (1951) is a detailed and painstaking study in the best French tradition which, however, added little that was new except for the dubious rejection of Kyd's authorship of *Soliman and Perseda* and the equally doubtful ascription of *Arden of Faversham* to Kyd. Philip Edwards's short *Thomas Kyd & Early Elizabethan Tragedy* (1966) usefully placed Kyd within the dramatic traditions of his time, while Arthur Freeman's *Thomas Kyd: Facts and Problems* (1967) is a detailed and generally balanced study to which all modern Kyd scholars are indebted. The central problem with Freeman's book, however, is that, apart from the biographical chapters, it largely confines itself to *The Spanish Tragedy* and *Soliman and Perseda*, thereby leaving out an important, albeit problematic, part of Kyd's work. Even though Freeman holds that *Don Horatio* may well have been written by Kyd and thinks it is probable that *The First Part of Hieronimo* constitutes a revision of *Don Horatio* (pp. 175–7), he does not discuss the play nor relate it to the contemporary vogue for two-part plays. He further disposes of the lost *Hamlet* as a 'primarily Shakespearian' (p. 175) problem and shows little interest in *Cornelia* beyond its dedication. Freeman's aim 'to provide a broad basis for the study of Kyd's works' (p. viii) was only partly achieved.

One of the purposes of this study then is to present a comprehensive scholarly and critical introduction to Kyd's works that reviews, amends, and updates previous work on Kyd. As a study of this kind is by its nature dependent upon earlier criticism, it is legitimate to ask what my new contributions are. Scholarly matters such as date, sources, text, language, company connections, the additions to *The Spanish Tragedy*, and Nashe's famous attack on Kyd have repaid scrutiny and yielded new insights. Other parts of my study are more original, for instance the investigation of the textual history of *The First Part of Hieronimo* and of its relationship to *Don Horatio* (chapter 1); the discussion of the bearing of the forepiece upon *The Spanish Tragedy* and of Kyd's place in the history of the Elizabethan two-part play (chapter 1); the analysis of the dialectical structure (chapter 4) and of the best early adaptation (chapter 5) of *The Spanish Tragedy*; the twentieth-century stage history of the same play (chapter 5); and the examination of the dramaturgy of *Soliman and Perseda* (chapter 8).

In what follows, most of my investigations will focus on Kyd's dramatic works.[36] However, as I disagree with earlier identifications of Kyd's patron – the one biographical issue with a definite impact upon Kyd's dramatic career – I discuss the matter in an appendix. Chapters 1 to 9 deal with the five plays attributable to Kyd in what I take to be their chronological order: *Don Horatio* (c. 1586/87) (via *The First Part of Hieronimo*), *The Spanish Tragedy* (c. 1587), the lost *Hamlet* (c. 1588/89), *Soliman and Perseda* (c. 1588/89), and *Cornelia* (1593/94).

Chapter 1 gives a new account of the textual and theatrical history of *Don Horatio* – which was played in conjunction with *The Spanish Tragedy* in 1592 – and the textually corrupt *First Part of Hieronimo* (printed in 1605). The latter play, I argue, is a reworking for the Children of the Chapel of c. 1603/04 of what appears to have been Kyd's forepiece to *The Spanish Tragedy*, preserving most of the 'political level' of the Kydian original but with a new 'private level'. While the revised part is burlesque in style and completely incompatible with *The Spanish Tragedy* in plot, the original part is continuous and at times indeed finely in tune with its sequel, allow-ing interesting insights into how Kyd seems to have constructed his two-part play. Not only Marlowe's *Tamburlaine*, but also the contemporary Kydian diptych, thus stands at the head of the Elizabethan vogue for two-part plays. Shakespeare's *2* and *3 Henry VI* as well as paired plays of which the second part is a revenge tragedy – Marston's *Antonio and Mellida* and *Antonio's Revenge*, Chapman's *Bussy D'Ambois* and *The Revenge of Bussy D'Ambois,* and possibly Chettle's lost *Danish Tragedy* and *The Tragedy of Hoffman: or a Revenge for a Father* – appear to follow a pattern first established by Kyd's *Don Horatio* and *The Spanish Tragedy*.

There are four chapters on *The Spanish Tragedy*: chapter 2 surveys introductory matter, in particular sources, date, text and language. In chapter 3, I investigate the 'origins' – the dramatic traditions as well as the political and socio-historic pressures – out of which the play grew. Chapter 4 is purely critical and highlights some of the play's central tensions while simultaneously trying to integrate some of the useful criticism of the past. Chapter 5, finally, explores the play's theatrical destiny after the death of Kyd, especially the additions to the play first published in 1602, the various continental adaptations as well as the play's revival on the twentieth-century stage.

The short chapter on the lost *Hamlet* takes a fresh look at the passage in Thomas Nashe's preface to Robert Greene's *Menaphon* upon which Kyd's claim to its authorship depends, adducing new evidence why Kyd, and only Kyd, appears to be the target of Nashe's diatribe. I further attempt to separate the little that possibly can be inferred from Shakespeare's play about Kyd's from all that cannot.

Chapters 7 and 8 deal with *Soliman and Perseda*, the former with introductory matters (authorship, date, sources, text, company and auspices), the latter a critical analysis of the play's artistry. In partic-ular, I explore the play's careful two-part structure, its daring generic blend, and Kyd's skilful and instructive transformation of a loose narrative into a tightly dramatised play on the threshold to the great Elizabethan drama.

In the following chapter, I situate *Cornelia*, Kyd's translation of Robert Garnier's *Cornélie*, in the context of the drama of its time and show that both its thematic interest and its language occupy an organic place within Kyd's works. My study concludes with a brief consideration of Kyd's non-dramatic works, in particular *The Householder's Philosophy*, a translation of Tasso's *Il Padre di Famiglia*, and with a survey of Kyd's dramatic apocrypha.

Notes

1 T. W. Baldwin, *Small Latine and Lesse Greeke*, 2 vols. (Urbana, Ill., 1944), I, p. 415.

2 Thomas Dekker, *A Knights Conjuring*, ed. Larry M. Robbins (The Hague, 1974), p. 155. Most of *A Knight's Conjuring* is identical with Dekker's *Newes from Hell* (1606), published the previous year. Dekker disguised the pamphlet as new by adding some nine pages at the beginning and at the end and by dividing the text into nine chapters. The passage quoted above is part of Dekker's additions to *Newes from Hell*. As *A Knight's Conjuring* is not included in *The Non-dramatic Works of Thomas Dekker*, ed. Alexander B. Grosart, 5 vols. (London, 1884–86, reissued New York, 1963), I quote from Robbins's edition.

3 See T. W. Baldwin, 'Thomas Kyd's Early Company Connections', *PQ*, 6 (1927), 311–13, and Freeman, p. 13.

4 Bentley is also mentioned by Nashe in *Pierce Penniless*: '*Tarlton, Ned Allen, Bentlie*, shall be made known to *France*, *Spain*, and *Italie*' (McKerrow, I, p. 215). See also Chambers, II, pp. 105–7, 303. For an account of Bentley's life, see Edwin Nungezer, *A Dictionary of Actors* (New Haven, 1929), p. 45.

5 For a full and original study of this acting company, see Scott McMillin and Sally-Beth MacLean, *The Queen's Men and Their Plays* (Cambridge, 1998). Though the specific bearing of this study on Kyd's known plays is slight, its attempt to study a portion of the English drama of the 1580s and early 1590s in its own right rather than as 'pre-Shakespearean' is highly valuable.

6 No extant English plays can be assigned to either Watson or Achelley. However, William Cornwallis affirmed in 1592 that Watson 'could devise twenty fictions and knaveryes in a play which was his daily practyse and his living' and Harington's *Ulysses upon Ajax* (1596) refers to 'the froth of witty Tom Watson's jests, I heard them in Paris fourteen years ago: besides what balductum [trashy] play is not full of them' (quoted in Chambers, III, p. 506). The only other playwrights connected with the Queen's Men are the actors Richard Tarlton and Robert Wilson. The second part of Tarlton's *Seven Deadly Sins* (c. 1585), of which the 'platt' (plot summary) is extant, homiletically exposes Envy, Sloth, and Lechery in three independent playlets. Robert Wilson's *Three Ladies of London* (printed 1584) is a straightforward morality play 'wherein is notably declared and set foorth, how by the meanes of Lucar, Love and Conscience is so corrupted, that the one is married to Dissimulation, the other fraught with all abhomination. A perfecte patterne for all Estates to looke into' (title page, quoted in Chambers, III, p. 496).

7 The Queen's Men made eight appearances at court between 1583 and 1585, performing the now lost *Phyllida and Corin*, *Felix and Philiomena*, *Five Plays in One*, and *Three Plays in One* besides unnamed plays. It seems plausible to assume that Kyd contributed to these plays.

8 Note though that 'industrious' also had the now obsolete meaning 'showing intelligent or skilful work' (*OED*).

9 Edwards, *Kyd*, p. 5.

10 See T. S. Eliot, *Selected Essays*, p. 118.

11 Whitelocke is quoted in Baldwin, *Smalle Latine and Lesse Greeke*, I, pp. 420–1.
12 See Freeman, p. 9.
13 See Michael Shapiro, *Children of the Revels: The Boy Companies of Shakespeare's Time and Their Plays* (New York, 1977), p. 14.
14 For the projected poem on St Paul, see Kyd's letter to Sir John Puckering (MS. *Harl.* 6849, fols. 218–19), printed in Freeman, pp. 182–3. On Mulcaster, see Richard L. DeMolen's four articles: 'Richard Mulcaster and the Elizabethan Theatre', *Theatre Survey*, 13 (1972), 28–41; 'Richard Mulcaster's Philosophy of Education', *Journal of Medieval and Renaissance Studies*, 2 (1972), 69–91; 'Richard Mulcaster and Elizabethan Pageantry', *SEL*, 14 (1974), 209–21; 'Richard Mulcaster: An Elizabethan Savant', *Shakespeare Studies*, 8 (1976), 29–82. See also William Barker's edition of Mulcaster's *Positions Concerning the Training Up of Children* (Toronto, 1994).
15 In *Playes Confuted in Fiue Actions*, quoted from Arthur F. Kinney, *Markets of Bawdrie: The Dramatic Criticism of Stephen Gosson* (Salzburg, 1974), p. 161.
16 D. A. Russell and Michael Winterbottom (eds), *Classical Literary Criticism* (Oxford, 1972), p. 64.
17 G. G. Smith, 'Marlowe and Kyd. Chronicle Histories', in Sir A. W. Ward and A. R. Waller (eds.), *The Drama to 1642, Part One*, The Cambridge History of English Literature, V (Cambridge, 1910), p. 163.
18 *English Drama from Early Times to the Elizabethans* (London, 1950), p. 160.
19 T. S. Eliot is the most prominent but by no means the only critic of Elizabethan drama to have argued that Marlowe was not 'as great a dramatist as Kyd' (*Selected Essays*, p. 118).
20 Collins, I, p. 58.
21 The fullest treatment of the revenge tragedy genre and of Kyd's role in instigating it is still Fredson Bowers's *Elizabethan Revenge Tragedy 1587–1642* (Princeton, 1940), in particular the chapter 'The School of Kyd' (pp. 101–53). Unfortunately, Bowers did not include Shakespeare's *Hamlet* in his study and his account of Kyd's *Hamlet* (pp. 85–98) is marred by the mistaken assumption that *Hamlet* Q1 allows far-reaching inferences about it. For a more recent survey of the revenge tragedy genre up to 1642, see Wendy Griswold, *Renaissance Revivals: City Comedy and Revenge Tragedy in the London Theatre 1576–1980* (Chicago, 1986), pp. 55–100.
22 See, for instance, *Titus Andronicus*, ed. Jonathan Bate, Arden Shakespeare (London, 1995), pp. 86–7.
23 See also Arthur Freeman, 'Shakespeare and *Solyman and Perseda*', *MLR*, 58 (1963), 481–7, and L. L. Brodwin, *Elizabethan Love Tragedy 1587–1625* (London, 1971). It has also been argued that *Romeo and Juliet* shows 'Kyd's lessons of the irony of endeavours, of the self-cancelling actions, of the intricacy of the web of love, hate and fortune' (Edwards, *Kyd*, p. 43).
24 *Hamlet*, ed. Harold Jenkins, Arden Shakespeare (London, 1982), pp. 97–8. See also Bullough (VII, pp. 16–18), who points out 'over a score of parallels', and E. E. Stoll, '*Hamlet* and *The Spanish Tragedy*', *MP*, 35 (1937–38), 31–46.

25 An interesting case has also been made for *The Spanish Tragedy* exercising on *Richard III* 'what I take to be a decisive influence' (Emrys Jones, *The Origins of Shakespeare* (Oxford, 1977), p. 196, see pp. 196–206). See also Philip Edwards, 'Shakespeare and Kyd', in K. Muir, J. L. Halio, and D. J. Palmer (eds.), *Shakespeare: Man of the Theater* (Newark, 1983), pp. 148–54. For Kyd's influence upon 2 and 3 *Henry VI*, see chapter 2.

26 See Lukas Erne, 'W. E. Burton's *Dramatic Works of Thomas Kyd* of 1848', *NQ*, 242 [n.s. 44] (1997), 485–7.

27 See *The History of English Dramatic Poetry*, 3 vols. (London, 1831), III, pp. 205–12.

28 *Ibid.*, III, p. 207.

29 *Ibid.*, III, pp. 209–11.

30 *Play Sources: The Original Stories on which were Founded the Tragedies of 'Arden of Faversham' and 'A Warning for Fair Women'* (London, 1913), pp. vii–viii.

31 See W. W. Greg, 'The Works of Thomas Kyd', *MLQ*, 4 (1901), 185–90. Greg's review gives a good impression of the quantity and the seriousness of Boas's mistakes in establishing his texts. Charles Crawford's *Concordance to the Works of Thomas Kyd* (London, 1906–10) is based on Boas's edition and thus shares its mistakes and limitations.

32 In Arthur Freeman, 'Inaccuracy and Castigation: The Lessons of Error', in Anne Lancashire (ed.), *Editing Renaissance Dramatic Texts, English, Italian, and Spanish* (New York and London, 1976), pp. 97–120.

33 Arthur Freeman's projected Clarendon edition has, alas, long been abandoned, but his bibliographical article 'The Printing of *The Spanish Tragedy*', *The Library*, 5th Series, 24 (1969), 187–99, as well as his 'Inaccuracy and Castigation: The Lessons of Error' referred to above will be of help to a future editor.

34 Freeman, p. 156.

35 To these should be added Serena Cenni's *Il Corpo insepolto: Discorsività e affettività in 'The Spanish Tragedy' di Thomas Kyd* (Trento, 2000), of which I became aware after completing my manuscript. My thanks go to Fernando Cioni for drawing my attention to this book and to the author for providing me with a copy.

36 For the most detailed discussion of the known facts of Kyd's life, see Freeman, pp. 1–48, and Arthur Freeman, 'Marlowe, Kyd, and the Dutch Church Libel', *ELR*, 3 (1973), 44–52.

CHAPTER 1

Don Horatio and
The First Part of Hieronimo

The anonymous play *The First Part of Ieronimo. With the Warres of Portugall, and the life and death of Don Andræa* (hereafter '1 *Hieronimo*') was printed in quarto format in 1605 by William Jaggard and published by Thomas Pavier.[1] Scholarship on 1 *Hieronimo* has been dominated by the question of its origin and its relationship to the forepiece to *The Spanish Tragedy* referred to in the diary of the theatre manager Philip Henslowe. Among the performances by Lord Strange's Men listed there, the diary features the following entries:[2]

Rd at spanes comodye donne oracioe the 23 of febreary	xiij s vj d
Rd at the comodey of doneoracio the 13 march 1591	xxviiij^s
Rd at Jeronymo the 14 of march 1591	iij li xj s
Rd at Joronymo the 20 marche 1591	xxxviij s
Rd at doneoracio the 30 of marche 1591	xxxix s
Rd at Jeronymo the 7 of ap^rell 1591	xxvj s
Rd at the comodey of Jeronymo the 10 of ap^rell 1591	xxviij s
Rd at Joronymo the 14 ap^relle 1591	xxxiij s
Rd at the comodey Jeronymo the 22 of ap^rell 1591	xvij s
Rd at Jeronymo the 24 of ap^rell 1592	xxviij s
Rd at Jeronymo the 2 of maye 1592	xxxiiij s
Rd at Jeronymo the 9 of maye 1592	xxvj s
Rd at Jeronymo the 13 of maye 1592	iij^li 4^s
Rd at the comodey of Jeronymo the 21 of maye 1592	xxviij s
Rd at Jeronymo the 22 of maye 1592	xxvij s
Rd at Jeronymo the 27 of maye 1592	xxiij s
Rd at Jeronymo the 9 of June 1592	xxviij s
Rd at Joronymo the 18 of June 1592	xxiiij s
Rd at the comodey of Jeronymo the 20 of June 1592	xv s
Rd at Joronymo the 30 of desember 1592	iij^li viij^s
Rd at Jeronymo the 8 of Jeneway 1593	xxij s
Rd at Jeronymo the 22 of Jeneway 1593	xx^s

Scholars in the past had problems identifying the different titles. Sidney Lee, in the *DNB*, believed that 'Ieronymo' refers to *1 Hieronimo*, and that by 'spanes comodye donne oracioe', 'comodey of doneoracio', 'doneoracio', and 'comodey Jeronymo', Henslowe meant *The Spanish Tragedy*.[3] Today most scholars agree that the contrary is true.[4] 'Ieronymo' is the title under which Kyd's contemporaries knew and parodied *The Spanish Tragedy*. Also, the entries document that the companion-piece was clearly less popular and the takings more modest. When 'Jeronymo' or 'Joronymo' was revived in 1597 for a run of thirteen performances, the 'doneoracio' (hereafter '*Don Horatio*') had disappeared from the repertoire. On three occasions, *The Spanish Tragedy* was performed immediately after its companion-piece: 13 and 14 March, 22 (Saturday) and 24 (Monday) March, and 21 and 22 May. This, too, suggests that *Don Horatio* was a forepiece to, or formed a two-part play with, *The Spanish Tragedy*.

Critics have disagreed about whether *The Spanish Tragedy* was written before or after *Don Horatio*. One reason for assuming the former play to be a sequel is the passages that allude to a conflict preceding the beginning of *The Spanish Tragedy*. The matter to which they refer – centring on an affair between Bel-imperia and Andrea, and Castile's wrath at its discovery – is never explained or developed. I quote the relevant passages:

Andrea.   In secret I possess'd a worthy dame,
        Which hight sweet Bel-imperia by name.   (I.i.10–11)

Lorenzo.   [*to Pedringano*] Thus stands the case; it is not long
        thou know'st,
        Since I did shield thee from my father's wrath
        For thy conveyance in Andrea's love,
        For which thou wert adjudg'd to punishment.   (II.i.45–8)

Lorenzo.   [*to Bel-imperia*] Why then, remembering that old
        disgrace
        Which you for Don Andrea had endur'd,   (III.x.54–5)

Castile.   Welcome Balthazar,
        Welcome brave prince, the pledge of Castile's peace:
        And welcome Bel-imperia. How now, girl?
        Why com'st thou sadly to salute us thus?
        Content thyself, for I am satisfied,
        It is not now as when Andrea liv'd,
        We have forgotten and forgiven that,
        And thou art graced with a happier love.   (III.xiv.106–13)

1 Hieronimo, however, does not appear to deal with any of these events. After the King has created Hieronimo Marshall of Spain,

news is given of Portugal's refusal to pay tribute to Spain. Andrea is
sent to the Portuguese court as an ambassador. Injured in his pride,
Lorenzo plans a plot on Andrea's life (I.i). Andrea takes leave of Bel-
imperia and entrusts her to Horatio's care (I.ii). Lorenzo hires
Lazarotto, a 'discontented courtier', to murder Andrea on his return
from Portugal. The villains' conversation is overheard by Hieronimo
and Horatio, who plan to thwart Lorenzo's plot (I.iii). Arrived at the
Portuguese court, Andrea's claim for tribute is rejected. He declares
war on the Portuguese and challenges Balthazar to meet him during
the battle (II.i). Forging further Machiavellian plans, Lorenzo asks
Alcario to disguise himself as Andrea in order to woo Bel-imperia
(II.ii). Hieronimo and Horatio write a letter to Andrea to inform him
of Balthazar's intentions (II.iii). Lorenzo's plans fail as Lazarotto
mistakenly kills the disguised Alcario. Lazarotto's murder is discovered, but the courtier is silenced by Lorenzo who, after promising to
obtain a pardon, has him killed (II.iv and II.v). Andrea, only just
returned from Portugal and preparing for the battle, is again bidding
farewell to Bel-imperia (II.vi). Leaders of the two armies meet in
verbal skirmishes before the beginning of the actual fight (III.i).
During the battle, Andrea is killed by Balthazar and his soldiers, but
Horatio revenges his friend's death by taking Balthazar captive and
leading the Spanish army to victory (III.ii). As the funeral procession
passes over the stage, Revenge denies the request of Andrea's ghost
to speak to Horatio (III.iii). After Andrea's funeral, the Spanish
army, Horatio, Lorenzo, and their prisoner are set to return to
Spain. Hieronimo speaks the epilogue (III.iv).

   Critics have hitherto tried to account for the origin of
1 *Hieronimo* in two radically opposed ways: one group has argued
that 1 *Hieronimo* (or the text from which it originates) and *The
Spanish Tragedy* form a two-part play by Kyd composed in the order
in which the events are dramatised. The other group has held that
1 *Hieronimo* is a clumsy attempt by an anonymous and moderately
gifted writer to make money from the popularity of *The Spanish
Tragedy*. Adepts of the first group are F. G. Fleay, Sidney Lee, Dr
Markscheffel, Gregor Sarrazin, Josef Schick, and, among more
recent critics, Andrew S. Cairncross.[5] The supporters of the latter
group include Rudolf Fischer, F. S. Boas, E. K. Chambers, Félix
Carrère, Philip Edwards, Arthur Freeman, and John Reibetanz.[6]

   Fleay's, Lee's, and Sarrazin's views were not based on any firm
evidence. Schick pointed out significant 'stylistic resemblances in
tropes and figures, parallel passages, ridiculous puns, common
geographical mistakes' (p. xviii) which could argue for Kyd's

authorship. In the introduction to his edition of *1 Hieronimo* and *The Spanish Tragedy* as a two-part play, Cairncross gives the reasons for his revival of a view that had not found any prominent supporters since the beginning of the century:

> In the last half-century, however, we have had the revolution in the study of Elizabethan texts caused by the 'memorial' theory of corrupt quartos like *1 Hieronimo*; and, if we assume that this is a memorial version of an original first part by Kyd, we may now return to a modified form of the earlier view.   (p. xiv)

He arrives at the following conclusion:

> It therefore seems reasonable to suggest as the original of which *1 Hieronimo* is a memorial version a longer good text by Kyd, *The Spanish Comedy*, which preceded *The Spanish Tragedy* and combined with it to form a two-part play.   (p. xix)

Unfortunately, Cairncross does not show in detail in what ways the text of *1 Hieronimo* conforms to what we know about memorially reconstructed texts. He shrewdly observes 'the curious contradiction between the skilled, complicated construction and occasional strength of expression and characterization, on the one hand, and the many irregularities and defects of the play, on the other', but his summary statement that this 'can be simply explained by imperfect reporting or memorial reproduction of a competent original play by Kyd' (pp. xv) is not demonstrated with sufficient rigour. Cairncross applies with too much confidence the category of 'memorial reconstruction': 'The text is indeed extremely corrupt. It is only some 1200 lines long. Even in the absence of a good text for comparison, it seems clear that it is "memorial"' (p. xv). Surely, texts can be subjected to a corrupting influence in other ways than by 'memorial reconstruction'. Laurie E. Maguire has recently shown that critics and editors have been too hasty to resort to 'memorial reconstruction' when no better answer could be found.[7] Cairncross's edition seems a case in point. Nevertheless, he has usefully reminded critics that the external evidence – the entries in Henslowe's diary and the references in *The Spanish Tragedy* apparently pointing to earlier events – should be borne in mind in any discussion of the origins of *1 Hieronimo*.

The argument against Kyd's involvement in *1 Hieronimo* and in favour of the priority of composition of *The Spanish Tragedy* was first articulated by Rudolf Fischer's *Zur Kunstentwicklung der englischen Tragödie von ihren ersten Anfängen bis zu Shakespeare*, an excellent study of which, disappointingly, neither Freeman nor

Cairncross seem to have been aware. Fischer usefully opposes the political level ('politischen Theil') of the play to its private level ('familiären Theil'), a distinction we do well to bear in mind. He argues that the political level is handled rather adroitly – 'nicht gerade ungeschickt' (p. 102) – by the anonymous playwright whereas the private level is qualified as odd – 'eigenthümlich' (p. 103).

Fischer convincingly demonstrates to what extent the private level is modelled upon *The Spanish Tragedy*. The intrigues in the two plays run virtually parallel: Lorenzo hates Andrea (Horatio) out of envy for his honour and because of Andrea's amorous liaison with Bel-imperia. He hires an accomplice, Lazarotto (Pedringano), in order to have his rival killed at an encounter with Bel-imperia. Following the murder, Lorenzo gets rid of his accomplice after keeping him quiet by promising to obtain a pardon from the King. Lorenzo is the same Machiavellian villain in both plays, Pedringano and Lazarotto, Lorenzo's tools, are made of the same farcical-comical stuff. The structural debts can be traced even to single words: in both plays, the King, when first addressing Hieronimo, asks him to 'frolic'.[8] Fischer's conclusion is unequivocal: 'It seems impossible to advocate Kyd's authorship of *The First Part of Hieronimo*, chiefly owing to the composition of the play which bears obvious traces of the use and copying it made of *The Spanish Tragedy*' (p. 111, my translation).

Boas's view is largely informed by Fischer's analysis, but he adds useful circumstantial evidence: *1 Hieronimo* may owe its existence to 'the excitement caused by the revival of *The Spanish Tragedie* in 1602 with Ben Jonson's Additions to bring out this so-called "First Part" – a medley of farce and melodrama' (p. xlii). He points out incompatibilities inherent in the plots of the two plays. For instance, the love affair between Andrea and Bel-imperia in *1 Hieronimo* is not a secret as we are told in *The Spanish Tragedy* (I.i.10, II.i.47), and Hieronimo's farcical paternal pride in *1 Hieronimo* is not in keeping with his dignified character in *The Spanish Tragedy*.

Chambers, Carrère, and Edwards basically agree with Fischer and Boas and add little to their argument. Chambers deviates slightly from Boas by cautiously stating that the quarto of 1605 may be 'a later version of the same theme' (IV, p. 23) as the play recorded by Henslowe.[9] Edwards declares *1 Hieronimo* to be 'clearly written after *The Spanish Tragedy* and based on it, and almost certainly intended as a burlesque' (*ST*, p. 138). Freeman discovered evidence corroborating a dating around the year 1602. He detects echoes from plays written around the turn of the century and owned by the King's Men, notably *Julius Caesar* (II.iii.26 and II.iii.45) and *Hamlet* (I.iii.106), He also points out that II.iii is 'a semi-parodic imitation' of a scene in Chapman's *The Gentleman Usher* (c. 1602).[10] In the same scene, he finds a play on the name of a boy actor, William Ostler (p. 176), who performed for the Children of the Chapel. Even though agreeing with the earlier critics on the matter of the late date, Freeman significantly differs in his view of the play's relationship to the play recorded by Henslowe: 'I think it is unlikely that anyone fabricated *The First Part* out of thin air, and far more probable that the extant play represents a revision or rewriting of the original "spanes commodye", and hence that it is fairly close, at least in plot, to the early fore-piece' (p. 176).

To sum up: Boas, Freeman and Cairncross, the play's most influential critics in the twentieth century, all disagree on the provenance of *Don Horatio* and *1 Hieronimo* as well as on the sequence of events:

Boas: 1 *Don Horatio* (presumably by Kyd)
           2 *The Spanish Tragedy*
           3 *1 Hieronimo*, not based on *Don Horatio*

Freeman: 1 *The Spanish Tragedy*
           2 *Don Horatio* by anon. some time before 1592
           3 *Don Horatio* revised and printed as *1 Hieronimo*
              ('fairly close, at least in plot, to the early fore-piece')

Cairncross: 1 *Don Horatio* (by Kyd)
            2 *The Spanish Tragedy*
            3 *1 Hieronimo*, put together after 1600, a memorial
               reconstruction of *Don Horatio*.

Ironically, both Freeman's study and Cairncross's edition were published in 1967, and nobody has attempted to settle the dispute since. John Reibetanz's article (1972) deals with the play as published in 1605. He does not examine the play, however, from the angle of Kyd criticism, but in the context of the 'war of the theatres' which raged during the first years of the seventeenth century.[11] Apart from this shift of emphasis, Reibetanz is in agreement with Boas and does not address Cairncross's and Freeman's views. Emma Smith's edition of *The Spanish Tragedy* includes the text of *1 Hieronimo*, but Smith summarily dismisses Cairncross's argument and sees the 'prequel' simply as part of the 'afterlife' of *The Spanish Tragedy*.

The purpose of the present survey of criticism has been to bring out the complex and conflicting evidence, the total sum of which no single critic seems to have been able to explicate. Boas cannot account for the 'stylistic resemblances in tropes and figures, [or the] parallel passages' that Schick mentions, and he has to argue that *Don Horatio* melted into thin air. Freeman's theory fails to account for the allusions in *The Spanish Tragedy* that imply the spectators' knowledge of anterior incidents. Cairncross's theory of memorial reconstruction, finally, falls short of justifying the features of *1 Hieronimo* that are irreconcilable with *The Spanish Tragedy*.

Although none of the above critics is entirely wrong, I will offer a new account of the provenance, authorship, and textual constitution of *1 Hieronimo* as well as of its relationship to *Don Horatio*. This explanation introduces a distinction between two textual layers, one 'original' and one 'revised', which I shall term 'A' and 'B'. This distinction alone can account for the conflicting evidence.

For the sake of clarity, I will begin by presenting my conclusions: the two diametrically opposed views of previous critics – one claiming that Kyd wrote *Don Horatio* and that *1 Hieronimo* is a version of it, the other holding that *1 Hieronimo* was written much later in an attempt to profit from the popularity of *The Spanish Tragedy* and is not related to *Don Horatio* – only become compatible if we realise that *1 Hieronimo* is made up of two textual layers of a completely different generic nature and with radically different relationships to *The Spanish Tragedy*. One level, 'A', is compatible in plot, tone, and characterisation with its companion-piece. It is indeed finely harmonised with the plot details of its sequel and dramatises the material of which the opening scenes in *The Spanish Tragedy* represent a faithfully reported summary. The other textual level, 'B', is in every respect incompatible with *The Spanish Tragedy*. Whereas the first layer is generically mixed, a 'tragical-comical-historical-pastoral' in the words of Polonius, the second is an intentional burlesque.

The first level, I will argue, is a textually corrupt version of parts of *Don Horatio*, the first half of a continuous and interrelated diptych of which the second part is *The Spanish Tragedy*. Kyd thus appears to have been the writer of a large-scale two-part play of which more is extant than has hitherto been supposed, and it seems that Kyd, along with Marlowe, triggered the vogue for the contemporary two-part play. The intrinsic value of what is extant of *Don Horatio* does not add much to Kyd's reputation. It is nevertheless of considerable importance to the study of Kyd, and inferences about

The Spanish Tragedy can be drawn from it of which I will mention here only three instances: the vicious circle of revenge has long begun when Andrea speaks the prologue to *The Spanish Tragedy*, the play's complex and puzzling structure results from the connection with the prequel, and the subplot seems to grow out of its more complex counterpart in the first part. *The Spanish Tragedy*, that is, needs to be read with what is extant of *Don Horatio*.

Let me return to the two textual layers A and B of *1 Hieronimo*. What are their characteristics? A was written around the time of the composition of *The Spanish Tragedy*, and was probably part of *Don Horatio*. The action is neither incompatible with *The Spanish Tragedy* in general nor with the allusions to what happened earlier in particular. It is by all means Kydian in style and finely harmonised with *The Spanish Tragedy*. Passages pertaining to A feature characters that reappear or (if dead) are mentioned in *The Spanish Tragedy*. The tone of A is essentially serious, in keeping with the non-comic parts of *The Spanish Tragedy*. Despite the generally corrupt text, A has fairly regularly scanning verse, a mixture, like *The Spanish Tragedy*, of blank verse and rhyme, with slightly more rhyme than its companion piece. Style and language are reminiscent of (albeit not of quite the same quality as) *The Spanish Tragedy*.

The textual layer termed B was written substantially later, after the turn of the century. It is neither by Kyd nor Kydian. Its action is not compatible with *The Spanish Tragedy* and evidently does not try to be. Its genre is a mixture of farce, parody, and grotesque. Its characterisation is not harmonised with *The Spanish Tragedy*, most notably in the case of Hieronimo who is turned into a ridiculous buffoon. B contains all the references to Hieronimo's small stature and all the echoes of what must have been recent plays when B was composed, *Julius Caesar*, *Hamlet*, and Chapman's *Gentleman Usher*. It carries further noticeable features such as topical references and repetitions of phrases. Its language mixes prose and verse which is frequently less regular or scans more roughly than that of A.

A and B more or less correspond to Fischer's political and private level. A centres on Andrea's progress in the 'wars of Portugal' (as the play's subtitle has it), from his election as ambassador and his presence at the Portuguese court to the final battle and his funeral, interspersed with passages that show him torn between his public duties and his private affections for Bel-imperia. B, on the other hand, deals with Lorenzo's envy and his plot against Andrea's life in which he involves Alcario and Lazarotto.

If we want to understand how the burlesque reworking of Kyd's

original *Don Horatio* came into being, we need to turn to a passage
from John Marston's play *The Malcontent* with which scholars have
not ceased to grapple. The third quarto of *The Malcontent*, printed
like the previous two in 1604, added various passages to Q1 and Q2,
most notably an induction featuring actors of the King's Men:

> *Sly.* I would know how you came by this play.
> *Cundale.* Faith sir the book was lost, and because twas pittie so
>   good a play should be lost, we found it and play it.
> *Sly.* I wonder you would play it, another company having interest
>   in it?
> *Cundale.* Why not Malevole in folio with us, as Ieronimo in
>   Decimo sexto with them? They taught us a name for our
>   play, wee call it *One for Another*.
> *Sly.* What are your additions?
> *Burbidge.* Sooth not greatly needefull, only as your sallet to your
>   greate feast, to entertaine a little more time, and to abridge
>   the not received custome of musicke in our Theater.   (Induction)

'Folio' and 'Decimo sexto' refer to the size of the adult and child
actors. *The Malcontent* was originally written for the boy actors of
the Children of the Chapel who had leased the Blackfriars buildings
from Richard Burbage. Critics have struggled to reconcile the
conflicting evidence suggesting, on the one hand, that the Children
of the Chapel apparently stole a play – referred to as 'Jeronimo' –
from the King's Men, and, on the other, that there are various references in *1 Hieronimo* which seem to indicate that the play was
performed by a boys' company. Now if we consider that
1 Hieronimo consists of two textual layers, one 'old' (which I have
termed 'A') and one 'new' (which I have termed 'B'), a case for a
coherent interpretation can be made: *Don Horatio* appears to have
been a Chamberlain's/King's play. When it passed into the hands of
someone who adapted it for the Children of the Chapel, cutting
much of the original play and adding an original intrigue, views on
the legality of the undertaking may have differed.[12] Whereas the
King's Men considered it a breach of their rights and retaliated by
appropriating *The Malcontent*, the Children's company may have
thought of it as an original play. Examples such as *Selimus* and
Locrine or *King John* and *The Troublesome Reign of King John*
indicate that playwrights felt free to draw upon other plays and the
boundaries between what was objected to and what was tolerated
seem to have been fluid.[13]

My interpretation is supported by the nature of the two textual
levels: for instance, by the complete absence of references to the
actors' small statures and of burlesque material in general from the

'old' portion (A). In addition, an attempt on the borders of legality
and an attempt to burlesque a play from the adult companies seems
to be in keeping with the part the Children of the Chapel took in the
wars of the theatres, as exemplified by the biting satire in Jonson's
Poetaster.

What thus appears to have happened is that someone who had
come into the possession of a manuscript of *Don Horatio* largely
rewrote the play for the Children of the Chapel. The anonymous
reviser omitted the 'private level' of the original play which must have
dealt among other things with Andrea's secret love for Bel-imperia
and Castile's wrath at its discovery, as we learn from *The Spanish
Tragedy*. For this he substituted Lorenzo's unsuccessful plot against
Andrea's life (B). The 'political level' of *Don Horatio*, however, was
largely left intact in *1 Hieronimo* (A), albeit possibly abridged and
further transformed by additions related to Hieronimo.[14] For
example, the battle scenes making up most of Act III basically belong
to A, but Hieronimo's presence at the battle is an addition. Some of
his lines are noticeably grafted upon the original text, as, for instance,
Hieronimo's soliloquy at the beginning of the battle scene, III.ii.:

> *Ieronimo.*   O valiant boy, stroake with a Giants arme
>   His sword so fals vpon the Portugales,
>   As he would slise them out like Orenges,
>   And squeese their blouds out. O aboundant ioy,
>   Neuer had father a more happier boy. *Exit* IERONIMO. (III.ii.1–5)[15]

As the (re-)writing was manifestly aimed at burlesquing the hero of
The Spanish Tragedy, even the political portions of *Don Horatio*
seem not to have been spared when the writer saw a possibility to
ridicule Hieronimo. While some scenes or passages can be attributed
to A or to B with some confidence, the occasional intrusions of B
into the play's political portions sometimes make it extremely difficult to distinguish one textual layer from the other. The numerous
corruptions also contribute to this difficulty.

A and B can also be distinguished by their respective casts.
Hieronimo (spelled 'Ieronimo'), Horatio, Andrea, the King of Spain,
Lorenzo his nephew, Bel-imperia ('Bellimperia'), the Spanish Lord
General, the King of Portugal, and Balthazar his son (called
'Balthezer' in *1 Hieronimo*) appear in both. Characters belonging to
A, the Kydian part, are Castile (the brother to the King of Spain),
Rogero (a Spanish courtier), Pedringano, Villupo ('Don Volluppo' in
1 Hieronimo) and Alexandro (two Portuguese Noblemen), all of
whom reappear or are mentioned in *The Spanish Tragedy*. Added to

these should be Christophil, who has only one line in *The Spanish Tragedy* (III.ix.15), and Phillippo and Cassimero, two ghost characters appearing in a stage-direction at III.iv.0.2. Without *Don Horatio*, it is not clear why these characters were introduced with names and they seem to have played a minor role in the first part which was omitted in the reworking. The characters confined to B consist of Lazarotto (a discontented courtier, a 'malcontent'), the Duke of Medina, and Alcario (son of the Duke of Medina, in love with Bel-imperia). What is notable about them is not so much that they do not reappear in *The Spanish Tragedy* (two of the three are killed anyway), but that they are never made mention of, even in situations where the lack of retrospection seems unaccountable.[16]

A is consistent with and sometimes carefully harmonised with *The Spanish Tragedy* as several passages demonstrate. The following short scene (II.vi) occurs before the decisive battle against the Portuguese in the course of which Andrea will be killed:

Bel-imperia.   You came but now, [and] must you part agen?
         You told me that your sperit should put on peace;
         But see, war followes war.
Andrea.   Nay, sweet loue, cease,
         To be denide our honour, why, twere base
         To breath and liue; and wars in such a case   5
         Is euen as necessary as our bloud.
         Swordes are in season then when rightes withstood.
         Deny vs tribute that so many yeeres
         We haue in peace tould out? why it would raise
         Spleene in the host of Angels: twere enough   10
         To make [the] tranquile saints of angry stuffe.
Bel-imperia.   You haue ore wrought the chiding of my breast;
         And by that argument you firmly proue
         Honor to sore aboue the pitch of loue.
         Lend me thy louing and thy warlicke arme,   15
         On which I knit this softe and silken charme
         Tyed with an amorous knot: O, may it proue
         Inchaunted armour being charmed by loue;
         That when it mounts vp to thy warlick crest,
         It may put by the sword, and so be blest.   20
Andrea.   O what deuinity proceeds from loue.
         What happier fortune, then, my selfe can moue?
         Harke, the drum beckens me; sweet deere, farwell.
         This scarfe shall be my charme gainst foes and hell.
Bel-imperia.   O, let me kisse thee first.
Andrea.   The drum agen.   25
Bel-imperia.   Hath that more power then I?
Andrea.   Doot quickly then:
         Farewell.
                                Exit ANDREA.

Bel-imperia.   Farewell. O cruell part;
       Andreas bosome bears away my hart.   *Exit* BELLIMPERIA.

The scene does not stand in contradiction to any of the allusions to
prior events reported in *The Spanish Tragedy*. Andrea and Bel-
imperia are alone and nothing indicates that their love relationship
is generally known. It is possible that the scene was originally longer,
and minor metrical imperfections, such as line II.vi.27 (which is one
foot short), can be explained by the corrupt text. In general,
however, the verse scans well and the passage has by all means a
Kydian ring. It is reminiscent of Horatio's encounter with Bel-
imperia (*The Spanish Tragedy*, II.iv.1–49) and of Ferdinando's with
Lucina (*Soliman and Perseda*, II.i.1–25). The seemingly random
alternation of rhyme and blank verse may seem odd, but closely
corresponds to both of the above-mentioned scenes, as a comparison
of the rhyme scheme in the opening verses of each scene will demonstrate:

1 Hieronimo, II.vi:	a	b	b	c	c	d	d	e	f	g
The Spanish Tragedy, II.iv:	a	b	b	c	c	d	e	f	g	h
Soliman and Perseda, II.i:	a	b	c	c	d	e	e	e	f	g

The scene bears further characteristics typical of Kyd. Physical
action is dexterously integrated into the language: the tying of the
scarf (*1H*), the 'love combat' (*ST*), and the handing over of the
carkanet, i.e. a collar or necklace of gold or jewels (*S&P*). There is
nothing parodic or burlesque about the scene. It is as straightfor-
wardly Kydian as any, even though of perfunctory brevity and
devoid of the highlights that occur in Kyd's greatest play.

   In addition to these likenesses in style and dramatic technique, a
plot detail links the scene to *The Spanish Tragedy*. It seems odd that
this important connection has never been pointed out. When in
1 Hieronimo Andrea has died in the battle and Horatio has captured
Balthazar, the scarf present in the above excerpt returns:

Horatio.   Come then, my friend, in purple I will beare
       Thee to my priuate tent, and then prepare
       For honord Funerall for thy melting corse.
              He takes his scarfe and ties it about his arme.
       This scarfe ile weare in memorie of our soules,
       And of our muteall loues; heere, heere, ile wind it,
       And full as often as I thinke one thee,
       Ile kisse this little ensigne, this soft banner,
       Smeard with foes bloud, all for the maisters honer.
                                        (*1H*, III.ii.161–8)

In *The Spanish Tragedy*, I.iv, when Horatio reports to Bel-imperia the circumstances of her lover's death in battle, he says:

> *Horatio.*   This scarf I pluck'd from off his liveless arm,
>   And wear it in remembrance of my friend.
> *Bel-imperia.*   I know the scarf, would he had kept it still,
>   For had he liv'd he would have kept it still,
>   And worn it for his Bel-imperia's sake:
>   For 'twas my favour at his last depart.   (*ST*, I.iv.42–7)

Kyd was an expert in the use he made of stage props: rope, knife, box, paper, pen and many more objects are employed in *The Spanish Tragedy*. Besides being literally tied about the characters' arms, the scarf in *1 Hieronimo* and *The Spanish Tragedy* metaphorically ties sequences together, thereby giving them additional meaning. Several critics have noticed the importance of the scarf as a reoccurring prop in *The Spanish Tragedy* without, however, referring to *1 Hieronimo*.[17] If a two-part play was intended when the last scenes of *Don Horatio* were written, Horatio's kiss of Andrea's scarf may well have been intended to foreshadow the transference of Bel-imperia's affection onto the surviving friend of her former lover. The scarf thus stretches over the full two-part play, passing from Bel-imperia to Andrea (*1H*, II.vi.16–24), from the dead Andrea to Horatio (*1H*, III.ii.164–8), from the dead Horatio to Hieronimo (*ST*, II.v.51–6) who inadvertently offers it to Bazulto (III.xiii.86–9) and finally shows it to the courtly audience after his deadly play (*ST*, IV.iv.122–9). The carkanet in *Soliman and Perseda* fulfills a similar role as it passes from Perseda to Erastus (I.ii.32), who loses it (I.iv). It is found by Ferdinando (I.iv.43–5), presented to Lucina (II.i.22), and discovered at her neck by Perseda (II.i.47). Finally, Erastus wins it back (II.i.231.1) and has it redelivered to Perseda (II.ii.8.1).

Further correspondences between *1 Hieronimo* and *The Spanish Tragedy*, principally dealing with the battle between the Spanish and the Portuguese armies, can be passed over more swiftly. Here is how *1 Hieronimo* dramatises Andrea's death:

> *They fight, and* ANDREA *hath* BALTHEZER *downe. Enter* PORTUGALES
>   *and releiue* BALTHEZER *and kil* ANDREA.
> *Andrea.*   O, I am slaine; helpe me, *Horatio.*
>   My foes are base, and slay me cowardly;
>   Farewell deere, dearest *Bellimperia.*
>   Yet heerein ioy is mingled with sad death:
>   I keepe her fauer longer then my breath.   *He dies.*
> *Sound Alarum,* ANDREA *slain, and Prince* BALTHEZER *vanting on him.*
>
>   *Enter* IERONIMO, HORATIO *and* LORD GENERALL.
>   (*1H*, III.ii.106.1–111.3)

This incident is taken up twice by *The Spanish Tragedy*, firstly in the General's report to the King, then in Horatio's report to Bel-imperia:

> *General.* The victory to neither part inclin'd,
>   Till Don Andrea, with his brave lanciers,   65
>   In their main battle made so great a breach,
>   That, half dismay'd, the multitude retir'd:
>   But Balthazar, the Portingales' young prince,
>   Brought rescue and encourag'd them to stay:
>   Here-hence the fight was eagerly renew'd,   70
>   And in that conflict was Andrea slain –
>   Brave man at arms, but weak to Balthazar.
>   Yet while the prince, insulting over him,
>   Breath'd out proud vaunts, sounding to our reproach,
>   Friendship and hardy valour, join'd in one,
>   Prick'd forth Horatio   (*ST*, I.ii.64–76)

> *Horatio.*   their fight was long,
>   Their hearts were great, their clamours menacing,
>   Their strength alike, their strokes both dangerous.
>   But wrathful Nemesis [. . .]
>   Brought in a fresh supply of halberdiers,
>   Which paunch'd his horse and ding'd him to the ground.
>   Then young Don Balthazar with ruthless rage,
>   Taking advantage of his foe's distress,
>   Did finish what his halberdiers begun,
>   And left not till Andrea's life was done.   (*ST*, I.iv.13–26)

Fischer (p. 111) and Boas (p. xliv) held that the accounts in the two plays are at odds with each other and argue against Kyd's authorship of *1 Hieronimo*. The absence of halberdiers and horses can be explained by the limitations of stage realism, imperfections which members of an audience are asked to piece out with their thoughts. Apart from this, *1 Hieronimo* and Horatio's report in *The Spanish Tragedy* agree in nearly every detail. Whether Balthazar finished off what the other Portuguese began, or whether he got back and vaunted on Andrea once he was already dead seems a petty detail, and one Horatio – who arrives after his friend's death according to the stage-direction – would be unlikely to judge accurately. Nor, surely, would this have mattered much to Kyd.

After Andrea's death, Horatio strikes back at the Portuguese prince:

> HORATIO *has Prince* BALTHEZER *downe; then enter* LORENZO *and
>   seizes his weapon.*
> *Horatio.*   Hand off, *Lorenzo*; touch not my prisoner.
> *Lorenzo.*   Hees my prisoner; I seizd his weapons first.
> *Horatio.*   O base renowne,
>   Tis easie to seize those were first laid downe.

> Lorenzo. My lance first threw him from his warlicke steede. [...]
> Horatio. Well, peace; with my bloud dispence,
>   Vntill my leedge shall end the difference. [...]
> Horatio. Speake, prince, to whether doost thou yeeld?
> Balthezer. The vanquisht yeilds to both, to you [the] first.
> Horatio. O abiect prince, what, doost thou yeild to two?
>
> (1H, III.ii.126.1–43)

The quarrel between Lorenzo and Balthazar continues in *The Spanish Tragedy*, I.ii:

> King. To which of these twain art thou prisoner?
> Lorenzo. To me, my liege.
> Horatio.   To me, my sovereign.
> Lorenzo. This hand first took his courser by the reins.   155
> Horatio. But first my lance did put him from his horse.
> Lorenzo. I seiz'd his weapon and enjoy'd it first.
> Horatio. But first I forc'd him lay his weapons down.
> King. Let go his arm, upon our privilege.   *Let him go.*
>   Say worthy prince, to whether didst thou yield?   160
> Balthazar. To him in courtesy, to this perforce:
>   He spake me fair, this other gave me strokes:
>   He promis'd life, this other threaten'd death:
>   He wan my love, this other conquer'd me:
>   And truth to say I yield myself to both.   (*ST*, I.ii.153–65)

Similarly, both plays stress Horatio's funeral for his dead friend. *The Spanish Tragedy* has:

> Andrea. By Don Horatio, our Knight Marshal's son,
>   My funerals and obsequies were done.   (*ST*, I.i.25–6)

> Horatio. I took him up and wound him in mine arms,
>   And welding him unto my private tent,
>   There laid him down and dew'd him with my tears, (*ST*, I.iv.34–6)

> Horatio. I saw him honour'd with due funeral: (*ST*, I.iv.41)

Like the passage dealing with the scarf, these references are of little importance in themselves, and a spectator or reader is unlikely to remember them. They have their significance though as they look back to an action that had greater prominence in *Don Horatio*:

> Horatio. Come then, my friend, in purple I will beare
>   Thee to my priuate tent, and then prepare
>   For honord Funerall for thy melting corse.   (*1H*, III.ii.161–3)

The stage-direction in *1 Hieronimo* at the beginning of III.iii reads:

> *Enter two, dragging of ensignes; then the funerall of* ANDREA: *next* HORATIO, *and* LORENZO, *leading prince* BALTHEZER *captiue; then the* LORD GENERAL *with others mourning.*

Finally, the last scene begins as follows:

> *Horatio.*   These honord rights and worthy duties spent
> Vpon the Funerall of *Andreas* dust,
> Those once his valliant ashes – march we now
> Homeward with victory to crowne Spaines brow.   (*1H*, III.iv.1–4)

Andrea's funeral – briefly mentioned in *The Spanish Tragedy* – was therefore an important contribution to the pervasive pageantry in *Don Horatio*.

A further correspondence between *1 Hieronimo* and *The Spanish Tragedy* that needs to be mentioned is that Don Pedro, brother to the Portuguese King, and Don Rogero, a Spanish courtier, who both fight in the battle (*1H*, III.i.0.1, III.ii.19), are mentioned by name in the General's report to the King in *The Spanish Tragedy* (I.ii.40, I.ii.43).[18] Finally, Cairncross, in his edition, points out that Andrea's 'Are all things abord?' and the King's 'Our selfe in person/ Will see thee safe aboord' (*1H*, I.ii.52; II.i.89–90) contain the same geographical oddity as *The Spanish Tragedy*, where the Portuguese Viceroy is said to have 'cross'd the seas' in order to get from Portugal to the court of Spain (*ST*, III.xiv.11).

The internal evidence outlined above as well as the external evidence inherent in the entries in Henslowe's diary, in Marston's *Malcontent*, and the allusions to prior events reported in *The Spanish Tragedy* all argue for Kyd's authorship of the textual layer which I have termed 'A'. To the Kydian portion A belong II.i, II.vi, III.i, III.ii, and III.iv without some short parodic additions related to Hieronimo, and probably parts of I.i and I.ii.[19] It thus seems that a certain number of verses, possibly about four hundred, which were written by Kyd around the time of and in conjunction with *The Spanish Tragedy* survive in the text of *1 Hieronimo*.

As we have seen, the multiple close correspondences in plot, characterisation, style, and tone between A and *The Spanish Tragedy* argue against a hackwriter's having burlesqued Kyd's masterpiece in order to profit from its popularity early in the seventeenth century. This seems to have been the precise motive, however, behind the writing of B. In order to analyse its characteristics and demonstrate its incompatibility with *The Spanish Tragedy*, I shall touch upon features of plot as well as characterisation and genre.[20]

In I.iii of *1 Hieronimo*, Hieronimo and Horatio overhear Lorenzo and Lazzarotto's plot to murder Andrea. They are infuriated at the prince's villainy and write a letter to Andrea to warn him. If *1 Hieronimo* and *The Spanish Tragedy* formed a continuous two-part play, it would be difficult to account for the fact that there is no mention of this in *The Spanish Tragedy*. Hieronimo's scepticism when he receives Bel-imperia's letter stating that Lorenzo and Balthazar killed Horatio would be especially inexplicable: 'My son slain by Lorenzo and the prince!/ What cause had they Horatio to malign?' (*ST*, III.ii.33–4).

Furthermore, we learn from *The Spanish Tragedy* that the love relationship between Andrea and Bel-imperia was a secret and that its discovery triggered her father's wrath (*ST*, I.i.10–11, II.i.45–8). In the 1605 text, however, there is nothing secret about the relationship between Andrea and Bel-imperia. When Castile hears Lazarotto reveal the whole story, he does not show any signs of surprise (II.v.27–41). A further feature of *1 Hieronimo* that makes it appear less than plausible that it was conceived before *The Spanish Tragedy* is that the King is acquainted with Horatio in *1 Hieronimo*, placing him 'next vnto his royall bosome' (I.i.63), whereas he does not recognise him in *The Spanish Tragedy* (I.ii.114–15).

Arguing that *1 Hieronimo* is a memorial reconstruction of *Don Horatio*, Cairncross tried to anticipate these objections by suggesting that 'a hack writer using the material of *The Spanish Tragedy* was likely to produce a version of a fore-piece consistent with it; a memorial version by one or more actors, on the other hand, was likely to show gaps and inconsistencies, as in recognized Elizabethan bad quartos' (p. xvii). *Hamlet* Q1 may well be a 'bad' quarto, a memorial reconstruction by an actor who, it seems, played Marcellus. Yet, its relationship to Q2 and F appears to be of a very different kind from that of *1 Hieronimo* to a forepiece consistent with *The Spanish Tragedy*. The order of scenes in *Hamlet* Q1 differs slightly from the more authoritative texts: one short scene has no correspondence in Q2 and F; the language is at times corrupt and many speeches are shortened. The plot, however, is that of Q2 and F. It seems unlikely that actors would have failed to remember some of the essentials of the play's story-line.

We might thus expect even a badly remembered version to contain aspects of the conflicts alluded to. Cairncross has to take considerable liberties with the evidence in order to make it suit his argument. His point that Andrea's 'In secret I possess'd a worthy dame' (*ST*, I.i.10) may imply that it was 'the "possession," not the whole affair, that was secret' (p. xviii) seems strained.

If we try to go along with Cairncross's argument, what would have been the procedure of reconstruction his 'one or more actors' followed? On the one hand, they would have had an extremely close look at *The Spanish Tragedy* to make their reconstruction compatible with such an unimportant feature as Andrea's scarf. On the other hand, they would have disregarded gross incompatibilities in plot such as Hieronimo's unawareness of Lorenzo's villainy and suggestions of Castile's wrath at the discovery of Andrea's love for Bel-imperia in *The Spanish Tragedy*. This is hardly plausible.

As for the differences in characterisation, Lorenzo's familiar intercourse with Alcario – he addresses Alcario as 'my soules spaniell, my lifes ietty substance' (*1H*, I.iii.1), for example – sharply contrasts with his aristocratic demeanour in *The Spanish Tragedy*. Bel-imperia, a 'most weeping creature' at the beginning of I.ii in *1 Hieronimo*, seems a parodic version of the very determined character in the second part of the diptych. The prime target of the intentional burlesque, however, is clearly Hieronimo. His opening lines show him to be little more than a buffoon: 'My knee sings thanks vnto your highnes bountie;/ Come hether, boy *Horatio*; fould thy ioynts' (*1H*, I.i.4–5). The parodic intent in several short speeches or soliloquies by Hieronimo – at the end of III.i, the beginning and the end of III.ii, and the end of III.iv – is evident; for example: 'So now kisse and imbrace: come, come,/ I am wars tuter; strike a larum, drum' (*1H*, III.i.133–4). On other occasions, Hieronimo's care for the memory of his son in *The Spanish Tragedy* is turned into ridiculous paternal pride:

> *Balthazar.* [*to Horatio*]   Hath war made thee so impudent and
> >   young?
> My sword shall giue correction to thy toong.
> *Ieronimo.*   Correct thy rascals, Prince; thou correct him ?
> Lug with him, boy; honors in bloud best swim.   (*1H*, III.ii.118–21)

Allusions to the small stature of the actor playing Hieronimo, no doubt a boy actor of the Children of the Chapel, add further comic business at the expense of the Knight Marshal (for example, *1H*, I.iii.114, II.iii.65, III.i.33–8, III.i.46, III.iv.10–11). Around the time when *The Spanish Tragedy* was once again in the theatre, augmented with Jonson's additions, the writer of B provided a parodic counterpart to Kyd's hero.

If, as I shall argue below, *Don Horatio* and *The Spanish Tragedy* were both written before 1588, they are likely to precede Kyd's *Hamlet*. In his edition of Shakespeare's play, Harold Jenkins suggests that the name of Hamlet's confidant Horatio goes back to *The Spanish Tragedy*.[21] More likely, the name was suggested by the loyal friend in *Don Horatio*, rather than the romantic lover in *The*

Spanish Tragedy. Horatio pondering suicide at the death of Andrea (*1H*, III.ii.149–52) is reminiscent of Horatio in *Hamlet* (V.ii.292–4). In general, the character constellation Andrea–Horatio–Bel-imperia–Lorenzo–Castile corresponds in many ways to Hamlet–Horatio–Ophelia–Laertes–Polonius. Like Hamlet and Ophelia, Andrea and Bel-imperia form a social mismatch and are actively opposed by her father. As the King makes Andrea ambassador to Portugal to claim the overdue tribute, so Claudius pretends to send Hamlet to England '[f]or the demand of our neglected tribute' (III.i.173).

It has already been pointed out that the text of the 1605 quarto shows signs of major corruption. Cairncross suggested that its cause was memorial reconstruction, a suggestion I have tried to discredit. A close look at a few examples may help us understand the nature of the text's faultiness:[22]

> *Medina.*   Who names *Alcario* slaine? aie me, tis he:
>   Art thou that villaine?
> *Lazarotto.*   How didst know my name?   (*1H*, II.v.13–14)

Here, a line in which the Duke of Medina mentions Lazarotto's name is likely to have dropped out of the text. This seems all the more plausible as verse II.v.13 is preceded and followed by a rhyming couplet which suggests that the missing line would have rhymed with verse II.v.13. Before the decisive fight between Horatio and Balthazar, Horatio's last words are:

> If thou beest valliant, cease these idle words,
> And let reuenge hang on our glittering swords,
> With this proud prince, the haughty *Balthezer*.   (*1H*, III.ii.124–6)

It is not quite clear how the last line follows upon the preceding two. Markscheffel conjectures:

> Enough! I speak no more, and Ill now war
> With this proud prince, the haughty *Balthezer*.[23]

These passages further discredit Cairncross's suggestion of memorial construction. Reporters are likely to miss puns, add actors' interjections, spoil images. Incoherent syntax as evidenced above, however, seems the result of poor copying rather than memorial reconstruction. At the ultimate reason for the faulty textual transmission – a disorderly, barely readable copy? a short-hand version? – one may only guess.

Many rhyming couplets have one verse consisting of a few syllables only. For example:

Ieronimo.   But my leedge,
          Heere must be kind words which doth oft besiedge   (*1H*, I.i.46–7)

J. Le Gay Brereton, lists six pages of doubtful readings with attempts at emendation in the 1605 text and in Boas's edition.[24] For instance:

Lazarotto.   I see an excellent villaine hath his fame
          As well as a great courtier.
Medina.   Speake, villain: wherefore didst thou this accursed deed?
                                                        (*1H*, II.v.15–17)

'Speake, villaine' should clearly be placed at the end of II.v.16. Although the text is corrupt beyond the redemptive help of any editor's emendations, Boas does too little, it seems, to rearrange some of the play's lines when the verse in the 1605 quarto looks more like doggerel.

The Spanish Tragedy was entered in the Stationers' Register on 6 October 1592, within eight months of the seven recorded performances of *Don Horatio*. The figures in Henslowe's diary suggest that the popularity of *Don Horatio* had been considerable, especially considering that it was coming of age in 1592. The intake for *Don Horatio* on 21 May 1592 ('xxviij s') was not beaten by the next four performances of *The Spanish Tragedy* ('xxvij s', 'xxiij s', 'xxviij s', 'xxiiij s'). Only four plays, *The Spanish Tragedy*, *The Jew of Malta*, *Henry VI* (often assumed to be Shakespeare's 'First Part'), and *Mully Mulloco*, were performed more often from the beginning of Henslowe's entries (19 February 1592) until acting stopped because of plague (22 June 1592).[25] It is not easy to explain what kept Lord Strange's Men from having both parts published as had happened with Marlowe's *Tamburlaine* two years earlier.[26]

A further question, to which there is no easy answer, concerns the titles by which Henslowe designates the forepiece. So far, I have simply referred to the play as 'Don Horatio'. In fact, the entries read:

      spanes comodye donne oracioe
      comodey of doneoracio
      doneoracio
      comodey of Jeronymo [3x]
      the comodey Jeronymo[27]

That the play was called a comedy does not pose a serious problem as Elizabethan generic distinctions were more vague than ours today. Nor is it difficult to account for 'Jeronymo' in the title, which was probably a result of the popularity of *The Spanish Tragedy* and does not necessarily reflect the importance of Hieronimo's role in the forepiece. The mention of Horatio, however, is not easy to explain, as nothing in the extant text or in *The Spanish Tragedy* indicates that he may have been the play's hero. Wrestling with the conflicting evidence, Freeman (p. 177) writes:

> Horatio is the lover of the tragedy proper, but not of the action summarized by Andrea's ghost, and if the fore-piece was the comedy of Horatio, one can explain the situation only as the outcome of an effort to capitalize on the popularity of the tragedy by 'inferring' a comedy concerning the romantic hero of the popular play in happier times.

This, however, appears to contradict the point he made a page earlier:

> I think it is unlikely that anyone fabricated *The First Part* out of thin air, and far more probable that the extant play represents a revision or rewriting of the original 'spanes commodye', and hence that it is fairly close, at least in plot, to the early fore-piece.

A play close in plot to *1 Hieronimo* is clearly not a comedy on Horatio 'in happier times'. The evidence is conflicting, but Freeman wants to have it both ways. Perhaps we should beware of making too much of Henslowe's precise wording. As 'titus & ondronicus' (for *Titus Andronicus*) in his diary illustrates, Henslowe did not go out of his way to get the titles exactly right. Moreover, most of *Don Horatio* is lost, and it is possible that Horatio played an important part in the lost romantic part. Alternatively, the title may have been intended to indicate the continuity of the two-part play, the first ending with Horatio's revenge for his friend's death, the second ending with Hieronimo's revenge for his son's death.

Theatre directors have long realised that *The Spanish Tragedy* gains from being considered in the context of its forepiece. *1 Hieronimo* makes clear that Andrea's death is not the accidental result of the ravages of the battle, but the outcome of Balthazar's challenge to Andrea at the Portuguese court (II.i.50–93). As the pride of the Portuguese is offended by Andrea's request for tribute, Balthazar presents the Spanish prince with 'my gage, a neuer fayling pawne' (II.i.52). The spiral of revenge dramatised in *The Spanish Tragedy* – moving from Andrea, to Bel-imperia, to Lorenzo, to Hieronimo – had its origin in an even earlier causal link in *Don Horatio*. The productions at the Citizens Theatre, Glasgow (1978) and at the Shakespeare Center in New York (1986) both made use of *1 Hieronimo* (see chapter 5) which makes it seem all the more surprising that most critics have refused to consider *The Spanish Tragedy* in the context of its forepiece.

If *The Spanish Tragedy* was conceived after *Don Horatio* as the passages referring to specific past events imply, its dramatic architecture becomes more intelligible. It has often been pointed out that the structure of *The Spanish Tragedy*, especially its beginning, is in some respects rather odd.[28] Granted, the first act, if well performed, can evoke an effective atmosphere of unease as the spectators try in vain to make sense of the outcome predicted by Revenge on the one hand (I.i.86–9) and the unfolding of the events on the other. Even so it is surprising that Hieronimo, under whose name the play was generally known during its time, is a secondary character until II.v., a minor figure at court, father of one of the central characters in the romantic plot, and the Master of the Revels who presents a masque to a courtly audience. Before II.v., his role resembles that of Egeus in the Folio text of *A Midsummer Night's Dream*.[29] Only after Horatio's murder does Hieronimo have the role of protagonist thrust upon him. Thereafter, the primary interest clearly centres around the revenge for the murder of Horatio, and not for the killing of Andrea. 'From this point', Bowers wrote, 'the ghost and his theme, which was to be the core of the play, are superfluous; and, indeed, need never have been introduced.'[30]

The play's singular dramatic architecture becomes clearer if we realise that *The Spanish Tragedy* was constructed to be continuous with but also understandable without the first part. In fact, the opening scenes represent a detailed and somewhat laborious transition from the chief concern of *Don Horatio* to that of *The Spanish Tragedy*. There is something highly meticulous about Kyd's plotting. In *Soliman and Perseda*, he goes to great lengths to adapt the story of the loss and recovery of the carkanet found in his source. Only once the chain is restored to its owner and Erastus goes into exile after murdering Ferdinando, does the central conflict involving Soliman, Perseda, and Erastus get under way. In *The Spanish Tragedy*, he similarly spends much time tracing the transition from the forepiece to Hieronimo's revenge. Kyd's painstaking dramaturgy may at times appear counterproductive, at the expense of greater dramatic dynamics. Kyd's weakness, however, is at the same time his strength, as it is bound up with his interest in complex causality which he dramatised like no other English playwright before him.

If *The Spanish Tragedy* is a sequel to a play that dramatised 'the Warres of Portugall' as the subtitle of *1 Hieronimo* has it, then the thematic relevance of the Portuguese subplot becomes more easily understandable.[31] Even Villuppo's treachery may have been prepared for in *Don Horatio*. In the verbal confrontation between the Portuguese and the Spaniards preceding the battle, Vollupo and Don Rogero challenge each other to meet during the combat. As the battle is raging, we see Rogero on the lookout for Vollupo:

> *Enter* ROGERO.
> Rogero. Ha, *Vullupo?*
> Balthezer. No; but a better.   (*1H*, III.ii.19–20)

As it turns out, Vollupo is the one character who is conspicuously absent from the battle. Don Rogero is finally killed not by Vollupo, but by Alexandro who is the target of Villuppo's treachery in *The Spanish Tragedy*. Even though Vollupo's villainy is nowhere commented upon, his absence from the battle is surprising, and the original text of *Don Horatio* may well have elaborated his character and further motivated the subplot in *The Spanish Tragedy*.

The repercussions of the impact of the forepiece upon *The Spanish Tragedy* extend as far as the final catastrophe. Hieronimo's killing of innocent Castile (IV.iv.201.1), whom Kyd had made a point of showing as a benevolent peacemaker between Lorenzo and Hieronimo (III.xiv), has understandably puzzled critics. Various explanations for Hieronimo's rash deed have been advanced: Bowers interpreted it as a reflection of contemporary abhorrence of private revenge, Freeman as redress of an imbalance ('Balthazar for Bel-imperia, Lorenzo for Horatio, Castile for Hieronimo'), while James P. Hammersmith argued that 'the thematic design of the play, not the plot, generates the inevitability of Castile's death'.[32] While none of this is wrong, it is important to add that Kyd's concern again appears to have been the unity of his dramatic diptych: the first part dramatised Castile's fierce opposition to Andrea and Bel-imperia's love – his wrath having been such that Bel-imperia still fears it late in *The Spanish Tragedy* (III.xiv.106–13) – while the second part contains the corresponding punishment administered by Revenge and approved of by the Ghost of the wronged Andrea.

If we therefore assume, as seems indeed likely, that Kyd wrote *The Spanish Tragedy* as a sequel, we are in a position to appreciate more fully the dramaturgical problem he faced: aware that the narrative of the second part was to move away from Andrea, the hero of the first part, he was nevertheless anxious to preserve a unity over the entirety of his two-part play. The use of the handkerchief which appears and reappears in various episodes throughout the two parts, thereby tying sequences and characters together, has been shown above. Another ingenious device which allowed Kyd to strengthen the unity of his two-part play was to provide *The Spanish*

Tragedy with a frame that would recall the first part. As Andrea's premature death in unfair battle (*1 Hieronimo*, III.ii.106–10; *The Spanish Tragedy*, I.iv.16–26) and Bel-imperia's consequent feelings of revenge (I.iv.65) bridge the two plays, so the Ghost of Andrea and Revenge carry the drama of *Don Horatio* over into its sequel and keep it alive throughout the play. After Horatio's death in II.iv, Revenge and the Ghost of Andrea on the one hand and the characters of the play proper on the other seem to have different concerns. While Hieronimo and even Bel-imperia are bent on revenging Horatio and have forgotten Andrea, the Ghost of Andrea reminds us that the play's initial concern was with having his death revenged. While the play proper stresses the central interests of *The Spanish Tragedy*, the frame keeps us aware of the wider perspective of the two-part play. Kyd's device is much more than a makeshift solution: it simultaneously allows him to dramatise the play's central tension between a determinist universe and a world of human causality in which man shapes and acts out his own destiny.

Two-part plays were a common feature of Elizabethan theatre. Shakespeare's *Henry IV* and Marlowe's *Tamburlaine* are the most famous but by no means the only examples. Even before c. 1587 when Marlowe and Kyd completed their two-part plays, George Whetstone's *Promos and Cassandra* had been published in two parts (1578) and Richard Tarlton's *Seven Deadly Sins* appears to have been performed in two parts. It was after 1587, however, that a real vogue for two-part plays began. Among the fully extant two-part plays are *1* and *2 Edward IV* (c. 1592/99), presumably by Thomas Heywood; Henry Chettle and Anthony Munday's *1* and *2 The Downfall and Death of Robert, Earl of Huntingdon* (1598); Marston's *Antonio and Mellida* and *Antonio's Revenge* (also called *1* and *2 Antonio and Mellida*) (1599/1601); Heywood's *1* and *2 If You Know Not Me, You Know Nobody* (1603/05); Dekker and Middleton's *1* and *2 The Honest Whore* (1604–05); Chapman's *Conspiracy of Charles, Duke of Byron* and *The Tragedy of Charles, Duke of Byron*; and Chapman's *Bussy D'Ambois* (1607) and *The Revenge of Bussy D'Ambois* (1610/11). In the years immediately following the two-part plays by Marlowe and Kyd, Robert Greene's *Alphonsus, King of Aragon* (c. 1587) announced in its last chorus a sequel that does not seem to have been written. In *The Three Lords and Three Ladies of London* (1589), Robert Wilson added a sequel to his earlier *The Three Ladies of London* (c. 1581); *The Troublesome Reign of John, King of England* was printed in two

parts (1591), presumably in order to recall the *Tamburlaine* plays
printed the year before; *Selimus* (c. 1591) was projected as a two-
part play of which only the first part appears to have been written;
and Strange's Men performed 1 and 2 *Tamar Cham* (of which only
a transcript of the plot of the first part survives). Finally, besides *1*
and *2 Henry IV* (1597–98), Shakespeare wrote two plays on the War
of the Roses, or on the 'Contention' between the houses of York and
Lancaster as the titles of the early quartos (1594/95) have it, which
may also be considered as a two-part play: *2* and *3 Henry VI*.

The Elizabethan two-part play has had its share of critical atten-
tion. G. K. Hunter analysed it in relation to Shakespeare's *1* and *2*
Henry IV, and Clifford Leech opposed the structure of *1* and *2*
Tamburlaine and their two-part offspring to that of Shakespeare's *2*
and *3 Henry VI*.[33] Despite the unambiguous evidence from
Henslowe's diary showing that *Don Horatio* and *The Spanish
Tragedy* were repeatedly performed on successive nights at a time
when Kyd was alive and well, neither of the two articles mentions
Kyd. Now that I have argued that *Don Horatio* partly survives in the
Kydian portion of *1 Hieronimo*, it seems particularly appropriate to
consider Kyd's hitherto neglected place in the history of the
Elizabethan two-part play.

Hunter and Leech argue that a number of Elizabethan two-part
plays were written under the influence of *Tamburlaine*. While I
agree, I would like to suggest, in a way which complements rather
than contradicts their arguments, that some two-part plays may also
owe certain debts to Kyd's *Don Horatio* and *Spanish Tragedy*.

It is surely remarkable that Kyd's is by no means the only two-
part play of which the second part is a revenge play. Marston's
Antonio's Revenge (c. 1599/1601), the sequel to *Antonio and
Mellida* (c. 1599/1600), acknowledges from the beginning its indebtedness to *The Spanish Tragedy*: the 'poniard' and the 'cord'
mentioned in the opening stage direction are reminiscent of
Hieronimo who enters with 'a poniard in one hand, and a rope in
the other' (III.xii). Like Horatio, Feliche has been murdered at night,
hung on stage, and his mangled body, like Horatio's, is hidden
behind a curtain before being shown to the audience. As G. K.
Hunter has pointed out, 'Andrugio, the deprived father of the play,
is obviously modelled on Kyd's Hieronimo'.[34] These examples could
be multiplied.

W. Reavley Gair, editor of *Antonio's Revenge* for the Revels
Plays, agrees that Marston's play 'adheres rigidly to [the] form of
revenge tragedy', but thinks that '*Antonio's Revenge* is exceptional

in that it is ostensibly the second part of a play which began as a comedy.'[35] Yet, judging by the extant evidence, Kyd's *Don Horatio*, which Henslowe repeatedly called a comedy, was just as generically mixed as *Antonio and Mellida*. So, while it has long been recognised that the second half of Marston's two-part play is in many ways a reworking of *The Spanish Tragedy*, as an intentional burlesque or not, critics do not seem to have considered that Marston also followed Kyd in writing a two-part play consisting of a generically mixed play and a revenge tragedy.[36]

The Tragedy of Hoffman, or Revenge for a Father, for which Chettle received payment from Henslowe on 29 December 1602, may be a further revenge tragedy that was written as a sequel. On 7 July of the same year Henslowe had paid Chettle one pound for the now lost 'danyshe tragedy' which Greg imagines 'was a fore-piece dealing with the story of Hoffman's father, such as the extant work throughout presupposes.'[37] Like *Antonio's Revenge*, Chettle's play does not hide its debts to *The Spanish Tragedy*: Hoffman, like Hieronimo, 'Strikes ope a curtaine where appeares a body', and a bloody handkerchief spurns the hero to vengeance.[38] As the brothers Mathias and Lodowick are clearly meant to recall the paired characters of the same names in *The Jew of Malta*, the echoes of the names Jeronimo, Lorenzo, Horatio, and Isabella in Jerome, Lorrique, Hoffman, and Lucibella may be more than coincidence. It seems at least possible that Chettle's two-part structure was also inspired by Kyd's.

Chapman's *Bussy D'Ambois* and *The Revenge of Bussy D'Ambois* constitute a third two-part play that conforms to the pattern established by Kyd and followed by Marston and possibly Chettle. Even though several years elapsed between the original writing of *Bussy D'Ambois* and *The Revenge of Bussy D'Ambois*, Chapman appears to have revised *Bussy* around the time he wrote *The Revenge*, smoothing out the transition between the two plays in the process; moreover, it has been argued that *The Revenge* 'was intended as a genuine dramatic sequel to the revised Bussy'.[39] Even though adopting the external form of the revenge tragedy, Chapman's dramatisation is as much his criticism of the genre as his own contribution to it, casting Clermont as the stoic and morally responsible counterpart to the impassioned revenger of *The Spanish Tragedy* and its progeny. That Chapman adopted the two-part structure of the prototype for this criticism may be significant.

Why did several playwrights follow Kyd by adding a revenge tragedy as a sequel to a first part? The revenge tragedy is a subgenre of the tragedy of intrigue, its peculiarity being that it dramatises the reaction to, rather than the instigation of, a crime – typically a murder. By definition, the revenge forms a sequel, a 'second part' in a course of events. Andrea, Andrugio, Hoffman's father, and Bussy have all been killed before the revenge tragedies begin and the ensuing action follows naturally upon what precedes. If the revenge is to preserve its dramatic urgency, not only the revenger but also the spectators must remember the cause. If an audience has seen the first part, possibly even on the eve of the sequel as audiences of *The Spanish Tragedy* could have in 1592, then the emotional background against which the revenge tragedy is placed is ideally present to the audience. The revenge tragedy sequel, even if it is an afterthought, as it certainly was in Chapman's case and may have been in Kyd's, therefore gains in unity by having its central concern already prepared for: the quest for vengeance.

According to Hunter, unity in the Elizabethan two-part play 'depends on a parallel setting-out of the incidents rather than on any picking-up of all the threads of Part One. The two-part plays we have examined all use this method, with a greater or lesser degree of success, and it is the only method I have been able to find'.[40] Nevertheless, Kyd was not content to construct his two-part play with a unity of theme, but elaborately dramatised the trajectory of his plot from the first to the second part in order to preserve dramatic unity in this regard. Although 'the greater number of surviving two-part plays of the Elizabethan period are not unified in any way', Kyd's clearly is.[41]

While Hunter did not find any two-part plays in which unity is foremost a matter of 'preservation of traits of character or strands of the plot', Clifford Leech singled out *2* and *3 Henry VI* as an example of two closely related plays with 'a continuous action running through the two Parts'.[42] It thereby resembles what the extant evidence allows us to gather about Kyd's two-part play, composed a few years earlier. Kyd and Shakespeare terminate the first part with an important battle, bringing about a provisional result after which the play can pause. Both effect a smooth transition from the first to the second part. At the beginning of *3 Henry VI*, the play, in Samuel Johnson's words, 'is only divided from the former for the convenience of exhibition; for the series of action is continued without interruption'.[43] The first part ends with Warwick and York determined to pursue the King, and the second part opens with the same two characters recognising that the King has managed to escape. Kyd's first part presumably ended with the

Lord General's declaration that 'The day is ours and ioy yeelds happy treasure;/ Set on to Spaine in most triumphant measure' (III.iv.5–6).[44] In the same vein, after Andrea has recalled the highlights of the first part, the sequel begins with the Spanish King's 'Now say Lord General, how fares our camp?' (I.ii.1). Apart from the introduction of the frame in *The Spanish Tragedy*, the action of both plays continues where the first part left off.

Even though *2* and *3 Henry VI* are not normally thought of as revenge plays, they do dramatise, like *Don Horatio* and *The Spanish Tragedy*, a spiral of revenge that stretches over both parts. In Kyd's two-part play, this spiral moves from Balthazar's offended pride at Andrea's request for tribute (*1 Hieronimo*, II.i), to his killing Andrea in unfair battle (*1 Hieronimo*, III.ii), to Bel-imperia's revenge through 'second love' (*The Spanish Tragedy*, I.iv), to the killing of Horatio (*The Spanish Tragedy*, II.iv), and, finally, to Hieronimo and Bel-imperia's revenge in the bloody play-within-the-play (*The Spanish Tragedy*, IV.iv). In Shakespeare's two-part play, York, having vainly claimed his right to the crown, kills Clifford in the battle of St Albans, whereupon Young Clifford vows revenge (*2 Henry VI*, V.ii) and kills both York's son Rutland (*3 Henry VI*, I.iii) and York himself (*3 Henry VI*, I.iv). York's sons, in turn, revenge their father by defeating the Lancastrians at the battle of Towton where Clifford is killed (*3 Henry VI*, II.vi) and, after further reversals, at Tewkesbury, whereupon Richard, Duke of Gloucester kills Henry VI in the Tower (*3 Henry VI*, V.vi).

Besides these structural analogies, some local resemblances are even more specific, suggesting that Shakespeare was consciously recalling Kyd's two-part play while composing his: Margaret, wailing over Prince Edward's stabbed body with 'How sweet a plant have you untimely cropped!' (*3 Henry VI*, V.v.61), recalls Hieronimo's 'Sweet lovely rose, ill-pluck'd before thy time' (II.v.46) as he mourns over Horatio who has just been butchered; Gloucester's 'If any spark of life be yet remaining' (*3 Henry VI*, V.vi.66) resembles Hieronimo's 'O speak, if any spark of life remain' (II.v.17); and Gloucester reproduces Hieronimo's wordplay on 'leave' (*3 Henry VI*, III.ii.34–5 and *The Spanish Tragedy*, III.xi.2–3). Both sequels refer to the same chapter of Elizabethan 'popular history':[45]

John of Gaunt,
Which did subdue the greatest part of Spain;   (*3 Henry VI*, III.iii.81–2)

Brave John of Gaunt, the Duke of Lancaster, [...]
He with a puissant army came to Spain,
And took our King of Castile prisoner.

           (*The Spanish Tragedy*, I.iv.164–7)

Shakespeare further takes up Kyd's device of the blood-stained napkin serving as an emblem of revenge by having Margaret dip it into Rutland's blood and present it to York before she stabs him (*3 Henry VI*, I.iv.80–2, I.iv.157–9, II.i.60–3). Compare, in particular, York's

See, ruthless Queen, a hapless father's tears.
This cloth thou dipped'st in blood of my sweet boy,
And I with tears do wash the blood away.   (I.iv.157–9)

and Hieronimo's

And here behold this bloody handkercher,
Which at Horatio's death I weeping dipp'd
Within this river of his bleeding wounds: (IV.iv.122–4)

Even the closing line of Shakespeare's two-part play looks like a conscious inversion of the final couplet in Kyd's:

For here though death hath end their misery,
I'll there begin their endless tragedy.   (*The Spanish Tragedy*, IV.v.47–8)

For here, I hope, begins our lasting joy.   (*3 Henry VI*, V.vii.46)

The certainty of Kyd's bleak afterworld is adapted to the uncertainties and hopes of Shakespeare's unstable historical landscape. Kyd and Shakespeare were the first dramatists of the public stage to write tightly and coherently organised two-part plays with a continuous plot; it seems that Shakespeare owed more than some occasional hints to his predecessor.

Notes

1   For Jaggard's printing of *1 Hieronimo*, see Laurie E. Maguire, 'The Printer and Date of Q4 *A Looking Glass for London and England*', *Studies in Bibliography*, 52 (1999), 155–60. Copies of the only seventeenth-century edition are in The British Library, the Victoria and Albert Museum, the Bodleian Library, the Folger Shakespeare Library, and the Huntington Library, according to the *STC*. The play was included in the reissues of Dodsley's *Old Plays* by Reed in 1780, Collier in 1825, and Hazlitt in 1874, in Walter Scott's *Ancient British Drama*, 1810, in Boas's *Works of Thomas Kyd* (1901), and in Emma Smith's recent old-spelling edition of *The Spanish Tragedy* (1998). (See my review of Smith's edition in *English Studies*, 81 (2000), 157–8.) Of Andrew Cairncross's edition of *1 Hieronimo* and *The Spanish Tragedy* (1967) more will be said below.

1 *Hieronimo*, contrary to all of Pavier's other plays, had not been entered in the Stationers' Register by which a publisher secured the rights to a play (see Gerald D. Johnson, 'Thomas Pavier, Publisher, 1600–25', *The Library*, 6th Series, 14 (1992), 47). As Pavier had owned the rights in *The Spanish Tragedy* since 1600, he may not have felt the need to enter the text of *1 Hieronimo*. On the often misunderstood topics of entrance and ownership of a copy, see Peter W. M. Blayney, 'The Publication of Playbooks', in John D. Cox and David Scott Kastan (eds.), *A New History of Early English Drama* (New York, 1997), pp. 398–405.

2 I quote from R. A. Foakes and R. T. Rickert (eds.), *Henslowe's Diary* (Cambridge, 1961), pp. 16–19. It should be noted that Henslowe carried over old-style year-dates well beyond 25 March (Lady Day). Following standard practice, the diary should read '30 of marche 1592', etc. The following year, he applied new-style year-dates (e.g.: '8 of Jenewarye 1593'), a practice that was becoming increasingly common.

3 XI, pp. 349–52.

4 The only scholar since Lee who did not take this for granted was Philip Edwards who doubted the existence of a forepiece despite the entries in Henslowe's diary (*ST*, pp. 137–8). His evidence is not convincing and he has not found any followers.

5 Fleay, *A Biographical Chronicle of the English Drama* (London, 1891), II, p. 27; Lee, 'Thomas Kyd', *DNB*, XI, p. 349; Markscheffel, 'Thomas Kyd's Tragödien', *Deutsche Schulprogramme*, 619 (1886), 1–20, and 'Thomas Kyd's Tragödien (Fortsetzung und Schluß)', *Deutsche Schulprogramme*, 627 (1887), 1–12; Sarrazin, pp. 54–8; Schick (ed.), *The Spanish Tragedy*, The Temple Dramatists (London, 1898), pp. xvi–xviii; Cairncross, pp. xv–xix.

6 Fischer, *Zur Kunstentwicklung der englischen Tragödie von ihren ersten Anfängen bis zu Shakespeare* (Strasbourg, 1893), pp. 100–12; Boas, pp. xli–xliv; Chambers, II, pp. 122, 210–11, III, p. 396, IV, pp. 22–3; Carrère, pp. 295–8; Edwards, *ST*, pp. 137–8; Freeman, pp. 175–7; Reibetanz, 'Hieronimo in Decimosexto', *RD*, 5 (1972), 89–121.

7 *Shakespearean Suspect Texts: The 'Bad' Quartos and Their Contexts* (Cambridge, 1996).

8 'But now Knight Marshal, frolic with thy king' (*ST*, I.ii.96); 'Frolick, Ieronimo' (*1H*, I.i.1).

9 Boas (p. xlii) argued that *Don Horatio* was short-lived and had completely disappeared by the time *1 Hieronimo* was written.

10 To the echoes Freeman mentioned, I would add II.iii.37, which seems to parallel *Hamlet* I.i.40, and I.iii.91–4, which anticipates *Hamlet* II.ii.237–9.

11 The 'war of the theatres', also known as the 'Poetomachia', refers to a series of plays written c. 1599–1601 by Ben Jonson for the Children of the Chapel and by John Marston and Thomas Dekker for the Children of St Paul's in which the playwrights ridiculed each other by means of satirical portraits.

12 Hans-Joachim Hermes (*Die Lieder im anonymen englischen Renaissance-Drama 1580–1603*, Salzburg Studies in English Literature (Salzburg, 1974), pp. 96–148) has convincingly argued that *The Maid's*

Metamorphosis, another anonymous play acted by a children's company around the turn of the century, consists of two textual layers, one original written before 1590, and one revised composed shortly before the play's appearance in print in 1600.

13 *Selimus* and *Locrine* have many lines in common, while *King John* and *Troublesome Reign* have exactly the same plot and share several lines and a good many phrases.

14 This is not the only instance of a play that was put together by the addition of new scenes to parts of an old play. Massinger's *Cleander* (1634) is a revision of Fletcher's *The Lovers' Progress* (1623); Heywood used parts of *The Golden Age* (1611) and *The Silver Age* (1613) for *The Escapes of Jupiter* (c. 1624). Sir Henry Herbert, Master of the Revels, allowed a company to 'add scenes to an ould play, and give it out for a new one', and received payments '[f]or adding of a scene to The Virgin Martyr', '[f]or allowing of a new act in an ould play', and for '[a]n ould play, with some new scenes' (see Eric Rasmussen, 'The Revision of Scripts', in Cox and Kastan (eds.), *A New History of Early English Drama*, p. 449).

15 Passages that seem to have been similarly added in order to make fun of Hieronimo are III.ii.171–6 and III.iv.7–16.

16 It is reasonable to assume that Isabella, Hieronimo's wife, appeared in *Don Horatio*, even though in the surviving quarto of 1605 she is confined to two short appearances (I.iii.90–103, II.iii.87–118) that seem to belong to B.

17 See Ejner J. Jensen, 'Kyd's *Spanish Tragedy*: The Play Explains Itself', *JEGP*, 64 (1965), 7–16; John Kerrigan, 'Hieronimo, Hamlet and Remembrance', *Essays in Criticism*, 31 (1981), 107; and Marion Lomax, *Stage Images and Traditions: Shakespeare to Ford* (Cambridge, 1987), pp. 34–44, Robert N. Watson, *The Rest Is Silence: Death As Annihilation in the English Renaissance* (Berkeley, 1994), pp. 64–7. For a recent article that does consider *1 Hieronimo* although without investigating its relationship to *The Spanish Tragedy*, see Andrew Sofer, 'Absorbing Interests: Kyd's Bloody Handkerchief As Palimpsest', *Comparative Drama*, 34 (2000), 127–53.

18 There is an inconsistency between the two plays in that Don Pedro dies in *1 Hieronimo* (III.ii.90.3) but is alive in *The Spanish Tragedy* (III.xiv, IV.iv.209), reappearing in a scene of reconciliation between Spain and Portugal in which the two kings and their two brothers salute each other. If *Don Horatio* was written first, Kyd may have chosen, late in the composition of *The Spanish Tragedy*, to reuse Don Pedro for the sake of symmetry (King and Viceroy, Castile and Don Pedro). If so, the only adjustment that would have been necessary is a slight change in one stage direction in the forepiece so as to omit Don Pedro's death, which is incidental to the plot of *1 Hieronimo*.

19 Added passages seem to be III.i.31–48, III.i.104–6, III.i.124–34, III.ii.1–5, III.ii.120–1, III.ii.132, III.ii.139–40, III.ii.144–6, III.ii.171–6, III.iv.7–16.

20 That the language of B is not Kydian needs no long demonstration: in II.iii, for example, Hieronimo and Horatio are made to speak prose throughout, a practice hardly attributable to Kyd.

21 *Hamlet*, ed. Jenkins, p. 163.

22 For the following examples and the emendations, I am largely indebted to Markscheffel, 'Thomas Kyds Tragödien' (1886), 15–16. The conclusions I draw, however, are mine.

23 Markscheffel, 'Thomas Kyds Tragödien' (1886), 15.

24 'Notes on the Text of Kyd', *ES*, 37 (1907), 87–99.

25 The play appears to have been performed as late as 1626 in Dresden under the title 'Komödie vom König in Spanien und dem Vice-Roy in Portugall' (Chambers, IV, pp. 23).

26 In fact, the early printing history of *1* and *2 Henry IV* is not so different. While the first part was printed in 1598 (twice), in 1599, and in six more quarto editions before 1642, the second part appeared in print in 1600 independently of its forepiece and was not reprinted outside the Folios before 1642.

27 Foakes and Rickert (eds.), *Henslowe's Diary*, pp. 16–19.

28 For instance by F. T. Bowers, *Elizabethan Revenge Tragedy 1587–1642*, pp. 66–8, Moody E. Prior, *The Language of Tragedy* (London, 1947), pp. 46–7, and W. Farnham, *The Medieval Heritage of Elizabethan Tragedy* (London, 1936), pp. 393–4.

29 Philostratus, Master of the Revels in Q, is absent from F and his lines are given to Egeus.

30 *Elizabethan Revenge Tragedy 1587–1642*, p. 68. Considering the relative critical neglect of the sequence prior to Horatio's murder, it is noteworthy that Frank Whigham's dense analysis of 'fantasies of power and control and achieved security' in *The Spanish Tragedy* centres upon the first two acts (*Seizures of the Will in Early Modern English Drama* (Cambridge, 1996), p. 22; see pp. 22–62). Roger Stilling, analysing the play's 'interplay of love and revenge' (p. 26), similarly centres his examination on the first two acts, in particular on the early love scenes (*Love and Death in Renaissance Tragedy* (Baton Rouge, 1976), pp. 26–40).

31 Edwards held that 'the Portuguese court could have been introduced more economically and the relevance of theme is very slight' (*ST*, p. liii). For attempts to argue for the relevance of the subplot without reference to the forepiece, see Ken C. Burrows, 'The Dramatic and Structural Significance of the Portuguese Sub-Plot in *The Spanish Tragedy*', *Renaissance Papers* (1969), 25–35. According to Burrows, the subplot has the purpose of 'reinforcing and highlighting, not only the grief of Hieronimo, but his total dilemma and action' (27). Another article stressing the relevance of the subplot is William H. Wiatt, 'The Dramatic Function of the Alexandro–Villuppo Episode in *The Spanish Tragedy*', *NQ*, 203 [n.s. 5] (1958), 327–9, rpt. in Max Bluestone and Norman Rabkin (eds.), *Shakespeare's Contemporaries*, 2nd edn (Englewood Cliffs, 1970), pp. 57–60.

32 Bowers, *Elizabethan Revenge Tragedy*, pp. 80–2; Freeman, p. 95; Hammersmith, 'The Death of Castile in *The Spanish Tragedy*', *RD*, 16 (1985), 3.

33 See Hunter, '*Henry IV* and the Elizabethan Two-Part Play', *RES*, 5 (1954), 236–48, and Leech, 'The Two-Part Play: Marlowe and the Early Shakespeare', *ShJ*, 94 (1958), 90–106.

34 G. K. Hunter, 'English folly and Italian vice: The moral landscape of John Marston', in *Dramatic Identities and Cultural Tradition: Studies in Shakespeare and His Contemporaries* (Liverpool, 1978), p. 107.

35 (Manchester, 1978), p. 22.

36 For the view that Marston's plays burlesque the revenge tradition, see R. A. Foakes, 'John Marston's Fantastical Plays: *Antonio and Mellida* and *Antonio's Revenge*', *PQ*, 41 (1962), 229–39.

37 W. W. Greg (ed.), *Henslowe's Diary*, 2 vols. (London, 1904/08), II, p. 223. This view had been advanced earlier by F. G. Fleay, *A Biographical Chronicle of the English Drama*, II, p. 76, and A. H. Thorndike, 'The Relations of *Hamlet* to Contemporary Revenge Plays', *PMLA*, 17 (1902), 135.

38 Henry Chettle, *The Tragedy of Hoffman*, ed. Harold Jenkins, MSR (London, 1951), I.i.8.1.

39 Albert H. Tricomi, 'The Revised *Bussy D'Ambois* and *The Revenge of Bussy D'Ambois*: Joint Performance in Thematic Counterpoint', *English Language Notes*, 9 (1971–72), 255. See also Gunilla Florby, *The Painful Passage to Virtue: A Study of George Chapman's 'The Tragedy of Bussy d'Ambois' and 'The Revenge of Bussy d'Ambois'* (Kävlinge, 1982), pp. 150–80.

40 '*Henry IV* and the Elizabethan Two-Part Play', 243.

41 *Ibid.*, 237.

42 Hunter, '*Henry IV* and the Elizabethan Two-Part Play', 247; Leech, 'The Two-Part Play: Marlowe and the Early Shakespeare', 100. Of course, 2 and 3 *Henry VI* can be considered part of a trilogy or a tetralogy rather than a two-part play. However, they can legitimately be viewed as a two-part play in subject (the War of the Roses in the reign of Henry VI), in printing history as the titles of the two early quartos suggest ('THE First part of the Contention betwixt the two famous Houses of Yorke and Lancaster' of 1594 and 'The true Tragedie of Richard Duke of Yorke [...] with the whole contention betweene the two Houses Lancaster and Yorke' of 1595), and probably in stage history ('harey the vj' in Henslowe is generally identified with 1 *Henry VI* and thus seems to have been staged separately).

43 *Johnson on Shakespeare*, ed. Arthur Sherbo, The Yale Edition of the Works of Samuel Johnson (New Haven, 1968), p. 597.

44 In 1 *Hieronimo*, this couplet is followed by a ten-line epilogue: '*Enter* Ieronimo *Solus*: Foregod, I haue iust mist them: ha' (III.iv.7), etc. It was clearly added as part of the burlesque revision in c. 1603/04.

45 On Kyd's use of popular history in *The Spanish Tragedy*, see Freeman, p. 55.

CHAPTER 2

The Spanish Tragedy:
an introduction

The Spanish Tragedy is a complex play. It is not only that critics have found it difficult to come to terms with some of its central issues. The play is also complex in the sense that a number of important questions must be tackled before a critical investigation can be undertaken with profit. Preliminary matters I shall discuss are authorship, sources, date, language, and the nature of the play's text.

Like many plays in the late sixteenth century, *The Spanish Tragedy* was printed anonymously and none of the later quartos bears the name of its author. In 1656, Edward Archer, a bookseller, attributed *The Spanish Tragedy* to 'Tho. Kyte'. The same catalogue attributes 'Hieronimo, both parts, H[istory]' to 'Will. Shakespeare' and the tragedy 'Cornelius' (*Cornelia?*) to 'Thomas Loyd' (Kyd?): telling illustrations of how rapidly Kyd was forgotten.[1] In Robert Dodsley's *Select Collection of Old English Plays* (1744) – the first 'modern' edition containing *The Spanish Tragedy* as well as the first reprint of *Cornelia* since the sixteenth century – the editor was in ignorance of the play's authorship: 'I know not who was the Author of this Play, nor exactly what Age it is.'[2] In 1773, Thomas Hawkins, editor of a collection of plays entitled *The Origin of the English Drama*, attributed the play to Kyd by referring to the following passage in Thomas Heywood's *Apology for Actors* (printed 1612):

> Therefore M. *Kid*, in the *Spanish* Tragedy, vpon occasion presenting itselfe, thus writes.
>> Why *Nero* thought it no disparagement,
>> And Kings and Emperours haue tane delight,
>> To make experience of their wits in playes. (E3ᵛ–E4ʳ)

Since Hawkins attributed the play to Kyd, his authorship has never been seriously doubted. In 1963, Levin L. Schücking unconvincingly argued that Kyd may have written *The Spanish Tragedy* in

co-authorship with Watson, basing his argument on doubtful parallels between *The Spanish Tragedy* and Thomas Watson's poem
'Meliboeus'.[3] Although Kyd is clearly indebted to Watson's
Hekatompathia in *The Spanish Tragedy* II.i.3–10 and even though
we know that Kyd and Watson were fellow-dramatists for the
Queen's Men up to 1585, there is very little ground on which to base
this attribution, and it is not surprising that Schücking has not found
any supporters. As Philip Edwards has rightly pointed out, the
dramatic unity of *The Spanish Tragedy* strongly argues against joint
authorship (*Kyd*, p. 26). Schücking's argument need not detain us
any further and the entirety of *The Spanish Tragedy* may safely be
attributed to Kyd.

In 1582, Stephen Gosson wrote that 'the *Palace of pleasure*, the
Golden Asse, the *Aethiopian historie*, *Amadis of Fraunce*, the
Rounde table, *baudie Comedies* in *Latine*, *French*, *Italian*, and
Spanish, haue beene throughly ransackt, to furnish the Playe houses
in London.'[4] Even though few people today would share the anti-
theatrical stance underlying Gosson's argument, modern criticism
agrees with his belief that Elizabethan drama is highly derivative. If
many playwrights turned to Holinshed's, Hall's and other chronicles
for their history plays, they often had recourse to novellas for
tragedies and comedies. Through the Italian and the French, these
narratives found their way into English collections, the most famous
of which, Painter's *Palace of Pleasure*, significantly heads Gosson's
list of dramatic sources. *Hamlet*, *Othello*, *The Merchant of Venice*,
The Merry Wives of Windsor, *All's Well That Ends Well*, *Measure
for Measure*, Greene's *James IV*, and Webster's *Duchess of Malfi*,
are only a few of the plays that owe much of their plot to novellas
of ultimately Italian origin. In particular, plays with elaborate plots
and a strong element of intrigue, like *The Spanish Tragedy*, were
often indebted to Italianate novellas.

Yet, one of the noteworthy features of *The Spanish Tragedy* is
that no chief narrative source has yet been identified. All the partial
sources that have been discovered have little impact upon the general
thrust of the plot. Andrea's account of his descent to the underworld
in the play's prologue is built upon Book VI of Virgil's *Aeneid*. The
tale of 'Soliman and Persida' from Wotton's *Courtlie Controuersie
of Cupids Cautels* (1578) underlies the play-within-the-play in the
final act. The Earl of Leicester's reckless way of disposing of one of
his servants, reported in print in *The Copie of a Leter* (1584), is the
source of Pedringano's execution. The recent Hispano-Portuguese

wars of 1578 to 1582 form the historical framework to *The Spanish Tragedy*. All of this leaves the play's main plot largely unaffected, however. Kyd's plot material is intricate: the love affair between Andrea and Bel-imperia in *Don Horatio*, Bel-imperia's transference of her love to Horatio, Lorenzo's and Balthazar's plot culminating in Horatio's violent death, and finally Hieronimo's and Bel-imperia's revenge. The complex mixture of intrigue and love stands firmly within the tradition of Bandello's novellas which found their way into England via France.

Freeman, following Fredson Bowers, held that 'it is clear that Kyd drew on [...] many uncorrelated writings in forging his play', and that we are lacking at the most 'another partial source'.[5] The recognised sources, however, account for very little of the play's plot. If we did not have access to the main source of *Hamlet*, a good many 'uncorrelated' minor sources would still be available, but it would nevertheless be wrong to assume that there is no main source. It is tempting, of course, for a Kyd scholar, to 'credit [Kyd] with powers of invention unparalleled among the dramatists of his time' (Freeman, p. 50), but this simply does not correspond to what we know about Kyd.

Freeman (p. 51) believes he has identified the missing source in the history of 'Alegre and Clarinda', the third tale in Wotton's *Courtlie Controuersie of Cupids Cautels*, in which Clarinda, the daughter of the Marquise de Gonzaga, is courted by both Adilon and Alegre, the latter having been taken prisoner during the siege of Milan. When Clarinda reciprocates Alegre's love, Adilon tries to kill him with a poisoned apple, but Alegre gives the apple to Clarinda who, having eaten from it, slowly dies while Alegre kills Adilon in revenge before dying himself of grief. The correspondences with *The Spanish Tragedy* are minimal, confined to the very beginning of both tale and play and even there imperfect. Whereas Bel-imperia never reciprocates Balthazar's love, Alegre and Clarinda's passion is mutual from the beginning. The character constellation at the arrival of Alegre in the Marquise's castle is imperfectly and most probably accidentally analogous to the initial situation in *The Spanish Tragedy*.

Freeman's belief that 'the Spanish setting is based on history so recent as practically to exclude the possibility of a tale grounded in it' (p. 50) is similarly flawed. There is no reason to believe that the lost source narrative need have been related to recent Spanish history. The device of placing a borrowed plot in a different setting is common enough. Nor is it true that Kyd's treatment of Wotton's tales is the same in *Soliman and Perseda* and *The Spanish Tragedy*: 'a close adherence at first to the source's situation and early action, with imaginative variation exercised in later acts' (Freeman, 51). Wotton's history of 'Soliman and Persida' provides all the plot essentials to *Soliman and Perseda*, whereas that of 'Clarinda and Alegre' would have provided none. On the contrary, Kyd's compositional technique in *Soliman and Perseda* and what can be conjectured from his *Hamlet* suggest, *pace* Freeman, that *The Spanish Tragedy* is strongly based on a now-lost narrative source. The few plays for which Shakespeare invented substantial parts of the story, like *Love's Labour's Lost* or *The Tempest*, offer little in terms of plot. As Boas (p. xxxi) suggested, it seems highly improbable that an English dramatist in the late 1580s would invent the plot of an Italianate intrigue play. It is even less probable that Kyd – who followed a single novella in both *Hamlet* and *Soliman and Perseda* – should do so in *The Spanish Tragedy*.

Freeman's design in crediting Kyd with 'genius' and great 'powers of invention' (p. 50) and denying that a source existed is typical of recent source studies. Of the two antithetical names of the Renaissance poet, the maker and the *trouvère*, most modern critics tend to stress the former and to neglect the latter. Enobarbus' justly celebrated 'The barge she sat in' speech is more or less a blank verse rendering of a passage in North's *Plutarch*. This should give us pause. In Shakespearean drama and in Elizabethan drama in general, the maker's artistic originality is, *per se*, as little synonymous with artistic excellence as the *trouvère*'s handling of his model.

All things considered, it seems likely that Kyd based the plot of *The Spanish Tragedy* on a narrative source which is and will remain lost. This is all the more unfortunate as, judging by *Soliman and Perseda* and, possibly, Kyd's *Hamlet*, the dramatically efficient use to which Kyd put his narrative sources played a significant role in creating the great English tragedies of the English Renaissance.

Of the play's minor and local sources, some have long been recognised and pose little difficulty. Boas (pp. xvii–xix) has identified most of Kyd's 'borrowings' from classical authors – Seneca, Virgil, Cicero, Ovid, and so on. Some of Kyd's further debts, such as the passage from Watson's *Hekatompathia* in II.i.3–10, Balthazar's euphuism in II.i, and the use of Wotton's *Courtlie Controuersie of Cupids Cautels* (1578) in the play-within-the-play are discussed by Freeman (pp. 50–70).[6] The identification of the origins of the Lorenzo–Pedringano episode is of particular interest as it shows Kyd aware of and commenting upon recent if not contemporary political events. *The Copie of a Leter*, a tract published in Paris in 1584, relates Leicester's alleged Machiavellian practices. It was smuggled into England, where it was suppressed by royal proclamation on 12 October 1584. Despite its consequent rarity, the stories were notorious and a multitude of manuscript versions seems to have circulated in London.[7] One episode deals with the story of Gates, a thief in the employment of Leicester. Fredson Bowers was the first to point out the striking parallels between Gates–Leicester and Pedringano–Lorenzo.[8] Gates, who had been promised a pardon by Leicester which never arrived, was hanged and Leicester escaped uncensored. With the lapse of state censorship, *Leicester's Commonwealth*, as the tract had come to be called, was reprinted twice in 1641. *Leicester's Ghost*, a paraphrase of the stories in the form of a poem which had been composed no later than 1605, was appended to *Leicester's Commonwealth*. One passage reinforces the connection between Gates and Pedringano: 'For his repriuall, like a crafty fox,/ I sent noe pardon, but an emptie box' (ll. 797–8). The author of *Leicester's Ghost* appears to recall the memorable incident of Pedringano's deception (III.v, III.vi).

Scott McMillin and Sally-Beth MacLean have recently argued for 'a special relationship between Leicester and the Queen's Men' bolstered by a shared Protestant ideology and political agenda.[9] If, as the evidence suggests, Kyd was a playwright for the Queen's Men after their formation in 1583 (see the introduction) but had moved to a rival company by the time he composed *The Spanish Tragedy*, we may here witness topical allusions which were at least partly motivated by allegiances to and rivalries between political factions with which the dramatic companies were bound up.

Discussions of the date and some of the sources of *The Spanish Tragedy* are necessarily related. An important question is whether Nashe, in his allusions to Kyd in the 'Preface' to Greene's *Menaphon* (1589), refers specifically to *The Spanish Tragedy*. A key passage is Nashe's sneer 'what can be hoped of those, that thrust *Elisium* into hell'. Having related the events leading to his recent death in battle in the prologue to *The Spanish Tragedy*, the Ghost of Andrea describes his journey through the underworld in an account which is clearly modelled upon Book VI of Virgil's *Aeneid*. Yet, if Kyd follows Virgil in the topology of the underworld, we cannot expect Nashe to object to it. Critics have struggled to make sense of Nashe's rhetorical question. Arguing that Nashe is alluding to *The Spanish Tragedy*, Boas wrote that Kyd 'represents the "faire Elizian greene"

as one of the regions of the nether world beyond Acheron, and the
abode of Pluto and Proserpine' (p. xxix). Of course he does, but so
did Virgil and many others before him, so this is clearly not the
problem. If we want to know whether Nashe may be alluding to *The
Spanish Tragedy* the prologue must be looked into more closely.

Few passages in Elizabethan drama have been parodied more
often. Beaumont's *The Knight of the Burning Pestle*, Heywood's
1 Fair Maid of the West, Shirley's *The Bird in a Cage*, and Rawlins's
The Rebellion are among the plays which parodied the passage.
Modern critics have shown little more sympathy for the beginning of
Kyd's play. The theatrical revivals of *The Spanish Tragedy* have
proved them wrong. Delivered adequately, Andrea's long speech can
be a very powerful opening, suggesting an uncanny atmosphere of
intrigue and impending tragedy. As to Kyd's adaptation of his
source, criticism has been inadequate and has scarcely gone beyond
the assertion that Andrea's description of the underworld is based
on Virgil. Kyd may be doing something rather more interesting.

Nobody has taken the pains, it seems, to compare in any detail
the underworlds depicted by Virgil in Book VI of the *Aeneid* and by
Andrea in the prologue to *The Spanish Tragedy*. In Virgil, Aeneas
and the Sibyl are taken across the river by Charon whereupon the
hero comes to the Plains of Grief situated between Styx and the two
ways that lead to the Elysium or Tartarus. The Plains are inhabited
by the spirits of those who have died prematurely, babies, men
wrongfully condemned to die, suicides, victims of love and the 'bello
clari' (VI, l. 478), i.e. the renowned warriors who have died. The
place is neither one of punishment nor one of blessedness. Having
crossed the Plains, Aeneas and the Sibyl come to the crossroads:

> hic locus est, partis ubi se via findit in ambas:
> dextera quae Ditis magni sub moenia tendit,
> hac iter Elysium nobis; at laeva malorum
> exercet poenas, et ad impia Tartara mittit.   (VI, ll. 540–3)[10]

Aeneas makes his way to Elisium. As he turns around to look back,
he sees an awe-inspiring castle:

> Rescipit Aeneas subito et sub rupe sinistra
> moenia lata videt, triplici circumdata muro,
> quae rapidus flammis ambit torrentibus amnis,
> Tartareus Phlegethon, torquetque sonantia saxa.
> porta adversa, ingens, solidoque adamante columnae,
> vis ut nulla virum, non ipsi exscindere bello
> caelicolae valeant; stat ferrea turris ad auras,
> Tisiphoneque sedens, palla succinta, cruenta,
> vestibulum exsomnis servat noctesque diesque.   (VI, ll. 548–56)[11]

The 'walls', the 'tower' and the 'gate' are precisely what Aeneas sees of Tartarus. After the Sibyl's account of Tartarus and its sinners, Aeneas proceeds to Elisium.

Aeneas' journey now needs to be compared to Andrea's. Having crossed Styx, Andrea meets Minos, Aeacus, and Rhadamanth – the three judges of the Underworld – 'amidst ten thousand souls' (I.i.32). As he moves on, Kyd's description consciously deviates from Virgil's: 'Three ways there were' (I.i.59), not only two as in Virgil. As in the *Aeneid*, the left-hand path leads to Tartarus (I.i.63–71). The right-hand path, leading to Elysium in Virgil, would take Andrea to the 'fields,/ Where lovers live, and bloody martialists' (I.i.60–1), where his soul would come to rest and 'spend the course of everlasting time' (I.i.43). He walks on the middle path, however, which leads to a mixture of Elysium and Tartarus:

> 'Twixt these two ways, I trod the middle path,
> Which brought me to the fair Elysian green,
> In midst whereof there stands a stately tower,
> The walls of brass, the gates of adamant. (I.i.72–5)

The 'fair Elysian green' is placed alongside the Tartarian 'tower', 'walls', and 'gates of adamant'. Surely, Kyd knew the topology of the underworld too well for this to be an accidental blunder. It seems that he consciously mixed Elysium and Tartarus or, in Nashe's words, 'thrust Elysium into hell'. Appropriately, the place which Andrea is taken to is not one of blessedness and rewarded virtue, but a purgatorial place from which Andrea's soul returns to the earth as a ghost doomed for a certain term to walk the night.

Despite what critics have said, the observation behind Nashe's sneer therefore seems accurate. I thus part company with McKerrow who could not 'see that the passage thrusts Elysium into hell, any more than does the Vergilian description upon which [...] it is based' (III, p. 450), and with George Ian Duthie who asked: 'why should Nashe object to Kyd's modelling his lower world upon Virgil's account, when upon Virgil was founded for many centuries, the whole Christian conception of the after-world?'[12] I also find myself in disagreement with Philip Edwards who argued that even though Kyd 'does take some liberties with Virgil's picture', 'Kyd does not confuse the "fair green" of the blessed with the "deepest hell" of the damned' (*ST*, p. 7). Kyd, I believe, *deliberately* confused elements of Elisium and Tartarus to describe the part of the netherworld led to by the 'middle path'.

Kyd's adaptation of Virgil may be a reaction to a thematically related passage in Garnier's *Cornélie*, a play Kyd was to translate a

few years later. In III.i, the heroine tells how the Ghost of Pompey
appeared to her as she was in a 'slumber', talked to her, but escaped
from her embraces (III.i.71–116). As she has finished her report, the
Chorus lectures Cornelia on the nature of ghosts (I quote Kyd's
faithful translation of this passage):

> 'For when our soule the body hath disgaged,
> 'It seeks the common passage of the dead,   135
> 'Downe by the fearefull gates of Acheron,
> 'Where, when it is by *Aeacus* adiudg'd,
> 'It eyther turneth to the Stygian Lake,
> 'Or staies for euer in th' Elisian fields,
> 'And ne're returneth to the Corse interd,   140
> 'To walke by night, or make the wise afeard.
> 'None but ineuitable conquering Death
> 'Descends to hell, with hope to rise againe;
> 'For ghosts of men are lockt in fiery gates,
> 'Fast-guarded by a fell remorceles Monster.   145
> 'And therefore thinke not it was *Pompeys* spryte,
> 'But some false *Daemon* that beguild your sight.   (III.i.134–47)

Whereas the Ghost of Andrea, faced with three paths, walks on the
middle path and is made to return to the scene of the living where
his revenge is acted out, this possibility is precisely excluded by
Garnier's Chorus. Souls remain once and for all in either heavenly
Elysium or hellish Tartarus. Both Garnier's and Kyd's ghosts appear
to hide a Christian dimension underneath their pagan appearance,
growing out not only of Seneca but also of contemporary theological controversies. Lavater's Protestant treatise *Of Ghosts and Spirits
Walking by Night*, which has long been suggested to have influenced
Shakespeare's treatment of the Ghost in *Hamlet*, was originally
written in Latin in 1570 and appeared in a French translation in
1571, three years before Garnier's play was first published.[13] The
Chorus's explanation for the ghost Cornelia perceives is the one
Shakespeare's Hamlet considers (II.ii.599–604) and Lavater advo-
cates: it is not a purgatorial spirit, returning from a place that is
neither heaven nor hell, but a 'false Daemon'. Especially in the final
lines, Garnier seems to go out of his way to make the doctrinal point
advocated by Lavater. Pompey's Ghost does not reappear in the
play, nor is the question of its nature and origin ever answered.[14]
The 'eternal substance of [Andrea's] soul' (I.i.1), however, *has*
returned to the human stage and correspondingly, Kyd dressed his
pagan netherworld not in vestments of Protestant but of Catholic
theology reaffirmed in the Council of Trent: 'Three waies there were'
(I.i.59) and the purgatorial middle way Andrea treads upon appro-

priately leads to a topological and theological mixture of heaven and hell.

Local echoes from *Cornélie* in *The Spanish Tragedy* have long been pointed out.[15] Compare the following passages:

Bellonne, ardant de rage, au plus fort de la presse
Couroit qui çà qui là   (Lebègue, ll. 1697–8)

Now while Bellona rageth here and there,   (I.ii.52)

Ils rompent pique et lance, et les esclats pointus,
Bruyant sifflant par l'air, volent comme festus.   (ll. 1684–5)

And shiver'd lances dark the troubled air.   (I.ii.54)

Aux uns vous eussiez veu la teste my-partie […]
Aux uns la cuisse estoit, ou l'espaule abbattue,   (ll. 1761–5)

Here falls a body scinder'd from his head,
There legs and arms lie bleeding on the grass.   (I.ii.59–60)

As Kyd seems to have had an intimate knowledge of Garnier's *Cornélie* years before he translated it, it is not implausible that the prologue of *The Spanish Tragedy* was influenced by Garnier's play.

It may be too bold to advance a case for Kyd having been a Catholic or having had Catholic sympathies on the basis of (a) the purgatorial 'middle path' in the depiction of his Virgilian underworld (and, possibly, the purgatorial ghost in his *Hamlet*), (b) his only thinly veiled portrayal of Leicester, the champion of the Protestant cause, in the villain Lorenzo, (c) the negative evidence of his absence from university (where he would have had to swear on the articles of the Church of England), and (d) his writing a play (*Hamlet*) which may well have been understood as critically commenting upon Queen Mary's execution (see chapter 6), but the possibility is certainly intriguing.

Kyd's debts to Garnier are in themselves of limited importance. They demonstrate, however, along with most of the play's other sources, that Kyd was conversant with the literature of his time: Wotton's tale of 'Soliman and Persida', Watson's *Hekatompathia*, Lylyan Euphuism, as well as Garnier's *Cornélie* were all not more than a few years old when Kyd composed *The Spanish Tragedy*. Rather than an archaic Senecan tragedy, Kyd's play shows full awareness and partly grows out of a wide variety of contemporary works.

The Spanish Tragedy has been called 'quite the most important single play in the history of English drama'.[16] It is important,

however, to acknowledge the assumptions concerning the dating of
the play which underlie this rather sweeping statement. The date of
composition is a matter of consequence and needs to be discussed at
some length. It would be of prime importance to determine if the
play, which refers in its very title to Spain, was written before or
after the defeat of the Spanish Armada in 1588. Also, a better
knowledge of the chronology of the plays written in this period may
help answer the question of what share Kyd had in 'inventing'
Elizabethan tragedy.

The Spanish Tragedy was entered in the Stationers' Register for
Abel Jeffes on 6 October 1592. When it had been staged by the Lord
Strange's Men earlier that year, Henslowe did not mark the play as
new. This suggests 1591 as a *terminus ad quem*. At the beginning of
II.i, Kyd borrowed a passage from Watson's *Hekatompathia* (entered
in the Stationers' Register in 1582), which sets the *terminus a quo* in
the early 1580s. Boas pointed out that the prolonged resistance of the
island of 'Terceira' (referred to in I.iii.82) to Spanish attacks in 1582
made the place-name known in England. This year may therefore be
safely assumed as the earliest limit for the play's composition. Much
room for conjecture remains. T. W. Baldwin placed the date as early
as 1583–4, J. Schick favoured a date between 1583–7, Boas and
Freeman between 1585–7.[17] Edwards has opted for a later date, 1590
(*ST*, pp. xxi–xxvii), while Mulryne cautiously states: 'In the absence
of firmer evidence we can only place the date somewhere between the
outer limits of 1582 and 1592, with a balance of conjecture in favour
of the later years' (p. xiv). It should be possible to determine the date
of composition with greater precision.

Weighing all the available data, an argument for a pre-Armada
date is more convincing, for reasons of both internal and external
evidence. Had it been written after the defeat of the Spanish Armada
in 1588, a play such as *The Spanish Tragedy*, with a penchant for
topicality and allusions to patriotic history, would have been likely
to exploit, in one way or another, the victory over Spain. The close
of the first act – Hieronimo's dumb show presented to the King – has
a distinct pre-Armada ring. Kyd deliberately gets off his dramatic
track in an obvious effort to appeal to English patriotic feeling. It
seems unlikely that Kyd would have brought forward half-invented
stories about past English victories over Spain if he could have
alluded to the real and recent glory. *Edward III*, Lyly's *Midas*, and
Robert Wilson's *The Three Lords and Three Ladies of London*,
written during or shortly after the naval conflict in 1588, all make a
point of referring to the Spanish Armada.[18]

There is no reason to doubt the approximate accuracy of Ben Jonson's dating of the play in *Bartholomew Fair* (1614): 'Hee that will sweare, *Ieronimo*, or *Andronicus* are the best playes, yet, shall passe vnexcepted at, heere, as a man whose Iudgement shewes it is constant, and hath stood still, these fiue and twentie, or thirtie yeeres' (Induction, ll. 106–9). This remark gives us a date of 1584–89. It is true that Jonson's stage-keeper cannot be taken as the most reliable authority and in the context of the play, he is more likely to stretch his point a little rather than the reverse. It would be surprising, however, if Jonson, who not only repeatedly parodied *The Spanish Tragedy* and wrote additions to the play, but, famously, also appears to have played the protagonist's part at some stage, had got the facts wrong.[19]

If I have correctly argued above that Nashe's sneer at 'those that thrust Elysium into hell' refers to *The Spanish Tragedy*, a strong case for a pre-Armada dating can be made. If Nashe, in 1589, alludes to *The Spanish Tragedy* and states that Kyd has turned from play-writing to Italian translations – thereby alluding to *The Householder's Philosophy*, published in 1588 and entered on 6 February 1588 – there is a strong presumption that *The Spanish Tragedy* was composed before the defeat of the Spanish Armada.

The following excerpt from Nashe's *Anatomie of Absurdities* represents corroborative evidence for a pre-Armada dating. In a passage in which Nashe runs down the 'the excessiue studies of delight' of those that 'forsake sounder Artes', he compares his target to 'him that had rather haue a newe painted boxe, though there be nothing but a halter in it' (I, p. 31). Nashe's words inevitably call up the Pedringano episode in *The Spanish Tragedy* (III.v and III.vi), and it is puzzling that nobody seems to have commented upon this passage. The empty box which Lorenzo sends to Pedringano does not, as the latter thinks, contain his pardon, but, metaphorically speaking, a halter. The real halter, an undeniably memorable presence on stage, referred to by Pedringano (III.vi.45) and punned on by Lorenzo (III.ii.92), has been around Pedringano's neck for some fifty lines when he is finally hanged.

Nashe's pamphlet was entered on 19 September 1588, within two months of the defeat of the Armada in July/August. If he is referring to Kyd's play, it must have been composed before the English victory. *The Anatomie of Absurditie* is a long tirade against unlearned writers who are not unlike the 'triuiall translators' of 'home-born mediocritie' Nashe was to attack a year later in his 'Preface' to Greene's *Menaphon*.

Edwards's argument for a date of composition as late as 1590 (*ST*, pp. 143–4) is built on the parallels between *The Spanish Tragedy* and Watson's elegy 'Melibœus' (1590), which Freeman (p. 73) has rightly dismissed as unconvincing. Edwards himself, a few years after his edition appeared, seemed to have changed his mind, holding that 'it probably belongs to the last years of the 1580s' (*Kyd*, p. 41). Another obstacle to Edwards's late date is Marlowe's *Jew of Malta* which is thought to have been influenced by *The Spanish Tragedy*. The following verbal parallels have been pointed out:

Hieronimo.	Away! I'll rip the bowels of the earth,	(III.xii.71)
Barabas.	Ripping the bowels of the earth for them,	(I.i.109)
Hieronimo.	The hopeless father of a hapless son,	(IV.iv.84)
Abigail.	The hopelesse daughter of a haplesse Jew,	(I.ii.317)
Bel-imperia.	No, he is as trusty as my second self.	(II.iv.9)
Barabas.	My trusty servant, nay, my second selfe;	(III.iv.15)[20]

In order to accommodate a late date of *The Spanish Tragedy*, Edwards argued that 'the question of precedence must remain open' (*ST*, p. 81), but the evidence clearly argues for Marlowe's indebtedness. It has been shown that under the influence of Kyd's play, he introduced a wealth of devices absent from his previous plays. The plot is intricate and radically departs from the linear and sequential structure of the *Tamburlaine* plays, the element of intrigue is strong, and the Machiavellian character (like Lorenzo in II.ii) is given punning asides (II.iii.319).[21] Even the 'night scenes' in *The Jew of Malta* may owe their origin to Kyd.[22] Marlowe's dramatic style was so clearly affected by *The Spanish Tragedy* that two critics have found Kyd's hand in *The Jew of Malta*.[23] There is very little to support their argument, but it may constitute corroborative evidence of Kyd's influence on Marlowe.[24]

I thus consider 1587 the likeliest date of composition. This would suggest that Kyd's play was probably written before Shakespeare's first plays and around the time Marlowe wrote *Tamburlaine*. This is supported by the absence of traces from any of Shakespeare's or Marlowe's plays.[25] In *Soliman and Perseda*, Kyd does parody a passage from *2 Tamburlaine*, and it is notable from the multitude of recent works of which *The Spanish Tragedy* shows awareness that his knowledge of contemporary literature was up to date. If we also accept that Nashe alludes to *The Spanish Tragedy* in *The Anatomie of Absurditie* (1588) and again in the 'Preface' to *Menaphon* in 1589 where he simultaneously asserts that Kyd has moved from playwriting to translating from the Italian (*The Householder's Philosophy*, 1588), 1587 is again a plausible date.

The text of *The Spanish Tragedy* poses a number of problems affecting, in particular, the last act. Unaware of the play's textual problems, Boas holds that in the last act, 'Kyd's finer instinct completely fails him' (p. xxxix). M. D. Faber, on the other hand, argues that 'Kyd's fourth act makes perfect sense psychologically, theatrically, structurally'.[26] Before agreeing with either Boas or Faber, it seems necessary to assess the available evidence.

The early textual and publishing history of *The Spanish Tragedy* is complex. The evidence from the records of the court of the Stationers' Company suggests the following chronology:[27] on 3 April 1592, *Arden of Faversham* was entered to Edward White in the Stationers' Register. By July, Abel Jeffes appears to have been in trouble with the authorities for publishing an edition of *Arden of Faversham*, an offence for which he was finally imprisoned according to an order of 7 August. By that time, Jeffes seems to have acquired the rights to *The Spanish Tragedy* and published the play (though without having it entered). Later in the same year, Edward White, too, was preparing an edition of *The Spanish Tragedy*. In order to defend his rights, Jeffes entered the play in the Stationers' Register on 6 October 1592:

Abell Jeffes	Entred for his copie vnder th[e h]andes of master HARTWELL and master Stirrop, a booke whiche is called *the Spanishe tragedie of Don HORATIO and BELLMIPEIA &c.* . . . . . *vj^d* *Debitum hoc/*

(Arber, II, p. 621)

White was not deterred and piratically published his edition. Before the end of the year, he was fined for his offense and the copies of his edition (along with those of Jeffes's edition of *Arden of Faversham*) were confiscated 'to thuse of the poore of the companye'.[28] No copy of Jeffes's edition is extant. The title page of White's edition, of which one copy, now in the British Library, has been preserved, appears to refer to Jeffes's edition however: 'Newly corrected and amended of such grosse faults as passed in the first impression.' It can thus be inferred that when White set up his edition, a printed text was already available.

This is the starting point from which Philip Edwards set out to argue an impressive case. His conclusions deserve to be quoted at some length:

1592 is a good text, deriving from a manuscript of the dramatist which had probably not been worked over for the stage. There is some corruption, irregularity, and inconsistency in the last act, though the 'affected area' is small. The inconsistency in the action, which relates to the play-within-the-play and to Hieronimo's behaviour just before his death, may suggest that the text contains elements of a revised and abridged version of the play. The presence of one unusually corrupt scene (III.xv) may suggest the use of inferior copy. If Jeffes' edition, which preceded White's, did indeed contain an 'unauthorized' text, the inconsistencies and the corruptions could be explained on the ground that the printer of *1592* used Jeffes' text as copy to supply defective parts of his manuscript copy.[29]

This would provide explanations for several inconsistencies which had previously troubled critics: Hieronimo's suggestion to perform the play-within-the-play in the last act in 'sundry languages' was added as part of Kyd's revisions, whereas the English text of the play in IV.iv, clashing with the promised multilingual show, goes back to Kyd's foul papers. Similarly, Edwards was able to account for the apparent contradiction in Hieronimo's behaviour after the play-within-the-play: in a speech no less than eighty lines long (IV.iv.73–152), Hieronimo reveals everything the King, Castile, and the Viceroy would possibly want to know, yet a few lines later, pressed by them, he promises never to reveal '[t]he thing which I have vow'd inviolate' (IV.iv.188). Following Schücking, Edwards explains that *1592* juxtaposes two endings, the long explanation originally composed by Kyd and the 'vow of silence' ending copied from Jeffes's revised and abridged edition.[30] The argument has been endorsed by Freeman, who calls Edwards's evaluation 'full and convincing' (p. 116), and has passed unchallenged, in its broad outlines, since the edition was published in 1959. The evidence is more ambiguous than Edwards and his followers may lead one to believe however.

To begin with, Edwards's explanations leave us with an unclear picture of what Jeffes's edition must have been like. It was a 'version of the play which was acted' (*ST*, p. xxxix) and '"bad" – that is to say, reported or assembled by "unauthorized" persons' (*ST*, p. xxxviii) constituting 'inferior copy' (*ST*, p. xxxix). The three passages argued to be based on Jeffes's are III.xv, IV.i.52–199, IV.iv.153–201. The first of these is indeed textually very corrupt and in places difficult to make sense of:

Enter *Ghoast* and *Reuenge*.
   Ghost.
Awake *Erictha*, *Cerberus* awake,

Sollicite *Pluto* gentle *Proserpine*,
To combat *Achinon* and *Ericus* in hell.
For neere by *Stix* and *Phlegeton*:
Nor ferried *Caron* to the fierie lakes,
Such fearfull sights, as poore *Andrea* see?
Reuenge awake.[31]

The Ghost of Andrea and Revenge cannot be expected to enter at the beginning of the scene, considering they sat down at the end of the prologue 'to see the mystery,/ And serve for Chorus in this tragedy' (I.i.90–1) and have been on stage throughout the play. Furthermore, 'in hell', ending the third line, has been transferred to the end of the following line in all modern editions. Edwards and Mulryne hold that a line dropped out after line four, whereas Schick, Boas and Cairncross emended 'Nor ferried' to 'O'er-ferried'. The scene requires emendation at several other places too: the final stage direction is 'Exeunt' even though Andrea has just said 'Rest thee, for I will sit to see the rest' (III.xv.39); and 'woe-begone' (III.xv.17), as all modern editors have it, is an emendation of the unintelligible 'degone' (1592), changed to 'begone' in 1594. 'Thsleep away what thou art warn'd to watch' (1592) is variously understood as 'To sleep; awake! what, thou art warn'd to watch!' (Edwards) or as 'To sleepe away what thou art warnd to watch' (Boas). Edwards explains that White must have had recourse to Jeffes's 'bad' and reported quarto for this scene (p. xxxviii) and he finds a possible 'inapposite recollection' in III.xv.24. If we pause for a moment to survey the evidence, however, most of the corruptions of III.xv are not those we would expect from a faulty memorial reconstruction. Why would a reporter mistakenly give the lines to the Ghost? add mistaken stage directions? transfer two words or forget a line, thereby completely spoiling the syntax? If, however, the deficiencies mirror the quality of the copy from which Jeffes set up his edition, we would expect to find similar irregularities in the other passages which Edwards attributes to the lost quarto. This is not the case, however.

The second passage Edwards argues is based on Jeffes's edition, IV.i.52–199, deals with the preparations for Hieronimo's play. He rightly points out that the passage 'shows great irregularity in the metre' (*ST*, p. xxxiv), and he concludes that this 'supports the view that inferior copy was being used' (*ST*, p. xxxix). Yet, the textual nature of this passage has very little in common with III.xv. Both the speech headings and stage-directions are faultless and the language does not need more emendation than elsewhere. The writing is clear and forceful, indeed one of the play's finest moments, as Kyd exhibits both his gift for biting irony and the immediacy and collo- quial ease of some of his language. If we consider that Kyd may have worried much less about metrical regularity in this passage of vivid exchanges than he did in set speeches, the lines have little to distin- guish them from the rest of the play.

In the last portion allegedly based on Jeffes's edition, Hieronimo vows silence and bites out his own tongue following his long speech after the play-within-the-play (IV.iv.153–201). The text of this passage is yet different again. It is good, free from major inaccura- cies and its metrical regularity is in keeping with the rest of the play. Edwards may find the passage aesthetically crude (*ST*, p. xxxv), but the adjective seems more apt to designate the subject than the artis- tic quality of this movement. Edwards thinks the passage to be based on Jeffes's 'bad' edition because it is 'remarkably deficient in stage- directions' (*ST*, p. xxxv).

If we follow Edwards's analysis, we end up with a vague if not contradictory impression of what Jeffes's edition may have been like: Verbally very corrupt as III.xv would suggest, or relatively free from such errors (IV.i.52–199, IV.iv.153–201)? Metrically deficient (IV.i.52–199) or not (IV.iv.153–201)? Deficient in stage-directions (IV.iv.153–201) or not (IV.i.52–198 contains no fewer than seven stage-directions)? Edwards does not address these issues. It seems useful to recall that even though Jeffes's edition *may* have had a debased text, this is by no means certain.[32]

Edwards's investigations set out from the contradictions in the text we have, and his conflation theory allows him to account for them: 'Hieronimo's silence will seem less queer if we suppose [...] that in IV.iv.153–201 we have, not confusion, but an alternative ending to the play' (*ST*, p. xxxvi). The argument seems attractive: for the sake of abridgement, the long explanation is replaced in performance by the 'biting out of the tongue' ending. At closer examination, however, this argument is doubtful. In fact, there is no contradiction between Kyd's 'first ending' (IV.iv.73–152) and the 'alternative ending' (IV.iv.153–201) which is not inherent in the 'alternative ending' on its own:

King.   Why hast thou done this undeserving deed?   165
Viceroy.   Why hast thou murdered my Balthazar?
Castile.   Why hast thou butcher'd both my children thus?
Hieronimo.   O good words!
    As dear to me was my Horatio
    As yours, or yours, or yours, my lord, to you.   170

My guiltless son was by Lorenzo slain,
And by Lorenzo and that Balthazar
Am I at last revenged thoroughly,
Upon whose souls may heavens be yet aveng'd
With greater far than these afflictions.   175
Castile.   But who were thy confederates in this?
Viceroy. That was thy daughter Bel-imperia,
For by her hand my Balthazar was slain:
I saw her stab him.
King.   Why speak'st thou not?
Hieronimo.   What lesser liberty can kings afford   180
Than harmless silence? then afford it me:
Sufficeth I may not, nor I will not tell thee.
King.   Fetch forth the tortures.
Traitor as thou art, I'll make thee tell.
Hieronimo.   Indeed,
Thou may'st torment me, as his wretched son   185
Hath done in murdering my Horatio,
But never shalt thou force me to reveal
The thing which I have vow'd inviolate:
And, therefore, in despite of all thy threats,
Pleas'd with their deaths, and eas'd with their revenge,   190
First take my tongue, and afterwards my heart.
[*He bites out his tongue.*] (IV.iv.165–91)

The passage presents both Hieronimo's biting out of his tongue and
all the information to which the King, Castile, and the Viceroy ever
have access. In his long speech, Hieronimo reveals nothing his listeners are not shown to know here: Hieronimo's revenge on Lorenzo
and Balthazar for their murder of Horatio, and Bel-imperia's
complicity.

In the edition of 1602, IV.iv.168–90 was replaced by new material,
but IV.iv.176–9 and IV.iv.168–75 were reintegrated in reverse order.
The resulting movement still contains the same inconsistency:
Hieronimo's confession of his revenge and its circumstances coupled
with the biting out of his tongue. The only lines which have been
removed deal with the enigmatic 'vow of silence'. As Peter B. Murray
showed, this is further evidence that there is nothing inconsistent
about the rest of the passage: 'From the deletion of Hieronimo's
refusal to violate a vow that we have never heard of earlier, we can see
that the reviser was concerned with clearing up what he took to be
inconsistencies in the play, and I think that it is therefore likely that he
saw nothing inconsistent in having the royal party ask why he has
killed – a question Hieronimo has just answered.'[33]

The play's final moments thus dramatise two endings only insofar
as Kyd consciously chose to superimpose two dramatic ideas:

Hieronimo's 'show' and 'oration' on the one hand, and his 'vow of silence' on the other. The first idea turns on Hieronimo's revelation, the horror of Horatio's corpse and the psychological torture of the King, Castile, and the Viceroy as he describes in detail the cause and the 'mechanics' of his revenge. The second idea explores silence and concealment, again aimed at the agony of Hieronimo's listeners and culminating in the horror of the biting out of his tongue and the stabbing of Castile. Both ideas make for powerful theatre. Even though they are logically incoherent, indeed contradictory, an audience, in the heat of the action, is unlikely to worry; I have not come across a single review of a modern production that objected to the inconsistency.

In more general terms, Edwards's point that '*The Spanish Tragedy* was at some stage revised to make it shorter and more suitable for the public stage' (*ST*, p. xxxvi) conflates revision and abridgement on the basis of very thin threads of evidence. *The Spanish Tragedy* is a few hundred lines longer than the average play of its times. Granted, it may have been abridged in performance as, probably, many of Shakespeare's plays,[34] yet, how likely is a playwright to revise a play for the sake of abridgement? Would it not be unusual to shorten the crucial scene in which the revenge is finally carried out rather than, say, the Viceroy's long lament in I.iii or the General's sixty-three-line account of the battle in I.ii? Modern productions have shown what an exciting moment Hieronimo's long explanatory speech after the play-within-the-play can be, as the on-stage audience grows increasingly aware that Hieronimo is no longer speaking from within the fiction. In order to reduce *The Spanish Tragedy* to the average length of contemporary plays, revision need not have been necessary and revision of the play's climax for the sake of abridgement is implausible. Edwards's contention that this is what has happened is impressionistically deduced rather than rooted in any firm evidence.

Edwards holds that 'the contradiction between the promise of foreign languages for the play-within-the-play and the English text which is in fact given can be understood if we postulate a revision for the sake of shortening and sharpening the play' (*ST*, p. xxxvi). It is true that the announcement inserted immediately before the play-within-the-play suggests that the performance in sundry languages was shorter:

> Gentlemen, this play of HIERONIMO in sundry languages, was
> thought good to be set down in English *more largely*,
> for the easier understanding to every
> public reader

(my emphasis). However, considering the English text is only fifty lines long and the passage introducing the idea of performing the play in 'sundry languages' takes up twenty-nine lines (IV.i.170–98), the revised version would hardly have been much shorter. Given a closer look, Edwards's case for abridgement again becomes very cloudy.

There are no sound reasons to doubt that the play of 'Soliman and Perseda' was ever performed in 'sundry languages'.[35] In IV.i.170–98 Hieronimo introduces the idea of the multilingual performance and, after Balthazar's initial resistance, has it approved by his fellow-actors. Hieronimo's statement after the performance is equally unambiguous: 'Here break we off our sundry languages/ And thus conclude I in our vulgar tongue' (IV.iv.74–5). Also, as none of Kyd's editors has pointed out, the King's ignorance of the role Lorenzo plays (IV.iv.33–4), which has just been announced by Balthazar-as-Soliman (IV.iv.30), shows that the audience cannot follow the play's linguistic content. The 'unknown languages' (IV.i.173) can hardly trouble the spectators, as the multilingual play is short, possibly with an effect similar to that of a dumb show. The audience off-stage is not dependent upon the language in the play-within-the-play in order to understand the plot which has already been paraphrased at some length (IV.i.110–26). Hieronimo's fourteen-line speech in Latin (II.v.67–80) may have been a greater obstacle to understanding for a popular audience than the multilingual play-within-the-play.

Various critics have explored the appropriateness of the sundry languages in Hieronimo's play. S. F. Johnson has analysed the relevance of the Babel *topos*, 'the fall of Babylon' (IV.i.195) and its tower, the confusion of languages as communication between the protagonist and the court has broken down.[36] Janette Dillon has explored the theatrical effect and efficiency of the sundry languages: it freezes 'the event in order to compel the spectator into a deep engagement with its horror'.[37] Kyd is not the only one who employed foreign languages at a moment of great emotional tension: as the two lovers are reunited in Marston's *Antonio and Mellida*, they express their rapturous emotions in eighteen lines of Italian (IV.i).

The origin of the English text of the play-within-the-play remains difficult to determine. The text shows clear traces of indebtedness to Wotton's novella which served Kyd again as the main source for *Soliman and Perseda*. It seems therefore sensible to assume that the English version of the play-within-the-play which found its way into

White's edition is Kyd's. Whether it was written alongside the multilingual text (for the players who had small Latin and less Greek?),
or whether it came into existence later seems difficult to determine.

I have only tentative explanations for the textual problems *The
Spanish Tragedy* poses. The evidence for a conflation of Kyd's foul
papers and Jeffes's 'bad', reported, printed text seems to me incon-
clusive. The unevenness of White's edition appears more likely to be
due to the state of Kyd's foul papers. Some passages may have been
written in a hurry and with less attention to metrical regularity.
Also, the printer's copy may have contained minor inconsistencies
owing to second thoughts and isolated changes which found their
way into the printed text.

Since White's edition does not seem to be a conflation of a
manuscript and a printed source, it may well be a simple reprint
of Jeffes's edition. White's assertion on the title page that his text
has been 'Newly corrected and amended of such grosse faults as
passed in the first impression' may not have to be taken seriously.[38] After all, White appears to have prepared his edition in
retaliation for Jeffes's edition of *Arden of Faversham* and must
have felt entitled to cry down the earlier edition, a strategy that
other publishers had adopted before him. What further supports
this interpretation is that the wording of Jeffes's entry in the
Stationers' Register ('*the Spanishe tragedie of Don HORATIO and
BELLMIPEIA &c*') resembles that of White's title page (THE/
SPANISH TRAGE-/ die [...] of *Don Horatio,* and *Bel-imperia*
[...]'). As the title in the Stationers' Register was normally copied
from the publisher's manuscript, this suggests that White's title
was simply copied from Jeffes's edition rather than set up from an
independent manuscript.[39]

If the unevenness of White's edition is due to the state of Kyd's
foul papers, then one of the affected areas could have been the
'Chorus' scenes at the end of each act. Acts I and II conclude with a
short exchange between Andrea and Revenge, the total of each scene
not exceeding a dozen lines (I.v, II.vi). At the end of the third act,
however, the 'Chorus' is substantially longer and includes a 'dumb
show' in the tradition of *Gorboduc*. This may have taken shape late
in the process of composition and the lines added – possibly on a
separate piece of paper – may have been in barely legible writing.
Even though this is mere speculation, it is not implausible. The
possible loss of a similar Chorus, constituting the end of what Kyd
intended to be the third act, supports this theory and would account
for the odd four-act structure with an over-long third act.

Boas's view that 'Kyd evidently wrote the play in four Acts' (p. 404) thus needs to be questioned. The third act of *The Spanish Tragedy* alone is longer than any two of the other acts together. This has led some critics to suspect that Kyd originally conceived the play in five acts.[40] The evidence for this is quite strong. Since Kyd is repeatedly keen to claim Seneca as a classical ancestor, it would be surprising if he did not follow him in the five-act division. *Soliman and Perseda*, even though less classical in its ancestry, clearly falls into five acts, each act finishing with the Chorus. Besides Seneca, New Comedy and neoclassical drama may also have suggested to Kyd the five-act structure to which *The Spanish Tragedy* conforms.[41]

In fact, the dramatic architecture of *The Spanish Tragedy* shows a careful five-act construction such as Kyd observed in Seneca.[42] The first act, the introduction, sums up what happened before the beginning of the play leading up to the play's first conflict caused by Bel-imperia's resolution to love Horatio in order to 'spite the prince' (I.iv.68). The last act, the *dénouement*, prepares and presents the fatal play-within-the-play. The plot between the first and the last act falls naturally into three parts: act II leads up to Horatio's murder; III.i to III.vii deals with the Pedringano and Serberine episode which is set between Bel-imperia's two letters to Hieronimo, the first causing him to doubt, the second bringing him to believe; and III.viii to III.xiv dramatises Hieronimo's descent into madness and culminates with his decision to take revenge into his own hands. Hieronimo's seventy-line bravura piece in III.vii, only briefly interrupted by the hangman reporting that Pedringano has been hanged, brings this sequence to an end. A 'Chorus' may have originally followed this scene, though another possibility is that Hieronimo's soliloquy was meant to replace it. The evidence thus adduced may not be strong enough for an editor to divide the play into five acts. If we want to understand Kyd's dramatic construction, we do well, however, to keep in mind that he is likely to have conceived *The Spanish Tragedy* as a five-act play.

It is well known that some of the more grandiloquent passages of *The Spanish Tragedy* were ridiculed by Kyd's successors, notably by Jonson (*Every Man in His Humour* (1601), I.iii.126–42, *Poetaster*, III.iv.214–58), but also in Shirley's *Changes*, Middleton's *Old Law*, and in the anonymous Cambridge play *The Return from Parnassus*, among others.[43] It is less well known that Kyd's play contributed substantially to an early miscellany with quotations from contemporary poets and playwrights: *Belvedere, or the Garden of the Muses* (1600), edited by A. M. (Anthony Munday?). Shakespeare's *Richard II* (forty-seven times) and *Edward III* (twenty-three times) are the only plays that are quoted more often than *The Spanish Tragedy* (twenty times), and even the eight quotations from *Soliman and Perseda* compare favourably with the seven from *Edward II* or the two from *Every Man in His Humour*.[44] From the very beginning then, opinions on the quality of Kyd's dramatic language seem to have differed.

While our understanding of Kyd's dramatic artistry has considerably improved in recent times, his language is still much misunderstood. The attitude manifested in early parodies has survived in a modern prejudice against Kyd's verse that dies hard. Superficial and uninformed critical opinion has seen in the language of *The Spanish Tragedy* rant, conventional rhetoric, mechanically patterned speech, and other alleged rhetorical absurdities, rather than any of Kyd's positive achievements.

The Spanish Tragedy is basically a blank verse tragedy interspersed with some prose (III.v, III.vi.41–89., III.vii.19–28) and a portion of rhymed verse (e.g.: II.i.1–40, II.iv.24–49). The play then is the first extant blank verse tragedy after *Gorboduc* (and *Jocasta* if we include translations), a title it has to share, considering the overlapping conjectural dates of composition and the absence of any detectable influence either way, with *Tamburlaine* (and, possibly, with *Dido, Queen of Carthage*). It seems therefore inaccurate to credit Marlowe solely with domesticating blank verse for the public stage.[45] The first early references to the new metre in London's playhouses occur in Nashe's 'Preface' to Greene's *Menaphon*, and it is more than likely that one ('Sufficeth them to bodge vp a blanke verse with ifs and ands' (III, p. 316)) refers specifically to Kyd.[46] Nashe's jibe is deliberately scathing as is the rest of his invective. Yet, Kyd's blank verse, like Marlowe's 'swelling bumbast of bragging blanke verse' (III, pp. 311), was clearly both novel and successful enough to awaken the professional jealousy of the rival dramatist. Kyd and Marlowe forged simultaneously the linguistic medium future dramatists were to inherit. If Marlowe's verse is justly praised above Kyd's, the distinct linguistic qualities and contributions of the author of *The Spanish Tragedy* must not be underestimated. In Howard Baker's words, 'Thomas Kyd's contribution to early dramatic blank verse, though it may not be earlier than Marlowe's, is certainly an independent contribution and one that proved to be of scarcely less value to the maturing Shakespeare.'[47]

What then is Kyd's 'independent contribution'? It will be readily conceded that Kyd's verse does not have the drive of Marlowe's 'mighty line', nor the power of Tamburlaine's great speeches, nor the beauty of the great passages in the first and the last acts of *Doctor Faustus* and *Edward II*. It is altogether less easily detached from its context and anthologised. This is so because Kyd's dramatic language is finely in tune with character and situation. As G. R. Hibbard has pointed out, in *1 Tamburlaine*, 'there are occasions when the style is at odds with the character or rather would be if character mattered'.[48] Not so in *The Spanish Tragedy*. The play's language respects decorum to a degree that not only Marlowe's, but also that of his other contemporaries – Lyly, Greene, and Peele – does not. In *Tamburlaine*, language creates drama, whereas in *The Spanish Tragedy*, drama creates language.[49] Here is Hieronimo, who has been woken up by Bel-imperia's cries for help, storming into his bower:

> Who calls Hieronimo? Speak, here I am.
> I did not slumber, therefore 'twas no dream, 5
> No, no, it was some woman cried for help,
> And here within this garden did she cry,
> And in this garden must I rescue her:
> But stay, what murd'rous spectacle is this?
> A man hang'd up and all the murderers gone, 10
> And in my bower, to lay the guilt on me:
> This place was made for pleasure not for death.
> *He cuts him down.*
> Those garments that he wears I oft have seen –
> Alas, it is Horatio my sweet son!
> O no, but he that whilom was my son. 15
> O was it thou that call'dst me from my bed?
> O speak, if any spark of life remain: (II.v.4–17)

What can make Hieronimo's soliloquy extraordinarily powerful – perhaps the emotional climax in the RSC production of 1997 – is not its poetry, but its fine concordance with the action out of which it grows. Unlike other soliloquies, it is not like an aria during which the action pauses after the *recitativo* dialogue has advanced the action. What Kyd introduces here to the English stage is the soliloquy that is acted rather than statically recited. Its effect is largely dependent upon its being seen, or visually imagined: Hieronimo rushing in 'in his shirt' (II.v.0.1), sword in one hand, torch in the other (title page of *1602*), his inability to see what is clearly visible to us articulated by the ironic 'Speak', the shock at the first discovery, his cutting down of the corpse from the arbour, the arising fear owing to 'Those garments', the transition from fearful doubt to terrible certainty, the desperate attempts at resuscitation. 'Suit the action to the word, the word to the action' is a precept Kyd seems to have been keenly aware of in Hieronimo's soliloquy.[50]

If Kyd suits his language intimately to action, situation, and character, the result is not so much a unified, recognizable idiom as a variety of idioms. The extent of this variety is remarkable. Kyd's language ranges from the straightforward prose of Lorenzo's page:

> My master hath forbidden me to look in this box, and by my troth 'tis likely, if he had not warned me, I should not have had so much idle time: (III.v.1–3)

and the farcical knock-about exchange between Pedringano and the hangman:

> *Hangman.*   Come sir.
> *Pedringano.*   So then, I must up?
> *Hangman.*   No remedy.
> *Pedringano.*   Yes, but there shall be for my coming down.
> *Hangman.*   Indeed, here's a remedy for that.
> *Pedringano.*   How? be turned off?
> *Hangman.*   Ay truly; come are you ready?   (III.vi.49–55)

to the gravity of the General's battle report as exemplified by the following simile:

> Both battles join and fall to handy blows,
> Their violent shot resembling th' ocean's rage,
> When, roaring loud and with a swelling tide,
> It beats upon the rampiers of huge rocks,
> And gapes to swallow neighbour-bounding lands.   (I.ii.47–51)

As Polonius puts it, 'Seneca cannot be too heavy, nor Plautus too light'. Of course, rhetorical figures and patterned speeches are not absent from this astonishing stylistic range, but it is important to recognise the degree of self-consciousness with which Kyd plays with these devices.[51] Here is self-styled 'Senecan Kyd':

> *Lorenzo.*   Sister, what means this melancholy walk?
> *Bel-imperia.*   That for a while I wish no company.
> *Lorenzo.*   But here the prince is come to visit you.
> *Bel-imperia.*   That argues that he lives in liberty.   80
> *Balthazar.*   No madam, but in pleasing servitude.
> *Bel-imperia.*   Your prison then belike is your conceit.
> *Balthazar.*   Ay, by conceit my freedom is enthrall'd.
> *Bel-imperia.*   Then with conceit enlarge yourself again.
> *Balthazar.*   What if conceit have laid my heart to gage?   85
> *Bel-imperia.*   Pay that you borrow'd and recover it.
> *Balthazar.*   I die if I return from whence it lies.
> *Bel-imperia.*   A heartless man and live? A miracle!   (I.iv.77–88)

Kyd's stichomythia is more than a rhetorical trick, a dead device taken over from Seneca. Bel-imperia is a strong-minded and self-willed woman, beauteous and imperial as her name suggests, neither married nor virginal, and nothing could introduce her character better than the way she linguistically bounces back at Lorenzo's and Balthazar's advances. Balthazar, characteristically, lacks this sharp concision:

> I think Horatio be my destin'd plague:
> First in his hand he brandished a sword,
> And with that sword he fiercely waged war,   120
> And in that war he gave me dangerous wounds,
> And by those wounds he forced me to yield,
> And by my yielding I became his slave.
> Now in his mouth he carries pleasing words,
> Which pleasing words do harbour sweet conceits,   125
> Which sweet conceits are lim'd with sly deceits,
> Which sly deceits smooth Bel-imperia's ears,
> And through her ears dive down into her heart,
> And in her heart set him where I should stand.   (II.i.118–29)

The length of the anadiplosis – a 'sort of repetition when with the worde by which you finish your verse, ye beginne the next verse with the same' – paired with the monotonously repeated 'And' and 'Which' is unbearable, but this is precisely Kyd's point.[52] Lorenzo reacts to the lethargic lover's drawn out and languid language just as impatiently as we do:

> Tush, tush my lord, let go these ambages,
> And in plain terms acquaint her with your love.   (I.iv.90–1)

> My lord, for my sake leave these ecstasies,   (II.i.29)

> Let's go my lord, your staying stays revenge.   (II.i.134)

Euphuism, another stylistic tic of the day, also serves Kyd to characterise the languid, effeminate Petrarchan lover:

> Yet might she love me for my valiancy,
> Ay, but that's slander'd by captivity.
> Yet might she love me to content her sire,
> Ay, but her reason masters his desire.
> Yet might she love me as her brother's friend,
> Ay, but her hopes aim at some other end.   (II.i.19–24)

Compare Lorenzo's direct Machiavellianism in corrupting Bel-imperia's servant:

> Then shalt thou find that I am liberal:
> Thou know'st that I can more advance thy state
> Than she, be therefore wise and fail me not.

Go and attend her as thy custom is,
Lest absence make her think thou dost amiss.   (II.i.102–6)

The aim Lorenzo pursues and the way he expresses it go hand-in-hand. Every word is to the purpose; the verse is pragmatic and devoid of flourishes.

Hieronimo's voice is more difficult to capture than Lorenzo's, Balthazar's, or Bel-imperia's.[53] As his roles extend from the public Knight Marshall and Master of the Revels to the private father, husband, and accomplice, so his language stretches from conversational prose to declamatory verse. At its worst, the latter betrays the overblown rhetoric which seems to lack sincerity when it is most needed:

O eyes, no eyes, but fountains fraught with tears;
O life, no life, but lively form of death;
O world, no world, but mass of public wrongs,
Confus'd and fill'd with murder and misdeeds;   (III.ii.1–4)

The Petrarchan ancestry of Hieronimo's lines has long been pointed out.[54] Yet, a device that works ingeniously to characterise the shallow Balthazar fails to make Hieronimo's profound bereavement credible. J. R. Mulryne rightly points out that '[a] modern reader finds it difficult to adjust to the larger-than-life emphasis, as well as the self-conscious artificiality of structure, in Kyd's stage rhetoric. Profound emotion wedded to exceptional artifice of structure appears to us contradiction and insincerity' (p. xxviii). At his best, however, Kyd expresses Hieronimo's grief with poignancy, as in his first soliloquy discussed above or as in the following passages in which strained language eloquently reflects strained emotions:

O sacred heavens! if this unhallow'd deed,
If this inhuman and barbarous attempt,
If this incomparable murder thus
Of mine, but now no more my son,
Shall unreveal'd and unrevenged pass,
How should we term your dealings to be just,
If you unjustly deal with those that in your justice trust?   (III.ii.5–11)

The protagonist's repeated and repeatedly failing attempts to come to terms with his son's death are enacted by the syntactical reiteration of the hypothetical clause, articulated three times before the sentence can move on. Just as Hieronimo's psyche can no longer contain his grief but finally cracks, so too does Kyd's blank verse finally give way and burst into a fourteener. A few lines later on, both the dramatisation of Hieronimo's grief and madness and the disruption of syntax reach a climax:

Eyes, life, world, heavens, hell, night, and day,
See, search, shew, send, some man, some mean, that may – (III.ii.22–3)

The very orderly rhetorical figure serves to make the syntactic break-down all the more forceful. In Hieronimo's despair, meaning as well as language are incoherent and fragmented. As noun and verb, subject and predicate are torn from each other, so Horatio has been torn from his life.[55]

If the situation requires it, however, Hieronimo's verse can also be the precise opposite: conversational rather than declamatory; smooth, straightforward, and colloquial. After Hieronimo's bloody play, he ceases to be the outraged and torn character of the earlier soliloquies. The directness and simplicity of his language contrasts strikingly with the artificiality of what precedes:

Here break we off our sundry languages
And thus conclude I in our vulgar tongue.   75
Haply you think, but bootless are your thoughts,
That this is fabulously counterfeit,
And that we do as all tragedians do:
To die today, for fashioning our scene,
The death of Ajax, or some Roman peer,   80
And in a minute starting up again,
Revive to please tomorrow's audience.
No, princes, know I am Hieronimo,   (IV.iv.74–83)

The language is as obvious, as direct and as transparent as Hieronimo's final assertion. G. R. Hibbard aptly summarises this quality of Kyd's language: 'His speech is not prose, nor is it prosaic, the rhythm and the touches of imagery ensure that and knit it into the rest of the play, but it does have the virtues of good prose: clarity and directness.'[56]

It is a critical commonplace today that 'the blank verse of *Tamburlaine* gave to English Renaissance drama its staple medium of expression'.[57] In one sense, this is frankly wrong. Taken as a whole, *Tamburlaine*'s 'mighty line' resembles the blank verse of very few if any English Renaissance plays. Theatricality and decorum, however, the twin marks of Kyd's dramatic idiom in *The Spanish Tragedy*, are marks that reappear in later playwrights. It has been argued that 'Kyd would have been a greater writer had he forged a single style capable of registering a wide range of levels of intensity, but the blend of voices which he produces is a very fine achieve-ment.'[58] It is true that Kyd would have been a greater writer, but he would not have been a better playwright. At its best, his language is eminently theatrical, subtly growing out of action, character, and situation, a quality which lies on the straight road to Shakespeare.

Notes

1 See Greg, pp. 1328–38. See also Emma Smith, 'Author v. Character in Early Modern Dramatic Authorship: The Example of Thomas Kyd and *The Spanish Tragedy*', *Medieval and Renaissance Drama in England*, 11 (1999), 129–42.

2 *The Spanish Tragedy* is in the second of twelve volumes.

3 'Zur Verfasserschaft der *Spanish Tragedy*', *Bayerische Akademie der Wissenschaften* (1963), 1–24.

4 *Playes Confuted in fiue Actions* (Kinney, *Markets of Bawdrie*, p. 169).

5 Bowers, *Elizabethan Revenge Tragedy*, p. 73; Freeman, p. 50.

6 Further sources have been suggested by Howard Baker ('The Formation of the Heroic Medium', in Paul J. Alpers (ed.), *Elizabethan Poetry: Modern Essays in Criticism* (London, 1967), pp. 126–68) who argues that the epic battle description in I.ii is modelled on Nicholas Grimald's 'Death of Zoroas' printed in Tottel's *Songes and Sonnettes*; by Andrew S. Cairncross ('Thomas Kyd and the Myrmidons', *The Arlington Quarterly*, 1.4 (1968), 40–5); and by G. K. Hunter ('Tacitus and Kyd's *The Spanish Tragedy*', *NQ*, 245 [n.s. 47] (2000), 424–5).

7 See the introduction to Thomas Rogers, *Leicester's Ghost*, ed. F. B. Williams, Jr. (Chicago, 1972). I quote from this edition.

8 'Kyd's Pedringano: Sources and Parallels', *Harvard Studies and Notes in Philology and Literature*, 13 (1931), 241–9.

9 *The Queen's Men and Their Plays*, p. 20.

10 'Here is the place, where the road parts in twain: there to the right, as it runs under the walls of great Dis, is our way to Elysium, but the left wreaks the punishment of the wicked, and sends them on to pitiless Tartarus.' The Latin and the English are quoted from *Virgil I: 'Eclogues', 'Georgics', 'Aeneid I–VI'*, ed. H. R. Fairclough, Loeb (London, 1916), pp. 542–5.

11 'Suddenly Aeneas looks back, and under a cliff on the left sees a broad castle, girt with triple wall and encircled with a rushing flood of torrent flames – Tartarean Phlegethon, that rolls among thundering rocks. In front stands the huge gate, and pillars of solid adamant, that no might of man, nay, not even the sons of heaven, may uproot in war; there stands the iron tower, soaring high, and Tisiphone, sitting girt with bloody pall, keeps sleepless watch o'er the portal night and day', Loeb, pp. 544–5.

12 *The Bad Quarto of 'Hamlet'* (Cambridge, 1951), p. 68.

13 The relevance of Lavater to the passage quoted from *Cornélie* has been pointed out and analysed by J. M. Maguin, '"Of Ghosts and Spirits Walking By Night" – a Joint Examination of the Ghost Scenes in Robert Garnier's *Cornélie*, Thomas Kyd's *Cornelia* and Shakespeare's *Hamlet* in the Light of Reformation Thinking As Presented in Lavater's Book', *CE*, 1 (1972), 26–40. Maguin, however, does not relate Lavater or the passage in *Cornélie* to the Ghost of Andrea in *The Spanish Tragedy*.

14 It may seem surprising that Garnier appears to have made a Protestant theological point in a play printed in Paris two years after the massacre. Is it possible that Garnier could rely on the pagan 'disguise' to make the passage innocuous? Unfortunately, Garnier's editors do not comment upon this interesting passage. It has been argued, however, that Garnier

temporarily had Protestant sympathies and a Protestant treatise published in 1591 contained an adaptation of a passage from *Cornélie* (see Robert Garnier, *Porcie, Cornélie*, ed. Raymond Lebègue (Paris, 1973), pp. 11, 28).

15 See Edwards, *ST*, pp. 10–11.

16 Thomas McAlindon, *English Renaissance Tragedy* (Houndmills, Basingstoke, Hampshire, 1986), p. 55.

17 Baldwin, 'On the Chronology of Thomas Kyd's Plays', *MLN*, 40 (1925), 343–9; Schick (ed.), *The Spanish Tragedy*, p. xxiii; Boas, p. xxx; Freeman, p. 79.

18 *Edward III*: 'The proud armado of King Edward's ships' (III.i.64, ed. Giorgio Melchiori (Cambridge, 1998)); *Midas*: 'Haue not I made the sea to groane vnder the number of my ships: and haue they not perished, that there was not two left to make a number?' (Bond, III.i.31–3); *The Three Lords and Three Ladies of London*: 'The Spanish forces, lordings, are prepar'd/ In bravery and boast beyond all bounds,/ T' invade, to win, to conquer all this land' (*A Select Collection of Old English Plays*, ed. W. C. Hazlitt, 4th edn (1874), VI, p. 447).

19 In Dekker's *Satiromastix* (1602), Tucca shouts at Horace, a thinly disguised parody of Jonson: 'I ha seene thy shoulders lapt in a Plaiers old cast Cloake, like a Slie knaue as thou art: and when thou ranst mad for the death of Horatio: thou borrowedst a gowne of *Roscius* the Stager [...] and sentst it home lowsie, didst not?' (I.ii.354–8). See Fredson Bowers, 'Ben Jonson, the Actor', *SP*, 34 (1937), 392–406.

20 The third parallel, not mentioned in Boas's or Edwards's editions, was pointed out by Susan E. Joy, 'The Kyd/Marlowe Connection', *NQ*, 231 [n.s. 33] (1986), 338–9.

21 See Joy, 'The Kyd/Marlowe Connection' and Muriel C. Bradbrook, *Themes and Conventions of Elizabethan Tragedy* (Cambridge, 1935), pp. 122, 159.

22 See Emrys Jones, 'The Sense of Occasion: Some Shakespearean Night Sequences', in Kenneth Muir, Jay L. Halio, and David John Palmer (eds.), *Shakespeare, Man of the Theatre* (Newark, 1983), pp. 98–104.

23 Ernest A. Gerrard, *Elizabethan Drama and Dramatists 1583–1603* (Oxford, 1928), p. 173 and Thomas Merriam, 'Possible Light on a Kyd Canon', *NQ*, 240 [n.s. 42] (1995), 340–1.

24 Thomas Heywood ascribes *The Jew of Malta* as unambiguously to Marlowe (Epistle Dedicatory to Q1633) as he ascribes *The Spanish Tragedy* to Kyd.

25 Edwards's suggestion (*ST*, pp. 141–2) that Kyd may have had a passage from 2 *Tamburlaine* in mind when writing *The Spanish Tragedy* has only the occurrence of the word 'mingled' in both passages to recommend itself and is unconvincing.

26 'The Spanish Tragedy: Act IV', *PQ*, 49 (1970), 444.

27 See W. W. Greg's introduction to *The Spanish Tragedy (1592)*, MSR (London, 1948), pp. vi–xiii.

28 *The Spanish Tragedy (1592)*, MSR, p. x.

29 Edwards, *ST*, p. xl. Something similar has been shown to have happened in the printing of the 'good' second quartos of *Romeo and Juliet* and *Hamlet* which were set up chiefly from authorial foul papers but also

with auxiliary use of the 'bad' Q1.

30 Schücking, *Die Zusätze zur 'Spanish Tragedy'* (Leipzig, 1938); Edwards, *ST*, p. xxxvi.

31 *The Spanish Tragedy (1592)*, I2^{r-v}.

32 See Leo Kirschbaum, 'Is *The Spanish Tragedy* a Leading Case? Did a Bad Quarto of *Love's Labours Lost* Ever Exist?', *JEGP*, 37 (1938), 501–12.

33 Murray, *Thomas Kyd*, p. 144.

34 See Leo Lukas Erne, '"The Two Hours' Traffic of Our Stage": Performance Criticism and the Length of Shakespeare's Plays', *ShJ*, 135 (1999), 66–76; Richard Dutton, 'The Birth of the Author', in R. B. Parker and S. P. Zitner (eds.), *Elizabethan Theatre: Essays in Honor of S. Schoenbaum* (Newark, Del., 1996), pp. 71–92; Stephen Orgel, 'Acting Scripts, Performing Texts', in Randall McLeod (ed.), *Crisis in Editing: Texts of the English Renaissance* (New York, 1994), pp. 251–94; Andrew Gurr, 'Maximal and Minimal Texts: Shakespeare v. The Globe', *SS*, 52 (1999), 68–87.

35 It has been doubted most recently by David Bevington in his Revels Student edition ((Manchester, 1996), p. 121) and earlier by, among others, Muriel Bradbrook (*Themes and Conventions of Elizabethan Tragedy*, p. 84).

36 S. F. Johnson, '*The Spanish Tragedy*, or Babylon Revisited', in R. Hosley (ed.), *Essays on Shakespeare* (Columbia, Mo., 1962), pp. 23–36.

37 Janette Dillon, '*The Spanish Tragedy* and Staging Languages in Renaissance Drama', *RORD*, 34 (1995), 34. See also Carla Mazzio, 'Staging the Vernacular: Language and Nation in Thomas Kyd's *The Spanish Tragedy*', *SEL*, 38 (1998), 207–32, which reads the play 'in light of contemporary debates about the heterogenous and intertwined fabrics of language, culture, and nation' (p. 213).

38 W. W. Greg ('*The Spanish Tragedy* – A Leading Case?', *The Library*, 4th Series, 6 (1926), 47–56) argued that Jeffes's edition was a 'bad' quarto and read the title page of White's edition literally. Leo Kirschbaum, ('Is *The Spanish Tragedy* a Leading Case?, 501–12) argued against Greg and tried to show that other title pages also promise 'augmented', or 'corrected' texts in order to promote the new edition by crying down the old. For other title page advertisements where nothing has been corrected or augmented, see Wells and Taylor, *William Shakespeare: A Textual Companion* (Oxford, 1987), p. 270, and Henry R. Woudhuysen's Arden 3 edition of *Love's Labour's Lost* (Walton-on-Thames, 1998), pp. 301–4. See also Paul Werstine's detailed analysis of Q1 *Love's Labour's Lost* suggesting that the first extant edition ('Newly corrected and augmented' according to the title page) was set up from printed copy, implying that Q1 is a reprint of the textually 'good' lost edition ('The Editorial Usefulness of Printing House and Compositor Studies', in G. B. Shand and Raymond C. Shady (eds.), *Play-Texts in Old Spelling: Papers from the Glendon Conference* (New York, 1984), 35–64).

39 Note that Kirschbaum ('Is *The Spanish Tragedy* a Leading Case?', 501–12) fails to mention this point which strengthens his argument that White's edition my have been set up from Jeffes's. Two examples will

suffice to illustrate that resemblance between the title in the Stationers' Register and the title page of the printed playbook suggests that the two titles have been copied from the same manuscript:

1. 'A pleasant Conceyted historie called "the Tayminge of a Shrowe"' (Stationers' Register, 2 May 1594); 'A Pleasant Conceited Historie, called The taming of a Shrew' (title-page, Q1594).

2. 'the woundes of Civill warre liuely sett forthe in the true Tragedies of MARIUS and SCILLA' (Stationers' Register, 24 May 1594); 'THE VVOUNDS of Ciuill VVar. Liuely set forth in the true Tragedies of *Marius and Scilla*' (title-page, Q1594).

See also the so-called 'staying entry' of 4 August 1600 in the Stationers' Register which lists, among other plays, 'HENRY the FFIFT' (Arber, *Transcript*, III, p. 37). Peter Blayney has ingeniously argued that this really refers to 2 *Henry IV* on the ground that the title page of the first quarto edition of 1600 reads 'THE Second part of Henrie the fourth, continuing to his death, and coronation of *Henrie the fift*' (my emphasis). Blayney's unpublished argument is reported in Andrew Gurr's New Cambridge edition of *Henry V* (Cambridge, 1992), pp. 217–20.

40 P. W. Biesterfeldt (*Die dramatische Technik Thomas Kyds*, pp. 83–7) was the first who argued a detailed case for the five-act structure of *The Spanish Tragedy*.

41 T. W. Baldwin has forcefully argued that the study of Terence at school 'taught the boys how to construct plays, and impressed upon them the formula for five-act structure' (*Shakespeare's Five-Act Structure* (Urbana, 1947), p. 788).

42 I disagree with Thomas W. Ross who holds that the 'four-act structure is admirably suited to the development of these events' (*The Spanish Tragedy*, Fountainwell Drama Texts (Edinburgh, 1968), p. 9).

43 Claude Dudrap, 'La Tragédie Espagnole face à la Critique Elisabéthaine et Jacobéenne', in Jean Jacquot (ed.), *Dramaturgie et Société*, 2 vols. (Paris, 1968), II, pp. 607–31.

44 See Charles Crawford, '*Belvedere*, or *The Garden of the Muses*', *ES*, 43 (1910–11), 198–228.

45 C. F. Tucker Brooke's influential essay on 'Marlowe's Versification and Style' (*SP*, 19 (1922), 186–205) did much to establish a one-sided picture of Marlowe's importance for the introduction of blank verse to English drama.

46 See G. R. Hibbard, '"From iygging vaines of riming mother wits" to "the spacious volubilitie of a drumming decasillabon"', in A. L. Magnusson and C. E. McGee (eds.), *The Elizabethan Theatre*, 11 (Port Credit, Ontario, 1990), pp. 55–73.

47 Howard Baker, *Induction to Tragedy: A Study in a Development of Form in 'Gorboduc', 'The Spanish Tragedy', and 'Titus Andronicus'* (Baton Rouge, 1939), p. 53.

48 Hibbard, '"From iygging vaines of riming mother wits" to "the spacious volubilitie of a drumming decasillabon"', 72.

49 See Sheldon P. Zitner, '*The Spanish Tragedy* and the Language of Performance', in Magnusson and McGee (eds.), *The Elizabethan Theatre*, 11, pp. 75–93.

50 See also Wolfgang Clemen's analysis of Hieronimo's soliloquy in

English Tragedy before Shakespeare (London, 1961), p. 109.

51 See Jonas A. Barish, '*The Spanish Tragedy*, or The Pleasures and Perils of Rhetoric', in *Elizabethan Theatre*, Stratford-upon-Avon Studies, 9 (London, 1966), pp. 59–85. Barish's article is a particularly acute study of Kyd's rhetorical practice, arguing that in *The Spanish Tragedy*, the rhetorical figures 'have ceased being mere aimless embroidery. They no longer represent self-indulgence on the playwright's part, nor do they suggest a flagging imagination. They now work actively to order the materials of the play. In addition to being "auricular" and "rhetorical", they have conceptual force. They help articulate the relationships among the characters; they aid the plot to incarnate itself as a physical event on a physical stage' (p. 67).

52 George Puttenham, *The Arte of English Poesie*, ed. Gladys Doidge Willcock and Alice Walker (Cambridge, 1936), p. 200. In *Soliman and Perseda*, there is more than one occurrence of this typically Kydian rhetorical figure. For a Marlovian anadiplosis, see *The Jew of Malta*, III.iii.44–6.

53 Eugene M. Waith's *The Herculean Hero* (London, 1962) can profitably be consulted in relation to Hieronimo's rhetoric as it explores the effect on the spectators of the rhetoric Shakespeare and others gave to their protagonist.

54 See Edwards, *ST*, p. 52.

55 See Rainer Lengeler, '"Mongrel tragi-comedy": Chaosdarstellung und Gattungsmischung in *The Spanish Tragedy* und *Romeo and Juliet*', in Heinrich F. Plett (ed.), *Renaissance-Poetik, Renaissance Poetics* (Berlin, New York, 1994), pp. 274–7, showing that Hieronimo's 'O eyes, no eyes' speech is not just about chaos, but that it enacts moral chaos.

56 Hibbard, '"From iygging vaines of riming mother wits" to "the spacious volubilitie of a drumming decasillabon"', 73. Hibbard's is a fine article that traces the evolution of English dramatic language from the 1560s of *Gorboduc* and *Cambyses* to Peele, Marlowe and Kyd in the 1580s.

57 Clifford Leech, *Christopher Marlowe: Poet for the Stage* (New York, 1986), p. 1.

58 Edwards, *Kyd*, p. 26.

CHAPTER 3

The Spanish Tragedy: origins

By the 1560s, native English drama had developed from the Mystery and Morality plays via the moral Interludes to secular plays such as *Cambyses*, *Apius and Virginia*, *Horestes*, and *Patient Grissell*, or romantic comedies such as *Common Conditions* and *Clyomon and Clamydes*. Though on the wane, Morality plays and Interludes still made occasional appearances as in *Impatient Poverty*, R. Wever's *Lusty Juventus*, or in Ulpian Fulwell's *Like Will to Like*. In the meantime, the two universities saw performances of various classical and neoclassical plays in Latin. For instance, a play on the subject of Dido by Edward Halliwell was performed in the chapel of King's College, Cambridge, before the Queen on 7 August 1564. Also, following vernacular neoclassical drama in Italy and France, tragedies such as *Gorboduc*, *Jocasta*, and *Gismond of Salerne* were produced. None of these plays would entertain a modern audience, but two decades later, Kyd wrote *The Spanish Tragedy* which remained popular for decades and still makes for powerful theatre today. Even though *The Spanish Tragedy* is a highly original and innovative play, it nevertheless grows out of a rich and multifaceted ancestry. It is these 'origins' of *The Spanish Tragedy* – its fusion, reconciliation, and transcendence of classical and native traditions – which I propose to examine in the following.

The Roman philosopher and dramatist Seneca (AD 1–65), more than anyone else, was the progenitor of English Renaissance tragedy. All of his plays were translated into English in the three decades before *The Spanish Tragedy* was written, and a collected edition of *Seneca his Tenne Tragedies* had been published in 1581. As the writers in the English Renaissance had little first-hand knowledge of Greek tragedy, neoclassical drama of the sixteenth century was basically Senecan in style. Features of Senecan drama survive in many

Elizabethan plays: revenge and violence, the ghost and the chorus, sententious rhetoric and narrative passages, division into five acts and stichomythia, to mention only a few.

Though Seneca's impact upon *The Spanish Tragedy* is obvious, to establish its nature and significance is a more difficult matter. We do well not to overestimate the importance of 'surface Senecanism', of features such as stichomythia and verbal parallels. On their own, they do not prove that the rhetoric, the dramaturgy, or the nature of tragic experience of Seneca's plays left a substantial imprint on *The Spanish Tragedy*. Moreover, Kyd clearly departs from Seneca in important matters: apart from the ghost, Senecan stock characters, such as *nutrix*, faithful servant, or tyrant, are largely absent; the two long messenger speeches are confined to the first act; and most of the action is staged rather than retrospectively related. While Seneca's is a drama of declamation that takes place in the listener's mind, Kyd's is basically a drama of action that takes place on stage.

The array of parallel passages and superficial features which John W. Cunliffe and H. B. Charlton mustered to demonstrate Seneca's all-pervasive influence therefore proves little.[1] On the other hand, it will not do either to deny or to minimise Seneca's influence on *The Spanish Tragedy*. Several critics did so on the grounds that earlier studies had failed to notice the multiplicity of intermediate sources and the complexity of the assimilative process through which Seneca came down to Kyd and Elizabethan drama at large.[2] More recently, Gordon Braden has shown convincingly that Senecan and Elizabethan drama share features which 'are not just a repertoire of varied effects, but have a corporate coherence as instruments of a particular style of selfhood', which is identified as 'the self's search for a radical, unpredicated independence'.[3]

A look at some of Seneca's dramatic writing shows that beyond isolated features of style which Kyd may owe directly to Seneca or not, the English and the Roman playwright share more generally a sense of the nature and the intensity of tragic experience. *Troades*, perhaps Seneca's finest dramatic achievement, is a case in point. After the sack of Troy, the victors have gathered their spoils and are ready to return to Greece, but the ghost of Achilles and the prophet Calchas demand that Polyxena, the daughter of Hecuba and Priam, and Astyanax, the little son of Hector and Andromache, be slain before they are allowed to sail home. It has long been noticed that Hieronimo, in the 'Vindicta mihi' soliloquy, quotes two lines *verbatim* from the play's magnificent central scene. In fact, the scene as a whole is well worth considering in relation to Kyd's play. It takes up more than a third of the whole tragedy and is situated exactly at the centre of the play. Divisible into three parts, it skilfully moves from Andromache and the Old Man (Senex), who have Astyanax hide in his father's tomb, to Ulysses' crafty interview with Andromache in which he finally discovers Astyanax's hiding place, and concludes with Andromache's lament at her final parting from her son. Even though Astyanax, unlike Horatio, is not dead, the central concern is the same as in *The Spanish Tragedy*: the protagonist's grief for the loss of a son. As in Kyd, madness, grief, justice, and retribution are the themes around which the scene turns. It further shares with *The Spanish Tragedy* a sense of some overpowering destiny that cannot be avoided: Kyd's Revenge announces the final outcome at the very beginning (I.i.87–9), and Seneca's audience knows that Andromache's attempts at saving her son will come to nothing. Particular similarities with the 'Senex' scene (III.xiii) can be noted. Both protagonists, in their laments, address their sons. As Hieronimo mistakes Bazulto for the Ghost of Horatio, Andromache, in her frenzy, believes she is in the presence of the Ghost of Hector (ll. 681–2). Kyd may well have had the suggestion for the name 'Senex' – an old man – which the speech headings have for Bazulto, from this very scene.

Contrary to most of his contemporary playwrights (with the possible exception of Marston), Kyd claims Seneca emphatically as his ancestor. The prologue featuring the Ghost of Andrea and Revenge clearly recalls the Ghost of Tantalus and Fury in the prologue to *Thyestes*. The opening lines of the third act follow Seneca's *Agamemnon* (ll. 57–73) so closely that Kyd could expect part of his audience to recognise his debt to Seneca. Similarly, in III.xiii, the book in Hieronimo's hand and the Latin borrowings from Seneca in the 'Vindicta mihi' soliloquy seem aimed at claiming 'descent' from the Roman dramatist. As most contemporary play-wrights – Greene, Marlowe, Peele, Nashe, and Lyly – were university-trained, Kyd, who could not boast a degree from Oxford or Cambridge, may have hoped to increase his respectability by proclaiming his debts to Seneca. Even though consciously parting from the purely rhetorical drama of Seneca's translators and the academic Senecan plays of the kind of *Gorboduc*, Kyd may have wanted his audience to see the play in the Senecan tradition. Skilfully blending classical Senecan with more recent native elements, Kyd seems to have tried to situate himself within a tradition at the very moment when he was radically redefining it.

Nashe's reaction to Kyd's appropriation of Seneca in the 'Preface' to Greene's *Menaphon* is not what Kyd was hoping for. Nashe denigrates Kyd precisely for his use of the Roman dramatist: '*Seneca* let bloud line by line and page by page, at length needes must die to our stage'.[4] The jibe suggests that Nashe, whether justly or not, perceived a Senecan presence in Kyd's plays which was stronger than some critics have found. Significantly, Nashe's words suggest that he is keen to highlight what he thought of as social presumption: moving away from the writing of Senecan plays, Kyd is 'renowncing all possibilities of *credit or estimation*, to intermeddle with Italian translations' (my emphasis).[5] Nashe thus simultaneously mocks Kyd's use of Seneca and grants, *ex negativo*, that it constituted a possible claim to 'credit or estimation'. Kyd's Senecanism and Nashe's attack on it seem to have had a strong social component.

One of the chief merits of critics like Hunter who argue against a monolithic Senecan influence is to point at the variety of other authors and works that may have influenced Kyd. Italian and French Senecan drama has obvious affinities with Kyd, and echoes from Garnier's *Cornélie*, which Kyd was to translate a few years later, have been noted above. In some ways, however, Garnier moved away from Seneca in a direction opposed to Kyd's. The French dramatist restricted dramatic action even more than Seneca and expanded the choral lyrics. Garnier's Senecanism outdid Seneca. In many ways Giraldi Cinthio's more theatrical drama thus seems closer to Kyd than does Garnier.[6] It has been suggested that Cinthio provided a model for Lorenzo.[7] It would be particularly interesting to know whether Kyd knew Cinthio's tremendously influential *Orbecche* which, like *The Spanish Tragedy*, is based on novelistic material. Several features are reminiscent of Kyd's play: we are told the future course of events before the beginning of the action proper. The Ghost of Selina announces that Oronte and his children will be murdered and that Orbecche will kill her father and eventually commit suicide. Like *The Spanish Tragedy*, *Orbecche* places a Chorus at the end of each act. More specifically, Sulmone pretends to have forgiven Orbecche and Oronto and performs an outward reconciliation before executing his revenge (III.iv), just as Hieronimo fakes reconciliation with Lorenzo and Balthazar before the fatal play-within-the-play (III.xiv, IV.i). Orbecche and Hieronimo use a similar device in their final moments: both pretend to resign – Orbecche by placing a knife in Sulmone's hands, Hieronimo by asking for a pen to write down his 'confession' – before using the very tool of apparent resignation as the instrument of both revenge and suicide. It would be rash, however, to claim that these similarities are more than accidental, for the two plays belong to a common genre and tradition with occasional similarities in plot devices.

Besides the tradition of Senecan drama ranging from the Roman dramatist to his Italian and French heirs, the native theatrical tradition and its legacy to *The Spanish Tragedy* needs to be examined. The influence that can be traced specifically is slight. Kyd departs from the traditional structure of the native drama. As David Bevington has shown, the latter was characterised by a 'sequential structure' in which subordination is a 'far less active principle of perception than coordination'.[8] Significantly, Kyd is almost completely absent from Bevington's study. The complex causality of Kyd's multilayered revenge scheme makes for a plot very unlike the basically linear one of the native drama.

In a more general sense, however, the native drama is a precondition for *The Spanish Tragedy*. Richard Edwards's *Damon and Pithias*, John Pickeryng's *Horestes*, Thomas Preston's *Cambyses*, and R. B.'s *Appius and Virginia* are extant plays of the 1560s which share with *The Spanish Tragedy* elaborate stage action, realistic methods of presentation (suggested by the stage directions) as well as popular appeal. The Italian and French drama of the sixteenth century was overshadowed by Scaliger's and Castelvetro's pseudo-Aristotelian poetics in a way English drama was not. Dramatists straying from the rules of neoclassical poetics met strong resistance. Cinthio, who ended most of his tragedies with a sudden turn for the better, had to apologise for the 'liberty' he was taking. Apart from the academic plays, English drama was not concerned with what tragedy was or should be according to theoreticians, nor was its course stopped by Sidney's protest against the violation of 'Aristotle's precept and common reason'.[9]

The Spanish Tragedy also departs from the conception of tragedy that goes back to Boccaccio's fourteenth-century *De casibus virorum illustrium* and John Lydgate's *Fall of Princes* (1431–38), and finds its chief sixteenth-century expression in *The Mirror for Magistrates* (first published 1559), a series of narrative tragedies by William Baldwin, George Ferrers, and others.[10] While the *De casibus* tradition shows characters at the mercy of inconstant fortune, Kyd subjects them to human causality. How different the two conceptions are can be seen by comparing *The Spanish Tragedy* to the ballad written on the same subject in the wake of the play's success. The latter, as Willard Farnham has noted, 'throws Kyd's drama into the simplest terms of *De Casibus* story':[11]

Hapless *Hieronimo* was my name,
On whom fond fortune smiled long:
And now her flattering smiles I blame;
Her flattering smiles hath done me wrong.   10
    Would I had dyed in tender yeares:
    Then had not beene this cause of teares.

I Marshall was in prime of yeares,
And wonne great honour in the fielde:
Vntill that age with siluered haires   15
My aged head had ouerspred.
    Then left I warre, and stayde at home,
    And gaue my honour to my sonne.   (ll. 7–18)

While the ballad, and *De casibus* narratives in general, tell the story of a downfall effected by 'inconstant Fortune', *The Spanish Tragedy* dramatises an intricate plot governed by the machinations of humans. The native metrical tragedies do not seem to have had a definite influence on Kyd's play.

After an evaluation of the influence of Senecan drama and of the native tradition, a distinctive feature of *The Spanish Tragedy* has still not been accounted for. Alfred Harbage has argued that 'the historical importance of *The Spanish Tragedy* resides chiefly in certain details of its action': 'the element of intrigue in Kyd's play, those considerable portions of it where the entertaining complication of the action becomes an end in itself. Perhaps Kyd's greatest innovation was to employ comic methods with tragic materials, thus creating a species of comitragedy'.[12] The importance of Kyd's 'comic methods' can hardly be overemphasised. Kyd is the acknowledged author of several tragedies but of no single comedy. Francis Meres places him among 'our best for Tragedie', but does not mention him as a writer of comedy.[13] He is generally known to have introduced the revenge tragedy to the English stage. If, however, we try to appreciate Kyd's achievement by imagining the state of English drama as it presented itself to him in the 1580s, his use of comedy is of prime importance. It clearly distinguishes him from Seneca's, from continental, and from earlier English Senecan drama. It also supplants the earlier native tragedy and tragicomedy, in that the comic material is not confined to a realm distinct from and subordinate to the play's main action, but rather is part of it. Like Basilisco in *Soliman and Perseda*, the comic character Pedringano is firmly placed within the play's main plot. His doings are not dramatised in a subplot that contrasts with the main action, but occupy five consecutive scenes from III.ii to III.vi. To downplay the role of the sequence as 'comic relief', as Freeman does (p. 91), is to misunderstand the innovative nature of Kydian comedy. In the 'third act' (III.i–III.vii), Kyd's complication of the intrigue for its own sake in the way of Latin comedy introduces a device to Renaissance tragedy present in many later plays, such as *Hamlet* and *Othello*, but absent from the *Tamburlaine* plays or Shakespeare's earliest attempts at tragedy, *Titus Andronicus* and *2 Henry VI*. Kyd hardly considered himself the inventor of Elizabethan Revenge tragedy, as the theme of revenge was an integral part of his dramatic ancestry. He may well have thought of his inclusion of comic material into the main plot of *The Spanish Tragedy* as a radical generic experiment, however.

The 'Lorenzo and Pedringano' movement (III.ii to III.vi) has been curiously neglected by critics. Its structural importance is considerable: Moving up to the 'jest' (III.v.14) of Pedringano's execution on a scaffold, it closes the play's first half, mirroring and anticipating the conclusion with the play of Hieronimo's execution of his opponents on a scaffold/stage. The five consecutive scenes show the course of justice in an ordered universe: crime (Pedringano's murder of Serberine) is followed by punishment (Pedringano is sentenced by Hieronimo and hanged).

The 'third act' (III.i to III.vii) is central to the play in more than one sense: not only does it contain the best and most substantial example of 'Kydian comedy' in *The Spanish Tragedy*, but it is also literally central in the way Kyd places it within the play's architecture. Freeman, who sees III.i to III.xv as one act, belonging 'mainly to Hieronimo' (p. 89), misses an important point about the play's structure. The comic sequence of scenes clearly forms a distinct movement that contrasts with its contiguous 'acts': Act II (II.i to II.v) – dramatising Horatio's murder at the hands of Lorenzo and Balthazar – is essentially tragic; 'Act IV' (III.viii to III.xv) – Hieronimo's increasing madness and grief – is essentially elegiac. In the second act, the central interest lies in the result, Horatio's death, which triggers Hieronimo's quest for revenge, while scenes III.viii to III.xv are chiefly concerned with character, as Hieronimo is portrayed with an emotional intensity which earlier tragedies lacked. The dramatic emphasis in the 'third act' is neither on the result nor on character. Lorenzo's stratagem has no longer any importance for the course of the ensuing action once Hieronimo has received Pedringano's posthumous letter. The contents of Bel-imperia's earlier epistle is confirmed, and the way is paved for Hieronimo's revenge. Nor does the 'third act' attempt three-dimensional portraits of Lorenzo and Pedringano. They are little more than types, the aristocratic, cunningly scheming Machiavellian and the 'guller gulled'. The interest lies in the stratagem itself, in intrigue for its own sake.

Lorenzo sets up his plot when Hieronimo's attempt to contact Bel-imperia arouses his suspicion (III.ii.56–77). As Pedringano and Serberine, Balthazar's servant, were the princes' only confederates in the murder of Horatio, he determines to eliminate them. He bribes Pedringano (III.ii.78–86) to kill Serberine 'this night' (III.ii.82) in St Luigi's Park, while commanding his page to send Serberine to the same place (III.ii.94–9). Alone, the villain confesses his intention to have the King's watch patrol the park at the appointed time (III.ii.100–4). The following scene stages in fewer than fifty lines the arrival of the three independent parties at the park, Pedringano's murder of Serberine, and his arrest by the guard. Early next morning (III.iv.1), Lorenzo and Balthazar are told by the page of Pedringano's murder of Serberine (III.iv.20–5). Balthazar, outraged, departs to the King to have Pedringano speedily sentenced and executed (III.iv.26–37), whereupon a messenger brings a letter from Pedringano (III.iv.50–4). Lorenzo sends him back to Pedringano, assuring him of his help (III.iv.55–9), and commands his page to carry a box with his pardon to Pedringano (III.iv.61–76). In a scene barely twenty lines long, the page, tickled by his curiosity, opens the box only to discover that it is empty (III.v.1–19). When Pedringano enters in the following scene (III.vi.16), Lorenzo's page has arrived and given him the false assurance of his pardon. Hieronimo makes Pedringano confess his guilt and orders his execution. Convinced that he will be saved *in extremis* by the pardon in the page's empty box, Pedringano keeps jesting with the hangman until he is finally hanged (III.vi.104).

The sequence packs a great amount of intricate action into fewer than three hundred lines. The page, the messenger, the watch, Pedringano, Serberine, and even Balthazar rush on and off stage as Lorenzo stage-manages his 'plot' (III.iv.40). The action advances with great economy and the language is direct, concise, and without the rhetorical ornament of Hieronimo's laments. When the action reaches its crisis, Pedringano is standing on the scaffold with the halter around his neck, still indulging in gallows humour. The tone is not that of tragedy, but of farce:

> *Pedringano.*   What, do you hang by the hour? If you do, I may
> chance to break your old custom.
> *Hangman.*   Faith, you have reason, for I am like to break your
> young neck.
> *Pedringano.*   Dost thou mock me, hangman? Pray God I be not
> preserved to break your knave's pate for this!

Hangman. Alas sir, you are a foot too low to reach it, and I
hope you will never grow so high while I am in the office.
(III.vi.57–64)

The humour is of a robust and physical kind, much like the slapstick
knock-about between Petruccio and Grumio in *The Taming of the
Shrew*:

Petruccio. Here, sirrah Grumio, knock, I say.
Grumio. Knock, sir? Whom should I knock? Is there any man
has rebused your worship?
Petruccio. Villain, I say, knock me here soundly.
Grumio. Knock you here, sir? Why, sir, what am I, sir, that I
should knock you here, sir?
Petruccio. Villain, I say, knock me at this gate,
And rap me well or I'll knock your knave's pate. (I.ii.5–12)

Apart from the broad, farcical humour, the sequence of scenes in
the 'third act' is likely to evoke a twofold response from the audience. On the one hand, spectators will derive the intellectual
pleasure of comic intrigue. As the audience shares Lorenzo's knowledge and enjoys his cunning schemes, moral judgement is partly
suspended and yields to approval of the trickster's (and the playwright's) cleverness. Harbage is certainly right in locating Kyd's
ultimate ancestors for this device in New Comedy, the ancient Greek
comic drama of the later fourth and third centuries which became
the model for Roman comedy.[14] It is difficult to determine to what
extent Kyd was influenced by Plautus and Terence themselves, or
their Renaissance derivatives, Italian *commedia erudita*, *commedia
dell'arte*, or English classical comedies such as *Gammer Gurton's
Needle* or *Ralph Roister Doister*. The *commedia dell'arte*, a possible
ancestor Harbage failed to consider, has been advanced by Frank
Ardolino.[15] Although I doubt Kyd was acquainted with the
'Pulcinella *lazzo*' Ardolino advances as the specific dramatic source,
it seems reasonable to assume that Kyd knew the *commedia dell'arte*
and its conventions and that he was affected by them.[16]

Apart from deriving the intellectual pleasure that flows from the
complex intrigue, an audience is also likely to react emotionally with
'a new and oddly mixed response – of amusement and horror, revulsion and admiration'.[17] As Pedringano is about to 'jest himself to
death' (III.v.17), the terribly serious and the comic interact. T. S.
Eliot called *The Jew of Malta* a 'terribly serious' farce, an apt
description of portions of *The Spanish Tragedy* as well as of *Soliman
and Perseda*. Pedringano's foolery oddly jars and comes to a sudden
end as the hangman 'turns him off' (III.vi.104.1).[18]

For an audience with strong Christian beliefs, Pedringano's end would also have been 'terribly serious' in a way to which most modern spectators are less sensitive. Pedringano becomes the subject of the ultimate Christian tragedy as, on the point of death, he refuses the hangman's advice to 'hearken to your soul's health' (III.vi.75). *The Spanish Tragedy* has been singled out as one of the least Christian plays of its period. Edwards, for example, holds that 'Marlowe never wrote a less Christian play' (*ST*, p. lii), and Freeman (p. 84), basically agreeing with Edwards, points out that the Christian concept of mercy is only present *ex negativo* in the word 'merciless' (IV.iv.106). Nevertheless, the Pedringano–Lorenzo sequence is firmly set within Christian parameters.

The theology of *The Spanish Tragedy* as a whole is difficult to work out and its inconclusiveness as well as its mixture of references to pagan and Christian religion are part of Kyd's design. In the central act, however, Kyd appears to have buried a playlet that owes much to the tradition of the Morality plays. Pedringano, like Everyman or Mankind, is the sinner faced with death and thus in danger of forfeiting his soul. He considers, but then rejects, prayer (III.vi.84–8). Half-Cain (slaying his brother-servant Serberine), half-Judas (as he accepts money for the betrayal of his former confederate and is finally hanged), Pedringano is the archetypal confirmed sinner. As Hieronimo puts it, his 'soul, that should be shrin'd in heaven,/ Solely delights in interdicted things' (III.vi.91–2). In the fast-moving plot, the characters around him are little less than roles and personifications rather than three-dimensional characters. Lorenzo, the Devil, cunning engineer of murder and corrupter of souls, cynically comments that 'They that for coin their souls endangered,/ To save my life, for coin shall venture theirs' (III.ii.113–14). Having committed murder, Pedringano, on Judgement day, has to face Hieronimo, the just Judge, who insists that 'blood with blood shall, while I sit as judge,/ Be satisfied, and the law discharg'd' (III.vi.35–6). The hangman, commissioned to end Pedringano's life, is a fitting emblematic equivalent of Death at his poignant encounter with Everyman.[19]

In the Morality play *The Pride of Life*, the haughty protagonist is told to prepare for death.[20] He stubbornly refuses, sends a challenge to Death and dies in the fight. His soul is conveyed to hell, before being saved by the intercession of the Virgin Mary. Apart from the ending which is surprising and theologically problematic, the play dramatises the same story as 'Act III' of *The Spanish Tragedy*. Of course, a full-length dramatisation of roughly the same tale was composed only a few years later in Marlowe's *Doctor Faustus*. Kyd and Marlowe are not likely to have known *The Pride of Life*, one of the few extant Morality plays along with *The Castle of Perseverance*, *Mankind*, *Wisdom*, and *Everyman*. Yet, they did know and made use of a dramatic tradition which was more powerful and widespread than its scarce remnants suggest.

We are now in a position to understand better why Kyd has the playlet turn on a *pardon* that fails to materialise: the word is meant to carry as much theological as legal meaning. While Pedringano is vainly waiting for the King's pardon, or the legal document containing the remission of his crimes, he refuses to beg humbly for God's pardon. Putting all his hopes in a secular indulgence, he fails to petition for and obtain the remission of his sins. Pedringano thereby becomes the double victim, that of intrigue tragedy and that of the Morality play. On the one hand, he is a tool in Lorenzo's intrigue tragedy, on the other, he is the subject of the ultimate Christian tragedy as he suffers death unprepared.[21]

Known to Kyd's contemporaries as 'Jeronimo' but printed as 'The Spanish Tragedy', the play dramatises simultaneously a private and a public tragedy. Hieronimo is not only Horatio's father, Isabella's husband, and a private avenger, but he also holds the office of Knight Marshal of Spain and is supreme judge of the country in which he tries in vain to obtain justice. Lorenzo, apart from being Bel-imperia's brother and a Machiavellian villain, is also Castile's son, the King's nephew and is in the direct line of succession to the Spanish throne. After Hieronimo has brought about his 'private' revenge, he has wiped out, as the King puts it, 'the whole succeeding hope/ That Spain expected after my decease' (IV.iv.203–4). The play derives much of its meaning from the mutual encroachment of the private and the public, the personal and the political.

As critics have long realised, it is surely significant that Kyd's tragedy is *The* Spanish *Tragedy*. The play, it appears, has not only literary but also political origins. Anglo-hispanic relationships were tense during the time of composition of *The Spanish Tragedy*. Catholic Spain and Protestant England, whose Queen had been excommunicated by Pope Pius V in 1570, had become bitter rivals by the 1580s and a Spanish invasion was believed imminent. Ronald Broude was the first who argued at some length that *The Spanish Tragedy* 'was built around a theme having special significance for Englishmen during the decade of the Armada'.[22] Critics have widely differed in their interpretations of Kyd's Spain, however. One group argues that 'throughout the play, Kyd portrays the Spanish monarch as a stable, judicious, conscientious, and compassionate leader', credits him with 'Solomon-like wisdom', and finds that the play exhibits 'a valid social order in Spain, where the gracious king does scrupulous justice and commands the full loyalty of Hieronimo and his son'.[23] The other group of critics stresses 'the wickedness of the Spanish royal house', holds that 'the Spain of Kyd's play is corrupt', the King 'swayed by partiality', and that 'Kyd presents a Spain too arrogant to note that it is ripe for downfall – due to be replaced as a leading imperial power by the lowly English'.[24]

It is true that the play is not free from associations with the anglo-hispanic conflict. Hieronimo's multilingual play brings about a metaphorical 'fall of Babylon' (IV.i.195), which must have reminded the audience of the Protestants' association of the corrupt Old Testament Babylon with the Roman Catholic Church. The name of the city having been 'Babel' in the Geneva Bible, the reference extends to the confusion of tongues at Babel (Genesis 11:1–9). God's punishment for the people's ambition and pride is thus skilfully worked into Hieronimo's play by means of the incomprehensible sundry languages. Also, it is certainly interesting to notice that Hieronimo's play has precisely those characteristics the reformers objected to in the Roman Mass, the linguistic unintelligibility and the 'real presence'.[25]

In general, however, the play precisely lacks the anti-Spanish tone that might be expected from a work composed around the time of the Armada. The Spanish king is depicted as a generous character who is conciliatory throughout towards the Portuguese. There seems nothing ironic about his 'We pleasure more in kindness than in wars' (I.iv.118), or his 'Spain is honourable' (I.ii.137).[26] Kyd goes out of his way to stress that the King's treatment of Horatio is fair. He rewards Lorenzo and Horatio for Balthazar's capture according to their merits, granting the latter Balthazar's ransom (I.ii.180–4), stresses that Horatio 'deserved to be honour'd' (I.iv.131) and sees to it that the ambassador dispatched to Portugal returns with Horatio's ransom:

> Amongst the rest of what you have in charge,
> The prince's ransom must not be forgot:
> That's none of mine, but his that took him prisoner,
> And well his forwardness deserves reward:
> It was Horatio, our Knight Marshal's son.   (II.iii.32–6)

This clearly is not a corrupt King bent on mistreating Horatio and

Hieronimo. Similarly, the play is careful to clear Castile from blame when, for example, he intercedes for Hieronimo with Lorenzo:

> I tell thee son, myself have heard it said,
> When to my sorrow I have been asham'd
> To answer for thee, though thou art my son:
> Lorenzo, know'st thou not the common love
> And kindness that Hieronimo hath won
> By his deserts within the court of Spain?
> Or seest thou not the king my brother's care
> In his behalf, and to procure his health?   (III.xiv.58–65)

If the 'Spanishness' of *The Spanish Tragedy* had originally contributed so much to the play's popularity as some critics assert, it would seem surprising that none – to my knowledge – of the innumerable early allusions to Kyd's play takes up its historical relevance or points to its alleged anti-Spanish prejudice. Contemporary authors alluded to the Ghost of Andrea, in particular to his opening monologue, to certain catch-phrases, to Hieronimo's madness, to his grief, to the rhetoric in his soliloquies, but not to corrupt Spain and the wiping out of her royal line. Judging by contemporary allusions, Kyd's play did not greatly activate the audience's hispanophobic prejudice.

A way to bypass this evidence is to assert that the play's 'real meaning' would only have been available to the initiated few. This line of argument is taken by Frank R. Ardolino, who holds that 'Kyd has created an apocalyptic revenge play which presents in a mysterious subtext the overthrow of the Antichrist, Babylon/Spain, by England in 1588'.[27] The play, Ardolino argues, is a 'Protestant Apocalypse': '*The Spanish Tragedy* contains many of the elements found in Revelation, including the four-act structure'; 'Kyd symbolically recreates the struggle with Spain in 1588'; he sees *The Spanish Tragedy* as 'a work containing hidden meanings available only to the initiated and concealed from the uninitiated' and goes on to explain these meanings in his study.[28] Ardolino's far-fetched analyses, attempting to show, for instance, that Hieronimo's revenge scheme re-enacts 'the famous Pazzi plot in 1478 to kill Lorenzo de' Medici', will hardly find many followers.[29] When it comes to dating the play, Ardolino subordinates all scholarly evidence to the needs of his analysis, sweepingly dismisses all previously adduced evidence and unconvincingly argues for 1592 as the date of composition.[30] In fact, there is little to support Ardolino's argument. Kyd carefully avoids a dichotomy between 'evil Spain' and the sympathetic revenger Hieronimo. In both Spain and Portugal, there is one Machiavellian figure, Lorenzo and Villuppo, apart from whom no character is either black or white.

Critics who have tied *The Spanish Tragedy* to the social reality in Kyd's London rather than to anti-Spanish sentiment have been more helpful in recovering some of the play's original meaning. C. L. Barber has inquired into the 'tensions between traditional, hierarchical society and the aspirations of the class from which Kyd himself derives', while James R. Siemon, in his sophisticated Bakhtinian analysis, identified the play as a highly perceptive depiction of social heteroglossia.[31] Their analyses contribute to recovering a social dynamic to which modern readers and audiences are no longer particularly sensitive and demonstrate that the characters cannot be fully understood if their private selves are detached from their social roles. Bel-imperia is not only a strong-willed woman but also a social rebel, 'meanly accompanied' (III.x.57) by her social inferiors Don Andrea and Don Horatio, and therefore 'in disgrace' (III.x.71). Balthazar masquerades as the Petrarchan lover, but the importance of his match with Bel-imperia is dynastic. Hieronimo's aspiration and his inability to make himself heard at court, finally, is a fate with which a middle-class audience would easily have identified.

Notes

1 John W. Cunliffe, *The Influence of Seneca on Elizabethan Tragedy* (London and New York, 1893); H. B. Charlton, *The Senecan Tradition in Renaissance Tragedy* (Manchester, 1946).

2 See Howard Baker's 'Ghosts and Guides: Kyd's *Spanish Tragedy* and the Medieval Tragedy', *MP*, 33 (1935), 27–35, and his *Induction to Tragedy*, Willard Farnham, *The Medieval Heritage of Elizabethan Tragedy* (Berkeley, 1936), G. K. Hunter, 'Seneca and the Elizabethans: A Case-Study in 'Influence', *SS*, 20 (1967), 17–26: 'We are left with a few well-worn anthology passages and a few isolated tricks like stichomythia [...] as relics of the once extensive empire of Seneca's undisputed influence' (p. 21); G. K. Hunter, 'Seneca and English Tragedy', in C. D. N. Costa (ed.), *Greek and Latin Studies: Classical Literature and Its Influence* (London and Boston, 1974), pp. 166–204. Hunter's articles are reprinted in G. K. Hunter, *Dramatic Identities and Cultural Tradition* (Liverpool, 1978), pp. 159–73, 174–213.

3 Gordon Braden, *Renaissance Tragedy and the Senecan Tradition: Anger's Privilege* (New Haven and London, 1985), pp. 66–7.

4 McKerrow, III, p. 31.

5 *Ibid.*

6 Giraldi Cinthio (1504–73) is best remembered today for his *Hecatommithi* (1565), a collection of prose romances which furnished Shakespeare with the plot of *Othello*. He is also the author of nine

tragedies, the most famous of which, *Orbecche*, was written in 1541. See A. J. Krailsheimer (ed.), *The Continental Renaissance 1500–1600* (Harmondsworth, 1971), pp. 252–4.

7 Freeman, pp. 56–7.

8 *From Mankind to Marlowe* (Cambridge, Mass., 1962), p. 3.

9 *Sir Philip Sidney: A Critical Edition of the Major Works*, ed. Katherine Duncan-Jones, The Oxford Authors (Oxford, 1989), p. 243.

10 Howard Baker argues that the narrative tragedies, in particular Sackville's 'Induction' and 'Buckingham' in the *Mirror of Magistrates*, had a definite artistic impact upon *The Spanish Tragedy* (In 'Ghosts and Guides: Kyd's *Spanish Tragedy* and the Medieval Tragedy', and in *Induction to Tragedy*, pp. 98–120). When Baker comes to the conclusion that '*The Spanish Tragedy*, in form, stems from the metrical tragedies' ('Ghosts and Guides', 35), however, he is methodologically as naive as those earlier critics he rightly criticises for attributing all of Kyd's debts to Seneca. Even though Revenge recalls the allegorical personifications of the medieval Morality plays, he is not medieval in dramatic ancestry, and the figure of the Ghost has rather too complex ancestors to pinpoint them unequivocally in the medieval narrative tragedies (see F. W. Moorman, 'The Pre-Shakespearean Ghost', *MLR*, 1 (1905–06), 85–95). Baker further argues that Kyd had an English precedent for a narrative induction to a tragedy modelled upon Aeneas' descent into hell: Sackville's 'Induction' to *The Mirror for Magistrates*. Sackville's description of the journey, however, is substantially different: for the greatest part he elaborates the passage in which Aeneas and the Sibyl at the entrance to the underworld are confronted by shapes of human misery (VI, ll. 268–81), which Sackville turns into allegorical personifications in the tradition of the Morality plays.

11 *The Medieval Heritage of Elizabethan Tragedy*, p. 394. The ballad is quoted from Boas, p. 343.

12 'Intrigue in Elizabethan Tragedy', in Richard Hosley (ed.), *Essays on Shakespeare and Elizabethan Drama: In Honour of Hardin Craig*, p. 37. T. S. Eliot had anticipated Harbage's point a few decades earlier: 'In the type of plot there is nothing classical or pseudo-classical at all. "Plot" in the sense in which we find plot in *The Spanish Tragedy* does not exist for Seneca' ('Seneca in Elizabethan Translation', in *Selected Essays*, p. 80).

13 G. G. Smith (ed.), *Elizabethan Critical Essays*, 2 vols. (Oxford, 1904), I, p. 319.

14 'Intrigue in Elizabethan Tragedy', 38.

15 Frank R. Ardolino, *Thomas Kyd's Mystery Play*, pp. 38–9.

16 K. M. Lea has pointed out that 'Pulcinella does not appear among the masks of the Commedia dell'arte until the beginning of the seventeenth century' (*Italian Popular Comedy: A Study in the Commedia dell'Arte, 1560–1620, with Special Reference to the English Stage* (New York, 1962), p. 91).

17 'Intrigue in Elizabethan Tragedy', 37.

18 *Selected Essays*, p. 123.

19 See ll. 85–183. References are to *Everyman*, ed. A. C. Cawley (Manchester, 1974).

20 Only a 502-line fragment of the play is extant, but the long prologue

summarises the play's action. See *The Cambridge Companion to Medieval English Theatre*, ed. Richard Beadle (Cambridge, 1994), pp. 258–62.

21 C. L. Barber identified a different 'Christian shaping' in the play, 'used to express family feeling in extremis' (p. 154) which may serve to complement my argument. Horatio, like Christ, is hung 'on a tree' and Isabella, like the Virgin Mary, embraces the wounded body beneath it (IV.ii.23). Hieronimo's 'From forth these wounds came breath that gave me life' (IV.iv.96) reinforces the parallels (*Creating Elizabethan Tragedy: the Theater of Marlowe and Kyd*, ed. Richard P. Wheeler (Chicago, 1988), pp. 153–4).

22 Ronald Broude, 'Time, Truth, and Right in *The Spanish Tragedy*', *SP*, 68 (1971), 131.

23 James T. Henke, 'Politics and Politicians in *The Spanish Tragedy*', *SP*, 78 (1981), 363; McAlindon, *English Renaissance Tragedy*, p. 248; Barber, *Creating Elizabethan Tragedy*, p. 134.

24 J. R. Mulryne, 'Nationality and Language in Thomas Kyd's *The Spanish Tragedy*', in Marie-Thérèse Jones-Davies (ed.), *Langues et Nations au temps de la Renaissance* (Paris, 1991), p. 69; Broude, 'Time, Truth, and Right in *The Spanish Tragedy*', 143; Eugene D. Hill, 'Senecan and Vergilian Perspective in *The Spanish Tragedy*, *ELR*, 15 (1985), 156.

25 See Huston Diehl, 'Observing the Lord's Supper and the Lord Chamberlain's Men: The Visual Rhetoric of Ritual and Play in Early Modern England', *RD*, 22 (1991), 160.

26 There are similarly pro-Spanish passages in *Soliman and Perseda*, I.ii.57 and I.iii.35–46.

27 *Apocalypse & Armada in Kyd's 'Spanish Tragedy'*, p. xiv.

28 *Ibid.*, pp. xii–xv.

29 *Ibid.*, p. 96.

30 *Ibid.*, p. 166.

31 Barber, *Creating Elizabethan Tragedy*, p. 25; Siemon, 'Sporting Kyd', *ELR*, 24 (1994), 553–83.

CHAPTER 4

The Spanish Tragedy:
framing revenge

The Spanish Tragedy is one of the great plays of the English stage. A leading critic of Renaissance drama has rightly called its theatrical design 'nothing less than great, strategically great'.[1] In its own time, the play had enormous success. Henslowe recorded no fewer than twenty-nine performances between 1592 and 1597, more than for any other play except *The Jew of Malta* and the lost *The Wise Man of West Chester*. Between 1592 and 1633, *The Spanish Tragedy* passed through at least eleven editions, more than any play by Shakespeare. It set the trend for the genre of revenge tragedy, thereby standing at the head of a considerable number of important plays that are all more or less indebted to it. The tremendous sway Kyd's play held over the popular imagination can perhaps be inferred from an anecdote in both Braithwaite's *English Gentlewoman* (1631) and Prynne's *Histrio-mastix* (1633): a lady who is close to death stubbornly refuses to turn her thoughts towards the next world and, thinking that there is no need to trouble herself with such thoughts yet, cries out: '*Hieronimo, Hieronimo*; O let me see *Hieronimo* acted'.[2] The sophistication of its dramatic artistry as well as the tremendous emotional impact the play had on its early modern audiences, and has shown still to exert in our own time, do not suffer from comparison with some of Shakespeare's plays.

Only recently has the seminal importance of Kyd's play – not solely in the history of English drama but as an achievement in its own right – been fully recognised. For a long time, critics of Kyd's masterpiece either passed over the play in silence or, if not, felt the need to apologise with the epithet 'pre-Shakespearean' for what they felt were its coarse features. Victorian sensibility was not easily compatible with Kydian rhetoric and dramaturgy. Nor did the increasing concern with theatrical naturalism favour a revival of interest. Generations of readers and critics too readily adhered to the view promoted by Jonson's many gibes at Kyd's play.[3] When, in the twentieth century, *The Spanish Tragedy* was rediscovered as an object worthy of critical investigation, it was largely for its historical importance, an emphasis which was sometimes more damaging than revalorising. Probably more than most other plays, *The Spanish Tragedy* suffered from being deprived of its true medium: the stage. Its revival on the professional stage has done more than much well-informed criticism to restore the play to its proper place.

To be sure, *The Spanish Tragedy* is a play of great historical importance. The first modern revenge tragedy, the first Machiavellian villain, the first play which successfully mixes tragic and comic elements, the first play-within-a-play: the list of 'firsts' attributed to Kyd's play is impressive. Much recent criticism could gain from a heightened awareness of Kyd's place in literary history. As students and critics, we naturally move from Shakespeare to Kyd whereas literary history moves from Kyd to Shakespeare. Students are sometimes disappointed by the limitations of Kyd's achievement in *The Spanish Tragedy* in comparison with Shakespeare's *Hamlet*. That a play has an exciting and well-wrought plot, complex characters, and poetic language with variety, immediacy and beauty is usually taken for granted by students approaching Kyd after Shakespeare. Yet, when Kyd approached the task of writing plays after *his* predecessors, none of this had been established on the English stage.

The Spanish Tragedy gains from being considered in the context of Kyd's career. As playwright for the Queen's Men from about 1583 and possibly for another company before, Kyd saw his plays performed only a few years after the opening of the Theatre, the first permanent building erected in London for the purpose of performing plays. His theatrical activities were embedded in a social institution which was not as established as it would become during Shakespeare's career. *The Spanish Tragedy* is one of the first extant plays to be written for adult players and performed on the public stage.[4] It is the product of a nascent enterprise whose place in society was still very much in need of definition. By investigating the power of theatrical illusion, *The Spanish Tragedy* engages in the searching discussion of the project out of which it grows.

Kyd's dramaturgical design and its importance for the play's meaning have not been fully acknowledged. Kyd sets the action within not only one but two frames. The first and obvious frame is constituted by the allegorical figure Revenge and the Ghost of Andrea. They start and end the play, comment at the end of each act and are constantly present in the theatre, an audience visible to the audience. Their view of the unfolding of events is one of determinism; the characters in the play within are no autonomous beings, but puppets who can only play out a pre-scribed plot whose conclusion is known to Revenge before the action starts:

> Then know, Andrea, that thou art arriv'd
> Where thou shalt see the author of thy death,
> Don Balthazar the prince of Portingale,
> Depriv'd of life by Bel-imperia: (I.i.86–9)

The histrionic vocabulary is used by Revenge to express the characters' inability to make their own decisions: 'Here sit we down to see the mystery,/ And serve for Chorus in this tragedy' (I.i.90–1). The off-stage spectators of *The Spanish Tragedy* undergo an experience closely related to that of the Ghost of Andrea and Revenge, the spectators of the Spanish tragedy. They witness tragic actions of which the outcome is already determined. Yet, although Andrea and Revenge perceive the goings-on in theatrical terms (likening the events to those of a 'tragedy' (I.i.91)), such events are, as Andrea points out, painfully real for them: 'Brought'st thou me hither to increase my pain?' (II.vi.1). What is theatre for the real-life audience is thought of as theatrical by the inset audience.[5] The similarity of experience for the intra- and extrafictional spectators may have been stressed by the placement of Andrea and Revenge in a box in the gallery adjacent to those of the paying audience.[6]

At the same time, the play's illustration of the *theatrum mundi topos* links the spectators' experience to that of the characters in the play within. As the fictional world of Spain and Portugal is shown to be 'a stage' and the characters 'merely players' in Revenge's play, the spectators are made aware that 'all the world's a stage and all the men and women merely players' in the divine theatre in which they cannot but enact the roles that have been pre-scribed by God. Rather than suggesting that the play is life-like, Revenge, overlooking and stage-managing the action, suggests that life is play-like.

Theatrical rhetoric, central to the first frame, stands in sharp contrast to theatrical activity which constitutes the second frame. In the first act – once the different strands of action have been introduced – and in the last act occur the two festive occasions in the play: the theatrical spectacles presented by Hieronimo. Standing at the beginning and the end of the development of the intrigue, they obviously mirror and comment on each other, a structural device

which a performance makes even more apparent.[7] The dumb show
played at the King's banquet in the first act (I.iv.138–74) extols the
military victory and recent peace, and displays Spanish magnanimity before the eyes of the Portuguese ambassador. The wedding
celebration, of which Hieronimo's play in the last act is a part, is
meant to consolidate the peace and ensure the future of the royal
line. Whereas the dumb show celebrates the union of two nations,
the play-within-the-play celebrates the union of two individuals.
Recalling and continuing the first celebration, the second one,
through Hieronimo's play, is turned into a public execution. While
Hieronimo's dumb show is conceived to display the King's power,
the play in the last act destroys it and wipes out an entire royal line.

The connection between the two events serves as a crucial element
in the play's construction that is highlighted by the text:

> Balthazar.   It pleas'd you
>   At the entertainment of the ambassador
>   To grace the king so much as with a show:
>   Now were your study so well furnished,
>   As for the passing of the first night's sport
>   To entertain my father with the like,
>   Or any such-like pleasing motion,
>   Assure yourself it would content them well.   (IV.i.60–7)

The two histrionic events mirror each other even more closely if we
realise that the effect the 'tragedy of Soliman and Perseda' must have
had upon its audience was very much like that of a dumb show. The
incomprehensible 'sundry languages' would have made the audience
concentrate on the visual aspects.

Hieronimo's dumb show at the end of the first act is only seemingly the innocent and benign counterpart of the catastrophic play at
the end.[8] In both performances, the King's power is destabilised not
only by what is represented, but also by his lack of control over its
exegesis. After the dumb show, the King admits that 'I sound not
well the mystery' (I.iv.139), and at the end of Hieronimo's play, he
asks: 'But now what follows for Hieronimo?' (IV.iv.72). In both the
first and the last act, a long speech follows in which Hieronimo not
only explains, but also produces the meaning of his show. That the
locus of meaning can easily be turned into the *locus* of power
becomes evident at the end of the play. In the dumb show, the
dangerous potential of theatrical representation and the purposeful
use to which it can be put is hinted at, thereby announcing the
instrumentalisation of Hieronimo's play in the last act. Called
'masque' (I.iv.138) by the King, it fails to be the display of regal

power and magnificence normally associated with this term.[9] This makes it difficult to understand why more than one critic interpreted Hieronimo's show as innocent and harmonious.[10] The stage direction reads:

> Enter HIERONIMO *with a Drum, three Knights, each his*
> *scutcheon: then he fetches three Kings, they*
> *take their crowns and them captive.* (I.iv.137.1–3)

The dumb show openly depicts the Elizabethan nightmare of usurpation. As Hieronimo consecutively explains the meaning of the three usurpations with accounts of English popular history, the King has at first no reason to be dissatisfied. The military success of Robert, Earl of Gloucester and Edmund, Earl of Kent over Portingale mirrors Spain's current triumph over the same enemy and thus indirectly celebrates the Spanish victory. Hieronimo's seven lines of explanation are twice followed by the King expressing his approval in four lines. The innocuous pattern is broken as Hieronimo moves on to the achievement of John of Gaunt:

> He with a puissant army came to Spain,
> And took our King of Castile prisoner.
> *Ambassador.*   This is an argument for our viceroy,
> That Spain may not insult for her success,
> Since English warriors likewise conquer'd Spain,   170
> And made them bow their knees to Albion.
> *King.*   Hieronimo, I drink to thee for this device,
> Which hath pleas'd both the Ambassador and me:
> Pledge me Hieronimo, if thou love the king.
> 　　　　　　　　　　　*Takes the cup of* HORATIO.
> My lord, I fear we sit but over-long,   （I.iv.166–75）

A production that is inattentive to the pattern which is built up only to be broken might well lose the dramatic tension inherent in the moment. Hieronimo's representation of Spanish defeat at the very moment when he is supposed to celebrate its victory and glory clearly leaves the King speechless. Even though there is no stage direction, the ambassador's lines must not be spoken before a pause shows the King eloquently silent. Trying to move on to less delicate matters, the King discloses his disquiet as he tries to conceal it: 'I fear we sit but over-long'. Hieronimo's masque clearly represents one usurpation too many.

The play is thus set within a tension between supernatural and human theatre. Whereas Revenge holds that the 'tragedy' (I.i.91; IV.v.48) in which the characters are acting has been entirely prescribed by an extra-human force, Hieronimo happened 'to write a

tragedy' (IV.i.78) himself, which he puts to effective use.[11] When
Revenge has fallen asleep and Andrea is impatient to see Revenge's
plot unfold, the allegorical figure assures him that his 'quietness is
feign'd' (III.xv.24) and that the tragedy will come about as predicted
by him. Hieronimo, however, '[d]issembling quiet in unquietness'
(III.xiii.30), also has an important role in the shaping of the events.
Being an excellent actor, he precisely refuses 'to be subject to
destiny' (III.xv.28). Instead, he has Lorenzo and Balthazar and, in an
extended sense, the King and Castile, 'play a part' (IV.i.83) in *his*
tragedy.[12]

In the past, this tension between divine and human theatre has
often been ignored in favour of an entirely determinist account of the
unfolding of events. In the mid-1960s, G. K. Hunter interpreted the
play not as freely willed actions, but as divinely predestined motions
within a 'dream-allegory' frame, and Philip Edwards held that 'the
technique of the play-within-the-play is only an accentuation of a
dramatic method [...] by which Kyd shows people living in mere illusion'.[13] Roughly a decade later, John Scott Colley saw the play as a
dramatisation of the theatre of God's judgement.[14] As late as 1986,
McAlindon argued that 'Kyd sees tragic action as the working-out of
an inexorable chain of events in which men seem the puppets of a
predetermined fate'.[15] This stresses the determinism suggested by the
frame, but does not account for the characters' intrigue and plotting
and the part they play in shaping their destinies. Clearly, Hieronimo
is not Oedipus. Kyd could hardly have made the point more emphatically than by casting Hieronimo as 'Author and actor in this tragedy'
(IV.iv.147) and by having other characters perform in his play, in
short, by stage-managing the Spanish tragedy himself. It is true that
revenge brings about the ending Revenge had predicted before the
actions started and in this sense, the action seems predetermined and
the characters are subject to destiny and acted upon by supernatural
forces. At the same time, however, Hieronimo and Bel-imperia take
matters into their own hands, thereby determining the course of the
events. G. K. Hunter held that in the play-within-the-play, '[t]he illusion of free will is suspended [...] character has become role, speech
has changed to ritual; the end is now totally predetermined'.[16] This
does not answer the question, however, of who has done the casting,
who has predetermined the end, Revenge, as the frame implies, or
Hieronimo and Bel-imperia, as the play within suggests. As Joel B.
Altman put it, 'Kyd did create a frame that points in one direction and
an action that points in another.'[17] It is in this tension between frame
and action that the play's fascination resides.

Comparing different conceptions of tragedy current in Elizabethan drama, J. M. R. Margeson points out that

> [t]he tragic stories of the *novelle* differ quite strikingly from both Senecan and *Mirror* tragedy in placing everything that happens on a human level of explanation. There is no need for a sense of destiny, a fatal curse, or the intervention of providence, when all the action depends upon intrigue and the cunning mind of a villain.[18]

The Spanish Tragedy dialectically combines a Senecan sense of destiny and a Protean sense of self-fashioning and human causality. The allegorical figure Revenge, announcing the fatal outcome from the outset, presiding over the predetermined actions in a way reminiscent of Seneca, is therefore one voice but not the only one. Revenge rather than the play *per se* takes the view that the characters are mere puppets who are to act out a pre-scribed plot. His control of the action as laid out in the frame and the course of the action in the play within go only seemingly hand in hand.

In interweaving and contrasting views of the theatre and turning them into a central constituent of his play, Kyd drew on dramatic, rhetorical and philosophical traditions of considerable standing. Long before Kyd, people used metaphors related to acting and playing to point out that they thought of their existence in theatrical terms. Present in the writings of Plato, Horace, and St Augustine, the *topos* goes back to both antique and early Christian authors. According to Curtius, it finds its chief expression, which lastingly influenced writers of the later Middle Ages and the Renaissance, in John of Salisbury's *Policraticus*, published 1159 and printed three times between 1476 and 1595.[19] Even the motto of the newly-erected Globe, '*Totus mundus agit histrionem*', seems directly indebted to this work.[20] A writer like Sir Walter Raleigh, who sees men as actor-puppets who cannot but act out the pre-scribed play they have been set in, follows in the rhetorical tradition of *Polycraticus*: 'God, who is the Author of all our tragedies, hath written out for vs, and appointed vs all the parts we are to play'.[21] Another instance is the famous poem attributed to Ralegh and set to music by Orlando Gibbons, first published in the latter's collection of madrigals in 1612:

> What is our life? A play of passion;
> Our mirth, the music of division,
> Our mother's wombs the tiring houses be,
> Where we are drest for this short Comedy.
> Heaven the judicious sharp spectator is,
> That sits and marks still who doth act amiss.
> Our graves that hide us from the searching sun,

Are like drawn curtains when the play is done.
Thus march we playing to our latest rest;
Only we die in earnest. That's no jest.[22]

The principal idea developed in these comparisons of world and
stage up to Jaques's 'All the world's a stage' speech in *As You Like
It* and beyond, is the illusion of human power. Theatrical metaphors
served to express the futility and transience of human existence in
this world. They were variations on the ancient *Vanitas topos*.
Distrust of worldly values went hand in hand with the prejudiced
view of the actor's enterprise.[23]

Most play metaphors in Tudor drama do no more than draw
upon and more or less mechanically reiterate a traditional *topos*.
The Spanish Tragedy, however, takes it up in its orthodox form only
to turn it into something more complex. Especially when *The
Spanish Tragedy* moves to its climax, the essentially static,
metaphorically expressed 'idea' of the play gives way to an interest
in the *effect* of play. Whereas the frame and several passages up to
the third act metaphorically assert that man cannot help being acted
upon, Hieronimo shows that the idea of the *theatrum mundi* can
take on a radically different meaning. The traditional *topos* asserts
that we are all subject to God's dramaturgy, but the Spanish tragedy,
that is, the wiping out of an entire royal line, is brought about by
human dramaturgy.[24]

When, at the end of the prologue, Revenge asserts that he and
Andrea 'will serve for Chorus in this tragedy' (I.i.91), the last word
has a metaphorical meaning (*OED*, 3), the histrionic resonance
serving to point out that the characters in the play proper are
heading for a predetermined, fatal future. This is in keeping with the
frame of ideas in which the ancestors of Kyd's Revenge – Tantalus
from Seneca's *Thyestes* and the allegorical figures of the Morality
plays – situate the play. When Hieronimo sets up his theatrical
project, however, the same word 'tragedy' takes on a different
meaning. Rather than being a metaphorical assertion, the term is
turned into its literal embodiment (*OED*, 1): performance.
Hieronimo's play becomes precisely the means to avoid being acted
upon in Revenge's tragedy. Whereas the term previously implied
determinism, it comes to stand for Hieronimo's refusal 'to be subject
to destiny' (III.xv.28). Once Hieronimo asserts that he is 'Author
and actor in this tragedy' (IV.iv.147), the histrionic vocabulary
points out that he acts from a subject position on the stage of life.
He has literally written the script of the play in which he acts, and
takes over the divine, authorial role from Revenge.

The tension between the determinist frame, showing the characters entirely at the mercy of supernatural powers, and the intrigue plot in the play within, where the characters shape their own destiny by histrionic means, articulates the position of *The Spanish Tragedy* at the cross-roads of two contemporary sets of influence. Harriett Hawkins tentatively suggested that *The Spanish Tragedy* may 'reflect contemporary religious theories which combined an emphasis on divine foreknowledge with an equal emphasis on the absolute free will and responsibility of men'.[25] The proposition seems to me pertinent and needs to be developed into more specific terms. Indebted to St Augustine's teaching, Calvinist theological determinism sees man's destiny, be it heaven or hell, as predetermined by God. On the other hand, the 'overreaching' Renaissance Man, the idea that Man was unique among God's creatures in shaping and determining his own being, was taught by Neo-Platonic thinkers such as Pico della Mirandola and Ficino. To Calvinism they opposed Pelagianism – the belief that man's powers are self-sufficient – continuing the opposition fought over in the fourth and fifth centuries between St Augustine and Pelagius. In Pico della Mirandola's *De dignitate hominis* (1486), God says to Adam: 'being thine owne fashioner and artificer of thyselfe, thou maist make thyselfe after what likenes thou dost most affecte'.[26] Where Calvinism stresses divine predestination, the Neo-Platonists stress human free will.[27]

Whether Man is seen as God's puppet or as the author of his own role and script, histrionic metaphors work to describe either view, a fact Kyd seized upon and constructed his play around. His exploration of the tensions within which he situates the play, divine foreknowledge and determinism on the one hand (frame), and Man's free will and responsibility for his moral actions on the other (play within), yields no easy answers. As Hieronimo takes his destiny into his own hands, displaying a histrionic understanding of the self, we sympathise with him. As he becomes author and actor in his tragedy, he takes on a role that stresses his resemblance to the Creator rather than the distance from creature to Creator emphasised by both the frame and Calvinism. At the same time, Kyd makes explicit the danger of substituting oneself for God when, in the crucial 'Vindicta mihi' soliloquy, Hieronimo moves within twenty lines from 'heaven will be reveng'd' (III.xiii.2) to 'I will revenge' (III.xiii.20).

The theatrical metaphors in *The Spanish Tragedy* do more, however, than reveal an interpenetration of life and drama, something innumerable Renaissance writers had done in non-dramatic

writing. At a time when the theatre as a social calling and an archi-
tectural reality was taking root in Elizabethan London, the plays
growing out of this enterprise were the obvious *locus* where a reevaluation of the meaning of theatrical metaphors could take place.
As dramatic practice became increasingly sophisticated, the adher-
ents of the theatre explored the function and purpose of drama and
had a growing belief in the shaping power which theatrical illusion
could exert on reality. As Harriett Hawkins put it, 'while the
members of Kyd's audience view everything that happens on the
stage as part of the fabulously counterfeit *Spanish Tragedy*, the
action of his play forces them to ask how they might feel if the events
seen on the stage suddenly turned out to be real'.[28] It is easy to see
that this is only a small step away from a belief that acting can be a
means to shape one's life rather than have it shaped by a divine
agon.[29] It is hardly surprising, therefore, that Shakespeare composed
the following lines shortly after the first staging of *The Spanish
Tragedy*:

> Why, I can smile, and murder whiles I smile,
> And cry 'Content!' to that which grieves my heart,
> And wet my cheeks with artificial tears,
> And frame my face to all occasions.   185
> I'll drown more sailors than the mermaid shall;
> I'll slay more gazers than the basilisk;
> I'll play the orator as well as Nestor,
> Deceive more slily than Ulysses could,
> And, like a Sinon, take another Troy.   190
> I can add colours to the chameleon,
> Change shapes with Proteus for advantages,
> And set the murderous Machiavel to school.   (*3 Henry VI*, III.ii.182–93)

A few years earlier, Lorenzo and Hieronimo had given Gloucester's
statement dramatic form with more emphasis and boldness than any
play before and paved the way for other explorations of the shaping
power of acting, such as Hamlet's attempt to catch the conscience of
the king in a play, or Rosalind's playing herself in the Forest of
Arden.

Past are the days when critics argued that Andrea and Revenge are
'harmlessly melodramatic', a judgement based on the view that *The
Spanish Tragedy* can 'interest us but not disturb us'.[30] Readers and
theatre-goers today agree that the dramatic frame of Kyd's play can
be highly disturbing. All too often it is still not properly understood,
however. The Ghost of Andrea is not the instigator of the play's
revenge he is often made out to be. Nothing in the text suggests that

he returns to the scene of the living to clamour for revenge. Whether his death in battle was achieved by unfair means or not, he does not seem to think so himself:[31]

> For in the late conflict with Portingale
> My valour drew me into danger's mouth,
> Till life to death made passage through my wounds.   (I.i.15–17)

In this he is unlike the other Senecan ghosts in contemporary plays such as *The Misfortunes of Arthur*, *Locrine*, *The Battle of Alcazar*, Shakespeare's *Hamlet*, and Kyd's own *Hamlet*. In *The Spanish Tragedy*, the Ghost of Andrea – obeying Proserpine's decree – returns to the scene of the mortals as a mere spectator.

Critics have found it equally difficult to determine the nature of Andrea's companion. Does Revenge stand for a supernatural 'real' outside the world accessible to the living characters? Is Revenge a 'real' character, sent from the underworld, determining the outcome of the action before it properly begins, or is he the embodiment of a strong, indeed a governing, passion within the different characters that drives them to act? Critics differ widely in the answers they give to these questions. Donna Hamilton has argued that 'Revenge does not direct or control anything, but represents the element of disorder and destruction that operates in the affairs of mortal men.'[32] Accordingly, 'when Revenge explains, "though I sleep,/ Yet is my mood soliciting their souls," he is speaking again of himself as a quality in men, not himself as a creature in control of men' (p. 206). Hamilton thus does not see Revenge as a supernatural agent at all, but only as the personification of a human passion, a 'mood soliciting their souls' (III.xv.20). Consequently, the characters in the frame, Proserpine, Pluto and Revenge, bear no responsibility for Hieronimo's actions. Their actions are 'not prescriptive, but descriptive' (p. 205) of that carried out by means of free choice. According to this reading, the play could very well stand without the frame.

At the other end of the spectrum, Philip Edwards holds that 'for a mere whim of Proserpine, kindly meant, Hieronimo and his family are wiped out along with "the whole succeeding hope" of the royal households of Spain and Portugal'.[33] Kyd, Edwards argues, 'has given total control over the living to the wife of the king of the dead'. Consequently, the play dramatises a divine malevolence as radical as that found in some of Seneca's plays, but while there is 'a dreadful logic' to Seneca's malevolent gods, the one in Kyd is entirely wanting and is replaced by utter 'meaninglessness' (p. 119).

We are thus faced with a dilemma. If the infernal deities entirely predetermine the living by exerting 'total control' over them, as

Edwards has it, any identification with these predetermined puppets would seem out of place. Yet, the title page of all early editions announces 'the pittifull death of olde *Hieronimo*', implying a reaction of sympathy and identification. This is corroborated by early references hinting at the emotional impact Hieronimo had upon the audience. Also, any evaluation of the morality of the characters' actions, Lorenzo's villainies, the King's benevolence or his lack of it, Hieronimo's revenge – despicable, objectionable, or justifiable depending on the critic – would be irrelevant if the play insisted on the characters' determinism. An audience, Elizabethan or modern, is not likely to be disturbed by the pointlessness of Proserpine's decree from which everything else ensues. Edwards's point is logically pertinent but ultimately of little importance to the audience.

Hamilton's argument is at first attractive: it locates the origin of the actions where we as spectators – used to suspending our disbelief for the time of a play and sympathising with the characters as if they were human beings – would place it, namely in the intentions and will of the characters. Also, certain striking correspondences between Revenge and Hieronimo, the agent of revenge, lend credibility to her interpretation. As Hieronimo takes time to wake up to his duty and delays revenge, so Revenge is 'slumb'ring' (III.xv.25) for a while. As Hieronimo is '[d]issembling quiet in unquietness' (III.xiii.30), so Revenge's 'quietness is feign'd' (III.xv.24). Yet, is the argument consistent with the way Kyd constructs the frame? If Revenge is only the personification of a human passion, then what do we make of Andrea and his references to the time when he still belonged to the world of the play within? Unlike the frame of *Soliman and Perseda* featuring Love, Fortune, and Death, that of *The Spanish Tragedy* is not so easily reduced to personifications.

Ultimately, neither Edwards's nor Hamilton's reading is satisfactory throughout. As the issues of divine determinism and free will are difficult to reconcile – as theological arguments over the centuries have demonstrated – so a frame suggesting complete determinism seems to clash with an inset action in which we judge the characters who are busy shaping their own destinies and feel sorry for the 'pittifull death of olde *Hieronimo*'. There appears to be no way of deciding. If we side with Hamilton, the frame is pointless; but if we side with Edwards, all other characters are meaningless, and with them the bulk of the play's criticism which takes for granted the characters' moral responsibility for their actions. Edwards and Hamilton, pre-determinism and self-determinism, frame and play within are both contradictory and complementary, articulating in conjunction an irreconcilable tension upon which *The Spanish Tragedy* hinges.

Kyd's boldness in setting up tensions with no wish to resolve them easily is also noteworthy in what Geoffrey Aggeler has identified as 'the eschatological crux' in *The Spanish Tragedy*, namely 'the discrepancy between the orthodox Christian beliefs expressed by the living characters with regard to the process of divine justice and what is revealed in the judgment scenes which frame the main plot'.[34] In fact, pagan and Christian deities are juxtaposed in the most puzzling manner. The characters, in particular Hieronimo, refer to pagan as well as Christian deities and beliefs. Despite noticing this simultaneous presence, critics have struggled to recognise its logic: 'The references to a Christian mythology seem so fitfully and arbitrarily interspersed with the pagan that I do not think one can separate them.'[35] This, however, misses the point, as the same critic, more than two decades later, realised himself when he argued pertinently that it is part of Hieronimo's trajectory to turn from one mythology, one set of references, and one understanding of justice to another.[36]

From the moment he discovers his dead son, Hieronimo repeatedly appeals to one set of powers, identifiable as heavenly, Christian, or both:

> O heavens, why made you night to cover sin?   (II.v.24)

> O sacred heavens! if this unhallow'd deed,
> If this inhuman and barbarous attempt,
> If this incomparable murder thus
> Of mine, but now no more my son,
> Shall unreveal'd and unrevenged pass,
> How should we term your dealings to be just,
> If you unjustly deal with those that in your justice trust?   (III.ii.5–11)

> But shall I never live to see the day
> That I may come, by justice of the heavens,
> To know the cause that may my cares allay?   (III.vi.5–7)

> Yet still tormented is my tortur'd soul
> With broken sighs and restless passions,
> That winged mount, and, hovering in the air,
> Beat at the windows of the brightest heavens,
> Soliciting for justice and revenge:
> But they are plac'd in those empyreal heights
> Where, countermur'd with walls of diamond,
> I find the place impregnable, and they
> Resist my woes, and give my words no way.   (III.vii.10–18)

O sacred heavens, may it come to pass
That such a monstrous and detested deed,
So closely smother'd, and so long conceal'd,
Shall thus by this be venged or reveal'd?   (III.vii.45–8)

It is, no doubt, part of Kyd's design that these references continue with regularity until the end of the play's first half, probably the end of the original third act. Up to this point, Hieronimo, even though deeply distraught, is essentially sane. Trying in vain to obtain justice himself, he still administers justice to others. Even though he may have doubts that justice will be done, he has not given up hope. Having been handed Pedringano's letter by the hangman, Hieronimo has just obtained the necessary evidence that Lorenzo and Balthazar were responsible for Horatio's death. The confirmation brought about by 'this' (III.vii.48), paving the way to revenge, may be the working of providence. Perhaps, Hieronimo appears to say, these are the crooked lines with which the heavens write straight. As long as Hieronimo has not given up hope in the workings of divine justice, he also believes in the possibility of obtaining public justice from the King. Granted, from the moment he discovers Horatio's body, he craves revenge: 'For in revenge my heart would find relief' (II.v.41). What Jeronimo means at this stage, however, has nothing to do with extralegal retaliation. James T. Henke has gone astray when he argues that 'Hieronimo is not interested in royal justice, but in murderous vengeance'.[37] As Ronald Broude has shown, in Renaissance England 'revenge had a more extended meaning than the modern one, a meaning more nearly equivalent to today's retribution'.[38] Consequently, the words 'revenge' and 'vengeance' could denote not only the private retribution of an individual, but also the public punishment exacted by the king or the state. Up to the end of the play's first part, Hieronimo seeks the latter, as the final lines of the part make clear: 'But wherefore waste I mine unfruitful words,/ When nought but blood will satisfy my woes?' (III.vii.67–8). So far, this may sound as if Hieronimo was already considering private revenge. As the next two lines make clear, however, he is not: 'I will go plain me to my lord the king,/ And cry aloud for justice through the court' (III.vii.69–70). Hieronimo's sanity and his hope for both heavenly and human justice – all characterising Hieronimo up to the end of the play's first half – go hand in hand.

When we next see Hieronimo, he is in a notably different state. If a hiatus can be determined in Kyd's depiction of Hieronimo's otherwise gradual transformation, it is between III.vii, where he makes plans and shows new courage, and his next appearance in III.xi where he erupts in wild speech:

> *Enter two Portingales, and* HIERONIMO *meets them.*
>
> 1.   By your leave, sir.
> *Hieronimo.*   Good leave have you, nay, I pray you go,
>   For I'll leave you, if you can leave me, so.   (III.xi.1–3)

It is not surprising that one of the Portingales concludes that 'this man is passing lunatic' (III.xi.32). Hieronimo's change is underscored by a change in imagery, with references to pagan hell replacing those of Christian heaven. In the same scene, Hieronimo describes the descent to the deepest hell where Lorenzo is to be found 'in a brazen cauldron fix'd by Jove' (III.xi.26). Later, he pictures his own descent to a pagan underworld (III.xii.6–16), and in the Senex scene, Hieronimo hopes that 'Proserpine may grant/ Revenge on them that murdered my son' (III.xiii.120–1). Shortly after, he imagines Bazulto to be a fury

> Sent from the empty kingdom of black night
> To summon me to make appearance
> Before grim Minos and just Rhadamanth,
> To plague Hieronimo that is remiss
> And seeks not vengeance for Horatio's death.   (III.xiii.154–8)

The shift in Hieronimo's trajectory from 'public' to 'wild' justice is most clearly dramatised in the 'Vindicta mihi' soliloquy (III.xiii.1–44) which has long been identified as a turning point in the play.[39] The initial quotation from Romans 12:19 is followed by an assertion of his faith in Christian providence:

> Ay, heaven will be reveng'd of every ill,
> Nor will they suffer murder unrepaid:
> Then stay, Hieronimo, attend their will,
> For mortal men may not appoint their time.   (III.xiii.2–5)

This succinctly articulates the belief he held until the end of the play's first half (III.vii). In the following lines, however, he turns to the copy of Seneca he carries in his hands: '*Per scelus semper tutum est sceleribus iter./* Strike, and strike home, where wrong is offer'd thee' (III.xiii.6–7). It is an intriguing detail that the two voices competing within Hieronimo are that of St Paul, on whose conversion Kyd planned to write a poem (according to his letter to Sir John Puckering), and that of Seneca, whose importance for Kyd's drama has been illustrated. The two contemporaries were long thought to have known each other, an erroneous belief strengthened during the Middle Ages by the discovery of a correspondence between them that was later judged spurious. Within twenty lines of deliberation, Hieronimo moves from the Pauline 'heaven will be reveng'd' (III.xiii.2) to the Senecan 'I will revenge' (III.xiii.20), from faith in Christian providence to a complete loss of it.[40] The natural conclusion follows: 'justice is exiled from the earth' (III.xiii.140). From this moment, Hieronimo's inner disposition has shifted to a point where bloody, private revenge only awaits execution.

Two basic stages can thus be distinguished in Hieronimo's trajectory, the first, leading up to III.vii, in which he is shown to be essentially sane and intent on public justice, and the second, starting with III.xi, with the protagonist seeking extralegal revenge and coming across as 'passing lunatic' (III.xi.32), madly digging the earth with his dagger, tearing the petitioners' papers, and mistaking Bazulto for Horatio. It is surely significant that during the first stage, Hieronimo appeals to Christian and/or heavenly powers, whereas in the second he turns to pagan deities.[41] Of course, these deities are the very ones that spur Andrea to revenge. Hence, it will not do to argue, as Edwards does, that 'Hieronimo's relation with the divine must be discussed in terms of a single providence, even though there are two different metaphors for this providence' (*Kyd*, p. 36), nor is it possible to assimilate the world of Andrea's hell to the world of Hieronimo's heaven, errors to which a number of critics have been prone.[42] The Christian and pagan references are not arbitrarily mingled but deliberately opposed to each other. Likewise, the play as a whole contrasts a Christian attitude – characterised by trust in providence and verbalised by Hieronimo's citation of Romans – with a pagan 'wild justice'. It is thus appropriate that the fatal outcome is brought about when Hieronimo succumbs to the passion for which Revenge stands.

The final dialogue between Andrea and Revenge about rewards and punishments in the after-life needs to be understood in the same context. Revenge, not the play, places Andrea's 'friends in ease, the rest in woes' (IV.v.46). Kyd's dramatisation of Hieronimo's delicate balancing act between the pursuit of justice and the rejection of God reveals the inadequacy of Revenge's facile black-and-white distinctions.[43]

One of the insights scholars owe to the recent stage revivals of *The Spanish Tragedy* is that the tremendous impact the play can have is not so much a matter of its spectacular features as of the personal drama of Horatio, Bel-imperia, Isabella, and Hieronimo. Like *Hamlet*, *The Spanish Tragedy* is very much a family play, exploring powerful emotions in what are the most basic human relationships. Experienced in a good production, *The Spanish Tragedy* is simply a very moving play. This should allow us to adjust the critical focus. Philip Edwards concluded that *The Spanish Tragedy* has 'a view of human life not remotely identifiable or compatible with a Christian view of providence' and that 'Kyd's play is a denial of God's care for man', a view I find impossible to share.[44] Kyd's play is not so much a cosmic drama about a world deserted by God as the personal drama of Hieronimo deserting God. Expecting to see heavenly justice accomplished, he despairs when in waiting and turns to the infernal deities instead. He invokes God's word and command ('heaven will be reveng'd' (III.xiii.2)), only to reject it and to substitute his own ('I will revenge' (III.xiii.20)); his tragedy ensues as a consequence, a pattern that affirms rather than questions a Christian view of providence. As he gives way to the passion of revenge, he turns to the very powers that send the Ghost of Andrea back to the world of the living in company with Revenge. Kyd's treatment of his hero, however, is not harsh but humane. Hieronimo's rejection of the Pauline precept is not in scorn and defiance, but in bereavement and near insanity. It is less grandiose but more intimate than Dr Faustus'. Our sympathy is with Hieronimo.[45] As the attribute 'pittifull' on the original title page suggests, his inability to recognise a benevolent divinity when confronted with evil is deserving of compassion rather than condemnation.

Notes

1 C. L. Barber, *Creating Elizabethan Tragedy* (Chicago, 1988), p. 131.
2 William Prynne, *Histrio-mastix, The Players Scourge* (London, 1633), fol. 556a.
3 In the 'Induction' to *Bartholomew Fair*, for instance, Jonson wrote: 'Hee that will sweare, *Ieronimo* [i.e. *The Spanish Tragedy*], or *Andronicus* are the best playes, yet, shall passe vnexcepted at, heere, as a man whose Iudgement shewes it is constant, and hath stood still, these fiue and twentie, or thirtie yeeres' (ll. 106–9). In the Induction to *Cynthia's Revels*, Jonson mocks a man 'whom it hath pleas'd nature to furnish with more beard, then braine' who holds that 'the old Hieronimo, (as it was first acted, was the onely best, and iudiciously pend play of Europe' (ll. 206–11). See also *Every Man in His Humour*, Q1601, I.iii.126–42, *Poetaster*, III.iv.214–58, and *The Alchemist*, IV.vii.63–72.
4 According to Harbage's *Annals of English Drama* (2nd edn), in which *The Spanish Tragedy* is dated 1587, only the anonymous *Famous Victories of Henry V*, performed at the Bull's Inn by the Queen's Men in 1586, precedes *The Spanish Tragedy*.
5 For a full analysis of the effects achieved by juxtaposing the different audiences in and of *The Spanish Tragedy*, fictional on-stage, fictional

off-stage, and non-fictional, see Barry B. Adams, 'The Audiences of *The Spanish Tragedy*', *JEGP*, 68 (1969), 221–36.

6 See Richard C. Kohler, 'Kyd's Ordered Spectacle: "Behold ... / What 'tis to be subject to destiny"', *Medieval and Renaissance Drama in England*, 3 (1986), 30.

7 See also Scott McMillin's observation that 'in his two appearances in the opening scenes, Hieronimo acts only at the bidding of the King, and his role is defined by two functions: his pride in a valorous son and his skill at devising pageants. Both functions return in terribly changed form at the end of the action, when Hieronimo stages a murderous playlet before his King and then reveals the object which has driven him to ruin the ceremonies of Spain, the corpse of his murdered son' ('The Figure of Silence in *The Spanish Tragedy*', *ELH*, 39 (1972), 37).

8 For Kyd's highly original treatment of the dumb show considered in the context of the history of the convention, especially his advance in the integration of the dumb show into the play proper, see Dieter Mehl, *The Elizabethan Dumb Show: The History of a Dramatic Convention* (London, 1965), pp. 63–71.

9 See James R. Siemon's fine analysis of the latent tensions in the dumb show ('Sporting Kyd', 562–6).

10 See McAlindon in *English Renaissance Tragedy*: Hieronimo's masque 'is in perfect harmony with the spirit of the feast' (p. 74). Anne Righter (Barton), in *Shakespeare and the Idea of the Play* (London, 1962), calls the dumb show 'the Marshal's innocent show of knights and kings' and asserts that 'the elements of illusion declare themselves honestly; they are what they seem' (p. 80).

11 The centrality of writing to *The Spanish Tragedy* as a whole has been demonstrated by Frederick Kiefer in *Writing on the Renaissance Stage: Written Words, Printed Pages, Metaphoric Books* (Newark and London, 1996), pp. 232–46.

12 Michael Henry Levin was the first critic to point out what a good actor Kyd's protagonist is: 'Hieronimo remains master of his emotions until his vengeance is complete. [...] he is a much better actor than Hamlet; he is never rash enough to alarm his intended victims, and he eventually deceives them so thoroughly that they embrace him as a friend' ('"Vindicta mihi!": Meaning, Morality, and Motivation in *The Spanish Tragedy*', *SEL*, 4 (1964), 309). For a comprehensive study of self-dramatisation and metatheatricality in the play, see Jonathan Bate, 'The Performance of Revenge: *Titus Andronicus* and *The Spanish Tragedy*', in François Laroque (ed.), *The Show Within*, 2 vols. (Montpellier, 1992), II, pp. 267–84.

13 Hunter, 'Ironies of Justice in *The Spanish Tragedy*', *RD*, 8 (1965), 89–104, rpt. in *Dramatic Identities and Cultural Tradition* (Liverpool, 1978), pp. 214–29; Edwards, *Kyd*, p. 33.

14 John Scott Colley, '*The Spanish Tragedy* and the Theatre of God's Judgement', *Papers on Language and Literature*, 10 (1974), 241–53.

15 McAlindon, *English Renaissance Tragedy*, p. 55.

16 Hunter, 'Ironies of Justice in *The Spanish Tragedy*', 102.

17 Joel B. Altman, *The Tudor Play of Mind* (Berkeley, 1978), p. 270. For another pertinent articulation of the tension between Revenge in the

frame and Hieronimo in the play within, see Jones, *The Origins of Shakespeare*, pp. 196–206: 'for Revenge the future is already present; for Hieronimo (after Horatio's death) the past is present. [...] The play is not simply a linear succession of episodes: in Kyd's construct the end is implicit in the beginning, and the beginning is recalled by the end' (p. 198) resulting in 'a form of drama more tightly knit than anything yet seen on Elizabethan stages' (pp. 204–5).

18 *The Origins of English Tragedy* (Oxford, 1967), p. 83.

19 Ernst Robert Curtius, *European Literature and the Latin Middle Ages*, tr. Willard R. Trask (London, 1979).

20 *Ibid.*, p. 140.

21 *History of the World*, ed. C. A. Patrides (London, 1971), 70.

22 I quote from Sir Walter Ralegh, *Selected Prose and Poetry*, ed. Agnes M. C. Latham (London, 1965), p. 56.

23 For the most comprehensive study of the age-old denigration of the theatre, see Jonas Barish, *The Anti-theatrical Prejudice* (Berkeley, 1981). Anne Righter (Barton), in *Shakespeare and the Idea of the Play*, pp. 77–81, explores various play metaphors and the play-like quality of life in *The Spanish Tragedy*. She does not distinguish, however, between Kyd's two different, indeed opposed ways of dramatising what she calls 'the interpenetration of life and the drama' (p. 81), the belittling of life as man is 'merely actor' and its full exploration as man shapes his own destiny *qua* acting.

24 Growing interest in the play's self-conscious theatricality and its dramatic artistry have opened up a new field of research on *The Spanish Tragedy* which has shown the sophistication of Kyd's use of props, stage imagery, and theatrical space: see D. F. Rowan, 'The Staging of *The Spanish Tragedy*', in *The Elizabethan Theatre*, 5, ed. G. R. Hibbard (London, 1975), pp. 112–23; Eleanor M. Tweedie, '"Action is Eloquence": The Staging of Thomas Kyd's *Spanish Tragedy*', SEL, 16 (1976), 223–39; Michael Hattaway, *Elizabethan Popular Theatre: Plays in Performance* (London, 1982), pp. 101–28; and Kohler, 'Kyd's Ordered Spectacle', 27–49. See also James R. Siemon's Bakhtinian analysis of Kyd's dramaturgy in 'Dialogical Formalism: Word, Object, and Action in *The Spanish Tragedy*', *Medieval and Renaissance Drama in England*, 5 (1991), 87–115. Like Shakespeare, Kyd was clearly a man of the stage with expert knowledge of his craft, and his theatrical reevaluation of the *theatrum mundi* metaphor appears to grow out of a concrete concern with theatre.

25 *Likenesses of Truth in Elizabethan and Restoration Drama* (Oxford, 1972), p. 35.

26 Quoted by C. S. Lewis, *English Literature in the Sixteenth Century Excluding Drama* (Oxford, 1954), p. 13.

27 This tension inherent in Renaissance thought is powerfully articulated by Ernst Cassirer, *The Individual and the Cosmos in Renaissance Philosophy*, tr. Mario Domandi (Philadelphia, 1963), especially in the chapter on 'Freedom and necessity in the philosophy of the Renaissance', pp. 73–122.

28 Hawkins, *Likenesses of Truth in Elizabethan and Restoration Drama*, p. 30.

29 Critics approaching early modern drama with the New Historicist tenet
    that the theatre participated in shaping the society out of which it grew
    have not failed to subject Hieronimo's play to scrutiny. Molly Smith
    ('The Theater and the Scaffold: Death as Spectacle in *The Spanish
    Tragedy*', *SEL*, 32 (1992), 217–32) has investigated what she calls
    'Kyd's merger of the spectacles of punishment and enacted tragedy' (p.
    218), while James Shapiro ('"Tragedies Naturally Performed": Kyd's
    Representation of Violence', in D. S. Kastan and Peter Stallybrass (eds.),
    Staging the Renaissance (New York and London, 1991), pp. 99–113)
    reads Hieronimo's 'Solyman and Perseda' as an example of a play that
    is subversive not because it was conceived as such but owing to the uses
    to which it is put. He holds that 'Hieronimo's old play, "long forgot"
    (IV.i.80), only becomes subversive within the context of a situation
    unimaginable when Hieronimo first wrote it' (p. 101). Shapiro's doubt-
    ful argument depends on taking Hieronimo's 'long forgot' at face value
    even though the Knight Marshal has just told us that he is '[d]issembling
    quiet in unquietness' (III.xiii.30), and that 'the plot's already in [his]
    head' (IV.i.51). In fact, there is no reason to believe that Hieronimo is
    appropriating an 'old' play. Shapiro appears to use *The Spanish Tragedy*
    to read his theory (subversion *qua* appropriation) rather than the
    reverse.
30 Farnham, *The Medieval Heritage of Elizabethan Tragedy*, pp. 393–4.
31 Critics have disagreed as to whether Andrea died in fair battle or was
    treacherously killed. I believe that the dramatisation of his death in
    1 Hieronimo reflects faithfully Kyd's original treatment in *Don Horatio*
    and it is therefore worthwhile examining:

> *They fight, and* ANDREA *hath* BALTHEZER *downe. Enter* PORTUGALES
> *and releiue* BALTHEZER *and kil* ANDREA.
> Andrea.   O, I am slaine; helpe me, *Horatio.*
> My foes are base, and slay me cowardly; [...]
> *Sound Alarum,* ANDREA *slain, and Prince* BALTHEZER
> *vanting on him.* (III.ii.106.1–111.2)

So Andrea *was* killed 'cowardly'. This more or less conforms to
Horatio's report to Bel-imperia mentioning Balthazar's 'Taking advantage of his foe's distress' (I.iv.24), but is notably different from the
report by the Spanish General, in which Andrea is said to be a '[b]rave
man at arms, but weak to Balthazar' (I.ii.72). I therefore disagree with
Peter Murray (*Thomas Kyd*, p. 48) and Ian McAdam ('*The Spanish
Tragedy* and the Politico-Religious Unconscious', *Texas Studies in
Literature and Language*, 42 (2000), 41–3) who believe that Horatio is
deceptive in order to further his cause with Bel-imperia. Scott McMillin
has lucidly commented on the different accounts of the battle: 'While
certain differences occur in the several versions of the battle which fill
Act I, Kyd's interest centers on the enactment of the speeches rather than
on discrepancies in their content. What Act I implies is that the past can
be controlled and brought into present meanings through acts of speech'
('The Figure of Silence in *The Spanish Tragedy*', 31). Note that William
Empson ('*The Spanish Tragedy*', *Nimbus*, 3 (1956), 16–29, rpt. in
Derek Hudson (ed.), *English Critical Essays: Twentieth Century*, Second

Series (London, 1958), pp. 215–35, in Ralph J. Kaufmann (ed.), *Elizabethan Drama: Modern Essays in Criticism* (New York, 1961), pp. 60–80, and in William Empson, *Essays on Renaissance Literature, Volume Two: The Drama*, ed. John Haffenden (Cambridge, 1994), pp. 17–37) absurdly suggested that Andrea's killing has been arranged to pave the way for a dynastic marriage between Bel-imperia and Balthazar, a point for which there is simply no evidence in the text. In a later piece that was only published in 1994, Empson reiterated his wrong-headed argument, holding that the censor struck out the scene with the missing information (William Empson, 'The Spanish Tragedy (II)', in *Essays on Renaissance Literature, Volume Two: The Drama*, ed. Haffenden, pp. 41–65).

32 'The Spanish Tragedy: a Speaking Picture', *ELR*, 4 (1974), 204.
33 'Thrusting Elysium into Hell: The Originality of *The Spanish Tragedy*', in A. L. Magnusson and C. E. McGee (eds.), *The Elizabethan Theatre*, 11 (Ontario, Canada, 1990), p. 119.
34 Geoffrey Aggeler, 'The Eschatological Crux in *The Spanish Tragedy*', *JEGP*, 86 (1987), 319.
35 Edwards, *Kyd*, p. 36.
36 Edwards, 'Thrusting Elysium into Hell', 120–1.
37 Henke, 'Politics and Politicians in *The Spanish Tragedy*', 365.
38 'Revenge and Revenge Tragedy in Renaissance England', *RQ*, 28 (1975), 39.
39 The speech has probably received more attention than any other single passage in the play. Bowers (*Elizabethan Revenge Tragedy*) held that the soliloquy in III.xiii 'marks the turning point from Hieronimo the hero to Hieronimo the villain' (p. 70). John D. Ratliff ('Hieronimo Explains Himself', *SP*, 54 (1957), 112–18), dissatisfied with Bowers's reading, argued that 'Hieronimo is here justifying his course for the audience and preparing them for the dramatically necessary delay in his revenge. He is not revealing himself as a villain: on the contrary, by explaining his conduct he is making the charge of villainy impossible' (p. 118). David Laird ('Hieronimo's Dilemma', *SP*, 62 (1965), 137–46) tried to show that the speech 'reflects a state of mind neither confused nor strained beyond reason but acutely and precisely capable of confronting the issues that the question of revenge would have inevitably raised for thoughtful men in the Renaissance' (p. 138). Scott McMillin ('The Book of Seneca in *The Spanish Tragedy*', *SEL*, 14 (1974), 201–8) made the pertinent point that the three Senecan passages from which Hieronimo quotes bear upon self-destruction rather than revenge. Hieronimo three times wrenches them from their original meaning to justify his course of action, a rhetorical move which, as Hieronimo must be aware, reflects the step he is deciding to take, as his revenge can only be brought about at the same time as his self-destruction.
40 In a short but excellent passage on *The Spanish Tragedy* ('Tyrant and Martyr: Religious Heroisms in Elizabethan Tragedy', in Maynard Mack and George deForest Lord (eds.), *Poetic Traditions of the English Renaissance* (New Haven and London, 1982), pp. 85–102, see esp. pp. 93–5), G. K. Hunter usefully sees Hieronimo's decision to take justice into his own hands in the context of the 'intense Calvinism' (p. 94) of

Kyd's times, arguing that 'Hieronimo's flight from the standard processes of a Christian society leads him to claim that he bears a special destiny to act as God's immediate surrogate ("*I* will repay"). But an inner voice presenting demands that society can neither understand nor fulfill is as much the mark of madness as of election' (p. 94). This makes sense, in particular, of Hieronimo's self-delusory belief that 'all the saints do sit soliciting' (IV.i.33) as he sets up the final slaughter. Ian McAdam, who reads 'Hieronimo's violent justification as, indirectly, an expression of Reformation attitudes' (p. 39), has developed a similar argument in '*The Spanish Tragedy* and the Politico-Religious Unconscious', 33–60.

41 Incidentally, Isabella, Hieronimo's wife and companion in bereavement, precisely duplicates the pattern established in Hieronimo as she calls on the heavenly powers in the first part of the play (II.v.57, III.viii.14–20) but invokes pagan hell before her suicide (IV.ii.26–8).

42 For instance Broude ('Time, Truth, and Right in *The Spanish Tragedy*'), Cairncross, and Hunter, ('Ironies of Justice in *The Spanish Tragedy*'). For a good discussion of the play's opposition between the justice of Heaven and the justice of Hades, see Charles A. Hallett, 'Andrea, Andrugio and King Hamlet: The Ghost as Spirit of Revenge', *PQ*, 56 (1977), 43–64, rpt. in revised form in Charles A. Hallett and Elaine S. Hallett, *The Revenger's Madness: A Study of Revenge Tragedy Motifs* (Lincoln and London, 1980), pp. 21–39.

43 For an interesting reading of the play's final lines, see Michael Neill, *Issues of Death: Mortality and Identity in English Renaissance Tragedy* (Oxford, 1997), pp. 212–15. Watson (*The Rest Is Silence*) misconstrues the play when he argues that 'all [Revenge] can promise, in the play's final words, is an "endless tragedy." [...] Andrea suffers the annihilation-anxiety common to many dramatic characters, who must relive their story endlessly in order to exist at all' (p. 73). What the play's ending promises is, *pace* Watson, that Andrea and his friends will be placed 'in ease' (IV.v.46):

> I'll lead my friend Horatio through those fields
> Where never-dying wars are still inur'd:
> I'll lead fair Isabella to that train
> Where pity weeps but never feeleth pain:
> I'll lead my Bel-imperia to those joys
> That vestal virgins and fair queens possess:
> I'll lead Hieronimo where Orpheus plays,
> Adding sweet pleasure to eternal days.   (IV.v.17–24)

The final scene of *The Spanish Tragedy* is hardly fit to illustrate Watson's thesis of a Renaissance 'fear of death as annihilation' (p. 1).

44 Edwards, 'Thrusting Elysium into Hell', 125, 123. I similarly disagree with Katharine Eisaman Maus who sees in the empty box of III.iv to III.vi 'a comment upon the hollow promises of a Christianity *The Spanish Tragedy* both evokes and renounces' (*Inwardness and Theater in the English Renaissance* (Chicago and London, 1995), 66). See her subchapter on '*The Spanish Tragedy*, or, the Machiavel's Revenge' (55–71).

45 Eleanor Prosser (*Hamlet and Revenge*, 2nd edn (Stanford, 1971)), holding that when Hieronimo takes revenge into his own hands he would have been universally condemned, and Fredson T. Bowers (*Elizabethan Revenge Tragedy*), arguing that Hieronimo, in the eyes of the audience, 'inevitably becomes a villain' (p. 77), have found few followers. Ernst de Chickera ('Divine Justice and Private Revenge in *The Spanish Tragedy*', *MLR*, 57 (1962), 228–32) holds the view at the other end of the scale, seeing Hieronimo as executing 'just revenge, or, in Bacon's words, "the most tolerable sort of revenge" since it is undertaken for those wrongs which there is no law to remedy' (p. 231). A balanced assessment is given by Murray: Hieronimo's revenge does turn him into a second Lorenzo, repeats the murder of his son, a point the play-within-the-play, where Hieronimo takes Lorenzo's part and Lorenzo Horatio's, makes with fine Kydian irony. Yet, he clearly remains a sympathetic character with whom the audience identifies (*Thomas Kyd*, pp. 54, 127). For a general study of revenge tragedy, see John Kerrigan, *Revenge Tragedy: Aeschylus to Armageddon* (Oxford, 1996).

The Spanish Tragedie

OR,

Hieronimo is mad againe.

Containing the lamentable end of *Don Horatio*, and *Belimperia*; with the pittifull death of *Hieronimo*.

Newly corrected, amended, and enlarged with new Additions of the *Painters* part, and others, as it hath of late been diuers times acted.

LONDON,
Printed by W. White, and are to be sold by I. White and *T. Langley* at their Shop ouer against the Sarazens head without New-gate. 1615.

1 Title page of *The Spanish Tragedie ... with new Additions*, London, 1615.

CHAPTER 5

The Spanish Tragedy: additions, adaptations, modern stage history

In all probability, *The Spanish Tragedy* was printed twice in 1592, Jeffes's edition having perished, but one copy of White's edition having survived. The play was reprinted with only minor differences in 1594 and 1599. In 1602, Thomas Pavier, who had acquired the rights in the play in 1600, published an enlarged edition with the following title page:

THE
Spanish Tragedie:
Containing the lamen-
table end of *Don Horatio*, and *Bel-imperia*:
with the pittiful death of olde
Hieronimo.
Newly corrected, amended, and enlarged with
new additions of the Painters part, and
others, as it hath of late been
diuers times acted.[...]

Further editions followed in 1603, 1610/11, 1615, 1618, 1623, and 1633, all ultimately deriving from the text of 1602.

Five passages are added in the text of 1602, totalling approximately 330 lines: fifty-four lines inserted after II.v.45, ten lines replacing Hieronimo's speech at III.ii.65–6, forty-eight lines inserted between III.xi.1 and III.xi.2, 169 lines (the famous 'painter scene') inserted between III.xii and III.xiii with the final stage direction replacing III.xiii.0.1, and forty-seven lines replacing IV.iv.168–90 but incorporating IV.iv.176–9 and IV.iv.168–75 from *1592* in reverse order.

As Kyd had been dead for eight years when the additions first appeared, he seems unlikely to have made them himself. Henslowe's diary presents us with the following entries which seem to shed light on the question of their authorship:[1]

Lent vnto m^r alleyn the 25 of septembz 1601 to lend vnto Bengemen Johnson vpon hn writtinge of his adicians in geronymo the some of...xxxx^s

Lent vnto bengemy Johnsone at the A poyntment of EAlleyn &
w^m birde the 22 of June 1602 in earneste of A Boocke called
Richard crockbacke & for new adicyons for Jeronymo the some of....x^li

Since the 1980s, much has been made of Jonson's apparent authorship of the extant additions.[2] Jonson's first daughter, Mary, was
born early in 1601 and died later that year. According to Anne
Barton, a play dealing with a father's grief for his dead child was
thus 'designed in one important respect to touch a responsive chord
in him'.[3] Significantly, David Riggs adds, 'all of the passages added
to Kyd's text focus on the allied themes of premature death and
parental bereavement, and these were subjects close to Jonson's
heart'.[4]

Barton and Riggs take for granted Jonson's authorship of the
additions. The way they think of the nature of Jonson's achievement,
his range and versatility of style as well as the relationship between
his life and writing are thereby strongly affected. Before drawing
inferences about Jonson as man and artist from his alleged authorship of the additions, it is necessary to review the evidence for
Barton's and Riggs's attribution.

It has long been pointed out that there are reasons to believe that
the extant additions are not those referred to by Henslowe.[5] Some of
the arguments advanced by critics are indeed weak and readily
disposed of. The style of the additions resembles nothing in Jonson's
writings, but he may well have written them in a style unlike that of
his own plays. A further argument against Jonson's authorship can
easily be countered: it has been suggested that the sum Henslowe
paid (£2 and a portion of £10) seems too large for little more than
three hundred lines. However, considering the additions' metrical
deficiencies, Pavier may have obtained them 'perhaps by transcript,
but conceivably through the actors'.[6] It would be just possible, then,
that the additions as they have come down to us represent an imperfect and partial transcript of the added material.

There are more serious reservations about Jonson's authorship,
however. It has been shown that V.i of Marston's *Antonio and
Mellida*, printed in 1602 but generally dated 1599, parodies the
famous painter scene.[7] There is additional evidence that *The Spanish
Tragedy* had already undergone revision in the 1590s. When the
play was revised by the Lord Admiral's Men in 1597, Henslowe
marked the play 'ne'.[8] Although his notation is not consistent in
meaning, revision is at least one possible explanation. Even
Henslowe's wording 'new adicyons' may imply an older set of additions. Moreover, Jonson himself hinted at a revision of the play in

Cynthia's Revels (1600, publ. 1601) before he came to write his own additions: 'the old Hieronimo, (*as it was first acted*) was the onely best, and iudiciously pend play of Europe' (my emphasis, Induction, ll. 209–11).

Barton and Riggs treat this evidence in somewhat cavalier fashion. Riggs summarily states that 'the arguments against Jonson's authorship are not compelling' (p. 87) and feels no need to discuss the case against Jonson's authorship. Barton lengthily counters the arguments that carry little weight, but passes quickly over the real problems. Her explanation of chronology is particularly unsatisfactory. She argues that Marston 'inserted a *last-minute* parody of the Painter scene [...] into *Antonio and Mellida*', and that Jonson was so 'stung by the attacks of critics who felt [...] that Kyd's play had been more coherent in its original form' that he added 'a sentence introduced *at the last moment* into the quarto of *Cynthia's Revels*' (p. 16, my emphasis).

Barton's wording may lead us to suspect that her chronology is stretched. More than that, however, it belies the facts. This is her reasoning: Marston saw or read Jonson's additions – for which Jonson received his second payment on 22 June 1602 – and added his parody before *Antonio and Mellida* was printed in 1602 whereupon Jonson made his last-minute addition to *Cynthia's Revels*. However, *Cynthia's Revels* had been entered in the Stationers' Register on 23 May 1601 and printed the same year. Barton's chronology does not square with the facts.

Elsewhere her discussion of the additions seems muddled: she takes exception to the critics' 'disinclination to believe that the entries in Henslowe's diary can really mean what they say' (p. 27). This, however, is clearly not the problem. Jonson, for all we know, did write additions to *The Spanish Tragedy*, but it seems unlikely that they were ever printed. Considering that the play was one of the most popular plays of its time and performed by several companies, there is nothing inherently implausible in the possibility that two revisions of *The Spanish Tragedy* were undertaken. Roslyn Knutson has shown that popular tragedies were a rare and precious commodity and updating them may have been a convenient way of preserving their marketability.[9] The stress on Hieronimo's madness in all five additions is best explained as an attempt to capitalise on popular interest in both the play's hero and scenes of madness.[10] Again, the 'themes of premature death and parental bereavement [...] were subjects close to Jonson's heart', as Riggs points out, but it seems a biographer's fallacy to build an argument on 'Jonson's heart' rather than on the material pressures of the stage business.

Edwards, in his disinterested analysis of the authorship of the additions, presents a strong case against Jonson. He stops short, however, of denying the possibility that Jonson wrote them, considering that Marston might have added the parodies of the painter scene later, even though it seems to him 'something of a strained conjecture' (*ST*, p. lxv). One argument makes the case for a late addition of the parody even weaker, however. The passage upon which the dating of *Antonio and Mellida* is normally based and Marston's parody of the painter scene belong to the very same self-contained scenic movement, namely the first fifty-odd lines of V.i, featuring Balurdo in the company of a painter. At the beginning of the scene, Balurdo inspects the two pictures with which the painter has entered:

> whose picture is this? *Anno Domini* 1599. Beleeve me, master
> *Anno Domini* was of a good settled age when you lymn'd him;
> 1599. yeares old? Lets see the other. *Etatis suae* 24. Bir Ladie he
> is somewhat younger. Belike master *Etatis suae* was *Anno*
> *Dominies* sonne.   (Act V)

The play's editor in the Revels Plays series comments that 'in 1599 Marston was in his twenty-fourth year and this portrait is almost certainly of him'.[11] A few lines later follows the passage which most clearly alludes to the painter scene:

> *Balurdo.*   Can you paint me a driveling reeling song, & let the
> word be, Uh. [...]
> *Painter.*   It cannot be done sir, but by a seeming kind of
> drunkennesse.   (Act V)

The fourth 'addition' to *The Spanish Tragedy* has:

> *Hieronino.*   Canst paint me a tear, or a wound, a groan, or a
> sigh?   (ll. 113–14)
>
> *Hieronino.*   Canst paint a doleful cry?
> *Painter.*   Seemingly, sir.   (ll. 128–30)

The 'late addition' theory would be less implausible if it were not inextricably bound up with other lines for which there is a strong presumption that they were written in 1599.[12]

Critics have advanced several alternatives to Jonson. Thomas Hawkins, the first editor to print the additions, thought they had been 'foisted in by the players' and relegated them to footnotes. Less than forty years later, Charles Lamb considered them 'the very salt of the play' and advanced Webster as possible author.[13] Coleridge suggested Shakespeare, an attribution which, groundless though it be, was revived in the twentieth century.[14] An equally unconvincing case has been made for Dekker.[15] A last suggestion that may be discarded was advanced by Cairncross, who thought that 'it may be worth speculating on the alternative possibility that the "additions" are not additions at all, but original passages cut and later restored to the text, and written by Kyd himself' (p. xxii). This is not plausible and the weight of both external and internal evidence argues clearly against it.

The question of the authorship of the additions may well have to remain unanswered. The metrically deficient text, possibly due to either an imperfect reconstruction or a hurried transcript, make an evaluation even more difficult. What, for instance, are we to make of the 'thefts' from *Titus Andronicus* and *Dr. Faustus* in the fourth and fifth additions?[16] Are they part of the original additions? Or did actor-reporters use lines readily available in their memories to fill in memorial gaps as happened with some 'bad' quartos? The latter possibility seems more likely without being certain. What can be asserted with some confidence is that the author of the additions had a good sense of humour. Here is how he ends the last of his contributions to *The Spanish Tragedy*:

> *Hieronimo.*   Now do I applaud what I have acted.
> *Nunc iners cadat manus.*
> Now to express the rupture of my part,

... and Kyd is made to finish the sentence.

What are these additions, then, and what difference do they make to the play? The first point to bear in mind is that the very word used to designate them is misleading. Even though the new passages are additions to the printed text, they were in all probability designed as replacements rather than additions. Schücking has convincingly argued that the painter scene was conceived to replace the Senex scene ('Bazardo' thus replacing 'Bazulto').[17] Both scenes hinge on the same idea: a man, whose son, like Hieronimo's, has been murdered, comes to the Knight Marshall to plead for justice, but is told that there is no justice in this world. While *1602* juxtaposes the two scenes, the players for whom the additions were written no doubt acted the painter scene but discarded the Senex scene.

The third addition probably substituted another passage of the original. In *1602*, it is clearly misplaced, inserted between the First Portingale's 'By your leave, sir' (III.xi.1) and Hieronimo's 'Good leave have you, nay, I pray you go,/ For I'll leave you, if you can leave me, so' (III.xi.2–3), thereby destroying Hieronimo's wordplay. Schücking plausibly suggested that Hieronimo's speech must have come considerably earlier in the play, at a moment when he is not yet aware that Lorenzo and Balthazar have murdered his son (Hieronimo refers to Balthazar as 'valiant' (l. 39) in the addition). The natural inference is that the new passage replaced Hieronimo's only speech between the discovery of his murdered son and the reception of Belimperia's letter: the 'O eyes, no eyes' soliloquy (III.ii.1–23).

It now emerges what the purpose of the badly named additions seems to have been. By the time they came to be written, Jonson, Marston, and Donne had made their débuts and the style of the dramatisation of Hieronimo's grief and madness must have seemed decidedly out of date.[18] The stylistic differences between Kyd's original and the new substitutions could hardly be more striking:

OLD:

> O eyes, no eyes, but fountains fraught with tears;
> O life, no life, but lively form of death;
> O world, no world, but mass of public wrongs,
> Confus'd and fill'd with murder and misdeeds;   (III.ii.1–4)

NEW:

> What is there yet in a son
> To make a father dote, rave or run mad?
> Being born, it pouts, cries and breeds teeth.
> What is there yet in a son? He must be fed,
> Be taught to go, and speak.   (3rd addition, ll. 9–13)

OLD:

> I'll down to hell, and in this passion
> Knock at the dismal gates of Pluto's court,   110
> Getting by force, as once Alcides did,
> A troop of Furies and tormenting hags
> To torture Don Lorenzo and the rest.
> Yet lest the triple-headed porter should
> Deny my passage to the slimy strond,   115
> The Thracian poet thou shalt counterfeit:
> Come on, old father, be my Orpheus,
> And if thou canst no notes upon the harp,
> Then sound the burden of thy sore heart's grief,
> Till we do gain that Proserpine may grant
> Revenge on them that murdered my son: (III.xiii.109–21)

NEW:

> Well sir, then bring me forth, bring me through alley and alley, still with a distracted countenance going along, and let my hair heave up my night-cap. Let the clouds scowl, make the moon dark, the stars extinct, the winds blowing, the bells tolling, the owl shrieking, the toads croaking, the minutes jarring, and the clock striking twelve. And then at last, sir, starting, behold a man hanging, and tottering and tottering, as you know the wind will weave a man, and I with a trice to cut

him down. And looking upon him by the advantage of my
torch, find it to be my son Horatio. There you may show a
passion, there you may show a passion.

(4th addition, ll. 145–56)

Kyd's long, highly rhetorical and declamatory sentences, summoning
a good part of the ancient underworld, are replaced by a more immediate and economic language, short clauses, in irregular verse or in
prose that is not far from regular speech. When Jonson, in 1600,
satirically stated that 'the old Hieronimo, (as it was first acted) was
the onely best, and iudiciously pend play of Europe', he may well
have distinguished between the original, 'out-dated' play (the object
of his gibe) and the updated version (excepted from his attack).

The three remaining additions, the first, the second, and the fifth,
total slightly more than hundred lines. According to Edwards, they
'have little to commend them; their literary quality is slight and they
do much damage to Kyd's careful unfolding of plot and character'
(*ST*, p. lxi). The fifth addition has the merit of replacing Hieronimo's
nonsensical 'vow of silence'. The spiteful Hieronimo, out to 'torture'
(5th addition, l. 30) Castile and the Portuguese Viceroy who have
just lost their sons, has little in common, however, with Kyd's 'pittifull' Hieronimo:

> You had a son too, he was my liege's nephew;
> He was proud and politic, had he liv'd,
> He might ha' come to wear the crown of Spain:
> I think 'twas so: 'twas I that killed him,
> Look you, this same hand, 'twas it that stabb'd
> His heart – do you see this hand? –   (5th addition, ll. 33–8)

Kyd's Hieronimo, to be sure, also expresses his satisfaction after
having revenged Horatio's death by killing Balthazar and Lorenzo;
he is '[p]leas'd with their deaths, and eas'd with their revenge'
(IV.iv.190). Nevertheless, he is far from displaying *Schadenfreude* at
Castile's, the King's, and the Viceroy's loss.

The first addition is, *pace* Edwards, a fine piece of dramatic
writing in which Hieronimo's mad flippancy powerfully jars with
the tragedy of his son's death:

> *Hieronimo.*   Ha, ha! Saint James, but this doth make me laugh,
>   That there are more deluded than myself.
> *Pedro.*   Deluded?
> *Hieronimo.*   Ay, I would have sworn myself within this hour
>   That this had been my son Horatio,
>   His garments are so like: Ha!
>   Are they not great persuasions?
> *Isabella.*   O would to God it were not so!   (1st addition, ll. 25–32)

Edwards is correct, however, in pointing out that the first addition fits badly into Kyd's dramatisation of Hieronimo's gradual development towards madness. In II.v, as Hieronimo and his wife discover their dead son, the scene moves from the hero's long display of passion in his soliloquy to a second movement of subdued mourning and emotional exhaustion: 'sighs are stopp'd, and all my tears are spent' (II.v.37). The lines immediately following the point at which the first addition was inserted are notable for Hieronimo's control and restraint:

> Sweet lovely rose, ill-pluck'd before thy time,
> Fair worthy son, not conquer'd but betray'd:
> I'll kiss thee now, for words with tears are stay'd.   (II.v.46–8)

The regular, almost monotonous rhythm is identical in the three lines with a *caesura* placed each time after the second foot. The Hieronimo of the first addition, in contrast, 'raves' (l. 8), as Isabella properly puts it:

> Confusion, mischief, torment, death and hell,
> Drop all your stings at once in my cold bosom,
> That now is stiff with horror: kill me quickly: (1st addition, ll. 45–7)

He has uncontrolled fits of laughter (l. 25) and sends Jaques to 'bid my son Horatio to come home' (l. 18). In the second addition, similarly, Hieronimo, asked by Lorenzo why he is inquiring for Bel-imperia, jocularly reveals that the reason 'is a thing of nothing,/ The murder of a son, or so' (2nd addition, ll. 8–9). The simple withdrawal of Kyd's Hieronimo is again more in keeping with a character shown to be still in control of himself. Kyd skilfully constructs his protagonist's mental and emotional trajectory from initial self-control to utter frenzy in III.xii where Hieronimo, whose petitions remain unheard by the King, madly digs the ground with his dagger.[19]

In twentieth-century productions of *The Spanish Tragedy*, only the painter scene is sometimes added to Kyd's text. The choice seems a wise one. Whatever the intrinsic quality of the dramatic writing of the other additions, they do nothing to improve Kyd's play. We may safely leave them where they belong: in the appendix to editions of *The Spanish Tragedy*.[20]

We have seen that *The Spanish Tragedy* was immensely popular at the end of the sixteenth century and remained so in the early seventeenth century. As none of Kyd's editors has pointed out, the play even seems to have been performed at court, or considered for performance, as late as the winter of 1619/20.[21] The remarkable success *The Spanish Tragedy* had in London was matched by the play's popularity abroad. Adaptations of *The Spanish Tragedy* were printed between 1618 and 1729 and performances took place from Holland to Bohemia and from Denmark to southern Germany. As early as 1601, the play was acted in Frankfurt, followed by recorded performances at Dresden in 1626 (*Tragoedie von Hieronymo Marshall in Spanien*), at Prague in 1651 (*Von dem jämmerlichen und niemals erhörten Mord in Hispania*) and at Lüneburg in 1660 (*Don Hieronimo Marschalk in Spanien*).[22]

No fewer than six adaptations have survived, three each in German and Dutch:[23] Firstly, Jakob Ayrer's German *Tragedia, von dem Griegischen Keyser zu Constantinopel vnd seiner Tochter Pelimperia mit dem gehengten Horatio*, written probably before the close of the sixteenth century and published in Nürnberg in 1618 as part of his *Opus Theatricum*.[24] Secondly, Everaert Siceram's Dutch narrative adaptation, covering I.i to III.x of the original, curiously inserted into his translation of Ariosto's *Orlando Furioso*, published at Antwerp in 1615.[25] Thirdly, Adrien van den Bergh's Dutch *Ieronimo*, published in Utrecht in 1621. Fourthly, the anonymous Dutch *Don Jeronimo, Marschalck van Spanjens*, first printed in Amsterdam in 1638 and reprinted there nine times until 1729. Fifthly, the anonymous German *Comoedia von Jeronimo Marschalck in Hispanien*, probably written between 1662 and 1666, extant in a manuscript that originally belonged to Michael Daniel Treu's company of itinerant players, and presumably performed in Lüneburg in 1666.[26] Sixthly, Kaspar Stieler's German *Bellemperie*, printed in Jena in 1680.

Ayrer's adaptation is based on Kyd's original, unrevised play. Apart from Horatio (Horatius), Bel-imperia (Pelimperia), Lorenzo (Laurentzius), and Balthazar (Balthasar), the proper names have been completely changed. Ayrer introduces several new characters such as Jahn, the fool, and Philomena, Pelimperia's confidante. On the other hand, he omits the supernatural frame, the General's speech, the Portuguese subplot, Castile (Laurentzius and Pelimperia are the King's children) and Isabella. A total of ten scenes of Kyd's original leave no trace in the adaptation. A few of Ayrer's changes are interesting: Pelimperia and Horatius plan to get married (ii.129–30) which adds a sense of urgency to the princes' attempt to thwart the match. The play-within-the-play is substantially longer, dealing with the Soldan's (Balthasar) refusal to have his sister (Pelimperia) married even though there are two contenders: the King of Babylon (impersonated by Malignus who corresponds to Kyd's Hieronimo) and the Knight of Rhodes (Lorentzius). Most of the time, however, Ayrer's adaptation strips the original of its interest and excitement and turns the protagonist into a flat character.[27] The conversations are short and perfunctory. All in all, the play is poor stuff.

The same can be said of van den Bergh's *Ieronimo*. It reduces the play to roughly 1300 lines, does away with the frame and the subplot and turns the principal characters into little more than fools. Flat in style, random in dramatic motivation, superficial in characterisation, the play is a pale reflection of Kyd's masterpiece.[28] As it adapts the 'painter scene' from the original, it must be based upon an enlarged edition of 1602 or later. Van den Bergh's important invention is the Ghost of Horatio, a device taken over by the anonymous Dutch dramatisation.

Stieler's *Bellemperie* derives from the anonymous Dutch *Don Jeronimo, Marschalck van Spanjens*, but adds two important characters, Skaramutza, the fool, and Gillette, Bellemperie's confidante.[29] A narrative introduction tells the story up to Horatio's murder, Bellemperie's confinement, and her seeming consent to marry the Portuguese prince. The play itself dramatises what remains of Kyd's work with various extraneous comic material, such as Skaramutza's wooing of Gilette, and with a considerable shift in dramatic focus. As the title indicates, the protagonist of Stieler's play is not the old Knight Marshal but the young princess. She informs Hieronimo of her past love affair with his son, drives him to revenge, does the plotting, writes the play of 'Solyman and Perseda', and assigns the roles. Whereas Hieronimo's soliloquies are cut, her grief is dramatised in new material. Yet, Stieler's treatment lacks Kyd's intensity and dramaturgical qualities, and the new comic material is generally more successful than the tragic scenes.

The above adaptations suffer in comparison with the two remaining dramatisations. The anonymous Dutch *Don Jeronimo, Marschalck van Spanjens* has been shown to derive from both Kyd's original and van den Bergh's adaptation. It was composed in 2252 rhyming iambic alexandrines of no mean quality.[30] It was edited by Schönwerth at the end of the last century, but owing to most critics' inability to read Dutch it has largely passed unnoticed.[31] In the meantime, however, a previously unknown manuscript, the anonymous German *Comoedia von Jeronimo Marschalck in Hispanien*, has been made available to the scholarly community.[32] It is a prose translation of the anonymous Dutch play containing only a few

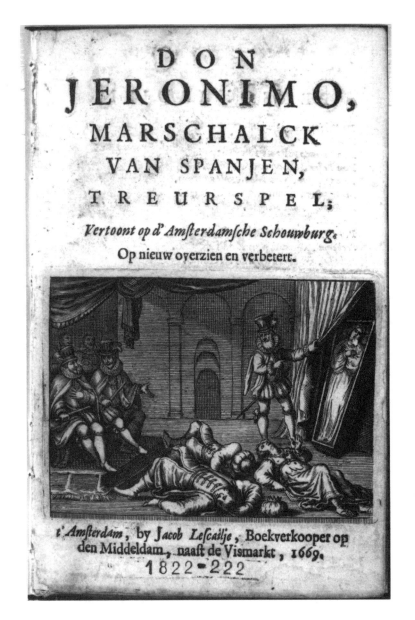

DON JERONIMO,

MARSCHALCK
VAN SPANJEN,

TREURSPEL;

Vertoont op d' Amsterdamsche Schouwburg.
Op nieuw overzien en verbetert.

t'*Amsterdam*, by *Jacob Lescailje*, Boekverkooper op
den Middeldam, naast de Vismarkt, 1669.

1822-222

2   Title page of the anonymous Dutch *Don Ieronimo, Marschalck van Spanjen*, 6th edition, Amsterdam, 1669.

alterations and a different act-division. The play constitutes by far
the best adaptation in German and allows inferences about the
quality of the Dutch play upon which it depends. The latter clearly
reveals a thorough understanding of Kyd's play. Rather than going
off in various directions by adding its own material, it grows organically out of *The Spanish Tragedy*.

Even though the adaptation dispenses with the supernatural
frame and the intrigue of Kyd's subplot involving Alexandro and
Villuppo, the plot follows *The Spanish Tragedy* for much of the
play: the conflict opposing Don Petro (Lorenzo) and Don Oratius
(Horatio) over their prisoner Don Lorenso (as Balthazar is confus-
ingly called), Belimperia's love for Oratius and Don Petro and Don
Lorenso's plot against it with the help of Petrongano (Pedringano),
the murder of Oratius and Jeronimo and Isabella's lament at its
discovery, Jeronimo's quest for vengeance and descent into madness
(including the 'painter scene') and the apocalyptic play-within-the-
play. The adaptation's adherence to the original can go as far as a
character's linguistic tic. The pathos in Lorenso's lines, for instance,
renders the highly rhetorical language Kyd gives to Balthazar:

> *Lorenso.* Ach ich Elender! ich schwimme auf den Unglücks
> Meer, und die Wellen des Todes ergißen sich albereit durch
> meinen engen Schlundt, ich verschmachte und erstirbe vor
> Durst, ich sauffe gegen Danck daß gesalzene Waßer in
> meinen Leib; O unleidliche
> Flamme! O hoffnungsloßer Streit!   (I.iii)

> *Lorenso.* Wretched me! I swim on the sea of misfortune, and the
> waves of death gush through my narrow throat, I languish and
> perish of thirst, I cannot but swallow the salty water; oh unbear-
> able flame! oh hopeless strife!

At times, the adaptor was not content to follow Kyd but elaborated the material he found. For instance, when the hangman
presents Jeronimo with Pedrongano's letter, the brief passage

> *Hangman.* You will stand between the gallows and me?
> *Hieronimo.* Ay, ay.
> *Hangman.* I thank your lord-worship.
> *Exit* HANGMAN. (III.vii.26–8)

is expanded and the hangman's fear of being held responsible for
Pedrongano's hanging is turned into a successful comic sequence.
Andrea's bloody scarf which, in *The Spanish Tragedy*, passes from
Horatio to Bel-imperia, then back to Horatio and to Hieronimo, is
used on an additional occasion when Belimperia wards off Lorenso's
advances by brandishing the scarf as a sign of her loyalty to the

deceased (I.iii). Like the revised text of *The Spanish Tragedy*, the
adaptation elaborates Hieronimo's grief and madness. Once
Jeronimo, like his counterpart in Kyd, enters in his shirt with a
sword and a torch, the adaptation exploits the implied darkness by
having Jeronimo mistake Oratius's corpse for an intruder:

> Noch eins, ich will alle Schatten dieser Bäume durchsuchen: stille
> hier ist ein Mensch, rede, weßwegen man mich izunter geruffen
> hat, was suchestu hier? rede oder dieser Stahl soll dir den garauß
> machen, er redet oder rührt sich nicht, er siehet ganz bestorben,
> stille er ist aufgehenckt. O ihr Götter!   (I.xi)

> Once more, I will search all the shadows of these trees: peace, here
> is a man, speak, why have I been called, what are you doing here?
> speak or this sword shall finish you; he doesn't speak nor move, he
> looks all dead, peace, he has been hanged. O ye gods!

Like Kyd's, the soliloquy is acted rather than only spoken and the
choppy syntax is expressive of Jeronimo's confusion. When Isabella
enters, the adaptation adds a second powerful passage as Jeronimo
mistakes her for a prostitute whose lover, he thinks, has murdered
Oratius during their encounter.

Most importantly, the adaptation dramatises a portion of the
events which Kyd left blank: Belimperia in sequestration. We see her
alone, pondering, then rejecting suicide. She opens one of her veins
and, using the blood as ink, writes a letter to Jeronimo, spurring him
to revenge. As she concludes, the Ghost of Oratius enters with a
sword in hand and the rope around his neck, but vanishes as she
tries to hold him. On his second appearance, he tells her he has come
to strengthen her resolve and to help her. He departs with her letter
to Jeronimo. When her brother enters, she disguises her inner
tumult. In the ensuing argument, Don Petro urges her to refrain from
a match that is not suitable to her nobility, while she asserts her own
right to decide. As he exhorts her to marry Lorenso, she first resists
before seemingly giving in.

In *The Spanish Tragedy*, Bel-imperia is carried off by Balthazar as
Horatio is murdered in II.iv; we lose sight of her until the beginning
of III.ix when she appears 'at a window' (III.ix.0.1): 'What means
this outrage that is offer'd me?/ Why am I thus sequester'd from the
court?' (III.ix.1–2). In between, Hieronimo, halfway through the 'O
eyes, no eyes' soliloquy, receives her 'bloody writ' (III.ii.26) which,
according to the stage direction, simply 'falleth' (III.ii.23.1), apparently from nowhere. The lack of an agon has suggested supernatural
intervention to several directors who had Revenge drop the letter.
The adaptation fills in the gap left by Kyd in a different way: Here,

Jeronimo's solitary lament is interrupted when the Ghost of Oratius enters, spurring him to revenge and dropping Belimperia's letter. Left alone, Jeronimo has doubts whether the apparition and the letter are more than deceptions and, like Hamlet, postpones action by resolving to seek stronger evidence.

The reworking of the material is intelligent. In showing how Belimperia's letter got to Jeronimo, it not only provides an answer where *The Spanish Tragedy* leaves a question, but it also introduces a theatrically effective Ghost at an appropriate moment. As has been pointed out, Kyd's Ghost is unusual insofar as he does not return to the scene of the living in order to further his revenge after an unjust death. He may have been conceived as a structural device, linking the two parts of Kyd's dramatic diptych. Considered on its own, the Ghost in *The Spanish Tragedy* clearly fits less well the conventions of the revenge tragedy than the one in the present adaptation. Bowers usefully summarised that '"Revenge tragedy" customarily [...] portrays the ghosts of the murdered urging revenge, a hesitation on the part of the avenger, a delay in proceeding to his vengeance, and his feigned or actual madness.'[33] *The Spanish Tragedy*, *Hamlet*, and other revenge plays share a number of dramatic devices and situations, but interestingly, it is the Ghost of Oratius in the adaptation rather than the Ghost of Andrea in Kyd's original that corresponds in dramatic function and role to old Hamlet's spectre and to the typical revenge tragedy ghost.

Belimperia's sequestration is not the only moment where the adaptation provides an answer to the question *The Spanish Tragedy* poses. The problem of the morality of revenge is addressed before the audience has time to worry about it: Jeronimo decides to

> folge der Spanischen Prister Geseze, welche lehret: wen ein Prinz nicht den ehrlichen Fußstapffen seines Vatern folget und Schlipfrige Wege gehet, auch zugleich in Geistlichen Sachen fehlet ist hoch nötig daß er zur Höllen gestürzet wird. (III.xi)

> conform to the laws of the Spanish priests which teach: if a Prince does not follow in the honest footsteps of his father but walks on a slippery path and sins in spiritual matters it is very necessary to thrust him into hell.

Contrary to Bowers and Prosser, who one-sidedly argued that an Elizabethan audience could not but condemn Hieronimo's actions, the adaptations in Holland and Germany took care to point out that Jeronimo had just and legal grounds on which to base his revenge.

Similarly, following the play-within-the-play, the adaptation provides an answer where Kyd's play leaves us guessing at why his courtly audience remains mute while Hieronimo explains his bloody stratagem at considerable length: Jeronimo has already explained that the princes are dead ('der Würmer Speiße'), that he has used the play to carry out his revenge for the princes' murder of his son, and has discovered Oratius's corpse (standing in a coffin), when Castile asks him to 'let the Princes rise' ('laßet die Prinzen aufstehen'). Only after Jeronimo's further explanation does it dawn on Castile that Jeronimo has long left the fictional realm. Hieronimo's enigmatic 'vow of silence' is sensibly discarded as in all later versions, beginning with the revised text of *The Spanish Tragedy*. Pressed to reveal who his confederates were (cf. *ST*, IV.iv.176), Jeronimo laconically states: 'Ich habe es schon gesagt' ('I have already told you'). In the ensuing bloodbath, Jeronimo also includes the King of Spain among his victims before killing himself, leaving the King of Portugal to speak solitarily the final lines.

On a few occasions, the adaptation arguably improves upon *The Spanish Tragedy*. It dramatises the inner conflict of characters – Pedrongano (III.iv) and Belimperia (II.iii and II.v) – other than the protagonist. Furthermore, some critics have objected to the slow start of Kyd's play, holding that the play takes two acts to get properly under way with the murder of Horatio. The German adaptation appears to have shared this concern as it dramatises in one act events that are spread out over two acts in *The Spanish Tragedy*. It is surely remarkable that the adaptation cuts precisely those passages some critics have tended to disparage, the long narrative introduction and the subplot, but adds and intensifies the very moment the author of the 1602 additions decided to dwell upon.

Moreover, a new act, the fourth, begins after the scene corresponding to III.vii in *The Spanish Tragedy*. Long before critics speculated about whether the beginning of the fourth act was lost in the printing of Kyd's play, the author of the German adaptation understood that a natural break occurs at this moment and appropriately marked it by beginning a new act.

Despite its dramaturgical qualities, which makes it by far the most substantial of the various Dutch and German reworkings, the adaptation is ultimately no match for *The Spanish Tragedy*. In comparison with Kyd's forceful language, the German prose is often coarse, merely fulfilling a functional purpose at the service of the action represented on stage. Consequently, many of Kyd's finer points are lost. Also, the original soliloquies being normally abridged or omitted, the protagonist comes across as a substantially thinner character. With the suppression of the supernatural frame, the play loses much of its disturbing quality. Kyd's disconcerting tension between a pagan and a Christian universe, vividly expressive of the protagonist's inner conflict, is replaced by an unequivocally Christian world. While the Ghost of Andrea returns from the pagan underworld, Oratius is clearly a Christian spirit. Nothing suggests he is a suffering, purgatorial ghost, however, doomed for a certain term to walk the night. Rather, he comes to further the causes of heaven – 'der Himmel nimbt sich unserer gerechten Sache an' (III.xi) – and to visit Heaven's punishment – 'Himmelß Straffe' (III.xi) – upon Don Petro. The epilogue, spoken by the King of Portugal, is in the same black-and-white tone:

> Hier siht man daß Gewaldt so große Herzen üben
> Nicht ungestraffet bleibt, diß komt von Neidt im lieben.   (V.vi)

> Force used by great ones shall not pass unchecked
> If they through jealous love have others wrecked.

The play is thus reduced to a simple 'mirror for magistrates' who are warned not to commit the sins of Don Petro and Don Lorenso.

In many ways, the adaptation can be understood as a 'critical reading' *avant la lettre* of *The Spanish Tragedy*, undertaken several centuries before critics started addressing some of the same issues. Much of the play's fascination lies in its intimate engagement and interpretation of the original. This accounts for the fact that the adaptation cannot compare with Kyd's masterpiece. Where *The Spanish Tragedy* poses questions, its remake provides answers, reducing to simple explanations the tensions and ambiguities which continue to fascinate critics and audiences alike.

Adaptations of *The Spanish Tragedy* on the Continent appear to have been performed until late in the seventeenth if not early in the eighteenth century. In England, however, the popularity of Kyd's play ceased with the closing of the theatres in 1642. It is not quite true, though, that *The Spanish Tragedy* stopped being performed until the twentieth century. The only known Restoration performance, ignored by all of Kyd's editors, is recorded in Pepys' diary and took place on 24 February 1667/68 at the Nursery Theatre in Hatton Garden:

> I took them [Mrs Pepys and Deb.] to the Nursery, where none of us ever was before; where the house is better and the Musique better then we looked, for and the acting not much worse, because I expected as bad as could: and I was not much mistaken, for it was so. However, I was pleased well to see it once, it being worth a man's seeing to discover the different ability and understanding of people, and the different growth of people's abilities by practice. Their play was a bad one, called *Jeronimo*

is Mad Again – a tragedy. Here was some good company by us who did make mighty sport at the folly of their Acting, which I could not neither refrain from sometimes, though I was sorry for it.[34]

The Spanish Tragedy did not appeal to the taste of Restoration audiences. The play which had been performed by the leading actors on London's main stages for about half a century before 1642 was now played in a marginal and temporary playhouse by mediocre actors.[35] The last recorded 'early' reference to *The Spanish Tragedy* occurred a few years later in the prologue to Charles Cotton's *The Scoffer Scoffed* (1675): 'Old Tales, old Songs, and an old Jest,/ Our stomachs easili'st digest;/ And of all plays, *Hieronimo*'s the best' (A2ʳ). The play was now decidedly considered *passée*. It did not return to the professional stage for more than three centuries.

As late as 1956 William Empson believed that *The Spanish Tragedy* 'would be very hard to put over on a modern audience'.[36] His discussion of its original staging – 'it looks as if the play-within-the-play was done on the inner stage, with the courtly audience on the balcony' (p. 17) – does not suggest that Empson was much of a theatre director, but his view is understandable. In the wake of Artaud's Theatre of Cruelty, stressing the ferocity of human life, and the beginnings of the Theatre of the Absurd, a dramatic tradition was being established into which *The Spanish Tragedy* fits better than at any time since the late sixteenth and early seventeenth centuries. The successful revival of *Titus Andronicus* in Peter Brook's production of 1955 may have been an indication that the time was ripe for the revival of its earlier sister-play.

The Spanish Tragedy had been staged earlier in amateur productions at Birkbeck College, London in 1921 and in 1931, in the Library of Christ Church College, Oxford, in 1932, at St John's College, Oxford, in 1951, and at the Edinburgh festival of the same year.[37] Performed by the Edinburgh University Dramatic Society, the last production suggested some of the excitement Kyd's play could still convey. One reviewer was 'not in the least surprised that such a play should have had a long reign on the Elizabethan stage'.[38] A number of amateur productions have since followed, including the first known attempt in the United States at the College of William and Mary in Williamsburg, Virginia, in 1976.[39] An Oxford Playhouse production in 1973, directed by Francis Matthews, was notable for its impressive set featuring a 'massive glittering wheel' on which Horatio was murdered, functioning as both an emblematic wheel of fortune and as 'a sadistic parody of Leonardo's Human Figure in a Circle'.[40] The action was set in 'a futuristic "Clockwork Orange" society full of police state uniforms, fluorescent eye make-up, tattooed body stockings and re-inforced concrete music' suggesting a world from which God, justice, and humanity had been exiled.[41]

The play returned to the professional stage in the same decade: the first production at the Mercury Theatre, London, opening on 24 September 1973, was directed by Philip Allen-Morgan, the second at the Citizens' Theatre, Glasgow, opening on 27 October 1978, by Robert David MacDonald.[42] The radical freedom with which the latter production treated the original material fully deserved its advertised qualification 'from the play by Thomas Kyd'. The text was substantially cut, including the 'Vindicta mihi' speech, but passages not only from the 1602 additions but also from *1 Hieronimo* were added. What generations of critics had neglected came naturally to people working in the theatre: *1 Hieronimo* was used to trace the origins of the revenge action and have Andrea killed on stage. Kyd's language, far from being an obstacle, was praised as 'surprisingly musical'.[43] The sinister stage set, suggesting to one reviewer 'an all-purpose execution-chamber', set the tone for an original production which stressed the play's spectacular and outrageous features.[44] Some ideas worked theatrically and at the same time genuinely informed the audience's understanding: Revenge, far from being a static figure, participated in the action as when dropping Bel-imperia's letter before Hieronimo's feet, and Balthazar's trajectory from prisoner to groom and heir to the throne was marked by carefully scaled costume changes. Other directorial ideas seemed less effective, such as the fragmentation of the 'wheel of Fortune' speech (I.iii) recited by a grotesque Viceroy at various moments during the play. Even though one reviewer felt that 'the play's outrageous strengths were perfectly clear', the freedom with which the original was treated may have betrayed a lack of trust in a play which had not yet proved itself on the modern stage.[45]

This mistrust was amended by the next professional production which delivered the text 'as printed in 1592, discreetly slimmed but with its action intact'.[46] Director Michael Bogdanov and the actors of the National Theatre were richly rewarded for their trust in Kyd's original. The warmly received 1982 production did a tremendous service to the play and most reviews convey the sense that 'seeing *The Spanish Tragedy* makes one realize how good a dramatist Thomas Kyd was'.[47] The success of the production was such that it was revived in 1984 and transferred from the intimate Cottesloe to the larger Lyttelton theatre.

The impressive set consisted of a large iron frame, a large chair, and an otherwise bare stage, the two tools being used throughout the performance by various characters. Serving at the same time as the scaffold on which Pedringano is hanged and the bower in which Horatio and Bel-imperia amorously meet, where Hieronimo's son is murdered by Lorenzo and Balthazar, and Isabella runs mad and commits suicide, the simple iron frame established powerful correspondences by means of visual links where the play suggests causal links. Likewise, the out-sized chair successively accommodated the Viceroy, the Knight Marshal, and Revenge, the first two deprived of the power their offices should entitle them to, Revenge in total control even though intermittently dozing off.

One thing the production made clear is that the play's apparent weaknesses and inconsistencies critics had been concerned with disappear on stage. The long set-pieces, Andrea's prologue and the General's speech as well as Hieronimo's soliloquies, sometimes inappropriately described as mere rant, prove no obstacle. On the contrary, 'what comes across as especially exciting is Kyd's own poetic voice – the "grand echoing lines" praised by Empson'.[48] Similarly, the opening scenes, often thought long if not tedious, reveal their own dramatic dynamics:

> The quality of suspense, or rather unease, generated in performance seems to arise from the fact that we the audience must try to find a meaningful pattern in the events and are deliberately frustrated. For we are, after all, watching these scenes in the company of the ragged and blood-stained ghost and his sinister companion, and yet there seems nothing in what happens to enable us to guess what Revenge foresees as emerging from it.[49]

Confined to the prologue and the last few lines of every act, the Ghost of Andrea and Revenge are easily removed from the mind's eye of the reader, but, in Bogdanov's production, were a persistent visual presence on stage. As the revenge plot got fully under way, Revenge, appropriately, was as busy a character as anyone, easily outdoing his counterpart in the Glasgow production, plotting the action by providing glove, letter, sword, dagger, and an empty box, and cunningly swapping a Seneca for Hieronimo's prayer-book.

The play's ending proved as little problematic as the beginning. The deadly play-within-the-play was performed in 'sundry languages' as the stage direction announces, and the Tower of Babel effect was startlingly effective. The courtly audience was seated in the gallery above the stage, clearly visible for the spectators, and their mistaken enjoyment of Hieronimo's deadly play contributed to the poignancy of the scene. As Hieronimo's long explanatory speech concluded the performance, the courtly audience kept laughing and clapping, again mistaking actor for character. Once the court party had realised the catastrophe, there was thus nothing inconsistent about their pressing Hieronimo for explanations he had already given. A last seeming inconsistency disappeared as the grief-maddened Hieronimo mindlessly butchered those around him before killing himself. He clearly did not look for a pertinent reason, as critics have, why he should or should not spare Castile.

Ultimately, the success of the National Theatre production resulted less from staging particulars than from the emotional impact of the tragic characters, especially Michael Bryant's Hieronimo. Well performed, the play is as much a tragedy of grief as a tragedy of revenge. Bogdanov and his actors illustrated that Kyd, rather than a mere dramatist of revenge thrillers and horror stories, 'shows later dramatists what it was to move audiences: not appal or astonish them (though he does all these) but *move* them to sympathy and pity, possibly to tears, and do so to a degree which was unforgettable'.[50]

Less than a year after Bogdanov's production there followed Kyd's professional début on the American stage. The Shakespeare Society of America, directed by Lillian Wilds, performed *The Spanish Tragedy* at the Globe Playhouse in Los Angeles from 20 July to 14 August 1983. As in the National Theatre production, Kyd's original text was only slightly cut and none of the 1602 additions was included. The long narrative beginning came across as 'altogether exciting', suggesting that the stage effectiveness of Kyd's language has been generally underestimated.[51] The production owed most of its success, however, to Jeff Pomerantz's impressive Hieronimo who easily managed the variety of 'mercurially shifting moods' required by the part.[52]

The next professional production followed in 1986, possibly on the play's four hundredth anniversary, performed by the Riverside Shakespeare Company at the Shakespeare Center in New York. As in the Glasgow production, the text was treated with freedom and complemented by passages from *1 Hieronimo*. The narrative introduction in Act I was replaced by its dramatic equivalent in *1 Hieronimo*. It is possible that something similar happened in Kyd's time when *Don Horatio* and *The Spanish Tragedy* were performed as a two-part play on consecutive nights.

The play was served less well by the decision to cut the supernatural frame. Anxious to pare down the play to what Director Ron Daley thinks 'speaks directly to people of the twentieth century', the production also omitted some of the famous passages such as Hieronimo's 'Oh eyes, no eyes' soliloquy.[53] This policy oddly contrasted with an effort to suggest period feeling by means of costumes and staging that tried to capture Kyd's original to the point of bringing to life the famous wood-cut of Horatio's violent death on the title page of the 1615 edition.[54]

The most recent professional production of *The Spanish Tragedy* opened in the Swan Theatre in Stratford-upon-Avon on 30 April 1997. Michael Boyd's Royal Shakespeare Company production was paired with Matthew Warchus's production of *Hamlet* in the Royal Shakespeare Theatre next door. This allowed for instructive comparisons between the two plays. Boyd made good use of the more intimate space at the Swan, repeatedly breaking down the boundaries between actors and audience, with Revenge visiting the pit and with the courtiers seated in the aisles during Hieronimo's bloody play. At the same time the set was simple and efficient: suspended iron pillars, aligned at the back of the stage, formed the wall of a claustrophobic inner space or, pushed forward and spread out, could suggest trees in the bower where Horatio is murdered or the park in which Pedringano kills Serberine.

The text was moderately and intelligently cut, minor alterations in III.xv and IV.iv clearing up what may be the result of textual corruption. Of the five additions added in 1602, only the superior 'painter-scene' was used. Rather than inserting it between III.xii and III.xiii, as *1602* does, or substituting the addition with III.xiii, as may have originally happened on stage, it was instead integrated into the Senex-scene (III.xiii), the painter and Senex becoming one and the same character.[55] The result was a long and powerful scene dramatising Hieronimo's gradual descent into madness.

Like the National Theatre production, Michael Boyd and his actors demonstrated how emotionally powerful Kyd's play can be. In particular, Hieronimo and Isabella grieving over their butchered son formed a highly moving stage picture, a disconcerting mixture of a *pietà* and a Holy Family.

Perhaps the chief merit of the production, however, was to show the breadth of Kyd's achievement by bringing to life characters and scenes that may well seem perfunctory in the text. Balthazar reminded the spectators that few princes were Petrarchan lovers, but many played them. Balthazar, rather than the actor, pretended to be a courtly lover reciting amorous conceits, revealing a more complex character who intermittently surfaced as when shouting out his frustration or grabbing Bel-imperia's breasts. The interesting tension between the smooth Petrarchan lover on the one hand and violence and perversion on the other added a third dimension to a character who can come across as thin and clichèd on the page.

The part of the Ghost of Andrea was similarly enhanced. Far from being confined to the role of mere spectator whose presence is easily forgotten, however, he lived, loved, and suffered through the events as they unfolded on stage, poignantly visible to us yet invisible to Bel-imperia as she redirects her love for Andrea to Horatio in order to further her revenge. Coerced into speaking the prologue, Andrea was the slave rather than the companion of Revenge and came across as a tragic figure whose suffering was made visible centre stage.

The Viceroy was far from a static and pathetic figure in a slim subplot. Rather, he was shown to be a despicable character, self-indulgent in his sorrows (highlighting Kyd's 'feed our sorrows with some inward sighs' (I.iii.6)), heartless, impulsive, and merciless in his decisions. Consequently, the subplot was not a parable of 'justice done' or of 'providence at work', commenting *ex negativo* upon the main plot where justice is not so readily available. Instead it painted a bleak picture of a court where tyranny and treachery reign. In contrast, the atmosphere at the Spanish court in the early scenes was altogether joyous, culminating in Hieronimo's masque at the end of Act I.[56] Here as elsewhere, the RSC production suggested intriguing alternative readings that have not been advanced by critics.[57]

The most memorable effect achieved by the production was not in one of the stagy highlights of the original, but in the seemingly innocuous final lines: as Revenge, dressed as a hangman, announced an 'endless tragedy', he lifted his mask and revealed Hieronimo underneath.[58] Revenge, the production suggests, is not a character but the psychic force that drives the characters, especially Hieronimo. I have shown in the previous chapter that Revenge can be and has been understood in two irreconcilable ways, as a supernatural exterior force (in Seneca's wake) or as an allegorised interior passion (in the tradition of the Morality plays). While the Glasgow, National Theatre, and Los Angeles productions opted for the first interpretation, the RSC production preferred the second. Accordingly, Revenge was sometimes visible, sometimes not, sometimes reduced to a metallic voice, at times slowly moving round the theatre as if sleep-walking, everywhere and nowhere, a pervasive passion governing the characters rather than an active agent stage-managing revenge. This introspective interpretation was in tune with Peter Wight's inward interpretation of the play's hero, conveying a

3   Peter Wight as Hieronimo and Tristan Sturrock as Horatio in Michael
Boyd's RSC production of *The Spanish Tragedy*, 1997.

psychological analysis of bereavement where some only suspected
Kydian rant.

The endless tragedy predicted by Revenge was appropriately
acted out. After a black-out, the tragedy returned to the beginning,
the play having completed a vicious circle only to continue. As in the
very beginning, the characters were seated in a claustrophobic room
reminiscent of Sartre's hell in *Huis Clos*; this time Horatio was
prompted by Revenge to speak the prologue.

Innovative, daring, yet both textually and theatrically solid,
Michael Boyd's RSC production showed that *The Spanish Tragedy*
still offers interpretative room where the long stage histories of most
of Shakespeare's plays defy novelty or tempt to cheap extravagance.
Directors and actors have now shown that 'far from being an
intriguing curiosity, *The Spanish Tragedy* turns out to be a play that
can still triumphantly hold the stage'.[59] We are again in a position
to appreciate Polymetes' tribute to Kyd's Hieronimo in Thomas
May's *The Heire* (1620):

> *Roscio.*   has not your Lordship seene
>   A player personate *Ieronimo*?
> *Polimetes.*   By th'masse tis true, I haue seen the knaue paint
>   griefe
>   In such a liuely colour, that for false

And acted passion he has drawne true teares
From the spectators eyes, Ladyes in the boxes
Kept time with sighes, and teares to his sad accents
As had he truely bin the man he seemd.   (B1ʳ)

It is to be hoped that Kyd's masterpiece will keep its place on the modern stage as one of the great plays of the English dramatic repertory.[60]

Notes

1 *Henslowe's Diary*, ed. Foakes and Rickert, pp. 182, 203.
2 See Anne Barton, *Ben Jonson, Dramatist* (Cambridge, 1984), pp. 13–28, and David Riggs, *Ben Jonson: A Life* (Cambridge, Mass., 1989), pp. 87–91.
3 Barton, *Ben Jonson*, p. 20.
4 Riggs, *Ben Jonson*, p. 87.
5 See Thomas Kyd, *The Spanish Tragedy with Additions 1602*, ed. W. W. Greg, MSR (London, 1925), pp. xviii–xix.
6 Edwards, *ST*, p. lxiv.
7 Schücking, *Die Zusätze zur 'Spanish Tragedy'*, pp. 33–5; Harry Levin, 'An Echo from *The Spanish Tragedy*', MLN, 64 (1949), 297–302; and Edwards, *ST*, p. 145. Note that Anthony Caputi (*John Marston, Satirist* (Ithaca, NY, 1961), pp. 260–1) suggested the second half of 1600 as the most likely date of composition of *Antonio and Mellida*, a date which would still be considerably earlier than Jonson's additions.
8 See *Henslowe's Diary*, ed. Foakes and Rickert, p. 55.
9 Roslyn L. Knutson, 'Influence of the Repertory System on the Revival and Revision of *The Spanish Tragedy* and *Dr. Faustus*', ELR, 18 (1988), 257–74.
10 Note that the 'fly killing' scene in *Titus Andronicus* (III.ii) explores the same aspects: Titus, his madness and his bereavement. Absent from Q1594 and first printed in the Folio of 1623, the scene is probably an addition that was written by Shakespeare himself.
11 John Marston, *Antonio and Mellida*, ed. W. Reavley Gair, The Revels Plays (Manchester, 1991), p. 143. Other reasons concur to suggest that *Antonio and Mellida* was indeed composed late in 1599 or early in 1600 (which, in 'Old Style', would have been referred to as '1599'). See *Antonio and Mellida*, ed. Gair, p. 24; Chambers, III, p. 429.
12 If this is not sufficient evidence against Jonson's authorship, a common words test comparing the additions to both Jonson's and Shakespeare's complete plays on the basis of fifty very common words has shown that 'the additions behave more like the Shakespearean texts than the Jonson ones' (D. H. Craig, 'Authorial Styles and the Frequencies of Very Common Words: Jonson, Shakespeare, and the Additions to *The Spanish Tragedy*', *Style*, 26 (1992), 199–220).
13 Charles Lamb, *Specimens of English Dramatic Writers* (London, 1808), p. 12.
14 *Table Talk*, 1, ed. Carl Woodring (Princeton, 1990), p. 355, in Kathleen

Coburn (ed.), *The Collected Works of Samuel Taylor Coleridge*, vol. 14;
Warren Stevenson, 'Shakespeare's Hand in *The Spanish Tragedy 1602*',
SEL, 8 (1968), 307–21.

15 See H. W. Crundell's three notes 'Dekker's Additions to *The Spanish
    Tragedy*', *NQ*, 164 (1933), 147–9, 'The 1602 Addition to *The Spanish
    Tragedy*', *NQ*, 167 (1934), 88, and 'The Authorship of *The Spanish
    Tragedy*', *NQ*, 180 (1941), 8.

16 Compare 'I pry through every crevice of each wall' (4th addition, l. 17)
    with: 'I pried me through the crevice of a wall' (*Titus Andronicus*,
    V.i.114), and 'Had I as many lives as there be stars,/ As many heavens
    to go to as those lives,/ I'd give them all, ay, and my soul to boot,' (5th
    addition, ll. 12–14) with 'Had I as many soules, as there be Starres,/ I'de
    give them all for *Mephostophilis*' (*Doctor Faustus*, I.iii.330–1).

17 Schücking, *Die Zusätze zur 'Spanish Tragedy'*, pp. 7–21.

18 See Schücking, *Die Zusätze zur 'Spanish Tragedy'*, p. 19.

19 Charles K. Cannon ('The Relation of the Additions of *The Spanish
    Tragedy* to the Original Play', *SEL*, 2 (1962), 229–39) offers a defense of
    the additions and their author's skill in integrating them into Kyd's play:
    'They are parts of a new whole, and the impression made by this new whole
    is a unified one' (p. 236). He argues that '[l]ike counterpoint to a raucous
    melody, those passages, so different in style from the original, carefully
    balance the noisy, brutal action and the raw rhetoric of the old drama with
    a plaintive sound suggesting something eternal and universal' (p. 231).

20 See also G. Wilson Knight's praise of the 'painter scene' in 'Visual Art in
    Kyd and Shakespeare', in *Shakespearian Dimensions* (Brighton, Sussex;
    Totowa, N.J., 1984), 92–109, 95.

21 See Frank Marcham, *The King's Office of the Revels, 1610–1622*
    (London, 1925), and E. K. Chambers' review of this in *RES*, 1 (1925),
    479–84. That the play remained popular is confirmed by the editions of
    1618, 1623, and 1633.

22 See Boas, pp. xcix–c and Elisabeth Mentzel, *Geschichte der
    Schauspielkunst in Frankfurt* (Frankfurt, 1882), pp. 7–24. The play was
    acted by the troupe of Robert Browne which performed on the
    Continent from 1590. Despite its title, Kyd's play has had a far less
    enthusiastic reception in Spain. Its first translation has still not been
    published but is now forthcoming – as part of a collection of revenge
    tragedies – from Gredos (translator José Ramón Díaz-Fernández).

23 For all but the fifth adaptation, see Rudolf Schönwerth, *Die nieder-
    ländischen und deutschen Bearbeitungen von Thomas Kyds 'Spanish
    Tragedy'*, Litterarisch historische Forschungen, 26 (1897) and Henri
    Plard, 'Adaptations de la *Tragédie espagnole* dans les Pays-Bas et en
    Allemagne (1595–1640)', in Jean Jacquot (ed.), *Dramaturgie et Société*,
    2 vols. (Paris, 1968), II, pp. 633–53. See also Ton Hoenselaars, 'The
    Seventeenth-Century Reception of English Renaissance Drama in
    Europe', *SEDERI* (Yearbook of the Spanish Society for English
    Renaissance Studies), 10 (2001), 69–87.

24 Boas printed Ayrer's play in the appendix of his edition.

25 J. A. Worp, 'Die Fabel der *Spanish Tragedy* in einer niederländischen
    Übersetzung des *Orlando Furioso* (1615)', *ShJ*, 30 (1894), 183–91.

26 *Jeronimo Marschalck in Hispanien: Das deutsche Wandertruppen-*

Manuskript der 'Spanish Tragedy', ed. Willi Flemming (Hildesheim, New York, 1973).

27 Ayrer at times seems to misunderstand the original. This may suggest that he did not have access to a printed text but merely saw the play performed. See Julius Tittmann, *Schauspiele aus dem 16. Jahrhundert* (Leipzig, 1868), p. 135.

28 Schönwerth, *Die niederländischen und deutschen Bearbeitungen von Thomas Kyds 'Spanish Tragedy'*, p. lxxxvi.

29 For *Bellemperia*, see Schönwerth, *Die niederländischen und deutschen Bearbeitungen von Thomas Kyds 'Spanish Tragedy'*, pp. xc–cxii and Judith P. Aikin, *Scaramutza in Germany: The Dramatic Works of Caspar Stieler* (London, 1989), pp. 71–6.

30 Schönwerth, *Die niederländischen und deutschen Bearbeitungen von Thomas Kyds 'Spanish Tragedy'*, p. xc.

31 Even Boas (pp. cii–ciii) and Freeman (p. 137) only mention it cursorily.

32 *Jeronimo Marschalck in Hispanien*, ed. Flemming.

33 *Elizabethan Revenge Tragedy*, pp. 63–4.

34 *The Diary of Samuel Pepys*, ed. Robert Latham and William Matthews, 11 vols. (Berkeley and Los Angeles, 1970–83), IX, pp. 89–90. Attention to this performance was first drawn by Freeman, pp. 130–1.

35 See William Van Lennep (ed.), *The London Stage 1660–1800: Part 1: 1660–1700* (Carbondale, Illinois, 1965), pp. xxxviii–xxxix.

36 Empson, '*The Spanish Tragedy*', 23.

37 Edwards, *ST*, p. lxviii.

38 '*The Spanish Tragedy* by Thomas Kyd', *The Times*, 25 August 1951, 6.

39 Tony Howard, 'Census of Renaissance Drama Productions', *RORD*, 20 (1977), 68–9.

40 G. K. Hunter, 'A Census of Renaissance Drama Productions', *RORD*, 17 (1974), 61.

41 Michael Billington, '*Spanish Tragedy* in Oxford', *The Guardian*, 29 November 1973, 10. Note that Andrew James Hartley – reviewing some of the ideas and decisions that went into an amateur production of *The Spanish Tragedy* which he and Kirk Melnikoff directed at the University of Boston in April 1994 – has given an instructive account of how to handle Kyd's language in the modern theatre ('Spaces for Characters in *The Spanish Tragedy*', *CE*, 58 (October 2000), 1–14.

42 Tony Howard, 'Census of Renaissance Drama Productions', *RORD*, 21 (1978), 64–6.

43 B. A. Young, '*The Spanish Tragedy*', *Financial Times* (30 October 1978), 11.

44 *Ibid.*

45 Howard, 'Census of Renaissance Drama Productions' (1978), 66.

46 Richard Proudfoot, 'Kyd's *Spanish Tragedy*', *Cambridge Quarterly*, 25.1 (Spring 1983), 71–6.

47 C. E. McGee, '*The Spanish Tragedy*', *Shakespeare Bulletin* (July/August 1984), 13.

48 Emrys Jones, 'Stage-Managing Revenge', *TLS* (15 October 1982), 1131.

49 *Ibid.*

50 *Ibid.* For further reviews of this production, see Nicholas de Jongh, '*The Spanish Tragedy*', *Plays and Players*, 351 (December 1982), 24–5,

Elizabeth Maslen, 'The Dynamics of Kyd's *Spanish Tragedy*', *English*, 32.143 (Summer 1983), 111–25, Tony Howard, 'Census of Renaissance Drama Productions 1982–83', *RORD*, 26 (1983), 76–7, '*The Spanish Tragedy*', *London Theatre Record* (9–22 September 1982), 512–15, '*The Spanish Tragedy*', *London Theatre Record* (18 June–1 July 1984), 550–2, G. M. Pearce, '*The Spanish Tragedy*', *CE*, 26 (October 1984), 101–3.

51 Joseph H. Stodder, 'Review of *The Spanish Tragedy*', *SQ*, 36 (1985), 477.

52 *Ibid.*

53 Harry Keyishian, 'An Interview with Ron Daley, Director of *The Spanish Tragedy*', *Shakespeare Bulletin* (May/June 1986), 11.

54 See Harry Keyishian, '*The Spanish Tragedy*', *Shakespeare Bulletin* (May/June 1986), 10–11.

55 The textual sequence was: III.xiii.1–163, addition 4, ll. 107–69, addition 4, ll. 54–106, III.xiii.164ff.

56 Hieronimo's masque, reduced to flickering light and the gazes of the courtly audience in Bogdanov's production, was here histrionic and spectacular, the visual feast an Elizabethan audience would have expected.

57 Considering the richness of informative interpretations in the production, some less fortunate ideas, such as the gratuitously incestuous relationship between Lorenzo and Belimperia, were more easily tolerated.

58 This device, incidentally, had been earlier used in a 1987 RSC production of *The Jew of Malta* (directed by Barry Kyle) in the same theatre where Ferneze, speaking the last words, removed his wig to reveal himself as the Machiavel of the prologue.

59 Quoted from Charles Spencer's review of the RSC production in *The Daily Telegraph* on 9 May 1997, reprinted, along with other reviews, in '*The Spanish Tragedy*', *The Theatre Record* (7–20 May 1997), 631–4. See also Peter J. Smith and Greg Walker, '*The Spanish Tragedy*, directed by Michael Boyd for the RSC', *CE*, 52 (October 1997), 113–14, and Elizabeth Schafer, 'Census of Renaissance Drama Productions', *RORD*, 37 (1998), 68–71.

60 In order to complete this twentieth-century stage history, I should add that a fictitious production of *The Spanish Tragedy* occurs in George Garrett's novel *Entered from the Sun* (San Diego, 1991) which deals with the Marlowe-murder-mystery. Another fictional treatment of Kyd's and Marlowe's last months is Robin Chapman's novel *Christoferus or Tom Kyd's Revenge* (London, 1993).

CHAPTER 6

Hamlet

The now lost pre-Shakespearean *Hamlet*, sometimes termed 'Ur-Hamlet' following the usage of German scholars in analogy to Goethe's *Ur-Faust*, must have been performed before Thomas Nashe finished writing the famous 'Preface' to Greene's *Menaphon* (printed 1589, entered 23 August 1589). For the sake of clarity, I will quote Nashe extensively:

> I'le turne backe to my first text, of studies of delight; and talke a little in friendship with a few of our triuiall translators. It is a cōmon practise now a daies amongst a sort of shifting companions, that runne through euery arte and thriue by none, to leaue the trade of *Nouerint* wherto they were borne, and busie themselues with the indeauors of Art, that could scarcelie latinize their necke-verse if they should haue neede; yet English *Seneca* read by candle light yeeldes manie good sentences, as *Bloud is a begger*, and so foorth: and if you intreate him faire in a frostie morning, he will affoord you whole *Hamlets*, I should say handfulls of tragical speaches. But ô griefe! *tempus edax rerum*, what's that will last alwaies? The sea exhaled by droppes will in continuance be drie, and *Seneca* let bloud line by line and page by page, at length must needes die to our stage: which makes his famisht followers to imitate the Kidde in *Æsop*, who enamored with the Foxes newfangles, forsooke all hopes of life to leape into a new occupation; and these men renowncing all possibilities of credit or estimation, to intermeddle with Italian translations: wherein how poorelie they haue plodded, (as those that are neither prouenzall men, nor are able to distinguish of Articles,) let all indifferent Gentlemen that haue trauailed in that tongue, discerne by their twopenie pamphlets: & no meruaile though their home-born mediocritie be such in this matter; for what can be hoped of those, that thrust *Elisium* into hell, and haue not learned so long as they haue liued in such spheares, the iust measure of the Horizon without an hexameter. Sufficeth them to bodge vp a blank verse with ifs and ands, & other while for recreation after their candle stuffe, hauing starched their beardes most curiouslie, to make a peripateticall path into the inner parts of the Cittie, & spend two or three howers in turning ouer French *Doudie*, where they attract more infection in one minute, than they can do eloquence all dayes of their life, by conuersing with anie Authors of like argument.[1]

The characteristic topicality of Nashe's writing may suggest that the play was written not too long before Greene's *Menaphon* was entered. There is little on which to base the dating of the play, but c. 1588/89 seems the best guess. Concerning the play's authorship, the possible allusions to Kyd's father being a scrivener, Kyd's debts to Seneca, his very name, his new occupation as a translator, his 'intermeddling' with an *Italian* translation, the 'home-born mediocrity' of this translation, and Kyd's 'thrusting Elysium into hell' in *The Spanish Tragedy*, I.i.72–5, make it more than likely that Nashe's target is indeed Kyd.

Critical opinion has been far more divided than one might suppose, however. In his edition of the works of Thomas Nashe, McKerrow sums up his analysis as follows:

> Nashe is, I think, speaking not of one writer, but of a group – probably, but not certainly, of dramatists. He did know of a Hamlet play, but the passage throws no light upon its authorship. There is no reason for supposing either Kyd or *The Spanish Tragedy* to be referred to.
>
> (IV, p. 451)

George Ian Duthie, in *The Bad Quarto of 'Hamlet'*, came to the conclusion that 'not one of the phrases which we have examined points directly at Thomas Kyd. One or two of them might possibly serve as corroboration of an attack on Kyd *inter alios*, if that could be shown from positive evidence to be intended' (p. 71).[2] McKerrow's and Duthie's stances may have to be understood as a slightly provocative counter-attack against what they felt had become an all-too-established critical orthodoxy since Boas and Schick. Nobody easily contradicts McKerrow's judgment, but there are obvious reasons for supposing that Kyd is the person to whom Nashe refers.

When it comes to trying to prove McKerrow and Duthie wrong, the arguments advanced by critics have concentrated on the wrong aspects of the Nashe invective. An extended critical debate has centred on the 'Kidde in *Æsop*' and the implications of Nashe's misattribution of the fable to Aesop rather than to Spenser.[3] Finally, the passage in itself proves or disproves nothing. What makes McKerrow's and Duthie's conclusions unacceptable and comes close to proving that Kyd is referred to is Nashe's allusion to those that 'intermeddle with Italian translations' and publish the results in the form of 'twopenie pamphlets'. Kyd's *The Householder's Philosophy* was entered on 6 February 1588. The fact that the translation has several 'gross blunders' (Boas, p. lxiii) perfectly fits Nashe's sneer. However, McKerrow and Duthie's discussions of Nashe's possible allusion to Kyd's translation are perfunctory: McKerrow writes that 'he was by no means the only translator from Italian' (IV, p. 450), a sentence that is taken over *tel quel* by Duthie (p. 67). Even Freeman, who argues against them, does not explore the issue, but solely states that '"triviall translators" who "intermeddle with Italian translations" might well be taken to include the translator of Tasso' (p. 43). We are hence left to suppose that there was a vast number of Italian translators and that our knowledge of Kyd's translation, which, moreover, fits the description 'twopenie pamphlet', does not give any substantial help in the identification of Nashe's target.

Research carried out on Tudor translations contradicts this impression. Julia G. Ebel's 'Numerical Survey of Elizabethan Translations' lists translations into English from various languages, based on the entries in the first edition of the *Short-Title Catalogue* and various supplements.[4] For the four years leading up to 1589 when *Menaphon* and Nashe's *Preface* were published, Ebel lists no more than five translations besides Kyd's. In comparison, for 1589 only, the list includes twenty-one translations from French. A first conclusion emerges: translations from Italian were substantially rarer than McKerrow, Duthie, and Freeman implied.

Mary Augusta Scott undertook an even more comprehensive study of *Elizabethan Translations from the Italian*.[5] She discusses all the translations that could be traced, altogether close to four hundred, ranging in time from 1525 to 1642 and in topic or genre from romances, poetry, and plays to 'science and the arts', 'voyages and discoveries', and 'history and politics'. Of the seventeen works listed under the period from 1586 to 1589, only six need to be considered.[6] Of these, two translations are by Bartholomew Young, a lawyer of the Middle Temple, who clearly does not fit the picture of one of the 'triuiall translators [...] that could scarcelie latinize their necke-verse'.[7] In the remaining four translations, Kyd is in the company of Thomas Hedley, Thomas Hill, and Thomas Hickock, none of whom is very likely to be alluded to by Nashe.[8]

It is possible to raise obvious objections against my argument: the lists which I have consulted are unlikely to be exhaustive; if a work was not entered in the Stationers' Register and is not extant today, it is unlikely that we would know anything about it. Also, a few translations may be disguised as original works.[9] Theoretically, Nashe may even be referring to an Italian translation that is more than four years old, although Nashe's topical style makes this seem rather unlikely: 'how poorelie they haue plodded [...] let all indifferent Gentlemen that have trauailed in that tongue, discerne by their twopenie pamphlets'. This hardly suggests that the pamphlet was published a long time ago. In any case, my general point would still be valid. Italian translations were a rare phenomenon in the years up to 1589 and Nashe could expect that his literary readership would easily identify an allusion to Kyd's *The Householder's Philosophy*.

McKerrow and Duthie argued that Nashe is referring to a group of writers, an assumption which was endorsed by Edwards in his edition of *The Spanish Tragedy* (pp. xxii–xxiii, 139–40). For a substantial part of the passage, however, the allusion to Italian translations makes this interpretation more than doubtful: Seneca's famished followers leap into a new occupation (thereby 'imitat[ing] the Kidde in *Æsop*'), namely Italian translation. Anyone who knows Italian can judge how bad the translation is. But what else can be expected from someone who thrusts Elisium into hell? This large part of Nashe's argument is intimately bound up with the translator from Italian, and Kyd – and only Kyd – is implied in these lines. He alone was born to 'the trade of *Nouerint*', was among 'our triuiall translators' who 'intermeddle with Italian translations' and had them published in 'twopenie pamphlets'.

That Kyd and, in particular, the 'gross blunders' in his translation from Tasso are the target of Nashe's invective is confirmed by a short passage that seems to have escaped the attention of previous commentators. After the lengthy passage quoted above, Nashe goes on to praise several translators, among them Erasmus and More, before returning to Kyd:

> [...] it is daily apparant to our domesticall eyes, that there is none so forward to publish their imperfections, either in the trade of glose or translations, as those that are more vnlearned than ignorance, and lesse conceiuing than infants. (**4ᵛ)

Beside the 'imperfections' in the rendering of Tasso's original, Nashe mocks the occasional glosses Kyd provided which indeed show off more ignorance than learning.[10] Two marginal notes in Latin contain inaccuracies (pp. 256, 281) and several are barely necessary, as when Kyd adds the comment 'Homer in his Odiss.' to a passage which mentions Homer, Penelope, and Circe (p. 273). A further note erroneously assigns to Book II of the *Aeneid* a passage that really belongs to Book I (p. 266).

We can now return to the famous part of Nashe's invective where he similarly mocks those 'that could scarcelie latinize their necke-verse if they should haue neede'. From here, Nashe continues: 'yet English *Seneca* read by candle light yeeldes manie good sentences'.

Why 'read by candle light'? Perhaps Kyd's worst blunder in his translation of Tasso (pointed out by Boas, p. 455) was his mistranslation of 'ad lumina' (till dawn) as 'by candlelight', a mistake Nashe did not fail to tease Kyd with. A few lines later, he even returns to Kyd's blunder by disparagingly referring to the result of his labours as 'candle stuffe'.

Nashe's gibes are at 'those that are more vnlearned than ignorance' and those that 'could scarcelie latinize their necke-verse', but the plurals hide again a single target. It is a rhetorical device Nashe also employs elsewhere: in *The Anatomie of Absurditie*, he seemingly satirises several writers who are 'pretending [...] to anatomize abuses and stubbe vp sin by the rootes' (I, p. 20). In fact, Nashe clearly alludes to the Puritan Philip Stubbes, author of *The Anatomie of Abuses*. Likewise, it is reasonable to assume that Nashe, in the 'Preface' to Greene's *Menaphon*, is thinking of Kyd only. If we remember that Nashe introduces his diatribe with 'I'le [...] talke a little in friendship with a few of our triuiall translators' and if we assume, as seems indeed likely, that these 'triuiall translators' are the same as those who 'intermeddle with Italian translations', it follows that the passage as a whole is directed at Kyd. In all probability, the play to which the arguably most famous piece of English literature is heavily indebted is thus indeed his.

One of the few things we know about Kyd's *Hamlet* is that, contrary to Belleforest's novella, it featured a ghost. A passage in Lodge's *Wit's Miserie* (1596) speaks of 'ye ghost which cried so miserally at ye Theator like an oister wife, *Hamlet, reuenge*'.[11] It seems plausible to take the direct address in Lodge's quotation to imply that the Ghost in Kyd's *Hamlet* was not confined to a narrative frame as he is in *The Spanish Tragedy*, but that, like Shakespeare's ghost, he took an active part in the play. Even though Shakespeare's Ghost probably owes his existence to Kyd's, it is a matter of mere conjecture to what extent Kyd's play raised the same complex issues concerning his nature.

An enormous scholarly effort has been put into an appraisal of Kyd's *Hamlet* and its relation to both the first quarto of Shakespeare's *Hamlet* (1603) and the later German version *Der bestrafte Brudermord* (*Fratricide Punished*). The most thorough study is still Duthie's *The Bad Quarto of 'Hamlet'* which convincingly argues that Q1 is not a substantive text, but derives from what is probably a shortened version of the play underlying the second quarto (1604/5).[12] Also, although it possibly contains some elements present in Kyd's *Hamlet* and absent from Q2, *Der bestrafte Brudermord* is principally based upon Q2. No important inferences about the lost *Hamlet* can therefore be drawn from the German play.

Attempts to recreate Kyd's *Hamlet* in detail with the help of Q1 – undertaken by several scholars, including Fredson Bowers in *Elizabethan Revenge Tragedy* (1940) and Félix Carrère in *Le Théâtre de Thomas Kyd* (1951) – are therefore bound to fail. Also, Boas's conviction that 'the last three acts [of Q1] are almost entirely pre-Shakespearean, and that the Stratford dramatist found the *scenario* of *Hamlet* fully sketched out for him by an earlier playwright' (p. l) is no longer tenable. If we choose to refrain from mere guess-work, the texts of Shakespeare's play allow no inferences about Kyd's play – perhaps with one exception.[13] Q1 contains a brief scene, situated after what corresponds to IV.v in modern editions, of which there is no equivalent in Q2 and F:

> *Enter* HORATIO *and the* QUEENE.
>
> Horatio.   Madame, your sonne is safe arriv'de in *Denmarke*,
>   This letter I euen now receiv'd of him,
>   Whereas he writes how he escap't the danger,
>   And subtle treason that the king had plotted,
>   Being crossed by the contention of the windes,   5
>   He found the Packet sent to the king of *England*,
>   Wherein he saw himselfe betray'd to death,
>   As at his next conuersion with your grace,
>   He will relate the circumstance at full.
> Queene.   Then I perceiue there's treason in his lookes   10
>   That seem'd to sugar o're his villanie:
>   But I will soothe and please him for a time,
>   For murderous mindes are alwayes jealous,
>   But know not you *Horatio* where he is?
> Horatio.   Yes Madame, and he hath appoynted me   15
>   To meete him on the east side of the Cittie
>   To morrow morning.
> Queene.   O faile not, good *Horatio*, and withall, commend me
>   A mothers care to him, bid him a while
>   Be wary of his presence, lest that he   20
>   Faile in that he goes about.
> Horatio.   Madam, neuer make doubt of that:
>   I thinke by this the news be come to court:
>   He is arriv'de, obserue the king, and you shall
>   Quickely finde, *Hamlet* being here,   25
>   Things fell not to his minde.
> Queene.   But what became of *Gilderstone* and *Rossencraft*?

> *Horatio.*   He being set ashore, they went for *England,*
>   And in the Packet there writ down that doome
>   To be perform'd on them poynted for him: 30
>   And by great chance he had his fathers Seale,
>   So all was done without discouerie.
> *Queene.*   Thankes be to heauen for blessing of the prince,
>   *Horatio* once againe I take my leaue,
>   With thowsand mothers blessings to my sonne.
> *Horatio.*   Madam adue.   (H2ᵛ–H3ʳ)

In Q2, the Queen does not appear in the corresponding scene (IV.vi).
A sailor delivers a letter from Hamlet to Horatio announcing his
return and hinting at the villainy of Rosencrantz and Guildenstern.
This is complemented by the beginning of V.ii (of which there is no
direct equivalent in Q1) where Hamlet relates to Horatio his discovery of Claudius' plot against him (ll. 1–74). In Q1, contrary to Q2,
the Queen is thus made aware of the 'subtle treason that the king
had plotted' to murder her son. As a consequence, her character
significantly deviates from the one we know from Q2 and F. She is
firmly on Hamlet's side, whereas she remains a more ambiguous
figure in the play as we know it. This is supported by brief passages
in the closet scene of Q1 which have no equivalent in the other texts:

> *Queene.*   But as I haue a soule, I sweare by heauen,
>   I neuer knew of this most horride murder: (G3ʳ)

In Q1, the closet scene ends as follows:[14]

> *Hamlet.*   And mother, but assist me in reuenge,
>   And in his death your infamy shall die.
> *Queene.*   *Hamlet,* I vow by that maiesty,
>   That knowes our thoughts, and lookes into our hearts,
>   I will conceale, consent, and doe my best,
>   What stratagem soe're thou shalt deuise.   (G3ʳ⁻ᵛ)

In Q2, the equivalent lines are:

> *Hamlet.*   To try conclusions, in the basket creepe,
>   And breake your owne necke downe.
> *Gertrude.*   Be thou assur'd, if words be made of breath
>   And breath of life, I haue no life to breath
>   What thou hast sayd to me.   (I4ᵛ)

Significantly, this more sympathetic treatment of the Queen
mirrors Belleforest's tale which was Kyd's source. Belleforest's
Hamlet also uses the word 'infamie' in exactly the same context.[15]
The following passage, excerpted from her lengthy *apologia* to
Hamlet in the sequence corresponding to the closet scene, shows
further similarities:

[...] swearing unto thee (by the majestie of the Gods) that if it had layne in my power to have resisted the tyrant, although it had beene with the losse of my blood, yea and my life, I would surely have saved the life of my lord and husband with as good a will and desire as, since that time, I have often beene a meanes to hinder and impeach the shortning of thy life, which being taken away, I will no longer live here upon earth. For seeing that thy sences are whole and sound, I am in hope to see an easie meanes invented for the revenging of thy fathers death.[16]

Like the Queen in Q1, Belleforest's Queen explicitly supports Hamlet's revenge on the King, whereas in Q2 and F, she only promises to keep secret what Hamlet has imparted to her. Belleforest and Q1 also share the Queen's profession of her innocence in the murder of her first husband. It is tempting to go so far as to identify a possible verbal echo of Belleforest in Q1: 'I vow by that maiesty', a phrase absent from Q2 and F, recalls Belleforest's 'swearing unto thee (by the majestie of the Gods)' (in the original: 'te jurant par la haute majesté des Dieux') appearing in roughly the corresponding place.[17] This, however, may also be a mere coincidence. Yet, the cumulative evidence suggests that a number of elements in Q1, chiefly related to the Queen's role, are markedly different from Q2 and F but apparently indebted to Belleforest. It cannot be assumed that the reporters of Q1 knew Belleforest. A possible inference is that they had knowledge of Kyd's play and that in reconstructing Shakespeare's play they had recourse to it for some features – in particular for the encounter between Horatio and the Queen before Hamlet's return from England. E. K. Chambers came up with the ingenious suggestion that 'the reporter might have been the Queen, as a boy, in the old play, and helped himself out with memories of that', a hypothesis elaborated by W. W. Greg.[18] This seems to me less plausible, however, than the possibility that Q1 imperfectly recovers a stage adaptation – perhaps undertaken by Shakespeare himself which would explain the presence of Belleforest – that already contained the scene with the Queen and Horatio. Since we are dealing with a text which, after all, is irretrievably lost, these conjectures will have to remain purely hypothetical.

Henslowe mentions a performance of *Hamlet* on 9 June 1594 at the Newington Butts theatre with the modest taking of 8s. He does not mark the play 'ne' (new). The low attendance need not imply that the play was a failure, and the reference in Lodge's *Wit's Misery* in 1596 suggests that the play was in fact well-known. Due to its inconvenient location, south of the Thames at a considerable distance from London Bridge, Newington Butts never became one of the principal theatres. In 1592, the Privy Council had ordered Strange's Men to stop playing there 'by reason of the tediousness of the waie and that of longe tyme plaies haue not there bene vsed on working daies'.[19] Two years later, the combined Admiral's and Chamberlain's company played at Newington Butts for a short season. The average taking was a modest 9s., little more than the income for the *Hamlet* performance.

As *Hamlet* was played by the combined Admiral's and Chamberlain's company and disappears from Henslowe's diary after the performance on 9 June 1594, there is a strong presumption that it belonged to the repertoire of Shakespeare's company. This is confirmed by Lodge's mention of 'the Theator' where the Chamberlain's Men played from 1594 to 1597. It is difficult to determine from which company it passed into the hands of the Chamberlain's Men. According to the title page of the second quarto, *Titus Andronicus* seems to have passed from Strange's/Derby's, to Pembroke's, to Sussex's, and finally to Chamberlain's Men. It is not impossible that Kyd's *Hamlet* followed the same trajectory.

Kyd's *Hamlet* may well have been a highly topical play when it was first performed. On 10 February 1567, Henry Stuart, Lord Darnley, Queen Mary's husband, was murdered in a plot which had been laid by James Hepburn, fourth Earl of Bothwell, confidant of Queen Mary. It seems likely that Mary was aware of the plot against her husband's life. On 15 May, little more than three months later, the Queen married Bothwell. Kyd's *Hamlet* was not created until two decades later; but in 1587, presumably shortly before Kyd composed *Hamlet*, a Latin poem was written in which the Ghost of Darnley addresses his son James VI. The Ghost of Darnley, James VI, Mary, and Bothwell closely correspond to Ghost of Hamlet's father, Hamlet, Gertrude, and Claudius.[20] Although the poem is not known to have been printed, it circulated in manuscript in Paris (where it was written), Scotland, and probably also in London.[21]

Kyd's source for the Pedringano episode in *The Spanish Tragedy* was in all probability *The Copie of a Leter* (1584), a book relating Leicester's alleged Machiavellian practices. It was published in Paris and smuggled into England, where it was suppressed by royal proclamation on 12 October 1584. Despite its consequent rarity, the stories were notorious since a multitude of manuscript versions circulated in London. The topicality of Kyd's *Hamlet* may have been even more daring. Casting James VI in the role of Hamlet seeking revenge for the murder of his parent is less than innocuous shortly after Mary's execution. Kyd's Senecan revenge tragedies seem, at first sight, to be securely removed from contemporary politics. Yet, for audiences readily on the look-out for topicality – more likely to see an allusion to contemporary matters when the author intended none than to miss a hint when the author intended one – Kyd's plays may have borne hidden treasures. Edmund Tilney, Master of the Revels, apparently found 'no offence in't', but others may have been more receptive to Kyd's topicality.

Notes

1 Robert Greene, *Menaphon* (London, 1589), **3^{r-v}. McKerrow follows the 1610 edition. See the discussions of this passage by Boas (pp. xx–xxiv) and Freeman (pp. 39–48).

2 Notice that E. A. J. Honigmann ('Shakespeare's "Lost Source-Plays"', *MLR*, 49 (1954), 293–307) similarly believes that '[f]rom Nashe's Epistle no valid clue for the authorship of the old *Hamlet* can be inferred' (p. 299), and goes on to suggest that the possibility of Shakespeare's authorship cannot be excluded.

3 Emil Köppel, 'G. Sarrazin's *Thomas Kyd und sein Kreis*' (*ES*, 18 (1893), 130) demonstrated that the fable to which Nashe is referring is not in Aesop, but in Spenser's May eclogue of *The Shepheardes Calendar*. V. Østerberg (*Studier over Hamlet-Teksterne* (Copenhagen, 1920)), paraphrased by J. Dover Wilson ('Nashe's "Kid in Aesop": A Danish Interpretation', *RES*, 18 (1942), 385–94), argued that the only reason why Nashe brings in this analogy is in order to pun on Kyd's name. His argument was challenged by Edwards (*ST*, pp. 139–40).

4 *The Library*, 5th Series, 22 (1967), 104–27.

5 (Boston, 1916).

6 I exclude reprints of works previously published (such as Arthur Brooke's *Tragicall historie of Romeus and Juliet*), stories 'told in the Italian manner' rather than genuine translations, and works translated into English from several languages (such as *The Arcadian Rhetorike*, a mixture of prose and verse translated from a great variety of sources, or Anthony Munday's *Palmerin d'Oliva*, a translation from Spanish, Italian, and French). I also exclude two Folios which, due to their size, hardly qualify as 'twopenie pamphlets'.

7 *Amorous Fiametta* (1587), a translation of Boccaccio's romance *L'Amorosa Fiametta*, and *The ciuile conuersation of M. Steeuen Guazzo* (1586).

8 Hedley is the author of *The Banishment of Cupid* (1587) translated from an Italian romance, Hill of *A Briefe and pleasant Treatise, Intituled: Naturall and Artificiall Conclusions* (1586), and Hickock translated *The Voyage and Travaile: of M. C. Frederick* (1588).

9 For instance, Fraunce's English translation of Watson's Latin *Amyntas* only acknowledged its debt on the title page of the fourth edition.

10 See also Boas, p. xviii.

11 *The Complete Works of Thomas Lodge*, ed. Edmund Gosse, 4 vols.

(Glasgow, 1883), IV, p. 62.

12 In the meantime, the pendulum has swung back and the possibility that the play behind *Hamlet* Q1 is earlier than the play behind the long texts Q2 and F is again examined. See the essays of Alan C. Dessen, G. R. Hibbard, and Steven Urkowitz in Thomas Clayton (ed.), *The 'Hamlet' First Published (Q1, 1603): Origins, Form, Intertextualities* (Newark, 1992). The case for Q1's derivative nature seems to me more convincing, however. Other scholars have even revived the theory that Q1 Hamlet may represent the *Hamlet* Nashe refers to in 1589 (see, for instance, Eric Sams, 'Taboo or Not Taboo? The Text, Dating and Authorship of *Hamlet*, 1589–1623', *Hamlet Studies*, 10 (1988), 12–46, and Leah S. Marcus, *Unediting the Renaissance: Shakespeare, Marlowe, Milton* (London, 1996), 132–76, esp. 147–9). In the light of these arguments, it needs to be stressed that in Nashe's 'Preface' to *Menaphon*, nothing supports and much contradicts the possibility of Shakespeare's authorship.

13 For a history of the unwarranted claims that have been made about the lost *Hamlet*, see Emma Smith, 'Ghost Writing: *Hamlet* and the Ur-Hamlet', in Andrew Murphy (ed.), *The Renaissance Text: Theory, Editing, Textuality* (Manchester and New York, 2000), 177–90.

14 Things are further complicated by the fact that these lines also recall a passage from *The Spanish Tragedy*, as Q1 repeatedly does. Preparing their revenge for Horatio's murder, Bel-imperia says: 'Hieronimo, I will consent, conceal,/ And aught that may effect for thine avail,/ Join with thee to revenge Horatio's death' (IV.i.46–8). It has been shown that the reporter(s) drew also on other plays that must have been in his/their mind(s) to fill in the gaps resulting from failing memory (see Chambers, *William Shakespeare*, 2 vols. (Oxford, 1930), I, p. 422).

15 See Sir Israël Gollancz, *The Sources of 'Hamlet'* (Oxford, 1926), p. 216.

16 I quote from 'The Hystorie of Hamblet' (1608), a more or less literal rendering of Belleforest printed by Bullough (VII, pp. 81–124).

17 See Gollancz, *The Sources of 'Hamlet'*, p. 220. Bullough does not print the text from Belleforest.

18 Chambers, *William Shakespeare*, I, p. 421; Greg, *Shakespeare and the Editorial Problem*, pp. 67–8. For a different explanation of the origin of this scene in Q1, see Giorgio Melchiori, '*Hamlet*: The Acting Version and the Wiser Sort', in *The 'Hamlet' First Published (Q1, 1603)*, pp. 195–210, esp. pp. 205–6.

19 Chambers, II, p. 405 and IV, p. 313.

20 The poem is printed by Bullough, VII, pp. 125–7.

21 See Bullough, VII, p. 19.

CHAPTER 7

Soliman and Perseda:
an introduction

Printed by Edward Allde for Edward White, the first edition of *Soliman and Perseda* is undated. It is generally assumed to have been printed not long after the play was entered in the Stationers' Register in November 1592. Its format is a quarto, but as the chain lines are vertical, indicating that the text was printed on double-sized paper cut in half, it is technically speaking an octavo-in-fours.[1] According to the title page, the full title reads: 'THE/ TRAGEDYE OF/ SOLYMAN AND/ PERSEDA. *Wherein is laide open, Loues/ constancy, Fortunes incon-/ stancy and Deaths/ Triumphs.*'

The second edition of 1599 is dividable into two issues (sometimes mistakenly assumed to be two editions). Some copies have stamped in 'Newly corrected and amended'. Even though it contains one major instance of textual corruption, O1 is clearly the authoritative text.[2] The problems an editor of the play faces thus cannot be compared with those inherent in the texts of some Shakespearean plays. It is all the more regrettable that there is still no satisfactory modern edition of *Soliman and Perseda*. The texts in Dodsley and Hawkins share the limitations of their times. Boas's text adopts numerous (mis-)readings from a type-facsimile of 1810 which he mistook to be an original. John S. Farmer was also taken in: his facsimile of *Soliman and Perseda* of 1913 reproduces the edition of 1810. J. J. Murray produced an edition of the play in a 1959 Ph.D. thesis, and the edition was published more than forty years later in the Garland series.[3] Freeman rightly pointed out that the edition of 1959 is unreliable both textually and critically, and, unfortunately, the publication of 1991 shows little improvement. We thus still lack a single satisfactory edition of what is in many ways an important play.

The printed text shows a number of features that indicate corruption in the process of textual transmission: an important number of lines scan poorly and many verses are a syllable short. Alfred Hart took this to suggest the presence of a reporter:

> Perhaps the best evidence of a reporter's presence is the large number of twelve-syllable lines [...]. In addition there are thirty unscannable lines of eleven syllables; in many of these the extra syllable is a monosyllabic enclitic such as 'but', 'and', 'for', 'why', etc. prefixed to an ordinary deca-syllabon. Most of these defects are undoubtedly the works of actors.[4]

Some passages are difficult to identify as either prose or verse (for example, I.iii.79–120), and the stage directions may suggest further irregularities. Many of the latter are headed by the word 'then', an odd feature only shared by the contemporary *Arden of Faversham* which has also been argued to be a report. One stage direction clearly takes up a word from the main text ('tumbled down', V.ii.129.1, cf. V.ii.128), a well-known feature of reports. Most importantly, perhaps, *Soliman and Perseda*, along with *The Taming of a Shrew*, *The Contention of the Two Famous Houses of York and Lancaster*, and *The True Tragedy of Richard Duke of York*, belongs to a group of plays performed by Pembroke's Men which have long been thought to be reported.[5] Even though Laurie Maguire's study of *Shakespearean Suspect Texts* has taught us to be wary of resorting too easily to the explanation 'memorial reconstruction', the evidence that *Soliman and Perseda* contains textual corruption of some kind is strong.

'[T]he tragedye of SALAMON and PERCEDA' (Arber, II, p. 622) was entered in the Stationers' Register to Edward White on 22 November 1592 which constitutes the *terminus ad quem* for the play's composition. As for the *terminus a quo*, the following passage indicates that *Soliman and Perseda* is later than *2 Tamburlaine* (c. 1587):[6]

> Why, sawst thou not how *Cupid*, God of loue,
> Not daring looke me in the marshall face,
> Came like a coward stealing after me,
> And with his pointed dart prickt my posteriors?   (IV.ii.43–6)

This is a parody of

> See where my slave, the uglie monster death
> Shaking and quivering, pale and wan for feare,
> Stands aiming at me with his murthering dart,
> Who flies away at every glance I give,
> And when I look away, comes stealing on: (*2 Tamburlaine*, V.iii.67–71)

While *Soliman and Perseda* thus alludes to *2 Tamburlaine*, it is, I believe, referred to by *The Jew of Malta* which allows us to narrow down its date of composition. Marlowe's play contains the following allusion to the siege of Rhodes:

> Small though the number was that kept the Towne,
> They fought it out, and not a man surviv'd
> To bring the haplesse newes to Christendome. (II.ii.49–51)

Recent editors of *The Jew of Malta*, Siemon (New Mermaids, p. 39) and Bawcutt (Revels Plays, pp. 5, 104), have pointed out that this is historically inaccurate. Bawcutt explains:

> In fact the Knights surrendered on terms and were allowed to leave by the Turks. There were literally dozens of accounts of these events available to Marlowe, in several languages, and he can hardly have failed to know the truth. (p. 5)

What has not been noticed is that Marlowe followed the recent *Soliman and Perseda*, which his audience would still have remembered, rather than any of the 'dozens' of historical accounts. The final scene of Kyd's play precisely dramatises Rhodes' refusal to give in to the Turks and stages the final battle. As Soliman realises that he is dying from the poison on Perseda's lips, he commands: 'Souldiers, assault the towne on every side;/ Spoile all, kill all; let none escape your furie' (V.iv.121–2). Marlowe's allusion to the death of the Duke of Guise on 23 December 1588 ('And now the *Guize* is dead' (Prologue, l. 3)) suggests that *The Jew of Malta* was composed not long after that date and scholars agree on 1589 or 1590 as the likely date of composition.

Shakespeare's *King John* is a further important play for the dating of *Soliman and Perseda*. The Bastard's well-known reference to 'Basilisco' (I.i.244) establishes Kyd's play to be older than Shakespeare's. The dating of *King John* is one of the thorny problems of Shakespeare scholarship and any year from 1589 to 1597 has been suggested as date of composition. While the majority of earlier critics opted for a relatively late date and argued that Shakespeare's main source was the anonymous *Troublesome Reign*, the view that *King John* pre-dates *Troublesome Reign* has found weighty supporters since the 1950s.[7] The first quarto of *Troublesome Reign* was printed in 1591, and the title page claims that the play had been 'sundry times' acted. If *Troublesome Reign* post-dates Shakespeare's play, *Soliman and Perseda* could hardly have been written after 1589.

In 'Shakespeare and *Solyman and Perseda*', Arthur Freeman tried to solve the problem of the order of *King John* and *The Troublesome Reign* by arguing that *Soliman and Perseda* is post-1591. The argu-

ment is not convincing. The only evidence he adduces in favour of
1591/1592 is the link he perceives between *Selimus*, a play that is
often attributed to Greene, and the scene dramatising the fraternal
killings in *Soliman and Perseda* (I.v). In *Selimus* (composed no
earlier than 1591), Acomat and Corcut both die at the hands of their
brother, whereas Soliman kills Amurath in revenge of his murder of
Haleb.[8] Kyd deals with these events in one scene, whereas the two
fratricides in *Selimus* are separated by several scenes and other
killings. Although it is true that the scene in *Soliman and Perseda* is
unaccounted for by the play's source, Kyd may have got the suggestion through many other channels than *Selimus*. Alleged Turkish
cruelty was proverbial and stories of fratricide among Turks
common knowledge. Kyd might just as well have had in mind
Amurath's historical killing of his five brothers in 1574. Accounts of
this would have been available to Kyd in several sources, for
instance in Whetstone's *English Myrror* of 1586 from which
Marlowe took suggestions for his *Tamburlaine*.

The Spanish Tragedy is the last play in relation to which the
dating of *Soliman and Perseda* has to be considered. Although critical opinion has not been unanimous, *The Spanish Tragedy* is
probably the earlier of the two plays by a few years. Kyd seems likely
to have first introduced the story of Soliman and Perseda in the play-
within-the-play in *The Spanish Tragedy*, and to have elaborated it
subsequently in an independent work. Kyd would hardly have felt
the need to summarise the story before Hieronimo's play if the spectators had already been acquainted with it. *Soliman and Perseda*
may well have been an attempt to capitalise on the enormous success
of *The Spanish Tragedy*.[9] I have argued that *The Spanish Tragedy*
was composed no later than 1587 which, in conjunction with the
indebtedness of *Soliman and Perseda* to *2 Tamburlaine*, would
establish the order of composition. The verbal parallels between the
two plays do little or nothing to determine the order of composition,
but apart from that the evidence is strongly in favour of a later date
for *Soliman and Perseda*.

The dating of *Soliman and Perseda* is hence best attempted in
simultaneously absolute and relative terms. On the one hand, it must
have been written before November 1592. On the other hand, the
play is post-*2 Tamburlaine*, pre-*King John*, and probably post-
Spanish Tragedy and pre-*Jew of Malta*. It seems therefore likely that
Soliman and Perseda was written in 1588 or 1589.

The early editions are anonymous and there is no unambiguous external evidence to settle the question of authorship once and for all. Computer analyses are not likely to prove anything either way, since an undoubted corpus of one play plus a translation from a French play is not much on which to base an investigation. Yet, the argument for Kyd's authorship advanced by Sarrazin (pp. 43–8), Boas (pp. lvi–lx), and Freeman (pp. 140–6) is difficult to resist. In Freeman's words: 'the case for Kyd is quite strong, perhaps as strong as the attribution of *Tamburlaine* to Marlowe' (p. 140). He readily dispenses with the implausible case for Peele, and no other known playwright suggests himself for possible authorship. He concludes: 'By the most conservative standards of cataloguing, of course, the play must remain "anonymous", but for the special purposes of scholars and readers in the period I think it safe to assign *Soliman and Perseda* to Kyd' (p. 146).

Since Hawkins first suggested Kyd's authorship in 1773, the most important but by no means the only argument for Kyd's authorship has been the great dramaturgical similarities with *The Spanish Tragedy*. The play dramatises the story of Soliman and Perseda using both Wotton's novella and Kyd's *The Spanish Tragedy* as Sarrazin (p. 42) has shown. Both plays feature allegorical figures in a dramatic frame. Like *The Spanish Tragedy* (I.iii), *Soliman and Perseda* introduces a subplot fairly early which, at that stage, is only loosely connected to the main plot. Both plays contain a love scene early in the play and the amorous encounter of Ferdinando and Lucina (II.i) is clearly modelled upon that of Horatio and Bel-imperia (II.iv). Alexandro and Erastus are both victims of mock trials. Both plays end in a weakly motivated blood bath. Perhaps more convincing still than these parallels is the evidence obtained from a close investigation of Kyd's narrative source: in an important number of cases, the author of *Soliman and Perseda*, when departing from his main source, is clearly influenced by the scenic form of *The Spanish Tragedy*. In short, no evidence contradicts and much evidence supports the case for Kyd's authorship of *Soliman and Perseda*.

None of Kyd's editors and critics has pointed out that there is a thread of external evidence linking the play with Kyd. This was first shown in Helen Gardner's edition of Donne's *Elegies and Songs and Sonnets*.[10] Gardner shows that underlying Donne's elegy 'The Bracelet: Upon the Losse of His Mistresses Chaine, for Which He Made Satisfaction' is the loss and recovery of the bracelet Perseda offered Erastus, as dramatised in Acts I and II of *Soliman and Perseda*. The poem mocks what must have seemed to Donne a hopelessly romantic play about 'that seely old moralitie,/ That as those links are tyed our love should be' (ll. 5–6).[11] Donne's 'loud-squeaking Cryer' (l. 55), who 'like a devill rore[s] through every street' (l. 57) to recover the chain, specifically alludes to the crier in I.iv and makes it difficult to doubt Gardner's argument. She goes on to suggest that the lines 'libells, or some interdicted thinge,/ Which negligently kept thy ruine bringe' (ll. 101–2) are 'a topical reference to the misfortunes that befell Kyd in 1593' (p. 112). Kyd's papers were searched for a 'libel that concern'd the state'.[12] He claimed that he had the 'vile hereticall Conceiptes' for which he was imprisoned from Marlowe.[13] That they had been, in Kyd's words, 'shufled wth some of mine' squares with Donne's 'negligently kept'. The papers found in his possession did bring his ruin insofar as he lost his patron, seems to have been tortured in prison and died the year after. Gardner conjecturally dates the poem 'not much after 1593' (p. 112).[14] All these coincidences considered, I agree with her conclusions that 'it is difficult not to see a reference in Donne's lines to Kyd's negligent keeping of a dangerous document' (p. 118) and that Donne appears to establish a connection between *Soliman and Perseda* and its author Thomas Kyd.

If Donne's poem cannot finally prove the case for Kyd's authorship, it corroborates strong internal evidence. If we want to have a clearer picture of Kyd's artistic qualities as well as of his historical importance, we do well to count the play among his works.

As with many contemporary plays, the early stage history which the extant records allow us to trace is riddled with holes and question marks. The title page of the early texts names no company. J. J. Murray (p. xxi) unconvincingly argued that Basilisco's ass could not have been accommodated on the public stage, a point Freeman easily refuted (p. 157). Shakespeare's, Donne's and Dekker's (see below) allusions to the play argue that the play was performed and popular.

Inter-play borrowings indicate that the play was probably performed by actors who were involved in the reconstruction of the *True Tragedy of Richard Duke of York* (*TT*), the 'bad' quarto of Shakespeare's *3 Henry 6* (*3H6*):[15]

S&P	Ah stay, no more; for I can heere no more.	(II.ii.28)
TT	O speake no more, for I can heare no more.	(B3ᵛ)
3H6	O, speak no more, for I have heard too much.	(II.i.48)
S&P	Their horse, I deeme them fiftie thousand strong;	(III.i.48)
TT	Their power I gesse them fifty thousand strong.	(B5ᵛ)
3H6	Their power, I think, is thirty thousand strong.	(II.i.177)

S&P	I, saist thou so? why, then it shall be so:	(IV.i.242)
TT	I, saist thou so boie? why then it shall be so.	(A7ʳ)
3 H6	[no equivalent]	

It appears that whoever prepared the manuscript from which *The True Tragedy* was set up occasionally had recourse to *Soliman and Perseda*. The *True Tragedy* was printed in 1595 and, according to the title page, had been acted by Pembroke's Men.

The compliment to the Queen in the closing lines of the play (V.v.37–41) suggests court performance, but we are left to wonder why the title page does not advertise this as other play-texts do. If *Soliman and Perseda* was performed at court, it may well have been one of the two plays acted by Pembroke's Men on 26 December (St Stephen's Day) 1592 and 6 January (the Feast of the Epiphany) 1593. The play had in fact been entered only a few weeks earlier (20 November 1592). That *Soliman and Perseda* may have become the property of the same company and remained so until at least 1597 is corroborated by Dekker's Horace – in *Satiromastix* (1601) – who claims to have played 'Zulziman' at 'Parris garden' (IV.i.122–3).[16] Pembroke's Men had made an agreement in 1597 to play at the Swan which stood in the Liberty and Manor of Paris Garden on the Bankside.[17]

If Pembroke's Men owned *Soliman and Perseda* until at least 1597, we still do not know for which company Kyd wrote his play. Pembroke's Men came into existence late in 1591, later, that is, than *Soliman and Perseda*.[18] Kyd wrote for the Queen's Men from c. 1583–85, but none of his extant plays can in any way be convincingly linked to this company. When Henslowe starts his diary early in 1592, *The Spanish Tragedy* and *Don Horatio* belong to Strange's Men and it is possible that *Soliman* had been owned by the same company. *Titus Andronicus* seems to have passed from Strange's/Derby's Men to Pembroke's Men before being acted by Sussex's Men on 28 January 1594 and subsequently by the Lord Chamberlain's Men.[19] Kyd's *Hamlet*, performed by the joint Lord Admiral's and Lord Chamberlain's Men in a short season at the Newington Butts in June 1594 along with *Titus*, and, according to Lodge's *Wit's Miserie*, again acted at the Theatre (that is, by the Lord Chamberlain's Men) in 1596, ended up with the same company. It is possible then that *Soliman and Perseda*, like *Titus*, and perhaps *Hamlet*, passed from Strange's Men to Pembroke's Men, but, unlike the two other plays, remained in their possession when the companies broke up and reformed in 1593/94.[20]

Kyd's chief source was the tale of Soliman and Persida from Henry Wotton's *A Courtlie Controuersie of Cupids Cautels* (1578), a translation of Jacques Yver's *Le Printemps d'Yver* (1572). The use Kyd makes of his source will be studied in the next chapter. J. J. Murray investigated the dramatic ancestors of Basilisco, the 'miles gloriosus', and of Pistan, the fool and suggested that Kyd may well be indebted to the Italian *commedia dell'arte* (pp. xvi–xx). The anonymous *Rare Triumphs of Love and Fortune* has been suggested as the source of the play's frame, consisting of the allegorical figures Fortune, Love, and Death (Freeman, p. 148). Dramatic frames with allegorical characters were far from rare, however, and Fortune, Love, and Death are repeatedly referred to and addressed by the main characters of Wotton's novella.

In the above examples, critics seem to have been too eager to find a definite source in instances where Kyd was in no need of one. In contrast, one clearly identifiable source has so far passed unnoticed. The passage in François de Belleforest's edition (Paris, 1575) of Sebastian Münster's *Cosmographie Universelle* is all the more interesting as Kyd's one-time writing companion Marlowe appears to have used the very same passage in *2 Tamburlaine*:

> I am sorry not to be familiar with the name of a certain Greek woman, despite the fact that she was not conspicuous for her chastity. This lady was mistress to the governor of the fort of Rhodes, who, as soon as she heard that her lord and lover had died fighting valiantly, and as he was also a man of honour, took the two children she had had by the said lord, and kissing and hugging them, imprinted the sign of the cross on their foreheads, and then cut their throats and threw their bodies on the fire, stating that there was no good reason why such lovely children sprung from such a distinguished father should serve for the amusement of infidels. After this action had been done (I do not know whether one ought to call it savage rather than great-hearted), she rushed to the place where lay the body of her lover, put on her lord's coat of mail and hoqueton [padded jerkin] which were still covered in blood, and taking his short sword in her hand, made her way into the midst of the enemy, where doing the kind of deeds that the bravest of men perform, she was killed by the Turks, whom she believed would shortly take the town by assault. That Christian victory astonished Suleiman quite forcibly.[21]

Kyd used this passage for the dramatisation of Perseda's death in the play's penultimate scene (V.iv). In Wotton (K2^{r-v}), Persida dies an untheatrical death by being shot through her stomach, and in the play-within-the-play in *The Spanish Tragedy*, Bel-imperia playing Perseda simply stabs Balthazar playing Soliman before killing herself (IV.iv.66–7). In *Soliman and Perseda*, however, Perseda appears upon the walls of Rhodes 'in mans apparell', defies Soliman, and then 'comes down to Soliman' where 'they fight' and 'Soliman kills Perseda':

> *The Drum soundes a parle.* PERSEDA *comes vpon the walls in mans apparell.* BASILISCO *and* PISTON, *vpon the walles.*
>
> *Perseda.*   At whose intreatie is this parle sounded?
> *Soliman.*   At our intreatie; therefore yield the towne.
> *Perseda.*   Why, what art thou boldlie bids vs yeeld?
> *Soliman.*   Great *Soliman*, Lord of all the world.
> *Perseda.*   Thou art not Lord of all; Rhodes is not thine.   20
> *Soliman.*   It was, and shall be, maugre who saies no.
> *Perseda.*   I, that say no, will neuer see it thine.
> *Soliman.*   Why, what art thou that dares resist my force?
> *Perseda.*   A Gentleman, and thy mortall enemie,
>   And one that dares thee to the single combate.   25
> *Soliman.*   First tell me, doth *Perseda* liue or no?
> *Perseda.*   She liues to see the wrack of *Soliman*.
> *Soliman.*   Then I will combate thee, what ere thou art. (V.iv.15.1–28)

After Perseda's long tirade against Soliman, the mortal conflict comes to a head:

> *Soliman.*   Iniurious, foule mouthd knight, my wrathfull arme
>   Shall chastise and rebuke these iniuries.
> *Then* PERSEDA *comes down to* SOLIMAN, *and* BASILISCO *and* PISTON.
> *Piston.*   I, but heere you, are you so foolish to fight with him?
> *Basilisco.* I, sirra; why not, as long as I stand by?
> *Soliman.*   Ile not defend *Erastus* innocence,
>   But [die] maintaining of *Persedas* beautie.
>   *Then they fight,* SOLIMAN *kills* PERSEDA. (V.iv.54–59.1)

It has generally been supposed that Kyd simply invented a different end for Perseda. However, Belleforest's historical account of the siege of Rhodes in 1522 is identical with the historical background to *Soliman and Perseda*. The characters too are perfectly identical. The fictional 'Soliman' corresponds to the historical 'Suleiman'; Erastus in Kyd's play is named 'Gouernour of Rhodes' (IV.i.181), and Perseda thus represents the same character as Belleforest's 'mistress to the governor'. In Belleforest and in the play, she dies fighting with a sword. In both, she is disguised and her female identity remains undiscovered to the end. Setting out from the fictional account in Wotton's tale, Kyd paradoxically seems to have found suggestions for the handling of this episode in a historical account of the events that lie behind Wotton and the play.

The source I have identified would be of no great importance if it were not that Marlowe and Kyd appear to have been influenced by the same page of the same work in *2 Tamburlaine* and *Soliman and Perseda*. Marlowe's being the earlier of the two plays, it does not seem implausible that Kyd's handling of Perseda's end is a result of his acquaintance with Marlowe. The fact that Kyd, in one of his letters to Sir John Puckering, denies having been acquainted with Marlowe before they shared lodgings in 1591 only adds further piquancy to this possibility.

Notes

1 The same applies to the second edition of *Soliman and Perseda* (1599) as well as to the first (undated) and second (1594) extant editions of *The Spanish Tragedy*.

2 The line 'That, for retaining one so vertuous' (III.i.34), appears at the top of E2^r instead of E3^r. For a full explanation, see Freeman, p. 155.

3 J. J. Murray (ed.), *The Tragedye of Solyman and Perseda* (New York, 1991).

4 *Stolne and Surreptitious Copies* (Melbourne, 1942), p. 384.

5 Hart, *Stolne and Surreptitious Copies*, pp. 352–90.

6 Cairncross (pp. 178–9), dating *Soliman and Perseda* 1587 and *2 Tamburlaine* 1588, fails to take this parody into account.

7 See E. A. J. Honigmann in the Arden edition (London, 1954) and L. A. Beaurline in the New Cambridge edition (Cambridge, 1990). A. R. Braunmuller, the play's editor in the Oxford Shakespeare Series, argues, however, that the play is post-*Troublesome Reign*.

8 For the dating of *Selimus*, see Chambers, IV, p. 46.

9 Furthermore, K. Wiehl ('Thomas Kyd und die Autorschaft von *Soliman and Perseda*, *The First Part of Jeronimo* und *Arden of Faversham*', *ES*, 44 (1912), 343–60) showed that stylistic features of *Soliman and Perseda* such as the comparative frequency of double endings, run-on lines and the proportion of blank verse to rhyme is closer to *Cornelia* than to *The Spanish Tragedy*.

10 John Donne, *The Elegies and The Songs and Sonnets*, ed. Helen Gardner (Oxford, 1965), pp. 112–13, 116, 118.

11 Compare, for instance, Erastus's 'the chaine,/ Wherein was linkt the sum of my delight' (I.v.119–20) or Perseda's 'the Carcanet/ Which, as my life, I gaue to thee in charge' (II.i.146–7).

12 Kyd's first letter to Puckering, MS. *Harl.* 6849, fols. 218–19, printed by Freeman, p. 181.

13 MS. *Harl.* 6848, fols. 187–9, quoted by Freeman, p. 26.

14 Incidentally, Donne's allusions to *Soliman and Perseda* lends plausibility to John Carey's interesting suggestion that 'thy fathers spirit' (l. 11) in Donne's 'Satire 3' may echo Kyd's *Hamlet* (*John Donne: Life, Mind and Art* (London, 1981), p. 28).

15 I quote from *The True Tragedy of Richard Duke of York*, ed. W. W. Greg, Shakespeare Quarto Facsimiles, no. 11 (Oxford, 1958). Alfred Hart (*Stolne and Surreptitious Copies*, pp. 352–90) was the first to notice the implications of the passages I quote. See also Karl P. Wentersdorf, 'The Repertory and Size of Pembroke's Company', *Theatre Annual*, 33 (1977), 71–85.

16 Dekker also refers to 'great *Sultane Soliman*' (V.ii.164–5) in the same play.

17 Andrew Gurr, *The Shakespearian Playing Companies* (Oxford, 1996), p. 107. Note that Horace is Dekker's satirical portrait of Ben Jonson who got himself into trouble with *The Isle of Dogs* in the same year (1597) at the same playhouse.

18 Gurr, *The Shakespearian Playing Companies*, p. 268.

19 The title page of the first quarto (1594) lists the first three, the title page of the second quarto (1600) all four companies in said order.

20 A residual group of Pembroke's Men survived after the trouble of 1593 as a touring company in the provinces (see Andrew Gurr, 'Three Reluctant Patrons and Early Shakespeare', *SQ*, 44 (1993), 169).

21 I quote the English translation from Vivien Thomas and William Tydeman (eds.), *Christopher Marlowe: The Plays and their Sources* (London, 1994), 157–8. The French original reads:

> Comme aussi ie suis marry de ne sçauoir le nom d'une femme Grecque, [In the left margin: 'Histoire fort Tragique.'] quoy que non segnalee de pudicité, laquelle estant l'amye du gouuerneur du fort de Rhodes, dés qu'eut entêdu que ce sien seigneur & amy estoit mort en combatant vaillament, comme aussi il estoit fort homme de bien: prit les deux enfants qu'elle auoit eu de ce seigneur, & les baisant & embrassant, leur empraignit le signe de la croix au front, puis leur coupa la gorge, & les ietta au feu, disant qu'il n'estoit pas raison que ces enfants tant beaux, & sortis d'vn pere tant illustre, seruissent aux plaisirs infames des Barbares: [In the left margin: 'Acte plein d'amour & generosité en vne femme.'] & fait cet acte (ne sçay si le doy plustost appeler brutal que magnanime) elle s'en court au lieu où estoit le corps de son amy, elle se vestit de la cotte, & Hoqueton d'armes de son seigneur, lequel estoit encore tout sanglant, & prenant son estoc au poing, s'en alla au milieu des ennemys, où faisant ce que les plus vaillants hommes executent, elle fut occise par les Turcs, lesquels elle pensoit que deussent lors emporter la ville. Cette victoire des Chrestiens etonna fort Solyman. (vol. II, p. 750)

Belleforest considerably revised and enlarged Munster's *Cosmographie Universelle* (Basel, 1555). In the latter, the siege of Rhodes is related only briefly (p. 1199). Thomas and Tydeman point out that Marlowe 'no doubt based on [this passage] those episodes involving the widowed Olympia and her successful resistance to the advances of the amorous Theridamas which form the substance of Act III Scenes 3 and 4, and Act IV Scene 2' (p. 80).

CHAPTER 8

Soliman and Perseda:
the play and its making

Criticism of *Soliman and Perseda* in its own right, excluding matters of 'facts and problems', adds up to little over thirty pages: Sarrazin spends a couple of pages on sketching some aspects of Kyd's use of his sources, J. J. Murray pays special attention to Basilisco and Piston, the braggart and the pedant and their dramatic ancestors, L. L. Brodwin briefly discusses the play as an early example of a love tragedy, Freeman spends a few pages on characterisation and on the mingling of comic and tragic themes in the play and Nick de Somogyi has recently analysed Basilico in the context of other Elizabethan braggart figures.[1] If we consider that Kyd is generally acknowledged to be the most important of Shakespeare's dramatic predecessors along with Marlowe and Lyly, and if we recall that *Soliman and Perseda* is the only extant stage play beside *The Spanish Tragedy* that can be attributed in its entirety to Kyd with a good degree of certainty, this critical treatment appears surprisingly inadequate. Two full-length studies have been devoted to close analyses of Kyd's dramaturgy in *The Spanish Tragedy*.[2] *Soliman and Perseda*, in contrast, has been blatantly neglected.

Source studies are not in vogue today. Modern criticism has rightly challenged some of the too narrow assumptions lying behind terms such as 'source' or 'influence'. There are obvious hermeneutic limits to an analysis of an artist's sources. Imponderables will remain and our insight into a writer's mental laboratory will always be limited. The 'sources' that go into a play and the 'influence' that is transposed in a play are always too complex to be fully understood by the critic. They are composed by a multitude of textual or other memories, conscious in the writer's mind or not, that no one can have access to. There are material aspects going into the composition of a play, however, that can be determined and isolated with a sufficient degree of certitude. It cannot be doubted that playwrights occasionally worked with books open on their desks and that elements of these books, after a complex process of adaptation and transformation, found their way into the plays. Our understanding of Elizabethan drama will be improved if we understand as much as possible about this process. As Madeleine Doran pointed out,

> one of the controlling elements in plot-building by Elizabethan dramatists was certainly the source stories they chose to dramatize. In general, plays based on novellas or on Roman or Italian plays are better knit, more unified and coherent, than those based on chronicles or episodic romances.[3]

Soliman and Perseda is one of the earliest extant plays based upon a novella and observing the process of dramatisation will allow us a glimpse at the artistry that vitally contributed to the growing sophistication of Elizabethan drama.

Before examining Kyd's dramatisation of his source, I briefly summarise the play's action: The three allegorical figures, Love, Fortune, and Death, appear at the beginning of the play and at the end of every act, arguing about their relative importance in the dramatised events. The action opens with Erastus, a knight of Rhodes, and Perseda, plighting their troth and exchanging a chain and a ring (I.ii). At a tilting contest organised to honour the wedding of the Prince of Cyprus with the daughter of the Governor of Rhodes, Erastus overcomes opponents from various countries, including the Turkish general Brusor and the braggart knight Basilisco, but loses Perseda's chain (I.iii). Following the discovery of his loss, Erastus laments his fortune (I.iv). At the court of Soliman, where Brusor's return is awaited, intrigue and treachery result in the death of two of Soliman's brothers (I.v). In Act II, Ferdinando, who has found Erastus's chain, bestows it upon his beloved Lucina. When Perseda sees Lucina wearing the chain, she suspects Erastus of unfaithfulness, rejecting his professions of innocence and asking Basilisco to avenge her. Erastus finally manages to recover the chain from Lucina, thereby awakening the jealousy of Ferdinando whom he kills in self-defence. He escapes punishment by fleeing to Constantinople (II.i). Piston, Erastus's servant, informs Perseda of Erastus's escape while bragging Basilisco still craves revenge on Erastus (II.ii). Having arrived at Soliman's court, Erastus is welcomed and overcomes Soliman in a friendly fight. Piston brings news from Rhodes (III.i), where Perseda and Lucina curse their fortune (III.ii). Having prepared a fleet, the Turks attack Rhodes, kill the Governor of Rhodes and his son-in-law, take Perseda and Lucina prisoner, and force Basilisco to 'turn Turk' (III.iii–III.v). Perseda is presented to the Emperor and threatened with death when she refuses to yield to his wooing. Erastus and Perseda meet again at the Turkish court. Moved by their innocent love, Soliman allows them to get married and to return to Rhodes, but soon regrets his magnanimity as his desire for Perseda is rekindled. Lucina and Brusor promise to further his cause (IV.i). Piston makes fun of Basilisco by debasing his empty boasts (IV.ii). Arrived at Rhodes, Lucina and Brusor treacherously lure Erastus back to Soliman's court (V.i), where two false witnesses accuse him of treason and the Lord Marshal has him executed. Regretting his wicked scheme, Soliman laments Erastus' death and kills his executioners and the Lord Marshal (V.ii). Piston brings news to Perseda of Erastus's execution. Realising that Lucina has played a part in the betrayal, Perseda asks Basilisco to kill Lucina and, when he cowardly recoils, performs the deed herself (V.iii). Soliman arrives in Rhodes to conquer Perseda, but, the gates being shut, has to wage a battle in which he accidentally wounds the disguised Perseda to death. When he understands what he has done, he kills Basilisco and Piston in despair and has Brusor executed. Having put deadly poison on her lips, Perseda allows Soliman to kiss her before she expires. As news of the sack of Rhodes arrives, Soliman speaks his dying words. The allegorical figures Love, Fortune, and Death speak the epilogue, Death arguing that he has been the dominant force in the action.

How, then, did Kyd handle his narrative source? Certain borrowings make clear that Kyd used Wotton's *Courtlie Controuersie* rather than Yver's French original *Le Printemps d'Yver*, and that Kyd must have worked with Wotton's tale open on his desk.[4] Kyd took over most of the names he found in Wotton: Soliman, Erastus, Brusor, and Lucina; he changed Persida to Perseda, Pistan to Piston, and Phillip to Phillippo.

In the first scene of the play proper, Kyd closely follows Wotton, adroitly turning a long account of the young lovers' origins into Erastus's expository opening speech. Kyd swiftly moves on to the lovers' exchange of chain and ring, again following Wotton, but significantly inverts the order in which the presents are offered. Whereas Wotton's Persida simply reciprocates the present, Kyd's Perseda, like Julia in *The Two Gentlemen of Verona* (II.ii), takes the active part. 'I, watch you vauntages?' (I.ii.30), she utters (which Boas (p. 437) paraphrases with 'Are you on the look out to get the better of me?') before giving him the ring. In a few lines, Kyd draws

Perseda's character markedly differently from the stereotypical figure of chivalric romance in Wotton.

After this initial encounter, Wotton reports the passage of ten months' time followed by the announcement of the tilting contest on the occasion of the prince's marriage. Kyd introduces the contest in the very same scene. The consistent speeding up of time, especially during the first half of the play, will deserve further attention. Erastus's character, too, is sketched rather differently. Wotton's young man participates secretly at the contest and after his triumph modestly refuses to reveal his identity until he is forced to do so. In the play Erastus informs Perseda of his purpose and confidently asserts: 'Ile winne/ Such glory as no time shall ere race out,/ Or end the period of my youth in blood' (I.ii.94–6). Kyd's Erastus is not only less appealing, but also of less central importance to the plot than Wotton's. The novella does not have a title, but it could well be called 'Erastus and Persida', whereas Kyd's play logically does not mention Erastus in its title.

Act I Scene iv constitutes the hitherto most complex interweaving of plot elements taken over from Wotton, elements suggested by the source and extended upon, and elements completely absent from the narrative. In the tale, Erastus, disguised as green knight, has been victorious against all opponents in the tournament. Phillip of Villiers, the *Commandeur* (the equivalent of Kyd's Philippo, Governor of Rhodes) asks him to reveal his identity. Erastus at first refuses, but the bridegroom unmasks him, thereby breaking the chain whose loss Erastus does not realise until later. He is congratulated and, after some amorous words to Persida, he is carried away in a procession to join the feast. Having to dramatise this material, Kyd faced an obvious problem. The scene is of small relevance to the main plot, but is nevertheless indispensable because of Erastus's loss of his chain. Kyd adapts the material in a way which allows him to tighten significantly the loosely constructed source material. He introduces Brusor – who only appears much later in the novella – as one of the participants at the tilting. Kyd also substitutes the bridegroom – who has no further importance in the tale – with Lucina, who takes an active part at a much earlier stage than in Wotton by making Erastus lose his chain. Finally, Kyd transforms the part of Ferdinando whom Wotton only mentions in passing as the 'Gentleman of the town' into whose hands Erastus's chain happens to fall and who, as he 'sought the good wil of a countrey Damosel [...] named *Lucina*' (G3r), hands it on to her. Kyd has Ferdinando participate in the tilting, where his poor performance contrasts unfavourably with Erastus's. The later antagonism between Erastus and Ferdinand is thus motivated by Lucina's admiration for Erastus's achievement and Ferdinand's consequent jealousy.

In the latter part of I.iv, Kyd again speeds up the action. Wotton's Erastus realises the loss of his chain when getting undressed in the evening and 'passe[s] the nighte in complainte of hys disaster' (G2^r). He does not send out his servant Pistan 'to make searche and diligente enquirie to vnderstande who has found his chayne' (G3^r) before the next day. Kyd compresses these events into one scene: Erastus's loss of the chain is only separated from Piston's search for it by a short intermezzo with Basilisco and Piston. Of course, it is not possible that within a few minutes Erastus should have noticed his loss and informed Piston who then contacted the crier. Like Shakespeare after him, Kyd deliberately disregards a naturalistic treatment of time. The question of precisely how much time passed during these events is immaterial. Kyd does not construct his plot to represent events with naturalistic fidelity, but to highlight a process of cause and effect.[5]

The scene ends with Erastus's soliloquy lamenting his misfortune (I.iv.114–37). Wotton has numerous laments of somewhat tedious length. Kyd chose to reduce their number radically for the purposes of his play. The choice is significant. Two or three decades earlier, a dramatist would have been likely to exploit fully every possibility of characters lamenting their fate in rhetorically high-flown and drawn-out speeches and soliloquies. Typical of the drama of action which he was instrumental in shaping, Kyd uses laments very sparingly. In the present instance where he does adapt a lament from his source, he carefully places it at the end of a scene bustling with action.

The opening scene of the second act is both the longest and the most complex of the play. A series of relatively small movements rapidly follow upon each other and advance the action at great speed. The scene constitutes the play's hinge, as it both terminates the plot concerned with the loss and recovery of Erastus's chain that dominates the first half and introduces Erastus's exile and separation from Perseda that is at the centre of the second half of the play. The scene has a symmetrical structure. Lines one to 166 dramatise Perseda's realisation of the loss of the chain; lines 186 to 338 deal with its recovery. Both halves lead up to a short but powerful climax: Perseda's outrage at her discovery of the chain around Lucina's neck (first half), and the fight between Erastus and Ferdinando in which the latter is killed (second half). The two parts of roughly equal length are connected by Erastus's soliloquy (ll.

167–85) in which he sums up what has happened before planning the action he is going to take.

Wotton furnished Kyd with very little of this carefully balanced structure. Concerning the first half of the scene, here is what Kyd found in the novella:

> Immediately after, there was a feast in the towne, at the which, this coun-
> trey Damosel named *Lucina*, (who customablie neuer escaped any) was
> presente, forgetting nothing in hir closet that might adorne hir person, or
> augmente hir naturall beautie. God knoweth if the chayne were hydden
> in hir pocket, but whersoeuer it was *Persida* espied it, whose rolling eyes
> glaunced in euery corner like the haggard Falcon, whose eye serueth for
> a sentinell, whilest shee pruneth hir plumage in the sunne. *Persida*,
> perceyuing a stranger beautified in hir feathers, grew in such choller, as
> fearing least hir countenaunce shoulde bewraye the disquiet of hyr
> mynde, she forsooke the company, and in excuse of hir departure sayde,
> that the streyghtnesse of hir gown greued hir so sore as she was very ill
> at ease therwith, and the better to counterfeite the matter, she caused
> *Agatha* to vnclaspe hir bodie: but alas she was griped with an other
> claspe more vneasye to be loosed. In thys perplexitie she threwe hir selfe
> vppon a bedde, and commaunded hyr mayde to depart, faynyng she
> woulde take some reste: but by no meanes she could entreate *Agatha* to
> leaue hir alone, which in deed had bene very perilous for the yong gentle-
> woman.   (G3ʳ⁻ᵛ)

Kyd changes the 'feast in the towne', which it would have been uneconomical to stage, to an amorous encounter between Ferdinando and Lucina (II.i.1–25). The close parallels between this episode and Horatio and Bel-imperia's 'love duet' in *The Spanish Tragedy* (II.iv.1–49) are striking. It seems significant that the author, when completely leaving the track given by his source, has recourse to a device which is present in *The Spanish Tragedy*. The same can be observed in the multinational pageant in I.iii (mirroring *The Spanish Tragedy* I.v), and in the relatively early introduction of the subplot set in a different country (*Soliman and Perseda* I.v and *The Spanish Tragedy* I.iii). This pattern, which becomes visible only through a study of Kyd's use of his main source, would be difficult to account for if one wanted to argue against Kyd's authorship of *Soliman and Perseda*.

The amorous encounter is interrupted by the arrival of Basilisco and Perseda. The passage leading up to Perseda's discovery of the chain around Lucina's neck is a good example of Kyd's skill in dramatising dialogue:

> *Basilisco.*   All haile, braue Cauelere. God morrow, Madam,   30
>   The fairest shine that shall this day be seene
>   Except *Persedas* beautious excellence,

> Shame to loues Queene, and Empresse of my thoughts.
> *Ferdinando.*   Marry, thrise happy is *Persedas* chance,
>   To haue so braue a champion to hir Squire.   35
> *Basilisco.*   Hir Squire? her Knight – and who so else denies
>   Shall feele the rigour of my Sword and Launce.
> *Ferdinando.*   O sir, not I.
> *Lucina.*   Heres none but friends; yet let me challenge you
>   For gracing me with a malignant stile,   40
>   That I was fairest, and yet *Perseda* fairer:
>   We Ladies stand vpon our beauties much.
> *Perseda.*   Herein, *Lucina*, let me buckler him.
> *Basilisco.*   Not *Mars* himselfe had eare so faire a Buckler.
> *Perseda.*   Loue makes him blinde, and blinde can judge no colours.
> *Lucina.*   Why then the mends is made, and we still friends.
>
>   (II.i.30–46)

The individual sequences are short and all four interlocutors participate. The conversation flows naturally. Singling out the importance
of this aspect of Kyd's dramaturgy, Clemen describes it as an 'inter-
play [...] in which the speakers are delicately attuned to one another
and establish a real contact'.[6]

   The first half of the scene ends with the confrontation between
Perseda and the newly-arrived Erastus (II.i.95–166). Kyd substantially shortens the encounter in Wotton (G3ᵛ–H2ʳ) and adds tension
by having Perseda initially dissemble her anger. The actual quarrel
at times leans heavily on Wotton and some details of direct indebtedness can be isolated:

> let hir attire & decke hir selfe with my spoyles   (G4ᵛ)
> Why didst thou deck her with my ornament?   (II.i.145)

> O false and disloyal *Erastus*   (G4ᵛ)
> For this thy periurde false disloyalty: (II.i.123)

> why are not the teeth (seruants of our sustenaunce) reuengers of
> all slaunderous lying tongs.   (G4ᵛ)
> If heauens were iust, thy teeth would teare thy tongue   (II.i.122)

> Or if a double hart outrageth the tong why is there not a
> wyndowe in each mans breast thorow the whiche the fraudulent
> deceites of this malicious guest may be discouered euen in
> the most secret cabyn of his habitation.   (G4ᵛ)
>   men should haue open brests,
> That we therein might read their guilefull thoughts.   (II.i.124–5)

It is also instructive to notice what Kyd chose to exclude. Hurt by
Persida's accusations, Erastus attempts suicide, but fails most
bathetically:

> And turning the poynt of his rapier (the miserable remedie of loue)

agaynst his valiaunt breast, prodigall of his soule, with a couragious feeblenesse pressed to balance his bodie therevpon, supposing by this piteous sacrifice to appease the rigour of his fierce friende: which in deede he had perfourmed, if *Agatha* perceyuing his desperate intent, running hastily, had not by great good happe stryken aside the pomell of the Rapier with hir foote, by meanes whereof, *Erastus* fell flat on the floore, the Rapier vnder him, without receyuing any harme, neuerthelesse with suche noyse as diuers came running into the Chamber: whereof the Louers something ashamed, fayned that the sicke Pacient fell into a sounde. Thus the playe was finished without tragedie, like a Cannon hauing made a false fire.   (H1^v–H2^r)

It is plausible to imagine that Kyd deemed this passage not in keeping with the tone of his play and decided not to use it.

At the stage equivalent to Erastus's soliloquy half way through the scene (II.i.167–85), the novella mentions another lapse of time. Erastus's plan is to 'to purchase the Damosels good wyll by amorous practises, wherein he played his parte so cunningly, as he quickly deserued the name of a friende' (H2^r), a project which takes a considerable amount. In the play the action ensues immediately. Kyd dramatises Erastus's recovery of the chain – which, according to Wotton, 'by good fortune he wanne' (H2^r) – in a dicing game that includes two characters, Guelpio and Iulio, who are absent from Wotton. Kyd has been criticised for this passage which shows Erastus winning back the chain through deceit (Boas, p. lxi). Although the sequence is not one of the play's highlights, the criticism is not entirely justified as Kyd was careful from the beginning to transform Wotton's chivalric and thoroughly honourable Erastus into a more ambiguous figure.

Up to this point, the play falls into parts which either follow Wotton closely or have no correspondence at all. The next three passages show a different relationship to the play's main source in that characters present in the source take on a largely independent life. Firstly, after Erastus's slaying of Ferdinando, Wotton's 'trustie seruant Pistan' accompanies Erastus on his flight from Rhodes to Constantinople while Kyd's stays in Rhodes (II.i.244–84). In a prose soliloquy (II.i.285–98) which prefigures Launcelot in *The Merchant of Venice* (II.ii.1–29), the servant considers disobeying his master and plunders the dead Ferdinando. Secondly, the following scene lacks a corresponding passage in the novella despite the fact that Perseda and Pistan (who appear in the scene along with Basilisco) go back to Wotton. Kyd has Pistan deliver the chain to Perseda and relate the circumstances of his flight (II.ii.1–27). In contrast, Wotton has Persida disappears from the story until she reappears as

Soliman's captive. Thirdly, all Wotton reports of Erastus's first encounter with Soliman in Constantinople is that he was presented unto him and won his favour. In the play, Brusor's report of Erastus's valour precedes the latter's arrival and his reputation is tested and confirmed by a friendly fight in which Erastus overcomes Soliman (III.i.1–111). In the next scene, Perseda and Lucina are back in Rhodes in the company of Basilisco and lament their fortune in a scene which has no direct debt to Wotton.

A closer look at Lucina and Brusor further illustrates how characters take on a life of their own in the course of the play. Lucina has only two brief appearances in the novella. In the first, Wotton relates in a couple of sentences how she received the chain and was seen with it by Perseda while the second narrates Erastus's recapture of the chain. Kyd makes her the instrument of Erastus's loss of the chain, shows her to be the motive for Ferdinando's antagonism to Erastus and presents her in a love scene with Ferdinando. She remains of central interest in the latter part of the play by being both Perseda's companion and counterpart, featuring in a total of seven scenes (I.iv, II.i, III.i, III.v, IV.i, V.i, V.iii).

As for Brusor, he is not introduced by Wotton before late in the tale when Soliman relies on his help to win back Perseda (K1[r]). The only other time we hear of him is when Soliman, after the death of Erastus and Perseda, has him hanged (K3[v]). In the play, Brusor has his first appearance in the tilting contest in Rhodes (I.iii) in which he takes part as a Turkish knight. Consequently, he is qualified to tell Soliman of Erastus's exploits before the latter's arrival in Constantinople (III.i). Like Lucina, he takes an active role in the shaping of the events in the second half of the play (III.iv, III.v, IV.i, V.i, V.ii, V.iv).

Kyd's design was thus such that the broad departure from the narrative in the latter parts of the play was carefully prepared by minor changes in the early scenes. The plot in Wotton's novella is basically linear. Most characters in the narrative make short appearances and disappear. Kyd excludes some and elaborates others, enlarging their impact on the action from isolated episodes to the play's entirety.

The following three scenes dramatise the siege and battle of Rhodes which Wotton passes over in a couple of sentences. The siege scene represents one of the typical dramatic episodes of pre- and early Shakespearean drama. Chronicle-plays, in particular, abounded in sieges; *2 Henry VI*, for instance, contains no less than thirteen. Hence, Kyd was in no need of a precise antecedent for these scenes and their stage-worthiness was tested and guaranteed. It is noticeable, however, that Kyd keeps them extremely short. His play clearly does not belong to the dramatic genre which in his time produced, at its best, *Tamburlaine* or, at its worst, *Edward I*. In her study of *Themes and Conventions of Elizabethan Tragedy*, M. C. Bradbrook usefully distinguishes between 'cumulative plots' and 'plots based on peripateia' (p. 41). The sources of the former are typically chronicles, of the latter novellas. Kyd's dramaturgy precisely departs from linear chronicles of wars and conquests to a tight dramatic structure strictly based on cause and effect dealing with intrigue and passion.

In IV.i, the second longest scene of the play, we see Kyd at the height of his poetic and dramatic power. Soliman's detailed description of Perseda, even though it assembles several stock ingredients of Renaissance catalogues of feminine charms, rises above the verse of much of the play (IV.i.75–89). The tyrant's wooing of his captive (IV.i.90–144) forms the climax. The scene clearly falls into two halves with Erastus's entry (IV.i.155.1) and the lovers' reunion at the centre. Each half, in turn, falls into two parts. The first quarter presents us with Soliman and Erastus who laments the fall of Rhodes. In the second, after Erastus's departure, Perseda and Lucina are brought in as captives, Lucina is given to Brusor and Perseda is unsuccessfully wooed by Soliman. In the third, the lovers are reunited and joined in marriage by Soliman; Erastus is named Governor of Rhodes and Perseda is crowned. In the fourth and last part, after the lovers' departure, Soliman regrets his decision and plans to reconquer Perseda with the help of Brusor and Lucina. The scene is carefully balanced with an emotional high point on either side of the scene's central hinge: Perseda awaiting the stroke of death from Soliman's hands and the marriage of the two lovers. Death, Fortune, and Love, allegorical figures in the chorus and central themes highlighted by the play's full title, are enacted and illustrated in juxtaposition. Perseda nearly falls prey to death before Fortune's wheel turns when Erastus arrives. Love (temporarily) triumphs as the marriage takes place.

How did Kyd handle his source in the present scene? Soliman's encounter with Erastus who laments Rhodes fall is Kyd's invention. The rest has a clear correspondence in Wotton, with the material presented in the same order in the two works. In the novella, however, the material corresponding to IV.i takes up much space (H4^r–K1^r), in fact, exactly a quarter of the whole history. The pace is leisurely and the emotions never reach a high peak. Kyd's adaptation then is one of dramatisation, condensation and acceleration.

Wotton ends the narrative sequence with the departure of the newly-wed couple. Weeks pass during which Soliman's passions revive. He writes a burning love letter to Perseda who, in her reply, courteously declines his offer. It is only at this stage that Brusor forges his cunning plan. By carrying on the scene after Erastus and Perseda have left, Kyd not only renews dramatic tension at the very moment when the central conflict seems to have been solved. He also makes the cause of the revival of Soliman's passion as clear as possible. Wotton *reports* that Soliman's memories of Perseda's dazzling beauty at the wedding ceremony rekindle the fires of his passion:

> And loue, whom he pretended to resist, planted his proude foote vpon the Princes heade: so as, whether by the supposed fauour he receiued at hir hande, who sought that day to honour him with all hir endeuour, which he construed to proceede of loue (as Louers take euery thing for their aduantage) or for that he stoode to neere this pleasant fire, he felt his heart so warmed, and his former intent so altered, as al his determination was wholly to please his pardoned captiue, who by a cruell reuenge, nowe emprisoned him so straightly, as although (reuiuing his auncient vertue) he was resolued to deliuer hir, yet with ioyned handes he was enforced to require grace.   (I3ᵛ)

Kyd *shows* this, adroitly merging the display of cause and effect:

> *Soliman.*   Giue me a crowne, to crowne the bride withall.
> *Then he crownes* PERSEDA.
>   *Perseda*, for my sake weare this crowne.
>   Now is she fairer then she was before;
>   This title so augments her beautie, as the fire,
>   That lay with honours hand rackt vp in ashes,   190
>   Reuiues againe to flames, the force is such.
>   Remooue the cause, and then the effect will die;
>   They must depart, or I shall not be quiet.
>   *Erastus* and *Perseda*, meruaile not
>   That all in hast I wish you to depart;
>   There is an vrgent cause, but priuie to my selfe: (IV.i.186–96)

In Wotton, Soliman's importance remains subordinate to the two lovers. In the play, he is the most complex character, only surpassed by Hieronimo in all of Kyd.

A further addition to the source is dramatically more basic but no less effective. In the narrative, Lucina has definitively disappeared from the story and Brusor has not yet made his first appearance when Lucina is brought in as a second captive, given to Brusor. Thereafter the two form a couple that serves as a counterpart to Erastus and Perseda. Motivated by Erastus's killing of Ferdinando,

Lucina, like Bel-imperia, furthers her revenge by turning to another man. Kyd's transformation of his source may again owe something to *The Spanish Tragedy*.

Of the four scenes in the last act, the first two dramatise a very short narrative portion in Wotton:

> But *Brusor* vnder colour of secret & waightie affaires, allured & ledde poore *Erastus* to *Constantinople*, where he was no sooner alighted from his horse, but the Marshall of the Emperours housholde attached & committed him close prisoner vnder sure garde. The King supposed to seyze vpon his Louer (as the hungry Hawke stoupeth like a leaden lump vpon hir pray) nothing mistrusting the feuer which detayned *Persida*, but he reckned without his hoste, and fared the worse for his snatching. At laste finding his fancie deceyued, blaming his haste, he deuised howe to satisfie his faulte. Neuerthelesse, resolued to strike whyle the yron was hotte, with speede prosecuted the processe agaynst the poore Gentleman, and by false witnesses of purpose prouided, *Erastus* was accused, and conuicted of treason & rebellion, for that he had consented (sayd they) to deliuer the Ile of *Rhodes* into the possession of the Christians: for which offence iudgement passed vpon him, and by the Emperours commandement he was beheaded.   (K1$^{\text{r-v}}$)

The short first scene is devoid of great intrinsic interest, and its sole purpose is to advance the action. Brusor lures Erastus to Constantinople (as in Wotton), whereas Lucina treacherously promises to keep Perseda company (added by Kyd). In the second scene, Kyd turns Wotton's sketchy outline into one of the play's dramatic highlights. Whereas the novella does not seem interested in more than getting Erastus out of the way, Kyd spices the sequence with the excitement of both a trial and an eavesdropping scene. The staging is of a sophistication that goes beyond Kyd's predecessors and is rare even in early Shakespeare. The scene displays the same interest in multi-layered action as the play-within-the-play in *The Spanish Tragedy*. The central action – involving the Lord Marshall, the two false witnesses, the Janisaries, and Erastus – is watched over by the hidden Soliman. Simultaneously, the trial and Soliman are spied on by Piston who escapes when Erastus is strangled. The atmosphere of spying and betrayal anticipates the conclusion of *The Jew of Malta*. As a two-layered eavesdropping scene, it announces *Troilus and Cressida* V.ii where Diomedes and Cressida are spied upon by Troilus and Ulysses and all four are watched by Thersites.

For the accumulated violence towards the close of the scene, Kyd's mind seems again to have reverted to *The Spanish Tragedy*. Hieronimo is not content with having his plan carried out and his enemies dispatched, but brings about a further slaughter that appears less clearly motivated. Similarly, Soliman, in a surprising turn of events, kills the two men he hired to bear false witness against Erastus and goes on to have the Lord Marshall killed.

Soliman's torn character is elaborated in the asides throughout the scene. They betray a complex inner conflict between affection for and magnanimity towards Erastus on the one hand and cruelty and lust on the other. Whereas Hieronimo displays his inner struggle in various soliloqies, Soliman's interiority is suggested in dramatically integrated asides and speeches.

Alexander in Lyly's *Campaspe* (c. 1580) offers an instructive contrast to Soliman. Granted, the two plays may seem difficult to compare: *Campaspe* is written for a private theatre, *Soliman and Perseda* for the public stage; Lyly writes euphuistic prose whereas Kyd composes patterned verse; the former play is a comedy, the latter a tragedy. Nevertheless, both plays are early examples of romantic drama set against a historical background. They are imaginative dramatic treatments of history and both oppose a male and a female protagonist.[7]

In his discussion of *Campaspe*, R. W. Bond concludes that 'the play's defect is one of passion. The dramatic opportunity for conflict in Alexander's breast between jealousy and magnanimity is quite missed' (II, p. 252). In fact, the conflict is hinted at briefly. When Alexander finally realises Apelles' passion for Campaspe, he says:

> Me thinks I might haue bin made priuie to your affection; though my counsell had not bene necessary, yet my countenance might haue bin thought requisite. But *Apelles*, forsooth, loueth vnder hand, yea & vnder *Alexanders* nose, and – but I say no more.
>
> (V.iv.97–101)

The interrupted sentence shows Alexander subduing his offended pride. A little later, he has rid himself of all jealousy: 'Thou shalt see that *Alexander* maketh but a toye of loue, and leadeth affection in fetters' (V.iv.132–3). Lyly follows his source, Book XXXV of Pliny's *Natural History*, in swiftly passing over Alexander's inner conflict. The feelings which would be a potential cause for dramatic tension are only briefly touched upon but not explored. The play states Alexander's surrender of Campaspe as a fact, and not as the result of a conflict in which cause and effect are highlighted and which suggests the character's interiority.

In *Soliman and Perseda*, Kyd faced the same problem Lyly had encountered a few years earlier. Like Lyly, Wotton has the male protagonist simply pass from one state to another. At first, he promises Erastus that 'I wyll vanquishe my proper affections' (I2ᵛ), and he yields Persida to Erastus. Yet after the wedding ceremony his passion is revived, and nothing can 'dissuade him from bitter repentaunce of his too frank offer and vnaduised liberalitie' (I3ᵛ). In a first stage, Soliman is completely magnanimous, in a second stage, he is wholly governed by jealousy and lust. Juxtaposed in Wotton, Soliman's emotions are superimposed in Kyd, thus creating a torn character. In particular, Soliman's asides during Erastus's trial poignantly dramatise an inner conflict that results in an inability to refer to himself other than in the third person: 'O vniust *Soliman*: O wicked time,/ Where filthie lust must murther honest loue' (V.ii.90–1). In Soliman's rant and grief after the strangling of Erastus, 'Whose life to me was dearer then mine owne' (V.ii.105), we have an embryonic version of Ferdinand's rage after the Duchess has been strangled in Webster's *Duchess of Malfi*. Kyd's complex handling of the character owes nothing to his source, which swiftly passes over the episode of Erastus's mock trial and execution. Soliman may seem like a second rate artistic creation when contrasted with Lear or Othello, but compared with characters in contemporary and earlier plays he looks like a remarkable achievement. Where *Campaspe* failed to explore a dramatic tension, Kyd can be said to have succeeded since he recognised and explored the possibilities for dramatic conflict offered by his source.

In the discussion of the play's sources, I have already investigated the dramatisation of Perseda's end. What is of importance for the present purpose is to determine the effect of Kyd's shift in emphasis. In the novella, Persida is killed accidentally by 'two bullets sent from a Musket' (K2ʳ), fired right after her tirade against the Monarch. In the play, however, Soliman kills Perseda while trying to gain access to her. '*Persedas* beautie' (V.iv.59) are Soliman's last words before he kills her. What he thinks of as a step towards the fulfillment of his desires constitutes in fact the destruction of his desires. The pattern is one of irony achieved through a discordant juxtaposition of cause and effect. Kyd dramatised Soliman's death with the same pattern in mind. As Perseda finally kisses Soliman and grants his passions what her dying body is still capable of, the seeming expression of love is in fact an instrument of death.

Wotton's Soliman mourns the death of the two lovers and buries them in a gorgeous tomb. Their death constitutes the tragedy and Soliman is a spectator left to mourn. In the play, however, Soliman ends up being both the subject and the object of the tragedy. Like Oedipus, he is the cause of his own downfall. Were it not for the early acts from which Soliman is all but absent, the tragedy should rightly be called 'Soliman'. The shift in emphasis from tale to play, especially its tragic conclusion, is exemplified by the difference in emphasis between *Romeo and Juliet* and *Othello*.

The point of the above analysis is not to argue that Kyd has consistently turned dross into gold, but that he helped shape tools of dramatisation which later dramatists inherited and refined. As we have watched Kyd transform, add, suppress, preserve, or develop sequences in the source, and as we have inquired into the reasons for the playwright's handling of his material, we have gained insight into one of the workshops in which Elizabethan theatre came into existence.

Kyd's language shows little direct indebtedness to Wotton. Kyd borrows a few words from his source, but in general, his highly patterned and rhetorical language is reminiscent of *The Spanish Tragedy*, whereas the ancestors of Wotton's euphuistic prose are George Pettie's novellas and ultimately North and Guevara. Two conspicuous features of Kyd's play are absent from the source: Basilisco, the braggart soldier of Latin Comedy, and the allegorical frame with Fortune, Love, and Death. Apart from these, Kyd relies on Wotton for much of his material. At the same time, Kyd is largely independent of Wotton in the shaping of individual scenes. He repeatedly imposes a tight and meaningful structure upon his source which is often accompanied with a speeding up of time. The chief effect of this is a foregrounding of causality. Departing from the structure of most earlier English plays, the play does not unfold in linear progression. Rather, it is closely knit and progresses through a series of causally determined jumps. Wotton's tale steadily advances with Erastus, Persida, and Soliman at its centre and with other characters appearing and disappearing. Kyd crucially substantiated the drama by more than doubling the number of principal characters. Piston, Ferdinando, Lucina, and Brusor, flat and perfunctory in Wotton, are carefully woven into the play's fabric. These seven characters, plus Basilisco, Kyd's addition, constitute the essentials of the play and the action turns around their alliances and intrigues.

Composed within a few years, *The Wars of Cyrus*, *Soliman and Perseda*, and *Edward III* offer three dramatic conflicts between a male ruler and a female captive or subordinate. In order to investigate the nature of Kyd's dramatic artistry, I will isolate three passages whose plotting and staging can profitably be compared.

The Wars of Cyrus is often thought to have been influenced by *Tamburlaine*, though it has also been argued that the play was written several years earlier.[8] It will suffice for my purposes to consider it as roughly contemporary with *Soliman and Perseda*. The main plot deals with the fate of Panthea, Abradates' wife. After being taken prisoner by Cyrus, she is put into the hands of Araspas, who woos her before threatening to win her by force:

Araspas.   Here is Araspas, louelie Panthea.   800
    For thee Ile leaue the field, then leaue thou him [*Abradates*];
    For thee Ile leaue the world, then loue thou me.
    Let Cyrus ioy in pompe and emperie;
    Sufficeth me to conquer faire *Panthea*.
    Let others glorie in their ground and golde;   805
    Panthea to me is twentie thousand worlds,
    And without *Panthea* all the world is trash.
Panthea.   For thee, Araspas, will I curse my starres,
    That suffers thee so to solicite me;
    For thee I will count the world as hell,   810
    Except thou leaue thus to solicite me.
Araspas.   How figuratiue is *Panthea* in her speach!
    Resembling cunning Rethoritians,
    Who in the person of some one deceasde
    Perswades their auditors to what they please.   815
    I cannot thinke that these be *Pantheas* words;
    She is [too] faire to giue so sharpe replie.
    But if these be the wordes of *Panthea*,
    Then must she change her face, and seeme lesse faire;
    For know that beautie is loues harbinger;   820
    Then, being beautious, *Panthea* needes must loue.
Panthea.   Would I were changde into some other shape,
    That I might fright thee with my hideous lookes!
    I, in the person of my self deceasde,
    Protest this heart shall neuer harbour loue;   825
    But if my lookes be this preparatiue,
    Ile beate my face against the haplesse earth
    Or deeply harrow it with these my trembling hands,
    Which I hold vp to heauen to chaunge thy minde
    Or hasten death to rid me from this sute.   830
Araspas.   Nay then, if amorous courting will not serue,
    Know whether thou wilt or no Ile make thee yeeld.
Panthea.   Though fortune make me captiue, yet know thou
    That *Pantheas* will can neuer be constrainde.
Araspas.   But torments can enforce a womans will.   835
Panthea.   Then should thy importunitie enforce,
    The sight of thee, Araspas, should constraine:
    For I protest before the gods of heauen
    No torment can be greater in my thought.
Araspas.   I, say so till ye feele them, *Panthea*.   840
Panthea.   I feele more torments then thou canst inuent;
    Who adde the more shall ease that I sustaine.
    All torments, be they neuer so exquisite,
    Are but ascending steps vnto my ende,

And death t[o] *Panthea* is a benefite.   845
What are thy threates but sugred promises!
Araspas.   Then shalt thou liue, and Ile importune thee.
Panthea.   I, now is *Panthea* menaced to the proofe.
Yet euery word thou speakes shall wound my heart,
And in despite of thee Ile die at last;   850
The earnester thou art, the sooner, too.
But to preuent it thus, I will flie from thee;
Cyrus shall know Araspus villanie.   *Exit* PANTH[E]A.
Araspas.   Thus therefore shall I pine, abandon loue?   (ll. 800–54)

The passage naturally falls into two parts, the first showing Araspas' 'amorous courting' (ll. 800–31), the second his threats to 'enforce' his will (ll. 832–54). The latter part constitutes a crescendo, moving from a general threat, to physical violence and finally to suggestions of sexual violence. The structure is skilful, but the drama takes place on a purely verbal level. With the one exception of Panthea's 'trembling hands,/ Which I hold vp to heauen' (ll. 828–9) nothing refers to stage action and the physical presence of the actors on stage. Disappointingly, the 'ascending steps' do not lead to a dramatic climax, but to a moment of bathos as Panthea candidly announces that she will fly from Araspus and goes on to do so. In language and action, the passage falls short of highlights. We seem to witness the contest of two 'Rethoritians' (l. 813), cleverly arguing about a point in dispute, but the passions fail to speak. Here, in comparison, is Soliman's wooing of Perseda:

Soliman.   Now, faire Virgin, let me heare thee speake.   90
Perseda.   What can my tongue vtter but griefe and death?
Soliman.   The sound is hunnie, but the sence is gall:
Then, sweeting, blesse me with a cheerfull looke.
Perseda.   How can mine eyes dart forth a pleasant looke,
When they are stopt with flouds of flowing teares?   95
Soliman.   If tongue with griefe, and eyes with teares be fild,
Say, Virgin, how dooth thy heart admit
The pure affection of great *Soliman?*
Perseda.   My thoughts are like pillers of Adamant,
Too hard to take an new impression.   100
Soliman.   Nay, then, I see, my stooping makes her proud;
She is my vassaile, and I will commaund.
Coye Virgin, knowest thou what offence it is
To thwart the will and pleasure of a king?
Why, thy life is doone, if I but say the word.   105
Perseda.   Why, thats the period that my heart desires.
Soliman.   And die thou shalt, vnlesse thou change thy minde.
Perseda.   Nay, then *Perseda* growes resolute:
Solimans thoughts and mine resemble
Lines parallel that neuer can be ioyned.   110

Soliman. Then kneele thou downe,
   And at my hands receiue the stroake of death,
   Domde to thy selfe by thine owne wilfulnes.
Perseda. Strike, strike; thy words pierce deeper then thy blows.
Soliman. *Brusor*, hide her, for her lookes withould me.   115
         Then BRUSOR *hides her with a Lawne.* [a kind of fine linen]
   O *Brusor*, thou hast not hid her lippes;
   For there sits *Venus* with *Cupid* on her knee,
   And all the Graces smiling round about her,
   So crauing pardon that I cannot strike.
Brusor. Her face is couerd ouer quite, my Lord.   120
Soliman. Why so: O *Brusor*, seest thou not
   Her milke white necke, that Alabaster tower?
   Twill breake the edge of my keene Semitor,
   And peeces flying backe will wound my selfe.
Brusor. Now she is all couered, my Lord.   125
Soliman. Why now at last she dyes.
Perseda. O Christ, receiue my soule.
Soliman. Harke, *Brusor*, she cals on Christ:
   I will not send her to him. Her wordes are musick,
   The self same musick that in auncient daies   130
   Brought *Alexander* from warre to banquetting,
   And made him fall from skirmishing to kissing.
   No, my deare, Loue would not let me kill thee,
   Though Maiestie would turne desire to wrath.
   There lyes my sword, humbled at thy feete;   135
   And I myselfe, that gouerne many kings,
   Intreate a pardon for my rash misdeede.
Perseda. Now *Soliman* wrongs his imperiall state;
   But, if thou loue me, and haue hope to win,
   Graunt [me] one boone that I shall craue of thee.   140
Soliman. What ere it be, *Perseda*, I graunt it thee.
Perseda. Then let me liue a Christian Virgin still,
   Vnlesse my state shall alter by my will.
Soliman. My word is past, and I recall my passions: (IV.i.90–144)

The passage represents a moment of real drama, the exterior theatrical thrill being sustained by the inner struggle in Perseda and Soliman. The passage is carefully constructed. In a first stage, the scene moves quickly and forcefully to Soliman's threat of physical violence (IV.i.90–115). Where the threat remains on a purely verbal level in *The Wars of Cyrus*, Kyd stages a climatic moment of near-execution (IV.i.111–35) which can have some of the dramatic thrill of Shylock getting ready to cut off his pound of flesh. As *The Spanish Tragedy* demonstrates, Kyd was enough man of the theatre to know and exploit the dramatic potential of executions. Like Perseda, Alexandro narrowly escapes execution as Villuppo's treason is revealed (III.i) and Pedringano is executed in one of the play's most memorable moments (III.vi).

Language and action go hand in hand when Perseda is made to kneel down, Brusor imperfectly covers her face and Soliman finally throws down his sword. Soliman's references to the sound of Perseda's voice (IV.i.92, 129) reinforce the link between language and the actors' physical presence. As in great Shakespearean scenes, the action pauses at the moment of greatest dramatic tension to give way to a passage of poetic beauty (IV.i.117–24). Significantly, it centres around the very lips which will cause Soliman's downfall when he is poisoned through a kiss. Here, Perseda's lips keep Soliman from killing her, whereas at the end, he will be killed by them. The poetic intrusion highlights and intensifies the dramatic tension. In its suspension of dramatic action through poetry at a moment of crisis, it prefigures one of the great moments of Shakespearean drama, Othello pausing before smothering Desdemona: 'Yet I'll not shed her blood,/ Nor scar that whiter skin of hers than snow,/ And smooth as monumental alabaster' (V.ii.3–5).

References to the defeat of the Spanish Armada suggest that *Edward III* was written not long after 1588, slightly later than *Soliman and Perseda*. Whereas the latter is likely to be the last extant original play by Kyd, an increasing number of critics have it that *Edward III* may well have been among Shakespeare's early dramatic efforts. Whether Shakespeare is part or sole author is still a matter of critical debate, but the Countess scenes, which alone interest us, are now generally acknowledged to be by Shakespeare.[9] Comparing the wooing scene (II.ii) with the above scene from *Soliman and Perseda* offers the fascinating possibility of seeing Shakespeare and Kyd at work on a related subject at roughly the same time.

Instead of attending to his military duties in France, Edward III is trying to conquer the Countess of Salisbury. Unlike Perseda, the Countess is already married, and so is the King. Nevertheless, the match is pressed by her father. In a first encounter, the King confesses his passion, but the Countess is granted some respite before he urges the utmost in their next meeting:

King Edward.   Now my soul's playfellow, art thou come
   To speak the more than heavenly word of yea   120
   To my objection in thy beauteous love?
Countess.   My father on his blessing hath commanded –
King Edward.   That thou shalt yield to me?
Countess.   Ay, dear my liege, your due.
King Edward.   And that, my dearest love, can be no less   125
   Than right for right, and render love for love.

Countess.   Than wrong for wrong, and endless hate for hate.
 But sith I see your majesty so bent,
 That my unwillingness, my husband's love,
 Your high estate, nor no respect respected,   130
 Can be my help, but that your mightiness
 Will overbear and awe these dear regards,
 I bind my discontent to my content,
 And what I would not I'll compel I will,
 Provided that yourself remove those lets   135
 That stand between your highness' love and mine.
King Edward.   Name them, fair countess, and by heaven I will.
Countess.   It is their lives that stand between our love
 That I would have choked, up my sovereign.
King Edward.   Whose lives, my lady?
Countess.   My thrice loving liege, 140
 Your queen, and Salisbury my wedded husband,
 Who, living, have that title in our love
 That we cannot bestow but by their death.
King Edward.   Thy opposition is beyond our law.
Countess.   So is your desire. If the law   145
 Can hinder you to execute the one,
 Let it forbid you to attempt the other.
 I cannot think you love me as you say,
 Unless you do make good what you have sworn.
King Edward.   No more: thy husband and the queen shall die. 150
 Fairer thou art by far than Hero was,
 Beardless Leander not so strong as I:
 He swum an easy current for his love,
 But I will through a Hellespont of blood
 To arrive at Sestos, where my Hero lies.   155
Countess.   Nay you'll do more: you'll make the river too
 With their heart bloods that keep our love asunder,
 Of which my husband and your wife are twain.
King Edward.   Thy beauty makes them guilty of their death
 And gives in evidence that they shall die,   160
 Upon which verdict I, their judge, condemn them.
Countess.   O perjured beauty, more corrupted judge!
 When to the great Star-chamber o'er our heads
 The universal sessions calls to 'count
 This packing evil, we both shall tremble for it. 165
King Edward.   What says my fair love? Is she resolved?
Countess.   Resolved to be dissolved, and therefore this:
 Keep but thy word, great king, and I am thine.
 Stand where thou dost – I'll part a little from thee –
 And see how I will yield me to thy hands.   170
 Here by my side doth hang my wedding knives:
 Take thou the one, and with it kill thy queen,
 And learn by me to find her where she lies;
 And with this other I'll dispatch my love,
 Which now lies fast asleep within my heart.   175
 When they are gone, then I'll consent to love. –

> Stir not, lascivious king, to hinder me:
> My resolution is more nimbler far
> Than thy prevention can be in my rescue;
> And if thou stir, I strike – therefore stand still   180
> And hear the choice that I will put thee to:
> Either swear to leave thy most unholy suit
> And never henceforth to solicit me,
> Or else, by heaven, this sharp-pointed knife
> Shall stain thy earth with that which thou wouldst stain,   185
> My poor chaste blood. Swear, Edward, swear,
> Or I will strike, and die before thee here.
> *King Edward.*   Even by that power I swear, that gives me now
> The power to be ashamèd of myself,
> I never mean to part my lips again
> In any words that tends to such a suit.   (II.ii.119–91)

The passage shows what separates Kyd from his greater successor. Shakespeare's verse flows with both naturalness and great power. The dialogue displays minds carefully attuned to each other:

> *Countess.*   My father on his blessing hath commanded –
> *King Edward.*   That thou shalt yield to me?
> *Countess.*   Ay, dear my liege, your due.   (II.ii.122–4)

The interjected 'and therefore this' (II.ii.167) or the reiterated 'Swear, Edward, swear' (II.ii.186) convey an immediacy with which the Countess expresses her emotions that is largely absent from Kyd. Feelings are not simply described in language but also displayed through the form which the language takes. A line such as 'And if thou stir, I strike – therefore stand still' (II.ii.180) is exemplary. Juxtaposing three clauses within one iambic pentameter, it combines simplicity in syntax and vocabulary with great dramatic tension. The Countess's speech (II.ii.167–87) is not only of poetic but also of theatrical power. Like Hieronimo's 'What outcries pluck me from my naked bed' soliloquy (II.v), it is acted rather than simply recited. Like Soliman's sword, her knives provide a dramatic centre that keeps up the tension for a considerable moment during which the action threatens to precipitate itself at any moment. The Countess' tools of possible destruction are not simply knives, but wedding-knives, symbols of love and unity at the very moment when they threaten to destroy love and unity. The passage is shot through with simple but powerful oppositions such as this, establishing an intricacy of ideas absent from Kyd. For example, holding the knives in her hands, the Countess requests Edward to pierce the bodies of their spouses lest she pierce her own body. Later on, she swears to kill herself unless he swears to stop pressing her. Most powerfully, the playwright builds the passage around the opposition, not referred to in his sources, between the King's law and natural law. 'Thy opposition is beyond our law' (II.ii.144), the King menaces the Countess; 'So is your desire' (II.ii.145), she fearlessly replies. Dominating the conflict through morality, wisdom, and reasoning, the magnificently conceived Countess is built upon this argument with which she can defy her social superior. The unity of conception on the level of ideas added to efficient theatricality and language raises the passage above Soliman's wooing of Perseda. It is difficult to imagine that it was not Shakespeare who thus outshone 'sporting Kyd'.

Kyd may well have looked to Wotton for a suggestion of how to structure his play. Immediately following the tale, its teller, Sir Fleur D'Amour, expounds its moral purpose and blames women for all misfortune in love. In particular, he dwells upon Persida's responsibility for the lovers' disaster:

> twice shee procured the ruine of hir friende and hir self. The first time, when hir poore Louer, losing by mischance hir chaine, euen in hys Ladies seruice was perpetually banished from hir gratious presence [...] The seconde tyme was, that these twoo louers being by heauenly fauoure miraculously coupled togither, enioying contrary to al hope, euen when they wer moste suppressed with misfortunes, the pleasure so muche desired, were againe separated by the faulte of the too beautifull bride, who pleasing the king ouermuche, approched the flame so neare the flare, as it caused the destruction of hir *Erastus*, and hir owne soone after.   (K4^v)

The play does not substantiate Sir Fleur D'Amour's point. Like Shakespeare, Kyd did not take over from his source any explicit didacticism. What he appears to have seized upon and highlighted, however, is its basic two-part structure: 'twice shee [...]'. Even though the structure is already present in the novella, it is set within a loose framework of primarily linear action. Kyd reinforces the two-part structure: he tightens it and explores the potential of meaning it can convey. If we do not realise that the first part prepares and mirrors the second, the first two acts will be difficult to account for and one of the play's sources of meaning will remain undiscovered.

The play shows twice that the occasion of greatest happiness is the root of greatest misery. On the first occasion, Erastus recovers the chain, but, accused of having stolen it, slays Ferdinando; on the second, he gains private happiness by marrying Perseda. Yet at the very moment when they are brought together, Soliman's desire, which is to prove fatal to their love, is rekindled. A close connection between the two parts is hinted at in Wotton. Having discovered the loss of his chain, Erastus laments: 'with what countenaunce dare I shewe my selfe in the presence of my louyng *Persida*, hauyng so reckleslye loste the iewell I oughte to haue preserued more dearely than my life' (G2ʳ). When Soliman regrets his magnanimity in letting Perseda be married to Erastus, the narrator comments that Soliman 'departed from a Iewell more precious and worthy of estimation vnto him, than the half of his Empire' (I3ᵛ). The play dramatises the same basic story twice. The literal statement in the first instance is turned into a metaphorical assertion in the second. Conversely, the loss of the literal 'iewell' (the symbol of love) in the play's first part metaphorically prepares for the loss of Perseda (the object of love) in the second part.

In both halves of the play, the plot follows a pattern of loss, recovery, and new loss. Erastus loses Perseda's love token and thus her love; he then wins it back in the dicing-game, only to lose her again when he is banished after killing Ferdinando. Similarly, after his separation from his love, Erastus is reunited with and married to Perseda only to lose her again as he is lured into Brusor's trap. Shakespeare's tragicomedies, *Pericles*, *Cymbeline* or *The Winter's Tale*, dramatise loss to make the final recovery all the more powerful. In *Soliman and Perseda*, temporary recovery only aggravates the final loss.

Much in *Soliman and Perseda* is subordinated to its careful structure. One of the play's problems is that the first part lacks a genuine tragic conflict and is likely to have little emotional impact upon an audience. The play needs Basilisco and Piston most badly in the first two acts. What is at stake is a mere love token that has accidentally been lost. 'My innocence shall clear my negligence' (I.iv.132) Erastus says, and the audience is never allowed any real doubts that he is right. A conflict only arises when, late in the play's first part, Erastus kills Ferdinando. It is true that in *Romeo and Juliet*, Romeo's killing of Tybalt (III.i) and his banishment do not occur earlier in the play than Erastus's. Yet, the enmity between Capulets and Montagues prepares for the central conflict from the beginning by providing the obstacle to the lovers' passion.

The *coup de théâtre* of Erastus's killing of Ferdinando constitutes the play's hinge. The conflict of the first part chiefly dealt with Erastus and Perseda complemented with and contrasted by Ferdinando and Lucina. Soliman and Brusor are only introduced in the play's margins. With the disappearance of Ferdinando, they come centre-stage and the character constellation is rearranged: Perseda is torn between Erastus and Soliman and Brusor takes Ferdinando's place at Lucina's side.

Emrys Jones has shown that many plays by Shakespeare and his contemporaries, whether clearly divided into five acts or not, naturally fall into two parts.[10] Few do so as obviously as *Soliman and Perseda*. In terms of length, the halves of Kyd's play are virtually equal. In Boas, the total number of lines of the first half is 1109, of the second it is 1118. Each half also has its temporal unity. Whereas the second is structured by a total of six journeys between Rhodes and Constantinople, the first is more or less continuous. Erastus and Perseda exchange gifts after which Erastus departs for the tilting (I.ii). The tournament (I.iii) is followed by the eulogies on Erastus who then realises the loss and has Piston search for the chain (I.iv). In the same scene, Ferdinando decides to visit Lucina and offer her the chain ('Therefore will I *now* goe visit her' (I.iv.43, my emphasis)). This we see him do in II.i. In the following scene, Piston's 'Did you euer see wise man escape as I have done?' (II.ii.1–2) suggests that it follows immediately upon the last scene. I am not suggesting that it is important for the audience to realise that the first two acts take place on the same day. A spectator would be unlikely to worry about the precise duration of the represented action or to pick up and remember the various temporal references; nor does the play unambiguously suggest that the two acts are confined to one day. Despite the above time scheme, Basilisco's 'God morrow' (II.i.30) seems to indicate the passage of at least one night after the tilting. As with several of Shakespeare's plays – most notoriously *Othello* – there is little point in musing about the playwright's demonstrable inconsistency (sometimes referred to as 'double time scheme'). It is of interest, however, to realise that the play's first half is governed by one temporal unity, and the second half by another.

In plays such as *Arden of Faversham* or *Tamburlaine*, the order of the attempts at murdering Arden or the order of the battles is not precisely random. It is aimed at some effect, growing tension or wonder, for instance. On the other hand, the plays would still make sense if the playwrights had chosen to present the events in a slightly different order. In plays like *Soliman and Perseda* or *The Spanish Tragedy*, however, the events come in a fixed order, determining and triggering each other, moving in rapid stages to a particular result. The emphasis is on haste, on temporal and emotional intensity. The action, in other words, forms a causal sequence. The causality of the action rather than a precise duration is expressed and emphasised through the apparent temporal juxtaposition of the different scenes. As one scene seems to follow immediately upon the next, temporal sequence suggests causal consequence.

The play's second part functions within a different temporal scheme. Whereas the first part could be reduced to one day, the represented time in the second part amounts to several months. Before the beginning of Act III, Erastus has travelled from Rhodes to Constantinople; two scenes later, the Turkish troupes have arrived before Rhodes; between the third and the fourth acts, the Turks and their prisoners return to Constantinople; after the end of the fourth act, the newly-wed Erastus and Perseda travel back to Rhodes; and after Erastus has been murdered, the Turks make head again for Rhodes. The actual duration of these travels, however, is of little interest to the audience. Subjectively, the impression created through Kyd's handling of time is again one of haste. Nowhere is a passage of time implied as in the fourteen years that pass between Acts III and IV of *The Winter's Tale* and *Pericles*. No character is shown waiting for someone else to arrive. Within the space of a few scenes, characters seem to move swiftly to and fro between Rhodes and Constantinople. Erastus takes a precipitated leave at the end of the second act, and Brusor calls Erastus to Soliman's court in all haste.

The Spanish Tragedy enacts a tension between the determinist universe suggested by the allegorical figure Revenge in the play's frame, on the one hand, and the play's protagonist, who shapes his own destiny, on the other. Hieronimo is both object and subject, puppet and playwright, in the universal theatre. In *Soliman and Perseda*, this tension does not exist. The play proposes to expound 'Fortune's inconstancy', and it does so unambiguously. The characters' progress from misery to happiness and back to misery is completely beyond their control. The harder the characters try to shape their destinies, the worse they fare, as when Soliman kills Perseda in an attempt to win her. The first part is not dramaturgically indispensable. Erastus's killing of Ferdinando and Lucina's consequent revenge motive could easily go into a much shorter exposition than the one in *The Spanish Tragedy*. The two parts are linked thematically more than dramatically. Thomas Heywood's *A Woman Killed with Kindness* dramatises two actions that remain entirely apart for most of the play. However, both main plot and subplot show the paradox of a burden imposed on characters through kindness, and the two stories mutually reinforce their governing idea. The two plots in *Soliman and Perseda* are serial rather than parallel, but the effect is similar. The play does not show an instance of the futility of human endeavours, but a general pattern. Whereas *The Spanish Tragedy* allows for the possibility that humans intervene, for better or for worse, in the shaping of their destiny, the outlook of *Soliman and Perseda* is ultimately one of fatalism and bleak cynicism.

I have hitherto postponed the discussion of Kyd's most important addition to his narrative source: Basilisco. Basilisco is a substantial character and he is placed within the play in a way which makes a difference to the work as a whole. His part is about as large as Erastus's in terms of the number of lines, but significantly bigger in terms of stage presence. Whereas the lovers are largely static characters who speak and lament, Basilisco performs the type of actions spectators are likely to remember: he enters 'riding of a mule' (I.iv.46) and in his armour (II.ii.44), Piston pricks his 'posteriors' (IV.ii.46) with a pin, he climbs up a ladder (I.iii.180.1), is pulled down to the ground by Piston and is made to swear an oath on Piston's dagger (I.iii.165). Significantly, Basilisco, not Soliman, Erastus, or Perseda, is the one character Shakespeare recalled in *King John*:

> *Lady Falconbridge.*   What means this scorn, thou most untoward
> knave?
> *Bastard.*   Knight, knight, good mother, Basilisco-like.   (I.i.243–4)

Shakespeare took for granted that his audience could recall Basilisco swearing on Piston's dagger:

> *Piston.*   I, the aforsaid *Basilisco* –
> *Basislisco.*   I, the aforesaid *Basilisco* – Knight, good fellow,
> Knight, Knight –
> *Piston.*   Knaue, good fellow, Knaue, Knaue –   (I.iii.168–70)

Shakespeare was not the only one to single out Basilisco. Thomas Nashe, in *Have with You to Saffron-Walden*, refers to Gabriel Harvey as a 'vaine Basilisco'.[11] As late as 1601, Mounsieur John fo de King in Marston's *Jack Drum's Entertainment*, another braggart, is addressed as 'Basilisco' (Act III). Like Basilisco, John fo de King cowardly shrinks from committing a murder and, like Kyd's antecedent, his courtship exposes him to ridicule.

Similar to Pedringano in *The Spanish Tragedy*, Basilisco owes a large debt to Latin and Italianate comedy. He is one of the descendants of Plautus' *miles gloriosus*. Like Pyrgopolynices, Terence's Thraso, and Matthew Merrygreek in *Ralph Roister Doister*, he boasts of his 'Herculian offspring' (I.iii.101). It seems likely that Kyd was also acquainted with sixteenth-century Italian comedies which, according to Gosson, 'haue beene throughly ransackt, to furnish the Playe houses in London'.[12] Gascoigne's *Supposes* (performed 1566), a translation of Ariosto's early *commedia erudita I Suppositi* (1509), introduced Italian comedy to England. 1584 saw the publication of Munday's *Two Italian Gentlemen*, a translation of Pasqualigo's *Il Fedele*. Munday's braggart is mentioned alongside Kyd's in Nashe's *Have with You to Saffron Walden*: 'such a vaine *Basilisco* and *Captaine Crack-stone* in all his actions & conuersation' (III, p. 102). The pairing is clearly not accidental. Their characters, their inflated rhetoric, as well as the dramatic situation they are placed in are close to each other, and Freeman suggests that 'direct influence seems at least plausible' (p. 148). Yet, if Kyd was influenced by Munday, he finally parted company with him: while Basilisco is given 'comi-tragic' dignity in his death, Crackstone is made the play's laughing-stock as he is caught in a net and has a chamber-pot emptied over his head.

Kyd quite possibly had access to a few Italian plays in the original, and it seems reasonable to assume that as playwright as well as translator of Tasso, he would have read them with great interest. In 1588, John Wolfe printed four of Aretino's five comedies, *Quattro Comedie*, containing the *Hipocrito*, *Il Marescalco*, *La Talanta*, and *La Cortegiana*.[13] *La Talanta* features a *miles gloriosus*, a boastful officer (Tinca), who is in competition with other men for the favours of Talanta. More Italian comedies might have been available to Kyd. The will of John Florio, translator of Montaigne's *Essais* (1603), contained 'numerous works of Cinthio, Bandello, Boccaccio, da Porto, Aretino, Machiavelli, Ariosto, Sanazzaro [sic], Castiglione, and many old "commendie [sic] dell'arte"'.[14]

J. J. Murray may well have been right in stressing Kyd's possible debts to the *commedia dell'arte*. He mentions several occurrences of the name Basilisco in Italian plays. Also, Piston's name for Basilisco – 'Seigniour *Tremomundo*' (IV.ii.31–2) – fits well the names normally given to the Captain in *commedia dell'arte* plays: 'Terremoto' (earthquake), 'Spezzaferro' (iron-breaker), 'Spacca-monti' (mountain-splitter).[15] This is all the more significant as *The Spanish Tragedy* contains an explicit reference to the improvisations of the *commedia dell'arte*: 'The Italian tragedians were so sharp of wit,/ That in one hour's meditation/ They would perform anything in action' (IV.i.164–6). The Privy Council proceedings of 1578 mention the presence of a *commedia dell'arte* company in London. Kyd was twenty years old and lived, for all we know, in London.

There is thus a strong presumption that he saw the Italian comedians live. Kyd's interest in complex stage action and a multitude of props well may have been fostered by the Italian comedians.

Murray suggests one of the plays containing a character called Basilisco as a 'copy-text source' (p. xix): Giovanni Battista della Porta's *commedia erudita La Furiosa*. The suggestion can be dismissed since *La Furiosa* is most likely to have been written around 1600 and was certainly not composed before 1591.[16] Murray seems right though in suggesting that Kyd was familiar with the conventions governing the *miles gloriosus/capitano* as dramatised in the Italian *commedia dell'arte* and *commedia erudita*, and that the name 'Basilisco' was suggested by one or several of them.

As early as 1773, Thomas Hawkins suggested that Basilisco 'should seem to be the original of Falstaff'.[17] Both are knights in rank, but not in behaviour. Like Falstaff, Basilisco boasts of exploits both military (I.iii.79–120) and amorous (I.iii.128–9), but he is shown to be a coward in action and is humiliated sexually. While Falstaff's lust is said to outlast performance, Basilisco is 'a little cut in the porpuse' (V.iii.5) as he prefers 'turning Turk' to death. He shares with Shakespeare's character an astounding capacity to turn defeat and humiliation into self-affirmation as the account of his forced circumcision illustrates:

> The Turkes, whom they account for barbarous,
> Hauing forehard of *Basiliscoes* worth, [i.e. 'heard before' (Boas)]
> A number vnder prop me with their shoulders,
> And in procession bare me to the Church,   15
> As I had beene a second Mahomet.
> I, fearing they would adore me for a God,
> Wisely informd them that I was but man,
> Although in time perhaps I might aspire
> To purchase Godhead, as did *Hercules*;   20
> I meane by doing wonders in the world:
> Amidst their Church they bound me to a piller,
> And to make triall of my valiancie,
> They lopt a collop of my tendrest member. [i.e. cut a slice]
> But thinke you *Basilisco* squicht for that?   (IV.ii.11–24)

His boasts and his self-delusion are so transparent as to make him endearing. The other characters are as little taken in as the spectators. Even though he carries a wooden sword like the Vice of the Morality plays, nobody is in danger of being corrupted by him. The laughter of which he is the object is benevolent. Unlike Pistol, another descendant of the *miles gloriosus*, he is essentially harmless. As with Falstaff, his inflated claims for honour go hand in hand with a deflation of honour. 'The Ubi Sunt rumination', as Willard Farnham pointed out, 'is not unworthy of comparison with Falstaff's famous meditation upon honour':[18]

> [*Falstaff.*]   Well, 'tis no matter; honour pricks me on. Yea, but how if honour prick me off when I come on? How then? Can honour set-to a leg? No. Or an arm? No. Or take away the grief of a wound? No. Honour hath no skill in surgery, then? No. What is honour? A word. What is in that word 'honour'? What is that 'honour'? Air. A trim reckoning! Who hath it? He that died o' Wednesday. Doth he feel it? No. Doth he hear it? No. 'Tis insensible then? Yea, to the dead. But will it not live with the living? No. Why? Detraction will not suffer it. Therefore I'll none of it. Honour is a mere scutcheon. And so ends my catechism.   (V.i.129–40)

> *Basilisco.*   Let me see: where is that *Alcides*, surnamed *Hercules*,
>   The onely Club man of his time? dead.
>   Where is the eldest sonne of *Pryam*,
>   That abraham-coloured Troian? dead.
>   [i.e. auburn-coloured (Boas)]   70
>   Where is the leader of the Mirmidons,
>   That well knit *Accill*[*es*]? dead.
>   Where is that furious *Aiax*, the sonne of *Telamon*,
>   Or that fraudfull squire of *Ithaca*, iclipt *Vlisses*? dead.
>   Where is tipsie *Alexander*, that great cup conquerour,   75
>   Or *Pompey* that braue warriour? dead.
>   I am my selfe strong, but I confesse death to be stronger:
>   I am valiant, but mortall;
>   I am adorned with natures gifts,
>   A giddie goddesse that now giueth and anon taketh: 80
>   I am wise, but quiddits will not answer death:
>   [i.e. subtle arguments (Boas)]
>   To conclude in a word: to be captious, vertuous, ingenious,
>   Are to be nothing when it pleaseth death to be enuious. [. . .]
>   I loue *Perseda*, as one worthie;
>   But I loue *Basilisco*, as one I hould more worthy,
>   My fathers sonne, my mothers solace, my proper selfe.   90
>   Faith, he can doe little that cannot speake,
>   And he can doe lesse that cannot runne away: (V.iii.67–92)

Basilisco's and Falstaff's speeches are made of simple, direct, and powerful language. The similarities in rhetorical construction are obvious. A litany of rhetorical questions are followed by a 'refrain' answer. The whole is concluded by an *apologia* of cowardice.

It is important to understand Basilisco not only as an interestingly drawn character in its own right, but as an important element that influences and shapes the work as a whole. Like Pedringano, he is not confined to a subplot but participates in the main plot, and unlike Pedringano, he remains prominent on stage throughout the play. He figures among the knights in the tilting contest (I.iii), is told by Perseda to revenge her on Erastus when she believes herself betrayed (II.i.73–6), has to yield to Brusor and his soldiers at the fall of Rhodes (III.v), is ordered by Perseda to kill Lucina (V.iii), fights at Perseda's side and is killed, like her, by Soliman (V.iv). To speak of 'a comic underplot, which contains the figure of Basilisco' seems strangely uncritical.[19] Nor does it seem useful or indeed possible to isolate the 'comic scenes' of the play as J. J. Murray does.[20]

Like Pedringano in *The Spanish Tragedy*, Basilisco reveals Kyd's interest in achieving a new and daring effect by mixing the tragic and the comic:[21]

> *Perseda.*   A kisse I graunt thee, though I hate thee deadlie.
> *Soliman.*   I loued thee deerelie, and accept thy kisse.
>   Why didst thou loue *Erastus* more than me?
>   Or why didst not giue *Soliman* a kisse   70
>   Ere this vnhappy time? then hadst thou liued.
> *Basilisco.*   Ah, let me kisse thee too, before I dye.
>   *Then* SOLIMAN *kils* BASILISCO.
> *Soliman.*   Nay, die thou shalt for thy presumption,
>   For kissing her whom I do hould so deare.
> *Piston.*   I will not kisse her, sir, but giue me leaue   75
>   To weepe ouer hir; for while she liued,
>   She loued me deerely, and I loued her.
> *Soliman.*   If thou didst loue her, villaine, as thou saidst,
>   Then wait on her thorough eternal night.
>   *Then* SOLIMAN *kils* PISTON.
>   Ah, *Perseda*, how shall I mourne for thee?   (V.iv.67–80)

In a superficial reading, Kyd may appear to be botching his job as the comic characters seemingly undermine the tragic climax. On stage, however, Basilisco's death is, at its best, strangely moving. The comic is subsumed within the tragic as the character is accorded tragic dignity. He is given the distinction of speaking blank verse, and dies not only with Perseda's kiss, but also with Kyd's regular iambic pentameter on his lips. The device of having the tragic and the comic clash seems therefore aimed not so much at parodying sentimentality as at creating what Harbage so aptly termed 'a new and oddly mixed response – of amusement and horror, revulsion and admiration'.[22]

Marlowe achieved a similarly striking clash of comic and tragic elements in *The Jew of Malta*, in the scene where the essentially comic Friar Bernardine is present at the death of the innocent Abigail:

> *Abigail.*   Death seizeth on my heart: ah gentle Fryar,
>   Convert my father that he may be sav'd,

> And witnesse that I dye a Christian.   [*Dies.*]
> 2. *Fryar.*   I, and a Virgin too, that grieves me most: (III.vi.38–41)

Here, too, the effect is one where the playwright has the serious and
the farcical boldly rub shoulders. Rather than simply constituting a
cheap joke, the passage should evoke a carefully blended response of
sympathetic compassion and corrective laughter.

Piston also has a share in the play's 'comitragic' genre.[23] Like
Basilisco, he plays a functional part in the main plot, in particular
when he eavesdrops on Erastus's mock trial and execution in
Constantinople (V.ii) and returns to Rhodes to inform Perseda
(V.iii). He is clearly more than a fool or a jester. At the same time,
however, he is unintentionally comic when he reports the tragic
news of Erastus's death:

> *Enter* PISTON.
> *Piston.*   O lady and mistris, weepe and lament, and wring your
>   hands; for my maister is condemnd and executed.
> *Lucina.*   Be patient, sweete *Perseda*, the foole but iests.
> *Perceda.*   Ah no; my nightly dreames foretould me this,   25
>   Which, foolish woman, fondly I neglected.
>   But say, what death dyed my poore *Erastus*?
> *Piston.*   Nay, God be praisd, his death was reasonable;
>   He was but strangled.
> *Perseda.*   But strangled? ah, double death to me: 30
>   But say, wherefore was he condemnd to die?
> *Piston.*   For nothing but hie treason.   (V.iii.22–32)

Freeman, who argues that Piston 'is capable of some seriousness –
e.g. in his report of Erastus's death to Perseda' (p. 164), seems to
miss the point. Piston makes us laugh at the same time that he makes
Perseda cry. His lack of sensitivity again serves to mix pathos and
farce.

Besides Erastus, Basilisco, and Piston, Lucina is the fourth character whose death is treated with 'comitragic' rather than tragic
effect:

> *Perseda.*   Thou shalt abie for both your trecheries.
>   It must be so. *Basilisco*, dooest thou loue me? speake.
> *Basilisco.*   I, more then I loue either life or soule:
>   What, shall I stab the Emperour for thy sake?
> *Perseda.*   No, but *Lucina*; if thou louest me, kill her.
>   *Then* BASILISCO *takes a dagger and feeles vpon the point of it.*
> *Basilisco.*   The point will marre her skin.
> *Perseda.*   What, darest thou not? giue me the dagger then –
>   Theres a reward for all thy treasons past.
>   *Then* PERSEDA *kils* LUCINA.

Basilisco.	Yet dare I beare her hence, to do thee good.
Perseda.	No, let her lie, a prey to rauening birds: (V.iii.46–55)

Basilisco could easily have been excluded from the scene of Lucina's killing in order not to mitigate its straightforward dramatic effect. Kyd is clearly interested in something else, however. Perseda's cold-blooded killing is made to jar with Basilisco's comic cowardice in order to highlight the difference between the two characters. Just as Basilisco's earlier boasts are recalled when he shrinks from the deed, so the young woman's determination is offset by the braggart knight's cowardice. Even the idle dagger in Basilico's hand cuts both ways, deflating the braggart's empty words, but also drawing extra attention to the full violence of the represented action: the point indeed mars Lucina's skin – and robs her of her life.

Like *The Spanish Tragedy*, *Soliman and Perseda* is generically a more radical and experimental play than has often been recognised. Even though it does belong among a group of Turkish plays (*Selimus*, *Alphonsus, King of Aragon*, and Peele's lost *The Turkish Mahomet*) written in the wake of the popularity of *Tamburlaine*, it also consciously departs from its precursors.[24] Greene's attempt to imitate *Tamburlaine* in *Alphonsus, King of Aragon* was a failure and may have provided a warning for Kyd. Without Basilisco, *Soliman and Perseda* is a play which, like *Tamburlaine*, mixes concerns of romance and Turkish chronicle-history. With Basilisco, *Soliman and Perseda* is something essentially different, for Kyd marries an element of comedy with the essentially tragic genre, a point the above-quoted parody (IV.ii.43–6) of a passage in *2 Tamburlaine* (V.iii.67–71) illustrates.

Whereas *The Spanish Tragedy* daringly mixes Senecan revenge tragedy with elements of comic intrigue, *Soliman and Perseda* blends serious love tragedy and light comedy. To argue that 'a strange element of comedy in *Soliman* [...] introduces us, if not to a new author, to a new phase of Kyd's art' is to fail to recognise that Basilisco organically follows upon Pedringano.[25] Only the neglect of these comic characters can account for the fact that some critics have been reluctant to accept Ben Jonson's 'sporting' as an appropriate epithet for Kyd. In either play, Kydian comedy has no affinity with the 'comic relief' which earlier plays such as *Cambyses* and *Horestes* provided by opposing two generically and dramatically distinct plots, one tragic and one comic. The actions in which Basilisco is involved do not provide 'a devalued back-ground added to bring out the superior qualities of "centerpiece" characters' as clown subplots did.²⁶ Basilisco is placed squarely within the main plot and any reading of the play needs to take him into account. It is especially the conventional love between Perseda and Erastus that is affected by Basilisco. Kyd deliberately keeps the relation between the colourless young lovers further removed from our concerns than Wotton's novella does. The spectators see the tilting contest, by which Wotton establishes Erastus's prowess, through the eyes of Basilisco and Piston watching from a ladder. Also, whereas Wotton unambiguously invites us to feel compassion for Persida as she curses her seemingly unfaithful lover, Kyd's Perseda asks Basilisco to revenge her by fighting Erastus. Our amusement at the hopeless mission is bound to interfere with our sympathy for Perseda's grief. Chiefly owing to Basilisco, *Soliman and Perseda* remains generically in a precarious balance between tragedy and comedy for much of the play and a recognition of this daring aspect of the play is central for an understanding of Kyd's achievement. It is only with Soliman's growing impact in acts four and five – his assault on Perseda's chastity, his inner torment after the mock trial and execution of Erastus, and his grief after he unknowingly causes Perseda's death in battle – that the play gains in tragic impact.

Notes

1 Sarrazin, pp. 40–3; Murray (ed.), *The Tragedye of Solyman and Perseda*, pp. xvi–xx; Brodwin, *Elizabethan Love Tragedy 1587–1625*, pp. 65–8; Freeman, pp. 158–66; Nick de Somogyi, *Shakespeare's Theatre of War* (Aldershot, 1998) pp. 148–54. For a few local points about Kyd's treatment of his narrative source, see also Max Bluestone, *From Story to Stage* (The Hague, Paris, 1974).
2 Biesterfeldt's *Die Dramatische Technik Thomas Kyds* and Murray's *Thomas Kyd*.
3 Madeleine Doran, *Endeavors of Art: A Study of Form in Elizabethan Drama* (Wisconsin, 1954), p. 336.
4 'But scalding sighes, like blasts of boisterous windes,/ Hinder my teares' (II.i.90–1) is taken from Wotton's 'a boysterous blaste of winde' (K2ᵛ). Yver simply has 'vent'. Similarly, 'Vnder couler of great consequence' (IV.i.245) is the result of 'But *Brusor* vnder colour of secret and waightie affaires' (K1ʳ) which is a relatively free translation of Yver's 'il amena le pauure Eraste à Constantinople, sous pretexte de quelque bonne intention' (p. 78). Finally, Kyd writes 'That Key will serue to open [...] the hart of Christendome' (I.v.14–16) which goes back to 'the inuincible key of christendome' (H3ᵛ), but not to 'un boulevard inexpugnable' (p. 58). Kyd also borrowed some of the references to Greek antiquity. Wotton has:

the victorious Emperoure notwythstandyng (in fauour of hys gentle knyghte, of whome he was alwayes myndefull) vsed more benignitie towardes them, than the rigour of Warres dothe vsually permitte. Euen as *Alexander* the great pardoned *Thebes* for the loue of *Pindarus*, and *Stagirius* [sic] for the good will he bare to *Aristotle*: or as the fortunate *Augustus* entreated rebellious *Alexandria* at the requeste of *Arrius*. (H3ᵛ–H4ʳ)

This is rendered by Kyd as follows:

> *Soliman.*   Well, well, *Erastus*, Rhodes may blesse thy birth.
>   For his sake onely will I spare them more
>   From spoile, pillage, and oppression,
>   Then *Alexander* spard warlike Thebes
>   For *Pindarus*: or then *Augustus*
>   Sparde rich Alexandria for *Arrius* sake.   (IV.i.54–9)

Wotton's tale of Soliman and Persida has not been reprinted in its entirety since the first appearance of *A Courtlie Controuersie* in 1578. Sarrazin provided a reprint of substantial parts of the tale (pp. 8–48). More recently, *A Courtlie Controuersie* has been included in the Chadwych-Healey *Early English Prose Fiction* CD-Rom (Cambridge, 1997). See also Lukas Erne, '"Throughly ransackt": Elizabethan Novella Collections and Henry Wotton's *Courtlie Controuersie of Cupid's Cautels* (1578)', *Cahiers Elisabéthains*, forthcoming.

5 See Emrys Jones, *Scenic Form in Shakespeare* (Oxford, 1971), pp. 41–65.

6 *English Tragedy before Shakespeare*, p. 104.

7 Significantly, the running-title of the early quarto texts is 'A tragical Comedie of Alexander and Campaspe', and Dodsley included the play in his collection under the title *Alexander and Campaspe*. As Ronald B. McKerrow pointed out, in cases when title page and running-title disagree, the latter is likely to reflect the author's intention (*An Introduction to Bibliography* (Oxford, 1927), p. 91).

8 See Irving Ribner, '*Tamburlaine* and *The Wars of Cyrus*', JEPG, 53 (1954), 596–73, and Chambers, IV, p. 52, but also James Paul Brawner ('*The Wars of Cyrus*': An Early Classical Narrative Drama of the Child Actors (Urbana, Illinois, 1942)) who dates the play considerably earlier than *Tamburlaine*. Quotations are from this edition.

9 For a disinterested summary of criticism on *Edward III*, see the introduction to Fred Lapides (ed.), '*The Raigne of King Edward the Third*': A Critical, Old-Spelling Edition (New York and London, 1980). The case for Shakespeare has been stated somewhat sweepingly in Eric Sams (ed.), *Shakespeare's 'Edward III'* (New Haven and London, 1996), and, with more discrimination, in Giorgio Melchiori's New Cambridge edition. I quote from Melchiori's edition.

10 *Scenic Form in Shakespeare*, pp. 66–88.

11 McKerrow, III, p. 102.

12 Kinney, *Markets of Bawdrie*, p. 169.

13 See Harry Sellers, 'Italian Books Printed in England before 1640', *The Library*, 4th Series, 5 (1924), 105–28.

14 Quoted from David Orr, *Italian Renaissance Drama in England Before 1625: The Influence of Erudita Tragedy, Comedy, and Pastoral on Elizabethan and Jacobean Drama* (Chapel Hill, 1970), p. 11.

15 Giacomo Oreglia, *The Commedia dell'Arte* (London, 1968), p. 103. For the mask of the *capitano*, see also Katherine M. Lea, *Italian Popular Comedy: A Study in the 'Commedia dell Arte', 1560–1620 with Special Reference to the English Stage*, 2 vols. (New York, 1962), I, pp. 41–52.

16 Louise George Clubb, *Giambattista Della Porta, Dramatist* (Princeton, 1965), p. 300. *La Furiosa* was first published in 1609 and not, as J. J. Murray (p. xix) has it, in 1726.

17 *The Origin of the English Drama*, I, pp. x–xi.

18 *The Medieval Heritage of Elizabethan Tragedy*, p. 395.

19 F. S. Boas, *An Introduction to Tudor Drama* (Oxford, 1933), p. 101.

20 *The Tragedye of Solyman and Perseda*, p. xxxiv.

21 There is an interesting discussion of this aspect of *Soliman and Perseda* in Freeman, pp. 164–6.

22 'Intrigue in Elizabethan Tragedy', 37.

23 I use the term 'comitragic' as the opposite of 'tragicomic' (cf. *OED*). If the latter genre integrates tragic action into a work with a happy ending, the 'comitragic' genre introduces comic material into a work with a tragic outcome.

24 For a survey of Renaissance Eastern plays, see Samuel Chew, *The Crescent and the Rose: Islam and England during the Renaissance* (New York, 1937), pp. 469–540.

25 G. G. Smith, 'Marlowe and Kyd: Chronicle Histories', 162.

26 Richard Levin, *The Multiple Plot in English Renaissance Drama* (Chicago, 1971), p. 111.

CHAPTER 9

Cornelia

The four plays that have been considered so far, *The Spanish Tragedy*, its forepiece, the lost *Hamlet*, and *Soliman and Perseda*, all share certain characteristics. They were written for and performed on the public stage. As the early references to the Ghost in Hamlet, to Basilisco's clowning and to Hieronimo's revenge suggest, they were notable for their stage action. They are intrigue plays, typically based on novelistic material. Their language stretches from the colloquial to the stately, from prose to verse. *Cornelia* is different in every respect: it is not an original work, but a translation of Robert Garnier's French tragedy *Cornélie* (first published 1574). It is aimed at an educated readership rather than a popular audience and, for all we know, was never performed.[1] Like all plays of the academic, neo-Senecan genre, it is characterised by an almost complete substitution of narrative for stage action and is declaimed rather than performed.

Entered on 26 January 1594 by Nicholas Ling and John Busby ('a booke called *CORNELIA*, THOMAS KYDD beinge the Authour', Arber, II, p. 644), Kyd's translation was printed later the same year with the following title page: 'CORNELIA./ AT LONDON,/ Printed by *Iames Roberts*, for *N. L./* and *John Busbie./* 1594.' Kyd's name is thus absent from the title page, but his initials stand at the end of the dedication to the Countess of Sussex, and the full name appears at the end of the text. The play seems to have sold badly. According to William Covell's *Polimanteia* (1595), 'tragicke *Garnier* ha[d] his poore *Cornelia* stand naked vpon euery poste' (Q3ᵛ). This refers to the practice of posting extra title pages as advertisements and suggests that *Cornelia* failed to find buyers despite commercial efforts. The play was reissued the same year. Several scholars have taken the reissue for a new edition, thus mistaking a sign of the play's commercial failure for a sign of its popularity.[2] The new title page was the first to bear Kyd's name: 'Pompey the Great,/ his faire/

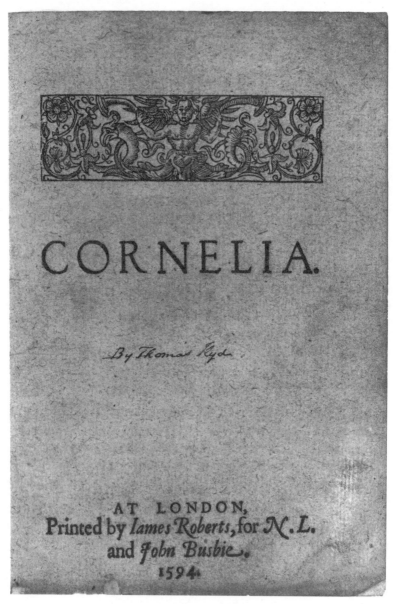

4   Title page of *Cornelia*, London, 1594.

Pompey the Great,

his faire
Corneliaes Tragedie:

Effected by her Father and Huſ-
bandes downe-caſt, death,
and fortune.

Written in French, by that excellent
Poet Ro: Garnier; and tran-
ſlated into Engliſh by Thomas
Kid.

AT LONDON
Printed for Nicholas Ling.
1 5 9 5.

5   Title page of *Cornelia*, reissued as *Pompey the Great, his faire*
Corneliaes Tragedie, London, 1595.

Corneliaes Tragedie:/ Effected by her Father and Hus-/ bandes
downe-cast, death,/ and fortune./ *Written in French, by that excel-/
lent/ Poet Ro: Garnier; and trans-/ lated into English by Thomas/
Kid./* AT LONDON/ Printed for Nicholas Ling./ 1595.' The fact that
a new and greatly changed title page was printed is unusual. By
Elizabethan standards, the original title page is exceptionally plain
and uninformative, and it is possible that it was held partly responsible for the poor sales figures. The publisher who reissued the play
may also have hoped to profit from the popularity of a play on the
public stage. In his diary, Henslowe lists on 8 November 1594 a new
play entitled 'sesar & pompie' which received eight performances by
the Admiral's Men until 25 June 1595. Significantly, *Cornelia*'s new
title page of 1595 prints 'Pompey the Great' in letters double the size
of those used for the following 'his faire Corneliaes Tragedie' even
though her husband does not appear on stage.

Cornelia, the protagonist of Garnier's play and Kyd's translation,
is not to be confused with the famous Cornelia who lived in the
second century BC, the daughter of Publius Cornelius Scipio, hero of
the Second Punic War and wife of Tiberius Semprionius Gracchus,
to whom she bore twelve children. Nor is she identical with Cinna's
daughter who married Julius Caesar in 83 BC, but died before his rise
to power. The historic figure Kyd's translation deals with is the
daughter of Scipio Metellus, who was married first to Publius
Licinus Crassus, then to the famous Pompey the Great. Following
Garnier, Corneille put the same character at the centre of his play *La
Mort de Pompée*.

Robert Garnier (1544–90), the greatest French dramatist before
Corneille, wrote eight plays between 1567 and 1583, seven tragedies
and one tragicomedy, *Bradamante* (1582), perhaps his best-known
play today. *Cornélie* is the third of Garnier's eight plays. For his
translation, Kyd did not use the first edition, nor the text printed in
the two earliest collected editions of Garnier's works published in
1580 and 1582, but the 1585 (or a later) edition, which show certain
cuts also present in Kyd.[3]

Long before the sixteenth century, the topic had been treated by
various writers. In a section of the 'argument' Kyd chose not to
translate, Garnier conveniently gives his literary references: 'Vous
verrez ce Discours amplement traitté en Plutarque ès vies de Pompée,
de César, et de Caton d'Utique, en Hirtius v[e] livre des Commentaires
de César: Au ve livre des Guerres civiles d'Appian, et XLIIIe de
Dion.' Strangely, Garnier fails to mention Lucan, his most important
source. Books VIII and IX of the *Pharsalia* probably did more than

any other ancient text to immortalise Cornelia.[4]

The 'plot' of *Cornelia* can be summed up in a few words, for its lack of complexity is in stark contrast with *The Spanish Tragedy*. The drama begins after the disastrous defeat of Pompey's troops on the plain of Pharsalus, Pompey's escape to Egypt, and his treacherous assassination. In Act I, Cicero comments on Rome's fate as she threatens to bring herself down in the ravages of civil war. The theme is taken up by the Chorus who interprets Rome's plight as the gods' vengeance for the crimes of her ancestors. In Act II, Cornelia laments her plight and considers suicide – to which Cicero replies that death is to be appointed by the gods. In III.i, Cornelia relates that the Ghost of Pompey has appeared to her, but she is contradicted by the Chorus who answers that she must have seen some false demon. In the following scene, Cicero foresees that Caesar's tyranny will eventually lead to his overthrow. In the concluding scene of the third act, Philip, who fought with Pompey against Caesar, brings to Rome the ashes of Cornelia's slain husband. She mourns his death and hopes for Caesar's fall. Scene IV.i opposes a fiery Cassius, eager to free Rome from her oppressor, Caesar, to Decimus Brutus who prefers to wait before taking action. The Chorus praises those who free the people from tyrants. In the following scene, Caesar rejoices after defeating his enemies, but is warned by Mark Anthony against a conspirator who will try to kill him. Most of the only scene of the concluding act (V.i) is taken up by the Messenger's speech, which reports Caesar's victory and Scipio's suicide. Cornelia, in her lament, concludes that she must live to bury and mourn the dead.

Approaching *Cornelia* from the angle of contemporary stage plays, what is not dramatised seems more remarkable than what is. Pompey has already been killed and Caesar's assassination, dimly foreshadowed, happens after the end of the play. The chief opponents, Cassius and Brutus on the one hand, and Caesar and Mark Anthony on the other, never meet. Cornelia laments for most of the play, with the sole alteration that whereas she laments her husband's death in Acts II and III, she also mourns for her slain father in the last act. The urn containing Pompey's ashes is the only potential stage prop. Within the five acts and eight scenes into which the play is divided, the action advances preciously little.

Rather than dramatising action, *Cornelia* deals with contemporary political ideas. Garnier described his play as a 'poème à mon regret trop propre aux malheurs de nostre siècle', and the play paints the dangers of civil war with no less clarity than *Gorboduc*.[5] To an age obsessed with the threat (England) or consequences (France) of civil unrest and concerned with the notions of ambition, good and bad rule, and the Monarchy and the Republic, Ancient Rome – and in particular the period of the great civil war – offered one of the chief 'Mirrors for Magistrates'. Towards the end of the sixteenth century, as English power was expanding, many would have seen Julius Caesar as an heroic figure, effecting a providential shift from the Republic to the Empire, and would have gone along with Dante in placing Cassius and Brutus in the ninth circle of hell. Following Lucan, Garnier and Kyd are less inclined to side with Caesar and paint a very different picture of his aspirations. In *Cornelia*, Rome is represented as in decline. Cicero's opening soliloquy addresses Rome as follows:

> See how the Rocks do heaue their heads at thee,
> Which if thou sholdst but touch, thou straight becomst
> A spoyle to *Neptune*, and a sportfull praie
> To th' Glauc's and Trytons, pleasd with thy decay.   (I. 88–91)

Two acts later, he anticipates with joy the time when Caesar will be overthrown:

> *Caesar*, thou shalt not vaunt thy conquest long,
> Nor longer hold vs in this seruitude,
> Nor shalt thou bathe thee longer in our blood.   (III.ii.66–8)

Similarly, the Chorus calls for 'another *Brutus* [...]/ Brauely to fight in *Romes* defence' (II.ii.406–7). Significantly, the only Chorus that does not disparage the future Emperor is 'A Chorus of Caesars friends' (IV.ii.167.1). Kyd, then, introduced to England an unusually skeptical view of Caesar and the beginnings of the Roman Empire.

Interestingly, Kyd and Marlowe, one-time companions and co-founders of modern English tragedy, both translated a work dealing with the Roman Civil War: *Cornelia* and the first book of Lucan's *Pharsalia*. Marlowe's translation, though probably not printed before 1600, was entered on 28 September 1593, only four months before Kyd's, but it is generally supposed that Marlowe had completed his translation much earlier, probably when still in Cambridge. While Lucan and Marlowe focus on the political horror of civil war, Garnier and Kyd look at the events from the personal perspective of Cornelia.

Shakespeare's vivid interest in the decline of the Republic bore fruit a few years later. It cannot be doubted that Shakespeare knew *Cornelia*, since his wide reading on the subject as well as his interest in Kyd's works are well attested. Especially IV.i and IV.ii, the first opposing Cassius and Decimus Brutus, the second Marc Anthony and Caesar, have obvious affinities with Shakespeare's *Julius*

Caesar. The dialogue in *Cornelia* IV.i between Cassius and Decimus Brutus shares certain characteristics with that between Cassius and Marcus Brutus in *Julius Caesar* I.ii. Furthermore, Boas pointed out that 'the character of Cassius [...] – a character of which only the barest hints are suggested by Plutarch – has its exact prototype in the Cassius of Garnier-Kyd, fiery yet shrewd, envious of Caesar, yet full of a genuinely patriotic passion for liberty' (p. lxxxiii). It is tempting to try to locate more specifically Kyd's influence, but the attempts that have been undertaken seem unconvincing.[6]

Little critical work has been done on Kyd's translation. To my knowledge, only Boas, Carrère, A. M. Witherspoon, and J. A. Roberts and J. F. Gaines have devoted more than cursory remarks to it.[7] With the exception of Roberts and Gaines, even these hardly ever go beyond listing Kyd's alleged mistranslations. Two fundamental misunderstandings underlie Carrère's analysis of *Cornelia* which may help explain more generally why critics have failed to do the work justice. In his dedication to the Countess of Sussex, Kyd qualifies his work as 'small endeuours' which Carrère (p. 315) mistakes as an acknowledgement of the weaknesses of his translation. In fact, Kyd's words display the common understatement of dedicatory rhetoric, comparable to Shakespeare's 'untutored lines' or 'unpolisht lines' in his dedications to the Earl of Southampton.[8] Carrère also misunderstands the last paragraph of Kyd's dedication: 'And so vouchsafing but the passing of a Winters weeke with desolate *Cornelia*, I will assure your Ladiship my next Sommers better trauell with the Tragedy of *Portia*.' A week of *reading* is vouchsafed to the Countess, not a week of *writing*, as Carrère (p. 315) has it. The following sentence makes Kyd's meaning plain: 'And euer spend one howre of the day in some kind seruice to your Honour'. Carrère's misreadings of Kyd's dedication are symptomatic of the spirit in which Kyd's *Cornelia* has been approached: if Kyd admits both his mistakes and his hurry, why should critics take the work seriously?

On close examination, Kyd's *Cornelia* is really more than a translation. Kyd often paraphrases rather than translates Garnier, unlike the Countess of Pembroke who, in her *Antonie*, translates virtually word by word. Not only is the handling of the original relatively free, but what are arguably the best eighteen lines are entirely Kyd's (see below). He omits a good many lines and adds others. As Roberts and Gaines have shown, *Cornelia* is in some ways an original play: 'His amendments constitute a second text, which can be considered independently of Garnier's version, and where the work of the writer can

be examined on many planes.'[9] Notably, a good number of changes
are concerned with the realm of the supernatural. References to
ghosts loom large in Garnier's play, but Kyd misses no opportunity to
add more. He adds several images of hell. As in *The Spanish Tragedy*,
he seems happy to add Christian to pagan references, as when he
invokes the Virgin Mary as 'heauens Queene' (II.401). He replaces
general mentions of fate with direct invocations of heaven. In general,
his aim seems to have been to impregnate his text with a stronger
sense of the supernatural than he found in the original.

From the point of view of the language, *Cornelia* is Kyd's
maturest work. Dodsley, who read widely in editing his twelve-
volume *Select Collection of Old Plays* (1744), pointed out that its
'stile and versification seem better than ordinary'.[10] The blank verse
scans well and flows naturally. Contrary to his earlier plays,
Cornelia contains a good many *enjambments* displaying the ease
with which Kyd had come to write blank verse:

> What end (O race of *Scipio*) will the Fates
> Afford your teares? Will that day neuer come
> That your desastrous griefes shall turne to ioy,   (II.116–18)

> Now *Scipio*, that long'd to shew himselfe
> Discent of Affrican (so fam'd for Armes),
> He durst affront me and my warlike bands,
> Vpon the Coastes of Lybia, till he lost
> His scattred Armie: and to shun the scorne
> Of being taken captiue, kild himselfe.   (IV.ii.67–72)

The verse in *The Spanish Tragedy* and *Soliman and Perseda* was,
with very few exceptions, heavily end-stopped. The technical
mastery Kyd had acquired also shows in his skilful translation of the
various rhymed stanzas. At the end of the third act, for example, the
Chorus muses on the workings of Fortune:

Garnier	Kyd
» Ore elle nous monstre le front	'One while shee bends her angry browe,
» De mille liesses fecond,	'And of no labour will allow;
» Ore elle se retourne,	Another while
» Et de son œil au change prompt	'She fleres againe, I know not how,
» La faveur ne sejourne.	Still to beguile.
» Instable en nos prosperitez,	'Fickle in our aduersities,
» Instable en nos adversitez,	'And fickle when our fortunes rise,
» De nous elle se joüe,	She scoffs at vs:
» Qui tournons sans cesse agitez	'That (blynd herselfe) can bleare our eyes,
» Au branle de sa roüe.[11]	To trust her thus.

With no mean dexterity, Kyd respects simultaneously the rhyme scheme, the varying length of the verses and the sense of the original. Meres, in *Palladis Tamia*, lists Kyd among a group of English poets. Even though Kyd's supposed poetic *oeuvre* is lost, his translation of Garnier's stanzas may allow us a glimpse of it.

It is one of the oddities of the history of Elizabethan drama that Kyd, best remembered today for the popular *Spanish Tragedy*, finished his dramatic career with the closet drama *Cornelia*. This strange fact becomes more easily understandable if we recall the biographical data to which his decision to undertake the translation seem intimately related. By May 1593, Kyd had gotten into trouble with the Privy Council who had found 'certain atheistical tracts' among his papers.[12] Even though Kyd claimed that he had the papers from Marlowe and that they had been 'shufled wth some of myne (vnknown to me) by some occasion of o^r wrytinge in one chamber twoe yeares synce', he was imprisoned and tortured.[13] As a consequence, he seems to have lost 'the favo^rs of my Lord, whom I haue servd almost theis vj yeres nowe', that is from 1587 until his imprisonment in May 1593.[14] It has been argued that *Cornelia*, entered on 26 January 1594 and probably written in the second half of 1593, should be seen in the context of Kyd's attempt to win back the protection of his former patron. Lady Bridget Fitzwalter, the Countess of Sussex, to whom Kyd dedicated his translation, thanking her for her 'fauours past', was the wife of Robert Radcliffe, the fifth Earl of Sussex.[15] Freeman (pp. 32–7) has suggested Radcliffe's father, Henry Radcliffe, the fourth Earl of Sussex until his death in December 1593, as possibly having been Kyd's patron. If, as I argue in the appendix, Kyd was not in the employment of the Earl of Sussex (but of the Earl of Pembroke), it is equally possible that the playwright, after his fall from grace, was looking for patronage elsewhere and therefore dedicated *Cornelia* to the Countess of Sussex.

Cornelia lies on the road English drama did not take. Obvious though this may be from the vantage point of modern literary history, it was perhaps less so in Kyd's own times. In Italy and France, the countries from which England inherited a share of its dramatic tradition, the courtly Senecan tradition bore rich fruit to which Cinthio's and Garnier's plays, among others, bear testimony. In England, 'Seneca's style' was advocated by Sir Philip Sidney, considered by many the paragon of his age.[16] What Willard Farnham calls 'a reactionary Senecan movement' probably looked more like the product of a literary *avant-garde* in its own time.[17]

Several other neoclassical plays were written around the turn of the century. Kyd's *Cornelia* had been preceded by *Antonie*, a translation of Garnier's *Marc Antoine*, undertaken by Mary Herbert, the Countess of Pembroke (the sister of Philip Sidney) in 1590, and was published in 1592. In 1594 appeared Samuel Daniel's *Cleopatra*, the first original play in the manner of Garnier, followed by a number of others, notably Fulke Greville's *Alaham* and *Mustapha*.[18] Earlier critics believed that this group of works grew out of a 'circle' or 'literary coterie' headed by Mary Herbert who took it upon herself, after her brother's untimely death in 1586, to attempt to reform the English tragedy in the way Sidney had called for when lamenting the 'gross absurdities' in contemporary drama and praising *Gorboduc* for its 'stately speeches and well-sounding phrases'.[19] This view is now rightly challenged.[20] Rather than fighting the public stage, Mary Herbert and her husband, the Earl of Pembroke, supported companies of players in the early 1590s just as her uncles Leicester and Warwick had done for a considerable time.

Similarly, it would be an oversimplification to consider *The Spanish Tragedy* and *Cornelia* as examples of two developments within the drama of the early 1590s and to claim that the one grew into Shakespeare, Jonson, and Webster – into plays widely admired and performed today – while the other was aborted after a few attempts and did not leave any traces. Public stage plays such as *The Spanish Tragedy* and closet dramas such as *Cornelia* may be seen more accurately as complementary rather than antagonistic in the influence they exerted. While the former could teach Shakespeare some of his stage craft, the latter may have shown him how to use plays as an eloquent medium to formulate and discuss some of the complex political ideas of his age.

Comparing the early reputations of *The Spanish Tragedy* and *Cornelia* yields telling insights into the relationship between literary recognition and popularity. Denigrated if not forgotten today, Kyd's translation found its admirers after its first publication. A funeral elegy for Lady Helen Branch, wife of the Lord Mayor, who died on 10 April 1594, pays a compliment to the authors of 'chaste *Lucretia*' and of 'sad *Cornelia*', inviting the authors to use their 'siluer pen' not to write about women in foreign countries, but about the life of the deceased, '[m]atter that well deserues your golden stile'.[21] The year after, William Covell, of Christ's College and Queens' College, Cambridge, wrote that *Cornelia* was 'excellently done by Th. Kid'.[22] Furthermore, the literary anthologies *England's Parnassus* (1600) and *Belvedere* (1600) pay *Cornelia* the tribute of citing twenty-one passages each from Kyd's translation.[23] Of the early reception of *The Spanish Tragedy*, in contrast, we best remember the scorn and ridicule Jonson and Marston heaped upon it. Yet, whereas *The Spanish Tragedy* went through eleven editions before 1642, *Cornelia* was not reprinted until the eighteenth century.

It is notable that *Cornelia* and *The Spanish Tragedy*, despite the gulf that separates them on a dramaturgical level, have more in common than their author. Cassius, in a moment of profound doubt about the benevolence, if not the existence, of the gods, suggests the radical scepticism expressed by Hieronimo as his failure to obtain justice drives him mad:

> Yet are there Gods, yet is there heauen and earth,
> That seeme to feare a certaine Thunderer.
> No, no, there are no Gods; or, if there be,
> They leaue to see into the worlds affaires:
> They care not for vs, nor account of men,
> For what we see is done, is done by chaunce.   (IV.i.15–20)

Hieronimo's gods, in comparison, are

> plac'd in those empyreal heights
> Where, countermur'd with walls of diamond,
> I find the place impregnable, and they
> Resist my woes, and give my words no way.   (III.vii.15–18)

The chief correspondences between the two plays, however, are to be found elsewhere: *Cornelia*, to some extent like *The Spanish Tragedy*, is basically a tragedy of grief. While Cornelia laments the loss of her husband and her father, Hieronimo grieves for the death of his son. Cornelia plays no role in the central political events but is told of actions to which she can only react. She is basically a spectator and her strong emotional involvement works as a catalyst for the reader's sympathy. Her passivity is mirrored by Hieronimo's inaction between the discovery of his murdered son and the last act when he takes revenge into his own hands. Their final courses of action are of course diametrically opposed: while Hieronimo destroys himself in the bloody revenge he takes, Cornelia mourns on and endures. Yet despite the plays' disparate conclusions, both characters are essentially rememberers or, in Kyd's word, 'remembrancers' (*Cornelia*, III.i.13).

Interestingly, Kyd's alterations of Garnier's original reveal affinities with *The Spanish Tragedy*. At one point in the last act, Kyd adds five lines, stressing Cornelia's bereavement in terms which are reminiscent of *The Spanish Tragedy*:

> Thy death, deere *Scipio*, Romes eternall losse,
> Whose hopefull life preseru'd our happines,
> Whose siluer haires encouraged the weake,
> Whose resolutions did confirme the rest,
> Whose ende, with it hath ended all my ioyes,   (V.361–5)

Compare this passage with the way Hieronimo mourns for his son:

> Here lay my hope, and here my hope hath end:
> Here lay my heart, and here my heart was slain:
> Here lay my treasure, here my treasure lost:
> Here lay my bliss, and here my bliss bereft: (IV.iv.90–3)

The one major addition to Garnier's text, the first eighteen verses of the third act, is no less characteristic of Kyd:

> The cheerefull Cock (the sad nights comforter),
> Wayting vpon the rysing of the Sunne,
> Doth sing to see how *Cynthia* shrinks her horne,
> While *Clitie* takes her progresse to the East;
> Where, wringing wet with drops of siluer dew,   5
> Her wonted teares of loue she doth renew.
> The wandring Swallow with her broken song
> The Country-wench vnto her worke awakes;
> While *Citherea* sighing walkes to seeke
> Her murdred loue trans-form'd into a Rose: 10
> Whom (though she see) to crop she kindly feares;
> But (kissing) sighes, and dewes hym with her teares: –
> Sweet teares of loue, remembrancers to tyme,
> Tyme past with me that am to teares conuerted;
> Whose mournfull passions dull the mornings ioyes,   15
> Whose sweeter sleepes are turnd to fearefull dreames,
> And whose first fortunes (fild with all distresse)
> Afford no hope of future happinesse.   (III.1–18)

The image in lines ten to thirteen recalls Hieronimo grieving over the dead body of Horatio: 'Sweet lovely rose, ill-pluck'd before thy time,/ [...] I'll kiss thee now, for words with tears are stay'd' (II.v.46–8). Even the rhetorical figure anadiplosis in III.i.12–14 is typical of Kyd (cf. *The Spanish Tragedy* II.i.118–29). The lines are among the finest in the play, probably more successful in their lyricism than any passage by Garnier, and the editor of *England's Parnassus*, whose other inclusions from *Cornelia* are all short, never exceeding six lines, paid Kyd the tribute of including the passage almost in its entirety.

Cornelia, a neoclassical play written by the author of the then-most famous play on the public stage, may well seem like the odd man out among Kyd's plays. It is quite possible that Kyd's translation of *Cornelia* would never have been written if he had not been in pecuniary need after getting into trouble with the authorities. It does not follow, however, that *Cornelia* can be considered as a play outside Kyd's genuine *oeuvre*. Kyd had been interested in Garnier's play long before he came to translate it. As we have seen in chapter 2, it is, in fact, the only contemporary play of which definite traces can be found in *The Spanish Tragedy*, and its influence on Kyd may have been of greater importance than that of any other play of his century. For language and certain passages and ideas, Kyd appears to have looked to *Cornélie* when writing *The Spanish Tragedy* and to *The Spanish Tragedy* when writing *Cornelia*. This relationship of mutual stimulation suggests, as I have pointed out in preceding chapters, that Kyd – rarely disinclined to take clues from his earlier plays – was an author who worked with a limited body of material which he then used and reused, transformed and adapted.

Notes

1 Contrary to the English translations, Garnier's original plays appear to have been acted. See Marie-Madeleine Mouflard, *Robert Garnier, 1545–1590: L'Oeuvre* (La Roche-sur-Yon, 1963), pp. 260–70.

2 See, for instance, Gordon Braden, 'Thomas Kyd', in Fredson Bowers,(ed.), *Elizabethan Dramatists*, Dictionary of Literary Biography, 62 (Detroit, 1987), p. 188. The same mistake is made by Bullough (V, p. 30) and others.

3 This was first pointed out by Markscheffel, 'Thomas Kyd's Tragödien' (1886), 4.

4 See, in particular, Cornelia's two great laments after Pompey's assassination, VIII, ll. 639–61 and IX, ll. 55–108.

5 In the dedication of *Cornélie*, ed. Lebègue, pp. 145–6.

6 Joan Rees ('*Julius Caesar* – An Earlier Play, and an Interpretation', *MLR*, 50 (1955), 135–41) analysed Shakespeare's possible debts to *Cornelia* IV.i and IV.ii; Carrère (pp. 443–4) gives a list of 'parallels' between *Cornelia* and *Julius Caesar*; and Kenneth Muir (*The Sources of Shakespeare's Plays* (London, 1977), pp. 119–20) compares passages in *Cornelia* about indiscriminate slaughter (I.198–200, II.142–3, IV.i.8–10 and IV.i.109) with Antony's vision of murderous chaos (III.i.262–78). In all cases, the 'parallels' are general rather than specific and probably unintentional. Note that it has also been argued that *Cornelia* – along with the Countess of Pembroke's *Antonie* and Samuel Daniel's *Cleopatra* – influenced Shakespeare's *The Rape of Lucrece* (Rolf Soellner, 'Shakespeare's *Lucrece* and the Garnier-Pembroke Connection', *Shakespeare Studies*, 15 (1982), 1–20).

7 Boas, pp. 414–36; Carrère, pp. 315–24, Witherspoon, *The Influence of Robert Garnier on Elizabethan Drama*, pp. 91–9; Roberts and Gaines, 'Kyd and Garnier: The Art of Amendment', *Comparative Literature*, 31 (1979), 124–33. Freeman, for instance, simply states that 'the transla-

tion is not altogether accurate' (p. 169) and, for the rest, quotes Witherspoon.

8 Dedications to the narrative poems *Venus and Adonis* (1593) and *The Rape of Lucrece* (1594).

9 'Kyd and Garnier', 133.

10 *A Select Collection of Plays*, XI, p. 64.

11 Robert Garnier, *Porcie, Cornélie*, ed. Lebègue, p. 197 (ll. 995–1004).

12 For a full account of this portion of Kyd's life, see Freeman, pp. 25–32.

13 Quoted from one of Kyd's two letters to Sir John Puckering, the effectual head of the Privy Council, MS. *Harl.* 6849, fols. 218–19, printed in Freeman, pp. 181–2. As Kyd's authorship of the unsigned letter, which provides details about Marlowe's alleged 'monstruous opinions', has been doubted on paleographical grounds (Robert D. Parsons, 'Thomas Kyd's Letters', *NQ*, 225 [n.s. 27] (1980), 140–1), it may be worthwhile referring to the judgment of Malcolm Parkes, former professor of paleography at the University of Oxford, who has pointed out (by private communication) that the consistency of a series of scribal habits and practices in the two letters strongly suggests that they were written by the same hand.

14 Quoted from Freeman, p. 182.

15 The subtitle 'The Lady Fitzwa[l]ter's Nightingale' of Robert Greene's *Philomela* (1592) was in her honour.

16 'A Defence of Poetry', in *Miscellaneous Prose of Sir Philip Sidney*, ed. Duncan-Jones and van Dorsten, p. 113.

17 *The Medieval Heritage of Elizabethan Tragedy*, p. 396.

18 The other neoclassical plays were Samuel Brandon's *Virtuous Octavia* (1598), Daniel's *Philotas* (1605), William Alexander's *Darius* (1603), *Crœsus* (1604), *The Alexandræan Tragedy* (1605), and *Julius Cæsar* (1607), and Elizabeth Cary's *Tragedy of Mariam* (1613).

19 'A Defence of Poetry', ed. Duncan-Jones and van Dorsten, pp. 113–14. T. S. Eliot was among those who held that 'the Countesse of Pembroke tried to assemble a body of wits to compose drama in the proper Senecan style, to make head against the popular melodrama of that time' ('Seneca in Elizabethan Translation', *Selected Essays*, pp. 92–4). For a full account of this view, see A. M. Witherspoon, *The Influence of Robert Garnier on Elizabethan Drama* (New Haven, 1924).

20 See M. E. Lamb, 'The Myth of the Countess of Pembroke: The Dramatic Circle', *The Yearbook of English Studies*, 11 (1981), 195–202, and Margaret P. Hannay, *Philip's Phoenix: Mary Sidney, Countess of Pembroke* (Oxford, 1990), pp. 119–26.

21 STC 12751: 'W. Har., Epicedium. A funerall Song, vpon lady Helen Branch. London, printed by Thomas Creede, 1594' (A2r). W. Har. cannot have been, as has been suggested, the poet Sir William Harbert (or Herbert), who was only eleven years old in 1594 (*DNB*, XXVI, pp. 225–6).

22 *Polimanteia* (STC 5883), Q3.

23 Charles Crawford (ed.), *England's Parnassus*, p. 377, and Crawford, '*Belvedere, or The Garden of the Muses*', 198–228, esp. 204–7.

CHAPTER 10

Other works and apocrypha

The Householder's Philosophy, a translation of Tasso's _Il Padre di Famiglia_, was published in 1588. The rare initials 'T. K.' on the title page combined with Nashe's gibe at a playwright who chose 'to leape into a new occupation' and 'intermeddle with Italian translations', leave no room for doubt as to Kyd's authorship.[1] The translation was entered in the Stationers' Register on 6 February 1588 as 'the Philosophicall Discourse of the householder' (Arber, II, p. 484). The title page reads:

The Housholders
Philosophie.
VVherein is perfectly and profitably described,
the true Oeconomia and forme of
Housekeeping.
With a Table added thereunto of all the notable
thinges therein contained.
_First written in Italian by that excellent Orator and Poet
Signior Torquato Tasso, and now translated
by T. K._
[ornament]
AT LONDON
Printed by J. C. for Thomas Hacket, [...]
M.D.LXXXVIII.

Some of the extant copies are bound together with 'A dairie Booke for good huswiues' that has its own title page and was separately entered (9 July 1588) and printed. In these copies, the words 'Whereunto is anexed a dairie Booke for all good huswiues' appear in minute letters on the title page of Kyd's translation. Only one copy preserves the title page in its original state (_STC_ 23702.5), while five others have the extended title page (_STC_ 23703).

Between the title page and the dedication on the one hand and the main text on the other, the tract contains a detailed seven-page index, referring to the different topics dealt with in the main text. Boas assumed that the index was Kyd's addition (p. 232), while Freeman believed that it was added by someone else (p. 172). Neither appears to have consulted Kyd's original: The text in Tasso's *Delle Rime, Et Prose* of 1583 (pp. 7–84) is followed by a 'tavola delle cose notabili' (pp. 85–96) which Kyd simply translated into his 'Table [. . .] of all the notable thinges', prefacing his text with what had been appended to Tasso's.

The source of Kyd's translation was *Il Padre di Famiglia* by the Italian poet Torquato Tasso (1544–95), author of the epic *Gerusalemme Liberata* (finished 1575) and the pastoral comedy *Aminta* (1573). It was first printed in 1583 and belongs to a series of prose works written between 1573 and 1587 to which the author himself referred as the 'dialoghi'.[2] Coupling 'philosophy with eloquence', in Tasso's own words, they are generally indebted to Plato's dialogues.[3] Behind *Il Padre di Famiglia*, however, looms more particularly Xenophon's *Oeconomicus*, the most famous ancient treatise on estate management which had a good number of descendants in the Renaissance. The *Oeconomicus* is written in the form of a dialogue (like most of *Il Padre di Famiglia*), one of the two interlocutors being Socrates. Tasso adds a (largely autobiographical) narrative of charming beauty that precedes the dialogue: journeying from Novara to Vercelli, Tasso is confronted by a river that has burst its banks. A gracious young man invites him to stay at his father's house where, assembled around a table, the father and the poet discuss various aspects of home and estate management.

Kyd's text contains a number of mistranslations which show the limits of both his Italian and his classical learning.[4] Yet the only editor of Kyd's tract since 1588 has found his prose 'spirited and vigorous' (Boas, p. lxiii), and Freeman has rightly pointed out that 'Kyd is closer to the chroniclers' direct narrative style than to the exfoliate belletristic style of Lyly or Sidney or Greene's prose romances' (p. 173).

Like *Cornelia*, *The Householder's Philosophy* is really more than a translation. Kyd occasionally adds and expands passages as when Tasso's comment on make-up

> con niun'altra maniera potrà meglio il marito far che non s'imbelleti che co 'l mostrarsi schivo de' belletti e de' lisci   (II, p. 357)

is 'translated' as

> he can practise no way better to dyswade her from such muddy making faire her face then with shewing himselfe a hater, contem-

ner, and carelesse of those that are faire with that filthy spunging,
proigning, painting, and pollishing themselues.   (p. 256, ll. 15–19)

Kyd's invective on the subject of usury is even fiercer. In a passage
with no correspondence in Tasso, he calls it

> an arteficiall gayne, a corrupter of a Common wealth, a disobeyer
> of the Lawes of God, a Rebell and resister of all humaine orders,
> iniurious to manie, the spoile of those that most vphold it, onely
> profitable to it selfe, more infectious than the pestilence, and
> consorted with so many perilous euils, as are hard or neuer to be
> cured.   (p. 280, ll. 33–8)

Boas compared this to the opening scene of *The Spanish Tragedy*
where 'usurers are chok'd with melting gold' (I.i.67) in deepest hell,
and thought that Kyd's diatribe against the malpractice 'may well
have been the fruit of bitter personal experience' (p. lxiv). Whether
any inferences about Kyd himself can be drawn from these writings
is of course no more than guesswork.

Nothing is known about the circumstances that prompted Kyd to
write the translation, but it seems reasonable to assume that the
work was commissioned. Thomas Reade, Esquire, the dedicatee of
the translation, has not been identified, nor is it likely, considering
his social status and the relative frequency of his name, that he ever
will be. Interest in Tasso was about to awake when Kyd carried out
his translation. Gabriel Harvey had referred to 'excellent Tasso' as
early as 1572 and the year 1584 saw the publication of Scipio
Gentili's Latin translation of parts of the *Gerusalemme Liberata*,
dedicated to Sidney.[5] We may legitimately wish, however, that Kyd
had translated a part of Tasso's epic or his dramatic verse rather
than a little-known prose tract.

Texts dealing with home and estate management were far from
unusual in the sixteenth century. Fitzherbert's *Book of Husbandry*
(*STC* 10994), first printed in 1523, went through twenty editions by
1600; Thomas Tusser's *A Hundreth Good Pointes of Husbandrie*
(1557) (*STC* 24372) was reprinted twice, then enlarged to *Five
Hundreth Points of Good Husbandry* (1573) (*STC* 24375), and
reprinted eleven times before the end of the century. Barnabe
Googe's translation of the work of Conrad Heresbach of Cleves
appeared as *Four Bookes of Husbandrie* in 1577 (*STC* 13196) and
was reprinted four times until the turn of the century. H. S. Bennett
explains that 'many a London merchant, having made his money in
trade and invested in a country place, was buying books which
described methods of leading successfully a rural life'.[6]

Kyd's translation did not attract the attention Tasso's other works did and while several works on 'husbandry' went through a great number of editions, Kyd's was not reprinted until the twentieth century. Mixing instruction and entertainment, it does not seem to have been instructive enough for esquires, nor entertaining enough for the *literati*. It remains an oddity that fits badly into Kyd's *oeuvre*.

What remains of the works attributed to Kyd is altogether more problematic. He may have written a poem on the subject of Queen Elizabeth's escape from the Babington, Tichborne, and Salisbury plots in 1586.[7] Commonly referred to as the 'Hendecasyllabon', it is ascribed to 'T. K.' and is included in a collection of five short poems entitled *Verses of Prayse and Joye written vpon Her Majesties preservation*, printed in 1586. Kyd's initials were scarce and, as Boas pointed out, 'thy hope, thy hap and all' is reminiscent of '[t]he hopeless father of a hapless son' (*The Spanish Tragedy*, IV.iv.84). On the other hand, the poetry is devoid of all intrinsic interest, a mechanical line-for-line answer to the poem Tichborne wrote in the Tower before his execution, and any educated person would have been able to compose it.

Only three of the extracts attributed to Kyd in Allott's anthology *England's Parnassus* (1600) are not taken from *Cornelia*. The one slightly longer passage, consisting of nine Senecan lines on the subject of tyranny, is included in Boas's *Works* (p. 294) and Schick, in a fit of fanciful conjecture, took it to be an extract from Kyd's *Hamlet*.[8] It has since been shown to be from Sylvester's 'Babilon'.[9] The two remaining passages, adding up to five lines, may of course still be Kyd's, but even if they are, they do not add much to his canon.

There is further evidence suggesting that Kyd may also have been a poet: in *Palladis Tamia* (1598), Meres, in drawing a parallel between two groups of English and Italian poets, lists Kyd along with Matthew Roydon, Thomas Achelley, Thomas Watson, Robert Greene, and George Peele. Bodenham, in the preface to *Belvedere*, published in 1600, places him among 'the modern and extant poets' from whom he quotes. Unfortunately, Bodenham's extracts are all anonymous and hence, although we are tantalizingly close to writings by Kyd, they cannot be identified as his.

According to Kyd himself, he projected a poem on the conversion of St Paul – as pointed out in one of the two extant letters written to Sir John Puckering – as well as another translation from Garnier, *Porcie*, mentioned in the dedicatory letter to the Countess of Sussex prefacing *Cornelia*. Nothing suggests that either of these works was ever written.

The Murder of Iohn Brewen (1592), a prose tract based on a contemporary crime and included in Boas's edition, no longer has a serious claim to be counted among Kyd's works as the name 'Tho. Kydd' added at the end of the text – 'in a contemporary hand', according to Boas – has been shown to be another of J. P. Collier's forgeries.[10]

Of all the anonymous plays that have from time to time been attributed to Kyd, *Arden of Faversham* deserves the closest attention. The three quartos of 1592, 1599, and 1633 are all anonymous and no other external evidence concerning the play's authorship has come to light. It was written between 1587 and 1592 – at a time, that is, when Kyd was still alive and active. The play is of a dramatic quality that is by no means incompatible with the author of *The Spanish Tragedy* and *Soliman and Perseda*. When Kyd was still believed to be the author of the journalistic prose pamphlet *The Murder of Iohn Brewen*, the source of *Arden of Faversham* – reports of a real murder in 1551 – was considered further evidence that Kyd may have written *Arden of Faversham*, a clue that may now safely be abandoned.

There are other grounds, however, upon which one might be tempted to argue a case for Kyd's authorship. *Arden* shares with *The Spanish Tragedy* a concern with love, passion, intrigue, and murder, and an intricate and exciting plot that moves at considerable speed. In particular, Lorenzo's murderous scheme is in tone and construction not unlike Alice and Mosby's intrigue culminating in the killing of Arden. Just as they play Michael and Clarke against each other, so too Lorenzo has Pedringano and Serberine neutralise each other. The language differs where a Senecan revenge tragedy and a domestic tragedy would hardly be expected to be similar, *Arden* lacking the grand, declamatory and rhetorically patterned passages of *The Spanish Tragedy*. Apart from this, the linguistic flexibility of both plays, conveying an impressive range of voices, is not without resemblance, and I would agree with Boas who found that

> in the cadence and diction of many passages, and in the combination of lyrically elaborate verse-structure with colloquial directness of speech, *Arden of Feversham* [sic] recalls the manner of Kyd far more nearly than that of Shakespeare, to whom it has been often groundlessly attributed.
>
> (pp. lxxxix–xc)

In the absence of any firm evidence, however, the above similarities are too little upon which to build a convincing argument for Kyd's authorship. In fact, *The Jew of Malta*, Marlowe's most Kydian play, shows as many affinities to *The Spanish Tragedy* as *Arden*. Despite some similarities, *Arden* and *The Spanish Tragedy* are different in other respects. The anonymous play does not show the interest in stage action or props that is characteristic of Kyd. While *The Spanish Tragedy* and *Soliman and Perseda* (and *Hamlet*) have an emotional centre onto which the audience's sympathy converges ('pittifull' Hieronimo; Perseda; the Prince) and with which the darker forces sharply contrast ('villainous' Lorenzo; Soliman and Brusor; Hamlet's uncle), *Arden*'s moral universe blurs these distinctions. Also, Nashe portrays Kyd as a Senecan playwright, a generic image to which *Arden* conforms badly if at all. The matter of attribution is further complicated by the text of *Arden* that has come down to us. As Alfred Hart was the first to show, it is of 'poor' quality and 'much of the verse is harsh or irregular'.[11] In the absence of a reliable text, authorship attribution becomes even more hazardous.

Some critics have been willing to attribute *Arden* to Kyd, notably T. S. Eliot, who stressed the 'affinity [of *Arden of Faversham* and *The Spanish Tragedy*] to our contemporary detective drama', and Carrère, who found in *Arden* the same kind of psychological analysis as in *The Spanish Tragedy*.[12] Even though I do not deny the presence of certain similarities between the two plays, they seem to me insufficient to warrant an attribution to Kyd.

Since the 1960s, Kyd has found less support as a claimant to the authorship of *Arden* than Shakespeare. In 1963, MacDonald P. Jackson was the first to advocate Shakespeare's case with a body of scholarship underlying the claim.[13] Of the play's recent editors, M. L. Wine concluded that 'of all the cases presented for and against various known playwrights that for Shakespeare emerges as the strongest' (p. lxxxviii), while Martin White stated that 'the most persistent and intriguing claim is, of course, that made for Shakespeare' (p. xiii). Even if we are willing to accept the claim for Shakespeare on grounds of internal evidence – as, no doubt, most scholars are not – the absence of *Arden* from the four Folio editions and from Meres's list of plays attributed to Shakespeare is strong external evidence against it.

Failing the future discovery of new evidence, the authorship question of *Arden* may well have to remain unanswered. Due to its dramatic qualities, interest in the play will subsist without the label of either 'Kyd' or 'Shakespeare' attached to it.[14] It is not impossible that *Arden* was composed by a playwright of whom little or nothing is known. Thomas Achelley, to give only one example, wrote plays

for the Queen's Men from c. 1583 to 1585.[15] According to Thomas
Nashe, 'most able' Thomas Achelley was 'extant about London' in
1589, and Meres, in his *Palladis Tamia* (1598), lists him among 'our
best for tragedie', yet none of his works for the public stage are
extant.[16] The case illustrates how little is known about the theatre of
Kyd's time and, however frustrating this may be, it can serve as a
caution for critics tempted to distribute the anonymous plays among
the better known playwrights.

Various other anonymous plays have in the past been linked to
the name of Thomas Kyd. Most of these attributions rest on no
persuasive evidence and can be passed over swiftly. A critic who
believed that Shakespeare's *The Taming of the Shrew* is a revision of
the anonymous *The Taming of a Shrew* attributed parts of the latter
play to Kyd.[17] Arthur Acheson believed the play to be originally by
Kyd (in fourteeners!) and revised by Kyd, Marlowe, Peele, and
Munday.[18] *Edward III* was first linked to Kyd by Gregor Sarrazin in
Shakespeares Meisterwerkstatt.[19] He compared the mariner's report
in III.i to the messenger's report in *The Spanish Tragedy* (I.ii.22–84)
and pointed out other stylistic similarities. *Edward III* may well be
indebted to *The Spanish Tragedy*. *Edward III* was also attributed to
Kyd by G. Lambrechts in 1963.[20] There is little to substantiate their
claim and the case for Shakespeare's (co-)authorship is far more
convincing. S. A. Tannenbaum's attribution of parts of the revised
Sir Thomas More to Kyd rests on a paleographical misinterpreta-
tion.[21] Freeman pointed out that a passage in *Selimus* (1592 or
earlier) closely parallels one in Kyd's *Cornelia* (1594) which, in turn,
is a faithful translation of the lines in Garnier. Struggling to accommodate the puzzling evidence, Freeman wrote that 'the possibility of
Kyd's involvement in writing *Selimus* is intriguing, and far from
preposterous in terms of style' (p. 169). However, the style is, *pace*
Freeman, nothing like Kyd's. It is declamatory throughout, and the
play shows no traces of Kyd's stage craft. The language implies little
stage action, like Greene's and Marlowe's, but unlike Kyd's. Also,
the case for Greene's authorship appears strong and it seems safe to
dismiss Freeman's suggestion.[22] Further plays with whose authorship Kyd was wrongly credited are *Titus Andronicus, The First Part
of the Contention, The True Tragedy of Richard the Third, King
Leir, The Rare Triumphs of Love and Fortune, Locrine, A Warning
for Fair Women,* and *The Troublesome Reign of King John*.[23]
Perhaps the most fanciful misattribution is that of a supposititious
Ur-Macbeth, imaginatively argued for by J. M. Robertson in the
heyday of Shakespeare disintegration.[24] Finally, Kyd was long

believed to be the author or co-author of a hypothetical *Ur-Andronicus*. Henslowe records ten performances between 11 April 1592 and 25 January 1593 by Lord Strange's Men of a play termed 'titus and vespacia'. Most scholars now agree that this lost play probably dealt with the destruction of Jerusalem AD 70 and, as *Titus Andronicus* has long been restored to the Shakespeare canon (with Peele, and not Kyd, contending for co-authorship), there is no need to suppose that Kyd ever had a hand in it.

'Industrious Kyd' (Dekker's *A Knight's Conjuring*) no doubt wrote more plays than the ones we know to be his. It seems unlikely though not impossible that any of them are to be found among the extant anonymous plays. As playwright for the Queen's Men before 1585, he must have contributed to the plays that were acted at court, such as the pastoral comedy *Phyllida and Chorin* on 26 December 1584 or the romance *Felix and Philiomena* on 3 January 1585. In all probability, we will never know whether one of these lost plays was by Kyd.[25]

Notes

1 Even in the absence of any external evidence, certain parallels to other works of Kyd would strongly suggest Kyd's authorship. See, in particular, Boas, pp. lxii–lxiii.

2 C. P. Brand, *Torquato Tasso: A Study of the Poet and His Contribution to English Literature* (Cambridge, 1965), pp. 179–80. For a scholarly edition of *Il Padre di Famiglia*, see Torquato Tasso, *Dialoghi*, ed. Ezio Raimondi, 3 vols. (Florence, 1958), II, pp. 333–89. I quote from Raimondi's edition.

3 See Brandt, p. 185.

4 Boas, pp. xviii and 446–57.

5 Watson's Latin *Amyntas* (1585) is not a translation of Tasso's play but an independent work; Abraham Fraunce's *Lamentations of Amyntas* (1587) is a translation from Watson. Carew's translation of the first five cantos of the *Liberata* (1594) and Fairfax's great translation of the entire epic (1600) appeared several years after *The Householder's Philosophy*.

6 *English Books and Readers 1558 to 1603* (Cambridge, 1965), p. 165.

7 See Boas, pp. xxv–xxvi, 339–42. For Tichborne's part in the conspiracy, his lament, his last letters, and his speech on the scaffold, see Richard S. M. Hirsch, 'The Works of Chidiock Tichborn', *ELR*, 16 (1986), 303–18.

8 In his 1898 edition of *The Spanish Tragedy*, p. xliii.

9 This discovery was made by Charles Crawford in his edition of Robert Allott's *England's Parnassus* (Oxford, 1913).

10 See R. M. Gorrell, 'John Payne Collier and "The Murder of John Brewen"', *MLN*, 57 (1942), 441–4. Unfortunately, several critics have

continued to base claims upon Boas's misattribution of the tract to Kyd, notably Félix Carrère in his edition of *Arden de Faversham* (Paris, 1950), p. 35, and C. A. Hallett and E. S. Hallett in *The Revenger's Madness*, p. 141.

11 Alfred Hart, *Stolne and Surreptitious Copies*, p. 374.

12 Eliot, 'Seneca in Elizabethan Translation', *Selected Essays*, p. 80; Carrère, ed., *Arden de Faversham*, pp. 33–4.

13 Jackson, 'Material for an edition of *Arden of Faversham*' (unpublished B.Litt. Thesis, University of Oxford, 1963).

14 The twentieth century has seen not only several theatrical revivals, but even an operatic adaptation: *Arden Muss Sterben*, or *Arden Must Die; An opera on the death of the wealthy Arden of Feversham*, according to the title of the English translation of the German Libretto (by Erich Fried (London, 1967)), was commissioned by and performed at the Hamburg State Opera.

15 See Thomas Heywood, *The Hierarchie of the Blessed Angells* (London, 1635), S1^v.

16 Nashe is quoted from his 'Preface' to Greene's *Menaphon* (McKerrow, III, p. 323).

17 See Carrère, pp. 261–8.

18 Arthur Acheson, *Shakespeare, Chapman, and 'Sir Thomas More'* (London, 1931), p. 209.

19 (Berlin, 1906), p. 124.

20 G. Lambrechts, '*Edward III*, oeuvre de Thomas Kyd', *Etudes Anglaises*, 16 (1963), 160–74.

21 Tannenbaum, *The Booke of 'Sir Thomas Moore'* (New York, 1927); W. W. Greg, '*The Booke of "Sir Thomas Moore"*: (A Bibliotic Study)', *The Library*, 4th Series, 9 (1928), 202–11.

22 See Chambers, IV, p. 46, and Irving Ribner, 'Greene's Attack on Marlowe: Some Light on *Alphonsus* and *Selimus*', *SP*, 52 (1955), 162–71, arguing that the two plays are not simply Greene's imitations of *Tamburlaine*, but an answer to Marlowe's unorthodox views of history and kingship.

23 For *Titus Andronicus*, *The First Part of the Contention*, see Carrère, *The True Tragedy of Richard the Third*, *King Leir*, and *The Rare Triumphs of Love and Fortune*, see Carrère, pp. 233–46, 269–88, 299–301 (for a balanced account of the authorship of *The Rare Triumphs of Love and Fortune*, see John Isaac Owen's edition (New York, 1979), pp. 40–61); for *Locrine*, see F. W. Moorman, 'The Pre-Shakespearean Ghost', *MLR* 1 (1906), 85–95; for *A Warning for Fair Women*, see A. F. Hopkinson (ed.), *A Warning for Fair Women* (London, 1893) and the very same A. F. Hopkinson (ed.), *A Warning for Fair Women* (London, 1904) (for the best rejection of Hopkinson's argument, see C. D. Cannon (ed.), '*A Warning for Fair Women*': *A Critical Edition* (The Hague, 1975), pp. 29–35); for *The Troublesome Reign of King John*, see William Wells, 'Thomas Kyd and the Chronicle-History' *NQ*, 178 (1940), 218–24, 238–43.

24 Robertson, *Literary Detection: A Symposium on 'Macbeth'* (London, 1931), pp. 5–7, 65–83, 151.

25 It may be useful to point out that Emma Smith's affirmation that Gerard

Langbaine, in *An Account of the English Dramatic Poets* (1691), credits Kyd with nine plays relies on a misreading ('Author v. Character in Early Modern Dramatic Authorship', 132). What Langbaine (mistakenly) affirms is that Robert Garnier, not Kyd, wrote a total of nine (in fact: eight) plays.

Kyd's Patron

Concerning Kyd's life, one vexed question with a definite impact upon Kyd's artistic career has so far remained unanswered. After Kyd had got into trouble with the authorities in 1593, was imprisoned and probably tortured, he wrote two letters to Sir John Puckering, Keeper of the Great Seal of England and effectual head of the Privy Council, asking him to intercede with his Lord, from whose grace he had fallen as a result of his imprisonment:[1]

> I maie still reteyne the favo^rs of my Lord, whom I haue servd almost theis vj yeres nowe, in credit vntill nowe, & nowe am vtterlie vndon w^thout herein be somewhat donn for my recoverie[2]

The identity of Kyd's patron has hitherto remained uncertain.

The year 1593 saw the appearance of a number of inflammatory libels against foreigners in London. On 11 May 1593 the Privy Council instructed officers to search suspects. Kyd, who was no doubt informed against, had his rooms searched. What the officers found is not what they were looking for but, instead, certain 'vile hereticall Conceiptes',[3] in fact parts of an Arian tract denying the deity of Jesus Christ. The day after, Kyd was imprisoned. In one of his letters to Puckering, Kyd explained that the heretical papers were Marlowe's:

> When I was first suspected for that libell that concern'd the state, amongst those waste and idle papers (wch I carde not for) & wch vnaskt I did deliuer vp, were founde some fragments of a disputation, toching that opinion, affirmd by Marlowe to be his, and shufled wth some of myne (vnknown to me) by some occasion of o^r wryting in one chamber twoe yeares synce.[4]

On 18 May 1593 Marlowe is called in by the Privy Council, but is freed just two days later. On 30 May 1593, Marlowe dies in a pub brawl in circumstances which will no doubt never be fully understood. Released from prison later the same year, Kyd writes his letters to Puckering, but his attempt to recover his former patron's favour is no success. After 'bitter times and priuie broken passions',[5] Kyd dies the year after.

Kyd's letter yields further interesting information about the nobleman:

> My first acquaintance wth this Marlowe, rose vpon his bearing name to serve my Lo: although his L^p never knewe his service, but in writing for his plaie^rs, ffor never cold my L. endure his name, or sight, when he had heard of his conditions, nor wold indeed the forme of devyne praiers vsed duelie in his L^ps house, haue quadred wth such reprobates.

The fact that Kyd's Lord was a patron of a company of players for whom Marlowe at one time wrote significantly reduces the number of candidates. Two names have principally been advanced: Ferdinando Stanley, Lord Strange (and, after his father's death in September 1593, Earl of Derby) fits the picture insofar as it can be inferred from Henslowe's diary that Marlowe wrote *The Jew of Malta* for the company he patronised.[6] Yet at a closer look, he is an unlikely candidate: *The Jew of Malta* was probably written in 1589, two years before Marlowe shared lodgings with Kyd and wrote for his patron. Freeman rightly raises further objections (p. 37), and in the meantime, more evidence has come to light: in a letter from Sir Robert Sidney (the younger brother of the late Sir Philip), governor of Flushing in the Netherlands, to Lord Burghley, Marlowe is quoted as saying that he is 'very wel known [to] my lord Strang'.[7] This contrasts with what Kyd says about his patron's acquaintance with Marlowe: 'his L^p never knewe his service, but in writing for his plaie^rs, ffor never cold my L. endure his name, or sight, when he had heard of his conditions'. While Marlowe stresses how close their acquaintance was, Kyd's letter makes it seem doubtful that they ever met.

The second candidate who has been advanced is Henry Radcliffe, Earl of Sussex.[8] The connection supporting this conjecture is Kyd's dedication of *Cornelia* early in 1594 to the Countess of Sussex, which has been understood as a further attempt to regain the favour of the family of his former patron. Sussex's Men appear to have been a fairly insignificant company, however, mainly touring the provinces; their first run of performances in a London playhouse was not before December 1593. Nothing links Marlowe to this company, and we may wonder if the leading playwright of his time would have written for it.

Even though neither Lord Strange nor the Earl of Sussex can be positively ruled out, there is another candidate who seems to me more plausible. Henry Herbert, second Earl of Pembroke, President of Wales from 1586, patronised the company for which Marlowe wrote *Edward II* as the title page of the first quarto of 1594 unambiguously attests. It seems significant that, contrary to the title page of *Titus Andronicus*, that of *Edward II* mentions one company only; this suggests that the play was originally written for Pembroke's Men. The precise date of *Edward II* has been a matter of some debate, but recent scholarly opinion confirms that 'the year 1591 emerges as the likeliest date'.[9] *Dido*, the two parts of *Tamburlaine*, *Doctor Faustus*, and *The Jew of Malta* were almost certainly composed earlier, while *The Massacre at Paris* can be dated with precision as it appears as 'ne' (new) in the repertory of Strange's Men on 30 January 1593. *Edward II*, on the contrary, appears to fit perfectly the date of composition implied by Kyd's letter. Unless we want to argue that the play Marlowe wrote for Kyd's patron is lost, *Edward II* and Henry Herbert, Earl of Pembroke seem to be the only plausible candidates for the play and the patron referred to by Kyd.

Carrère rejects Pembroke on the grounds that he did not seem to have been the patron of a company of players in 1591 (pp. 21–2), an argument Freeman endorses (p. 37).[10] The early history of Pembroke's Men is difficult to trace and no performance records from earlier than the second half of 1592 have been preserved. Yet, Andrew Gurr convincingly argues that Pembroke's Men came into existence earlier: 'in 1591 or early in 1592 Pembroke chose to change his long-held practice by giving his name and livery as patron to a wholly new London company'.[11] The creation of the company, Gurr argues, was triggered by the quarrel between Edward Alleyn and James Burbage in May 1591. When Alleyn and Strange's Men quit, 'Burbage may well have arranged to form a new company by applying to Pembroke to sponsor them' (p. 267). It is thus by no means implausible that Marlowe, when sharing a writing room with Kyd some time in the second half of 1591, was writing *Edward II* for Pembroke's and that Kyd's patron was indeed Henry Herbert.

We may now be in a better position to understand how Kyd, playwright for the public stage, came to translate the closet drama *Cornelia* from Garnier: a translation of Garnier's *Antoine* by Mary Herbert, the Countess of Pembroke, Henry Herbert's wife, had been published in 1592. Kyd may well have set out on his translation when he still hoped to win back his former patron's protection. When these hopes had failed by the time he had completed the translation, he dedicated it instead to the Countess of Sussex to whom he was beholden for some 'fauours past'.[12]

Notes

1 MS. *Harl.* 6849, fols. 218–19, MS. *Harl.* 6848, fol. 154, printed by Freeman, pp. 181–3.
2 It seems important to point out that Boas, whose *Works* of Kyd contain both a facsimile and a transcript of this letter, mistranscribed 'iij yeres' instead of 'vj yeres', an error he later acknowledged ('Corrections and Additions 1902–54', *Works*, 2nd edn (Oxford, 1955), p. cxviii).
3 This is quoted from a fragment preserved in *Harl.* MS. 6848, fols. 187–9 which reports Kyd's arrest on 12 May 1593.
4 For a provocative reading of Kyd's letter, see Jeffrey Masten, 'Playwrighting: Authorship and Collaboration', in John D. Cox and D. S. Kastan (eds.), *A New History of Early English Drama* (New York, 1997), pp. 357–82.
5 This is quoted from Kyd's dedication of *Cornelia* to the Countess of Sussex.
6 Strange's case has been argued by S. A. Tannenbaum (*The Booke of 'Sir Thomas Moore'* (New York, 1927), pp. 39–42), Carrère (pp. 20–4), and Frances Anne Smeath ('Great Reckonings in Little Rooms: Christopher Marlowe, Thomas Kyd, and Certain Circles of Association, 1583–1593', unpubl. Ph.D., Brigham Young University, 1979, pp. 26–33). It was endorsed by Charles Nicholl, *The Reckoning: The Murder of Christopher Marlowe* (London, 1992), pp. 225–33.
7 R. B. Wernham, 'Christopher Marlowe at Flushing in 1592', *English Historical Review*, 91 (1976), 345.
8 Freeman, pp. 34–7.
9 Christopher Marlowe, *Edward II*, ed. Charles R. Forker, The Revels Plays (Manchester, 1994), p. 16.
10 Note though that Pembroke was conjectured to have been Kyd's patron by Peter Alexander (*Shakespeare's 'Henry VI' and 'Richard III'* (Cambridge, 1929), p. 203).
11 Andrew Gurr, *The Shakespearian Playing Companies* (Oxford, 1996), p. 268.
12 Dedication of *Cornelia* to the Countess of Sussex.

SELECT BIBLIOGRAPHY

Concordance

Crawford, Charles, *A Concordance to the Works of Thomas Kyd*, Materialien zur Kunde des älteren englischen Dramas, 15 (Louvain: David Nutt, 1906–10)

Bibliographies

Díaz-Fernández, José Ramón, 'Thomas Kyd: A Bibliography, 1966–1992', *Bulletin of Bibliography*, 52.1 (1995), 1–13

Johnson, Robert Carl, 'Thomas Kyd', in *Minor Elizabethans*, Elizabethan, Bibliographies Supplements, 9 (London: The Nether Press, 1968), 33–41

Spurgeon, Dickie, 'Thomas Kyd', in Terence P. Logan and Denzell S. Smith (eds.), *The Predecessors of Shakespeare: A Survey and Bibliography of Recent Studies in English Renaissance Drama* (Lincoln: University of Nebraska, 1973), 93–106

Tannenbaum, Samuel A., *Thomas Kyd, a Concise Bibliography*, Elizabethan Bibliographies, 18 (New York: S. A. Tannenbaum, 1941; rpt. 1967)

Modern editions of Kyd's works

A Select Collection of Old Plays, ed. by Robert Dodsley, 12 vols. (London, 1744) (*The Spanish Tragedy*, vol. 2; *Cornelia*, vol. 11)

The Origin of the English Drama, ed. by Thomas Hawkins, 3 vols. (Oxford, 1773) (*The Spanish Tragedy* and *Soliman and Perseda*, vol. 2)

A Select Collection of Old Plays, 2nd edn, ed. by Isaac Reed, 12 vols. (London, 1780) (*Cornelia*, vol. 2; *The First Part of Hieronimo* and *The Spanish Tragedy*, vol. 3)

The Ancient British Drama, ed. by Sir Walter Scott, 3 vols. (London, 1810) (*The First Part of Hieronimo* and *The Spanish Tragedy*, vol. 1)

A Select Collection of Old Plays, 3rd edn, ed. by J. P. Collier, 12 vols. (London, 1825–27) (*Cornelia*, vol. 2; *The First Part of Hieronimo* and *The Spanish Tragedy*, vol. 3)

A Select Collection of Old English Plays, 4th edn, ed. by W. C. Hazlitt, 15 vols. (London, 1874–76) (*The First Part of Hieronimo, vol. 4*; *Cornelia*, *The Spanish Tragedy, and Soliman and Perseda*, vol. 5)

Kyd, Thomas, *Cornelia*, ed. by H. Gassner (Munich, 1894)

——*The Spanish Tragedy*, in John M. Manly (ed.), *Specimens of Pre-Shakespearean Drama*, 2 vols. (Boston, 1897)

——*The Spanish Tragedy*, ed. by Josef Schick, The Temple Dramatists (London: J. M. Dent & Sons, 1898)

——*Thomas Kyd's 'Spanish Tragedy': Kritischer Text und Apparat*, ed. by Josef Schick (Berlin: Emil Felber, 1901)

——*The Works of Thomas Kyd*, ed. by Frederick Samuel Boas (Oxford: Clarendon Press, 1901, rpt. with a supplement 1955)

——*The Spanish Tragedy: with Additions, 1602*, ed. by W. W. Greg, MSR (London: Oxford University Press, 1925)

——*The Spanish Tragedy, 1592*, ed. by W. W. Greg, MSR (London: Oxford University Press, 1948)

——*The Spanish Tragedy*, ed. by Philip Edwards, The Revels Plays (London: Methuen, 1959)

——*['The Spanish Comedy', or] 'The First Part of Hieronimo' and 'The Spanish Tragedy' [or, 'Hieronimo is Mad Again']*, ed. by Andrew S. Cairncross, Regents Renaissance Drama Series (Lincoln: University of Nebraska Press; London: Edward Arnold, 1967)

——*The Spanish Tragedy*, ed. by Thomas W. Ross, Fountainwell Drama Texts (Edinburgh: Oliver & Boyd, 1968)

——*The Spanish Tragedy*, ed. by J. R. Mulryne, New Mermaids, 2nd edn (London: A & C Black, 1989)

——*The Tragedye of Solyman and Perseda*, ed. by John J. Murray, The Renaissance Imagination (New York: Garland, 1991)

——*The Spanish Tragedy*, in *Two Tudor Tragedies*, ed. by William Tydeman, Penguin Books (Penguin: Harmondsworth, 1992)

——*The Spanish Tragedy*, ed. by David Bevington, Revels Student Editions (Manchester: Manchester University Press, 1996)

——*'The Spanish Tragedie' with anonymous, 'The First Part of Jeronimo'*, ed. by Emma Smith, Renaissance Dramatists (Penguin: Harmondsworth, 1998)

Modern editions of other early works

Arden de Faversham, ed. by Félix Carrère (Paris: Aubier, 1950)

Dekker, Thomas, *The Dramatic Works of Thomas Dekker*, ed. by Fredson Bowers, 4 vols. (Cambridge: Cambridge University Press, 1953–61)

Early English Prose Fiction, CD-Rom (Cambridge: Chadwyck-Healey Ltd., 1997)

Garnier, Robert, *Porcie, Cornélie*, ed. by Raymond Lebègue (Paris: Belles Lettres, 1973)

——*Oeuvres Complètes*, 2 vols., ed. by Lucien Pinvert (Paris: Librairie Garnier Frères, 1923)

Greene, Robert, *The Plays and Poems of Robert Greene*, 2 vols., ed. by J. Churton Collins (Oxford: Clarendon Press, 1905)

Jeronimo Marschalck in Hispanien: Das deutsche Wandertruppen-Manuskript der 'Spanish Tragedy', ed. by Willi Flemming (Hildesheim, New York: Georg Olms Verlag, 1973)

Jonson, Ben, *The Works of Ben Jonson*, ed. by C. H. Herford and Percy and Evelyn Simpson, 11 vols. (Oxford: Clarendon Press, 1925–52)

Lodge, Thomas, *The Complete Works of Thomas Lodge*, ed. by Edmund Gosse, 4 vols. (Glasgow, 1883)

Lyly, John, *The Complete Works of John Lyly*, ed. by R. W. Bond, 3 vols. (Oxford: Clarendon Press, 1902)

Marlowe, Christopher, *The Complete Works of Christopher Marlowe*, ed. by Fredson Bowers, 2 vols., 2nd edn (Cambridge: Cambridge University Press, 1973)

Marston, John, *The Plays of John Marston*, ed. by H. Harvey Wood, 3 vols.

(Edinburgh: Oliver & Boyd, 1934–39)

Nashe, Thomas, *The Works of Thomas Nashe*, ed. by Ronald B. McKerrow, corrected reissue ed. by F. P. Wilson, 5 vols. (Oxford: Blackwell, 1958)

Puttenham, George, *The Arte of English Poesie*, ed. by Gladys Doidge Willcock and Alice Walker (Cambridge: Cambridge University Press, 1936)

Seneca, *Tragedies*, tr. by F. J. Miller, Loeb Classical Library, 2 vols. (London: W. Heinemann, 1917)

Shakespeare, William, *Hamlet: First Quarto, 1603*, ed. by W. W. Greg, Shakespeare Quarto Facsimiles, no. 7 (London: Shakespeare Association, 1951)

——*The Complete Works*, ed. by Stanley Wells, Gary Taylor et al. (Oxford: Clarendon Press, 1986)

Tasso, Torquato, *Dialoghi*, ed. by Ezio Raimondi, 3 vols. (Firenze: G. C. Sansoni, 1958)

General criticism and scholarship on Kyd

Braden, Gordon, 'Thomas Kyd', in Fredson Bowers (ed.), *Elizabethan Dramatists*, Dictionary of Literary Biography, 62 (Detroit: Gale, 1987), 183–95

Carrère, Félix, *Le Théâtre de Thomas Kyd* (Toulouse: Edouard Privat, 1951)

Edwards, Philip, *Thomas Kyd & Early Elizabethan Tragedy* (London: Longman, 1966)

Erne, Lukas, 'W. E. Burton's *Dramatic Works of Thomas Kyd* of 1848', *NQ*, 242 [n.s. 44] (1997), 485–7

Freeman, Arthur, *Thomas Kyd: Facts and Problems* (Oxford: Clarendon Press, 1967)

——'Marlowe, Kyd, and the Dutch Church Libel', *ELR*, 3 (1973), 44–52

Merriam, Thomas, 'Possible Light on a Kyd Canon', *NQ*, 240 [n.s. 42] (1995), 340–41

Sarrazin, Gregor, *Thomas Kyd und sein Kreis* (Berlin, 1892)

Smet, J. de, *Thomas Kyd, l'Homme et l'Oeuvre* (Brussels, 1925)

Criticism and scholarship on The Spanish Tragedy

Adams, Barry B., 'The Audiences of *The Spanish Tragedy*', *JEGP*, 68 (1969), 221–36

Aggeler, Geoffrey, 'The Eschatological Crux in *The Spanish Tragedy*', *JEGP*, 86 (1987), 319–31, rpt. in Geoffrey Aggeler, *Nobler in the Mind: The Stoic-Skeptic Dialectic in English Renaissance Tragedy* (Newark: University of Delaware Press, 1998), 61–71

Ardolino, Frank R., *Thomas Kyd's Mystery Play: Myth and Ritual in 'The Spanish Tragedy'* (New York, Bern, and Frankfurt: Peter Lang, 1985)

——*Apocalypse and Armada in Kyd's 'Spanish Tragedy'*, Sixteenth Century Essays and Studies, 29 (Kirksville, MO: Sixteenth Century Journal Publishers, Northeast Missouri State University, 1995)

Baker, Howard, 'Ghosts and Guides: Kyd's *Spanish Tragedy* and the Medieval Tragedy', *MP*, 33 (1935), 27–35

——*Induction to Tragedy: A Study in a Development of Form in 'Gorboduc', 'The Spanish Tragedy' and 'Titus Andronicus'* (Baton Rouge: Louisiana State University Press, 1939)

Barber, C. L., *Creating Elizabethan Tragedy: The Theater of Marlowe and Kyd*, ed. by Richard P. Wheeler (Chicago: University of Chicago Press, 1988), chapter 3

Barish, Jonas, '*The Spanish Tragedy*, or The Pleasures and Perils of Rhetoric', in *Elizabethan Theatre*, Stratford-upon-Avon Studies, 9 (London: Edward Arnold, 1966), 59–85

Bate, Jonathan, 'The Performance of Revenge: *Titus Andronicus* and *The Spanish Tragedy*', in François Laroque (ed.), *The Show Within: Dramatic and Other Insets: English Renaissance Drama (1550–1642)*, 2 vols. (Montpellier: Université Paul-Valéry, 1992), 2. 267–84

Biesterfeldt, Peter Wilhelm, *Die dramatische Technik Thomas Kyds* (Halle/Saale: Niemeyer, 1936)

Bowers, Fredson, 'Kyd's Pedringano: Sources and Parallels', *Harvard Studies and Notes in Philology and Literature*, 13 (1931), 241–9

Broude, Ronald, 'Time, Truth, and Right in *The Spanish Tragedy*', *SP*, 68 (1971), 130–45

Burrows, Ken C., 'The Dramatic and Structural Significance of the Portuguese Sub-Plot in *The Spanish Tragedy*', *Renaissance Papers* (1969), 25–35

Cairncross, Andrew S., 'Thomas Kyd and the Myrmidons', *The Arlington Quarterly*, 1.4 (1968), 40–5

Cannon, Charles, K., 'The Relation of the Additions of *The Spanish Tragedy* to the Original Play', *SEL*, 2 (1962), 229–39

Cenni, Serena, *Il Corpo insepolto: Discorsività e affettività in 'The Spanish Tragedy' di Thomas Kyd* (Trento: Editrice Temi, 2000)

Colley, John Scott, '*The Spanish Tragedy* and the Theatre of God's Judgement', *Papers on Language and Literature*, 10 (1974), 241–53

Craig, D. H., 'Authorial Styles and the Frequencies of Very Common Words: Jonson, Shakespeare, and the Additions to *The Spanish Tragedy*', *Style*, 26 (1992), 199–220

Crundell, H. W., 'The 1602 Additions to *The Spanish Tragedy*', *NQ*, 164 (1933), 147–9

——'The 1602 Additions to *The Spanish Tragedy*', *NQ*, 166 (1934), 246

——'The Authorship of *The Spanish Tragedy* Additions' *NQ*, 180 (1941), 8–9

de Chickera, Ernst, 'Divine Justice and Private Revenge in *The Spanish Tragedy*', *MLR*, 57 (1962), 228–32

Diehl, Huston, 'Observing the Lord's Supper and the Lord Chamberlain's Men: The Visual Rhetoric of Ritual and Play in Early Modern England', *RD*, 22 (1991), 147–74, rpt. in *Staging Reform, Reforming the Stage: Protestantism and Popular Theater in Early Modern England* (Ithaca, N.Y., London: Cornell University Press, 1997), 94–124

Dillon, Janette, '*The Spanish Tragedy* and Staging Languages in Renaissance Drama', *RORD*, 34 (1995), 15–40

Dudrap, Claude, '*La Tragédie Espagnole* face à la Critique Elisabéthaine et Jacobéene', in Jean Jacquot (ed.), *Dramaturgie et Société*, 2 vols. (Paris: Centre National de la Recherche Scientifique, 1968), 2. 607–31

Edwards, Philip, 'Thrusting Elysium into Hell: The Originality of *The Spanish Tragedy*', in A. L. Magnusson and C. E. McGee (eds.), *The Elizabethan Theatre*, 11 (Ontario, Canada: P. D. Meany, 1990), 117–32

Empson, William, '*The Spanish Tragedy*', *Nimbus*, 3 (1956), 16–29, rpt. in Derek Hudson (ed.), *English Critical Essays: Twentieth Century*, Second Series (London: Oxford University Press, 1958), 215–35, in Ralph J. Kaufmann (ed.), *Elizabethan Drama: Modern Essays in Criticism* (New York: Oxford University Press, 1961), 60–80, and in William Empson, *Essays on Renaissance Literature, Volume Two: The Drama*, ed. by John Haffenden (Cambridge: Cambridge University Press, 1994), 17–37

——'*The Spanish Tragedy* (II)', *Essays on Renaissance Literature, Volume Two: The Drama*, ed. by John Haffenden (Cambridge: Cambridge University Press, 1994), 41–65

Faber, M. D., '*The Spanish Tragedy*: Act IV', *PQ*, 49 (1970), 444–59

Freeman, Arthur, 'The Printing of *The Spanish Tragedy*', *The Library*, 5th Series, 24 (1969), 187–99

Greg, W. W. '*The Spanish Tragedy* – A Leading Case?', *The Library*, 4th Series, 6 (1926), 47–56 partly rpt. in Greg, *Collected Papers*, ed. by J. C. Maxwell (Oxford, 1966), 149–55

Hallett, Charles A., 'Andrea, Andrugio and King Hamlet: The Ghost as Spirit of Revenge', *PQ*, 56 (1977), 43–64

Hamilton, Donna B., '*The Spanish Tragedy*: A Speaking Picture', *ELR*, 4 (1974), 203–17

Hammersmith, James P., 'The Death of Castile in *The Spanish Tragedy*', *RD*, 16 (1985), 1–16

Harbage, Alfred, 'Intrigue in Elizabethan Tragedy', in *Essays on Shakespeare and Elizabethan Drama: In Honour of Hardin Craig*, ed. by Richard Hosley (Columbia, Mo.: University of Missouri Press, 1962), 37–44

Hattaway, Michael, *Elizabethan Popular Theatre: Plays in Performance* (London: Routledge, 1982), chapter 4

Hawkins, Harriett, 'Fabulous Counterfeits: Dramatic Construction and Dramatic Perspectives in *The Spanish Tragedy*, *A Midsummer Night's Dream*, and *The Tempest*', *SS*, 6 (1970), 51–65, rpt. in *Likenesses of Truth in Elizabethan and Restoration Drama* (Oxford: Clarendon Press, 1972), 27–50

Henke, James T., 'Politics and Politicians in *The Spanish Tragedy*', *SP*, 78 (1981), 353–69

Hibbard, G. R., '"From iygging vaines of riming mother wits" to "the spacious volubilitie of a drumming decasillabon"', in A. L. Magnusson and C. E. McGee (eds.), *The Elizabethan Theatre*, 11 (Port Credit, Ontario: P. D. Meany, 1990), 55–73

Hill, Eugene, 'Senecan and Vergilian Perspective in *The Spanish Tragedy*', *ELR*, 15 (1985), 143–65, rpt. in Arthur F. Kinney and Dan S. Collins (eds.), *Renaissance Historicism: Selections from 'English Literary Renaissance'* (Amherst: University of Massachusetts Press, 1987), 108–30

Howarth, R. G., 'The 1602 Additions to *The Spanish Tragedy*', *NQ*, 167 (1934), 88

Hunter, G. K., 'Ironies of Justice in *The Spanish Tragedy*', *RD*, 8 (1965),

89–104, rpt. in G. K. Hunter, *Dramatic Identities and Cultural Tradition: Studies in Shakespeare and His Contemporaries* (Liverpool: Liverpool University Press, 1978), 214–229

Jensen, Ejner J., 'Kyd's *Spanish Tragedy*: The Play Explains Itself', *JEGP*, 64 (1965), 7–16

Johnson, S. F., '*The Spanish Tragedy*, or Babylon Revisited', in Richard Hosley (ed.), *Essays on Shakespeare and Elizabethan Drama: In Honour of Hardin Craig* (Columbia, Mo.: University of Missouri Press, 1962), 23–36

Joy, Susan E., 'The Kyd/Marlowe Connection', *NQ*, 231 [n.s. 33] (1986), 338–9

Justice, Steven, 'Spain, Tragedy, and *The Spanish Tragedy*', *SEL*, 25 (1985), 271–88

Kerrigan, John, 'Hieronimo, Hamlet and Remembrance', *Essays in Criticism*, 31 (1981), 105–26

Kirschbaum, Leo, 'Is *The Spanish Tragedy* a Leading Case? Did a Bad Quarto of *Love's Labours Lost* Ever Exist?', *JEGP*, 37 (1938), 501–12

Knight, G. Wilson, 'Visual Art in Kyd and Shakespeare', in *Shakespearian Dimensions* (Brighton, Sussex: Harvester Press; Totowa, N.J.: Barnes & Noble, 1984), 92–109

Knutson, Roslyn L., 'Influence of the Repertory System on the Revival and Revision of *The Spanish Tragedy* and *Dr. Faustus*', *ELR*, 18 (1988), 257–74

Kohler, Richard C., 'Kyd's Ordered Spectacle: "Behold . . . / What 'tis to be subject to destiny"', *Medieval & Renaissance Drama in England*, 3 (1986), 27–49

Laird, David, 'Hieronimo's Dilemma', *SP*, 62 (1965), 137–46

Lengeler, Rainer, '"Mongrel tragi-comedy": Chaosdarstellung und Gattungsmischung in *The Spanish Tragedy* und *Romeo and Juliet*', in Heinrich F. Plett (ed.), *Renaissance-Poetik, Renaissance Poetics* (Berlin: Walter de Gruyter, 1994), 271–85

Levin, Michael Henry, '"Vindicta mihi!": Meaning, Morality, and Motivation in *The Spanish Tragedy*', *SEL*, 4 (1964), 307–24

Maus, Katharine Eisaman, '*The Spanish Tragedy*, or the Machiavel's Revenge', in *Inwardness and Theater in the English Renaissance* (Chicago and London: University of Chicago Press, 1995), 55–71

Mazzio, Carla, 'Staging the Vernacular: Language and Nation in Thomas Kyd's *The Spanish Tragedy*', *SEL*, 38 (1998), 207–32

McAdam, Ian, '*The Spanish Tragedy* and the Politico-Religious Unconscious', *Texas Studies in Literature and Language*, 42 (2000), 33–60

McAlindon, Thomas, '*Tamburlaine the Great* and *The Spanish Tragedy*: the Genesis of a Tradition', *Huntington Library Quaterly*, 45 (1982), 59–81, partly rpt. in *English Renaissance Tragedy* (Houndmills, Basingstoke, Hampshire: Macmillan, 1986), chapter 2

McMillin, Scott, 'The Figure of Silence in *The Spanish Tragedy*', *ELH*, 39 (1972), 27–48, partly rpt. in Harold Bloom (ed.), *Elizabethan Dramatists*, Modern Critical Views (New York: Chelsea House, 1986), 27–45

——'The Book of Seneca in *The Spanish Tragedy*', *SEL*, 14 (1974), 201–8

Mulryne, J. R., 'Nationality and Language in Thomas Kyd's *The Spanish Tragedy*', in Marie-Thérèse Jones-Davies (ed.), *Langues et Nations au Temps de la Renaissance* (Paris: Klincksieck, 1991), 67–91, rpt. and rev. in Jean-Pierre Maquerlot and Michèle Willems (eds.), *Travel and Drama in Shakespeare's Time* (Cambridge: Cambridge University Press, 1996), 87–105

Murray, Peter B., *Thomas Kyd* (New York: Twayne Publishers, 1969)

Piesse, A. J., 'Kyd's The Spanish Tragedy', in Michael Hattaway (ed.), *A Companion to English Renaissance Literature and Culture* (Oxford: Blackwell, 2000), 206–14

Plard, Henri, 'Adaptations de la *Tragédie espagnole* dans les Pays-Bas et en Allemagne (1595–1640)', in Jean Jacquot (ed.), *Dramaturgie et Société*, 2 vols. (Paris: Centre National de la Recherche Scientifique, 1968), 2. 633–53

Ratliff, John D., 'Hieronimo Explains Himself', *SP*, 54 (1957), 112–18

Rowan, D. F., 'The Staging of *The Spanish Tragedy*', in *The Elizabethan Theatre*, 5, ed. by G. R. Hibbard (Toronto: Macmillan, 1975), 112–23

Sacks, Peter, 'Where Words Prevail Not: Grief, Revenge, and Language in Kyd and Shakespeare', *ELH*, 49 (1982), 576–601, partly rpt. in Harold Bloom (ed.), *Elizabethan Dramatists*, Modern Critical Views (New York: Chelsea House, 1986), 47–56

Schönwerth, Rudolf, *Die niederländischen und deutschen Bearbeitungen von Thomas Kyd's 'Spanish Tragedy'*, Litterarisch-historische Forschungen, 26 (Berlin, 1903)

Schücking, Levin Ludwig, *Die Zusätze zur 'Spanish Tragedy'* (Leipzig: S. Hirzel, 1938)

Shapiro, James, '"Tragedies Naturally Performed": Kyd's Representation of Violence', in D. S. Kastan and Peter Stallybrass (eds.), *Staging the Renaissance* (New York and London: Routledge, 1991), 99–113

Siemon, James R., 'Dialogical Formalism: Word, Object, and Action: *The Spanish Tragedy*', *Medieval and Renaissance Drama in England*, 5 (1991), 87–115

——'Sporting Kyd', *ELR*, 24 (1994), 553–83

Smith, Emma, 'Author v. Character in Early Modern Dramatic Authorship: The Example of Thomas Kyd and *The Spanish Tragedy*', *Medieval and Renaissance Drama in England*, 11 (1999), 129–42

Smith, Molly, 'The Theater and the Scaffold: Death as Spectacle in *The Spanish Tragedy*', *SEL*, 32 (1992), 217–32, partly rpt. in *Breaking Boundaries: Politics and Play in the Drama of Shakespeare and His Contemporaries* (Aldershot: Ashgate, 1998), chapter 2

Sofer, Andrew, 'Absorbing Interests: Kyd's Bloody Handkerchief As Palimpsest', *Comparative Drama*, 34 (2000), 127–53.

Stilling, Roger, *Love and Death in Renaissance Tragedy* (Baton Rouge: Louisiana State University Press, 1976), chapter 2

Tweedie, Eleanor M., '"Action is Eloquence": The Staging of Thomas Kyd's *Spanish Tragedy*', *SEL*, 16 (1976), 223–39

Watson, Robert N., *The Rest Is Silence: Death As Annihilation in the English Renaissance* (Berkeley: University of California Press, 1994), chapter 1

Whigham, Frank, *Seizures of the Will in Early Modern English Drama*,

Cambridge Studies in Renaissance Literature and Culture (Cambridge: Cambridge University Press, 1996), chapter 1

Wiatt, William H., 'The Dramatic Function of the Alexandro-Villuppo Episode in The Spanish Tragedy', NQ, 203 [n.s. 5] (1958), 327–9, rpt. in Max Bluestone and Norman Rabkin (eds.), *Shakespeare's Contemporaries*, 2nd edn (Englewood Cliffs: Prentice-Hall, 1970), 57–60

Zitner, Sheldon P., '*The Spanish Tragedy* and the Language of Performance', in A. L. Magnusson and C. E. McGee (eds.), *The Elizabethan Theatre*, 11 (Port Credit, Ontario: P. D. Meany, 1990), 75–93

The Spanish Tragedy *on the modern stage*

Bogdanov, Michael, director, '*The Spanish Tragedy*', *Theatre Record* (9–22 September 1982), 512–15

——'*The Spanish Tragedy*', *Theatre Record* (18 June–1 July 1984), 550–2

Boyd, Michael, director, '*The Spanish Tragedy*', *Theatre Record* (7–20 May 1997), 631–4

Hartley, Andrew James, 'Spaces for Characters in *The Spanish Tragedy*', *CE*, 58 (October 2000), 1–14

Jones, Emrys, 'Stage-Managing Revenge', *TLS* (15 October 1982), 1131

Maslen, Elizabeth, 'The Dynamics of Kyd's *Spanish Tragedy*', *English*, 32.143 (Summer 1983), 111–25

Proudfoot, Richard, 'Kyd's *Spanish Tragedy*', *Cambridge Quarterly*, 25.1 (Spring 1983), 71–6

Criticism and scholarship on Kyd's other plays and the Kyd apocrypha

Brodwin, Leonora Leet, '*Soliman and Perseda*', in *Elizabethan Love Tragedy 1587–1625* (London: University of London Press, 1971), 65–8

Freeman, Arthur, 'Shakespeare and *Solyman and Perseda*', *MLR*, 58 (1963), 481–7

Maguin, J. M., '"Of Ghosts and Spirits Walking By Night" – a Joint Examination of the Ghost Scenes in Robert Garnier's *Cornélie*, Thomas Kyd's *Cornelia* and Shakespeare's *Hamlet* in the Light of Reformation Thinking As Presented in Lavater's Book', *CE*, 1 (1972), 26–40

Rees, Joan, '*Julius Caesar* – An Earlier Play, and an Interpretation', *MLR*, 50 (1955), 135–41

Reibetanz, John, 'Hieronimo in Decimosexto', *RD*, 5 (1972), 89–121

Roberts, Josephine A. and James F. Gaines, 'Kyd and Garnier: The Art of Amendment', *Comparative Literature*, 31 (1979), 124–33

Smith, Emma, 'Ghost Writing: *Hamlet* and the Ur-Hamlet', in Andrew Murphy (ed.), *The Renaissance Text: Theory, Editing Textuality* (Manchester and New York: Manchester University Press, 2000), 177–90

Wilson, J. Dover, 'Nashe's "Kid in Aesop": A Danish Interpretation', *RES*, 18 (1942), 385–94

Other criticism and scholarship

Altman, Joel, *The Tudor Play of Mind: Rhetorical Inquiry and the Development of Elizabethan Drama* (Berkeley: University of California Press, 1978)

Arber, Edward, *A Transcript of the Registers of the Company of Stationers of London, 1554–1640*, 5 vols. (London: Stationers' Company, 1875–94)

Baldwin, T. W., *Shakespeare's Five-Act Structure* (Urbana: University of Illinois Press, 1947)

Barish, Jonas, *The Anti-theatrical Prejudice* (Berkeley: University of California Press, 1981)

Barton, Anne, *Shakespeare and the Idea of the Play* (London: Chatto & Windus, 1962)

Bevington, David, *From 'Mankind' to Marlowe: Growth of Structure in the Popular Drama of Tudor England* (Cambridge, Mass.: Harvard University Press, 1962)

Blayney, Peter W. M., 'The Publication of Playbooks', in John D. Cox and David Scott Kastan (eds.), *A New History of Early English Drama* (New York: Columbia University Press, 1997), 383–422

Bluestone, Max, *From Story to Stage: The Dramatic Adaptation of Prose Fiction in the Period of Shakespeare and His Contemporaries* (The Hague, Paris: Mouton, 1974)

Bowers, Fredson, 'Ben Jonson, the Actor', *SP*, 34 (1937), 392–406

——*Elizabethan Revenge Tragedy 1587–1642* (Princeton: Princeton University Press, 1940)

Bradbrook, M. C., *Themes and Conventions of Elizabethan Tragedy* (Cambridge: Cambridge University Press, 1935)

Braden, Gordon, *Renaissance Tragedy and the Senecan Tradition: Anger's Privilege* (New Haven: Yale University Press, 1985)

Brand, C. P., *Torquato Tasso: A Study of the Poet and His Contribution to English Literature* (Cambridge: Cambridge University Press, 1965)

Brooke, C. F. Tucker, 'Marlowe's Versification and Style', *SP*, 19 (1922), 186–205

Brooke, Nicholas, *Horrid Laughter in Jacobean Tragedy* (London: Open Books, 1979)

Broude, Ronald, 'Revenge and Revenge Tragedy in Renaissance England', *RQ*, 28 (1975), 38–58

Bullough, Geoffrey (ed.), *Narrative and Dramatic Sources of Shakespeare*, 8 vols. (London: Routledge, 1957–75)

Campbell, Lily B., 'Theories of Revenge in Renaissance England', *MP*, 28 (1930–31), 281–96

Chambers, E. K., *The Elizabethan Stage*, 4 vols. (Oxford: Clarendon Press, 1923)

Charlton, H. B., *The Senecan Tradition in Renaissance Tragedy* (Manchester: Manchester University Press, 1946)

Clayton, Thomas (ed.), *The 'Hamlet' First Published (Q1, 1603): Origins, Form, Intertextualities* (Newark: University of Delaware Press, 1992)

Clemen, Wolfgang, *English Tragedy before Shakespeare*, tr. by T. S. Dorsch (London: Methuen, 1961)

Doran, Madelaine, *Endeavors of Art: A Study of Form in Elizabethan Drama* (Wisconsin: University of Wisconsin Press, 1954)

Eliot, T. S., *Selected Essays, 1917–1932* (London: Faber and Faber, 1932)

Farnham, Willard, *The Medieval Heritage of Elizabethan Tragedy* (Berkeley: University of California Press, 1936)

Fischer, Rudolf, *Zur Kunstentwicklung der englischen Tragödie von ihren ersten Anfängen bis zu Shakespeare* (Strassburg: K. J. Trübner, 1893)

Foakes, R. A. and R. T. Rickert (eds.), *Henslowe's Diary* (Cambridge: Cambridge University Press, 1961)

Freeman, Arthur, 'Inaccuracy and Castigation: The Lessons of Error', in Anne Lancashire (ed.), *Editing Renaissance Dramatic Texts, English, Italian, and Spanish* (New York: Garland, 1976), 97–120

Greg, W. W., *A Bibliography of the English Printed Drama to the Restoration*, 4 vols. (London: Bibliographical Society at the University Press, 1939–59)

Griswold, Wendy, *Renaissance Revivals: City Comedy and Revenge Tragedy in the London Theatre 1576–1980* (Chicago: University of Chicago Press, 1986)

Gurr, Andrew, *The Shakespearian Playing Companies* (Oxford: Clarendon Press, 1996)

Hallett, Charles A. and Elaine S. Hallett, *The Revenger's Madness: A Study of Revenge Tragedy Motifs* (Lincoln: University of Nebraska Press, 1980)

Happé, Peter, *English Drama before Shakespeare* (London and New York: Longman, 1999)

Harbage, Alfred, *Annals of English Drama 975–1700*, revised by S. Schoenbaum, 2nd ed. (London: Methuen, 1964)

Hunter, G. K., '*Henry IV* and the Elizabethan Two-Part Play', *RES*, 5 (1954), 236–48

——'Seneca and the Elizabethans: A Case-Study in "Influence"', *SS*, 20 (1967), 17–26

——'Seneca and English Tragedy', in C. D. N. Costa (ed.), *Greek and Latin Studies: Classical Literature and Its Influence* (London: Routledge, 1974), 166–204, rpt. in revised form in G. K. Hunter, *Dramatic Identities and Cultural Tradition: Studies in Shakespeare and His Contemporaries* (Liverpool: Liverpool University Press, 1978), 174–213

——'English folly and Italian vice: The moral landscape of John Marston', in *Dramatic Identities and Cultural Tradition: Studies in Shakespeare and His Contemporaries* (Liverpool: Liverpool University Press, 1978), 103–32

——'Tyrant and Martyr: Religious Heroisms in Elizabethan Tragedy', in Maynard Mack and George deForest Lord (eds.), *Poetic Traditions of the English Renaissance* (New Haven: Yale University Press, 1982), 85–102

——*English Drama 1586–1642: The Age of Shakespeare*, The Oxford History of English Literature, 6 (Oxford: Clarendon Press, 1997)

Jacoby, Susan, *Wild Justice: The Evolution of Revenge* (London: Collins, 1985)

Jones, Emrys, *Scenic Form in Shakespeare* (Oxford: Clarendon Press, 1971)

——*The Origins of Shakespeare* (Oxford: Clarendon Press, 1977)

Kerrigan, John, *Revenge Tragedy: Aeschylus to Armageddon* (Oxford: Clarendon Press, 1996)

Kiefer, Frederick, *Writing on the Renaissance Stage: Written Words, Printed Pages, Metaphoric Books* (Newark: University of Delaware Press; London: Associated University Presses, 1996)

Leech, Clifford and T. W. Craig (eds.), *The Revels History of Drama in English: 1576–1613* (London: Methuen, 1975)

Lomax, Marion, *Stage Images and Traditions: Shakespeare to Ford* (Cambridge: Cambridge University Press, 1987)

Maguire, Laurie E., *Shakespearean Suspect Texts: The 'Bad' Quartos and Their Contexts* (Cambridge: Cambridge University Press, 1996)

Maguire, Nancy Klein (ed.), *Renaissance Tragicomedy: Explorations in Genre and Politics* (New York: AMS Press, 1987)

Margeson, J. M. R., *The Origins of English Tragedy* (Oxford: Clarendon Press, 1967)

McMillin, Scott and Sally-Beth MacLean, *The Queen's Men and Their Plays* (Cambridge: Cambridge University Press, 1998)

Mehl, Dieter, *The Elizabethan Dumb Show: The History of a Dramatic Convention* (London: Methuen, 1965)

Mouflard, Marie-Madeleine, *Robert Garnier, 1545–1590: L'Oeuvre* (La Roche-sur-Yon: Imprimerie Centrale de L'Ouest, 1963)

Muir, Kenneth, *The Sources of Shakespeare's Plays* (London: Methuen, 1977)

Munro, John (ed.), *The Shakespeare Allusion Book*, 2 vols (London: Chatto & Windus, 1909)

Neill, Michael, *Issues of Death: Mortality and Identity in English Renaissance Tragedy* (Oxford: Clarendon Press, 1997)

Soellner, Rolf, 'Shakespeare's *Lucrece* and the Garnier–Pembroke Connection', *Shakespeare Studies*, 15 (1982), 1–20

de Somogyi, Nick, *Shakespeare's Theatre of War* (Aldershot: Ashgate, 1998)

Waith, Eugene M., *The Herculean Hero in Marlowe, Chapman, Shakespeare and Dryden* (London: Chatto & Windus, 1962)

Wells, Stanley, Gary Taylor et al., *William Shakespeare: A Textual Companion* (Oxford: Clarendon Press, 1987)

Witherspoon, Alexander Maclaren, *The Influence of Robert Garnier on Elizabethan Drama* (New Haven: Yale University Press, 1924)

INDEX